Child First

Stephen Case · Neal Hazel
Editors

Child First

Developing a New Youth Justice System

Editors
Stephen Case
Criminology, Sociology and Social Policy
Loughborough University
Loughborough, UK

Neal Hazel
School of Health & Society
University of Salford
Salford, UK

ISBN 978-3-031-19271-5   ISBN 978-3-031-19272-2   (eBook)
https://doi.org/10.1007/978-3-031-19272-2

© The Editor(s) (if applicable) and The Author(s), under exclusive license to Springer Nature Switzerland AG 2023

This work is subject to copyright. All rights are solely and exclusively licensed by the Publisher, whether the whole or part of the material is concerned, specifically the rights of translation, reprinting, reuse of illustrations, recitation, broadcasting, reproduction on microfilms or in any other physical way, and transmission or information storage and retrieval, electronic adaptation, computer software, or by similar or dissimilar methodology now known or hereafter developed.

The use of general descriptive names, registered names, trademarks, service marks, etc. in this publication does not imply, even in the absence of a specific statement, that such names are exempt from the relevant protective laws and regulations and therefore free for general use.

The publisher, the authors, and the editors are safe to assume that the advice and information in this book are believed to be true and accurate at the date of publication. Neither the publisher nor the authors or the editors give a warranty, expressed or implied, with respect to the material contained herein or for any errors or omissions that may have been made. The publisher remains neutral with regard to jurisdictional claims in published maps and institutional affiliations.

Cover illustration: © Vectorium

This Palgrave Macmillan imprint is published by the registered company Springer Nature Switzerland AG
The registered company address is: Gewerbestrasse 11, 6330 Cham, Switzerland

Foreword by Rt Hon Mark Drakeford MS

In our earliest years, we are somebody's child or grandchild. As we get older, we are somebody else's pupil or patient. Even in an era where we are far more aware of children's rights and children's voices, it continues to be a struggle to see a child as an individual in her or his own right, rather than in relation to others.

For most people, the potentially adverse impact of this subordination is successfully enough negotiated through the 'sturm und drang' of adolescence. For those, however, whose conduct comes to be viewed through a hostile lens, the impact can be far more consequential and adverse. To become an object of the criminal justice system during childhood is especially fraught with danger. Now, a child becomes a *young offender*, forever doomed, it seems, to be seen through that very fractional lens, the instances of transgression being afforded a far greater weight than all the other actions of that young person put together. This is why the *Child First* approach, explored in its many facets in this book, is so important. It begins from the fundamental premise that a child in trouble with the law should be regarded in exactly that order—primarily as a child, and only then in relation to the criminal justice system.

Where this approach has been in operation for the longest time, as we would argue to be the case in Wales, it has been part of a real success story, reducing the number of children drawn into the system, and avoiding the most harmful consequences when this is unavoidably the case. The advantages of this approach are easily apparent for the child themselves, but it works for the rest of society as well. The further a child gets tangled up in the criminal justice system, the greater the likelihood that their own behaviour will become more harmful to themselves and others. It is enlightened self-interest, as well as concern for the child themselves, which makes the chapters in this book such a compelling read.

The golden thread which links all the contributions which follow is that which characterises all the best writing in this field: a commitment to the best standards of research and analysis, but a determination to stretch beyond theory building and into the complex and constrained worlds of policy choices and practice actions. As a result, there is much here to reward a wide variety of readers—from those primarily concerned to develop the concepts of a Child First approach, to those seeking to apply those concepts in the front rooms of children who find themselves in trouble with the law.

Rt Hon Mark Drakeford MS
First Minister of Wales

Foreword by Charlie Taylor

When I began my 2015 review of youth justice in England and Wales, I was not surprised to find that most of the children who were in the system had similar life stories to my pupils at the special school where I had been headteacher. What struck me however, was the attitude to children once they entered the criminal justice system where they were labelled as problematic young offenders, rather than children who were in need of help. This use of language was a manifestation of the way people felt about children who got involved in crime, even those whose job is to give them support. It also became a self-fulfilling prophecy for many for whom the label 'young offender' stuck.

At my school, our fundamental aim was to stop children from simply seeing themselves as a problem and to begin to help them imagine a future in which they could make a success of their lives. We did this in the way we spoke to them, challenging this self-description when we heard it, at the same time giving them some of the practical building blocks that would help them with this journey such as improving their learning, helping them to regulate their emotional response, supporting them to manage relationships and engaging with their parents or carers.

Once children entered the justice system, they were suddenly treated differently and too often the building blocks and support that would help them to live crime free lives were not in place.

This timely collection of essays seeks to address the challenge of providing the right help for children who find themselves in trouble. In particular, the way that the values and beliefs of the adults who are charged with supporting them can be a help or a hindrance in helping them move away from criminal behaviour. In recent years, the number of children locked up has reduced by nearly five times and those who commit more minor offences are now diverted away from the justice system. There will continue to be a very small number of children who will be convicted of the most serious offences and there remains a healthy debate about what the response should be in these rare cases.

Much progress has been made in recent years in changing the way that professionals talk and think about children who commit crime. Thanks to the work of people like Stephen Case, Neal Hazel and many of the other contributors to this book, attitudes have undoubtedly changed, but the pendulum can quickly swing back. This consolidated body of learning will serve a bulwark against any future temptation to bring large numbers of children back into the criminal justice system.

Charlie Taylor
HM Chief Inspector of Prisons
for England and Wales
and former Chair of the Youth
Justice Board

Foreword by Keith Fraser

Since being appointed Chair of the Youth Justice Board (YJB) in 2020, I have built upon the foundations laid by my predecessor, Charlie Taylor, embedding the Child First principle into practice. Prior to my appointment, I was a police constable rising to become a senior police officer. This gave me a real and unfiltered experience of the extreme challenges that children, victims and communities can face. But, and it's an important but, I also saw that no situation was hopeless and change could happen with a different approach. This approach, Child First, is based on evidence of what works in enabling children to flourish, while also reducing crime and improving public safety. I do not, however, shy away from the fact that there is more to be done.

I welcome the publication of this collection, which looks back at the development of Child First and signals potential next steps. There is an impressive range of contributors including researchers and, I am pleased to note, practitioners from within the YJB. The book reflects that success is achieved through collaboration and by translating research into policy and practice. Children themselves are at the heart of the approach. The chapters demonstrate this with the voice and experiences of children being central to how Child First is conceived and enacted.

I am personally committed to embedding and developing Child First practices. My experience of over three decades in policing has shown me the limits of criminal justice interventions and the benefits of taking a constructive, multi-agency approach that treats children as children. Child First is not about ignoring crime or behaviour that is wrong, it is about recognising that a punitive approach doesn't work. Child First is based on the evidence of what works—it is about being hard-headed and effective. I want to see children flourish into the best version of themselves and to make a positive contribution to society. By taking this approach, we will also reduce crime, have fewer victims, and make communities safer.

As the chapters in this book set out, there is more to be done. The YJB has an important role and will maintain the momentum through our statutory functions: to provide oversight of the youth justice system; to identify and share good practice; and to advise Ministers directly and via contribution to policy officials. This book offers compelling evidence, challenging questions and identifies gaps and opportunities. I will be recommending the book to those researching and working in youth justice, but I would also be interested to hear what children themselves think about the ideas presented. I hope that, like me, readers will be engaged and provoked not only into thinking about the challenges but also into taking action to embed Child First in practice.

Keith Fraser
Chair of the Youth Justice Board
for England and Wales,
Commissioner on the UK Race
and Ethnic Disparities
Commission and former senior
police officer

Contents

1 **Introduction** 1
Stephen Case and Neal Hazel

Part I Child First: Challenging Youth Justice Systems

2 **Challenging Punitive Youth Justice** 25
Tim Bateman

3 **Challenging the Risk Paradigm: Children First, Positive Youth Justice** 51
Stephen Case

4 **Challenging Historical Populism—Children First, Offenders Second: From Concept to Policy** 83
Kevin Haines and Sue Thomas

5 **Child First and Children's Rights: An Opportunity to Advance Rights-Based Youth Justice** 109
Ursula Kilkelly

Part II Child First: Developing Youth Justice Policy

6   Developing Child First Youth Justice Policy in England and Wales—A View from Inside the YJB and Westminster   137
    John Drew

7   Developing Child First as the Guiding Principle for Youth Justice   169
    Neal Hazel and Paula Williams

8   Child First in the Criminal Courts   203
    Kathryn Hollingsworth

Part III Child First: Developing Youth Justice Practice

9   Child First: Thinking Through the Implications for Policy and Practice   237
    Ben Byrne

10 The Place of Risk Within Child First Justice: An Exploration of the Perspectives of Youth Justice Practitioners   271
    Anne-Marie Day

11 Cementing 'Child First' in Practice   301
    Kathy Hampson

12 Embracing children's Voices: Transforming Youth Justice Practice Through Co-production and Child First Participation   333
    Samantha Burns and Sean Creaney

13 Postscript—Progress and Challenges for Progressing Progressive Child First Youth Justice   367
    Neal Hazel and Stephen Case

Index   387

Notes on Contributors

Dr. Tim Bateman is Reader in Youth Justice at the University of Bedfordshire. Prior to joining the University, he had extensive experience of social worker with children in trouble and of youth justice policy work. He has written widely on youth crime, youth justice and children in conflict with the law and his research is informed by a commitment to improve the treatment, and ensure the rights, of children who come to attention of the Youth Justice System. He is co-editor of *Safer Communities* journal, a long-standing contributor of the Youth Justice News section of *Youth Justice* journal, and Chair of the National Association for Youth Justice.

Dr. Samantha Burns is a Lecturer in Criminology within the Department of Sociology at Durham University. Her research interests have focused on children and young people's participation and co-production in the Youth Justice System, fuelled from both academic learning and work experience. She has worked in a variety of dynamic and engaging roles across education and youth work in both statutory and voluntary organisations over the last 10 years. She completed her Ph.D. in 2020 within the department of Social and Behavioural Sciences at City University in Hong Kong, and since being back in the UK has been working collaboratively on a range of research projects exploring services and interventions to improve outcomes for children, young people, and families informing policy in health, social care, education and criminal justice sectors. Alongside her current role at Durham University, she is currently Deputy Chair of the National Association of Youth Justice (NAYJ), an advisory board member for Peer Power Youth and member of the Risk Work in Young Lives network.

Ben Byrne has worked as a social worker and probation officer in London and the South East of England and has led services for young people, families and early help, as well as being a former youth offending team manager. He is Strategic Lead for Innovation and Improvement for the London Directors of Children's Services. This involves work across all 33 authorities to better help and protect London's children and families.

He is a trustee of the National Association for Youth Justice and served as a member of the Youth Justice Board for England and Wales from 2018 to 2021, where he led on the development of the 'Child First' principle. He is also an associate with Research in Practice and has worked on delivery of the Tackling Child Exploitation Support Programme across England. He has published works in relation to youth justice and safeguarding young people. His work is particularly associated with developing integrated, restorative and relational ways of working with young people and families.

Stephen Case is Professor of Youth Justice at Loughborough University. His research and scholarship have focused on the promotion of positive, 'children first', rights-based and anti-risk management approaches to working with children in conflict with the law. In addition to over 60 academic journal articles, he has published numerous books including 'Youth Justice: A Critical Introduction' (Case 2021—Routledge), 'Positive Youth Justice: Children First, Offenders Second' (Haines and Case 2015—Policy Press) and 'Understanding Youth Offending: Risk Factor Research, Policy and Practice' (Case and Haines 2009—Routledge). Professor Case has conducted funded research for the Youth Justice Board, UKRI, the Home Office, the Welsh Government, the ESRC, the Leverhulme Trust and the Nuffield Foundation. His most recent publications, 'Child First: The evidence-base' and 'Child First Strategy Implementation Project', are available at: https://www.lboro.ac.uk/subjects/social-policy-studies/research/child-first-justice.

Dr. Sean Creaney is a Criminologist and Senior Lecturer in the Department of Law and Criminology at Edge Hill University. His areas of knowledge and expertise include the theory and practice of co-production and Child First participation. He was previously a Trustee of the National Association for Youth Justice. He is a founding Advisory Board member of social justice charity Peer Power, an empathy-led charity focused on healing trauma and creating individual and system change. In 2021, he was a research consultant on a Youth Justice Board commissioned project that audited and explored the practice of participatory approaches and co-creation across Youth Justice Services. He co-authored the report, which provides guidance on how to utilise creative approaches to facilitate children's involvement in the design, delivery and evaluation of services. He played a key role in establishing the knowledge transfer partnership between Edge Hill University, Chester University and Cheshire Youth Justice Services, and currently sits as a voluntary member of the Cheshire Youth Justice Services Management Board. He is a member of the Editorial Advisory Board of the Safer Communities journal (Emerald) and was awarded Outstanding Paper in both the 2015 and 2021 Emerald Literati Network Awards for Excellence.

Dr. Anne-Marie Day is a Criminology Lecturer at Keele University. She has conducted research on children in care's experiences of the youth justice system, and more recently this has been focused on the custodial estate. She is currently working on a number of research projects covering areas including racial disparity in youth justice diversion; resettlement of children from custody; school exclusion and supporting children on the edge of care. She also has many years' experience as a practitioner and policymaker within criminal justice. She is a qualified Probation Officer and has worked in the community, courts and prison. She has also worked as a youth justice manager and for the Youth Justice Board as a Senior Policy Adviser. Currently, she is also a board member on the

Alliance for Youth Justice and is an expert adviser to the Howard League, the Youth Justice Board, Cheshire Youth Justice Service, and the Home Office.

Professor John Drew CBE is a social justice advisor and campaigner, specialising in the areas of youth justice and adolescent safeguarding. His current roles include chairing the Birmingham and Surrey Youth Offending Service management boards, and acting as the independent safeguarding scrutineer for HMIP Cookham Wood and the Oasis Restore Secure School. He is a senior associate of the Prison Reform Trust. His work with children in trouble began in 1970 when he was a voluntary youth worker at the New Planet City in Lancaster. From there he went on to spend ten years as a local authority children's social worker before moving into middle management in Lancashire, Essex and east London. John was Chief Executive of the Youth Justice Board from 2009 to 2013, and prior to that he spent ten years as a Director of Social Services in east London.

Professor Kevin Haines is Bedford Row Capital's head of social policy and focuses on leading the firm's ESG offering, developing due diligence processes to identify ESG-compliant firms looking to issue debt securities and communicating the firm's approach on ESG to investors. He previously led a distinguished academic career as a criminologist for over 30 years and most recently led the criminology department at the University of Trinidad and Tobago and before that the University of Swansea. In addition he has also been involved in high-profile projects including with the UK's former Department for International Development, in reforming the children's criminal justice system in Romania.

Dr. Kathy Hampson is an experienced Youth Offending Team (YOT) case manager (working with children from prevention to custody/resettlement), giving her vital hands-on experience of a wide range of justice-involved children and report-writing for Courts/Panels. During this time, she completed her Ph.D. looking at the emotional intelligence of children who have been offended. Following this she worked strategically with YOTs in Wales on resettlement processes and practice, which entailed research with children on their experiences, input into policy/legislation, and direct guidance/training for YOTs. She now works for Aberystwyth University (where she developed the first bespoke Master's programme in youth justice in England and Wales), and is an experienced researcher in youth justice matters, particularly exploring children's own understanding of their offending and experiences of the system. She has written extensively on youth justice matters, including online blogs, policy documents, research reports and peer-reviewed journals. She continues to train YOTs in effective practice with children.

Professor Neal Hazel is Chair of Criminology and Criminal Justice at the University of Salford. He has previously held posts as Director of the Institute for Public Policy and Director of the Centre for Social Research at the university. He has delivered more than 40 funded research projects, mainly in youth justice and family support, including several national surveys and evaluations. He specializes in providing useful policy and practice messages, most recently through his Beyond Youth Custody research with Nacro (www.BeyondYouthCustody.net). In January 2018, he was appointed by the Secretary of State for Justice to the Youth Justice Board, which is responsible for overseeing the Youth Justice System across England and Wales. He led the Board's policy development of 'Child First' as the guiding principle for the youth justice sector, and the 'Constructive Resettlement' framework for supporting reentry after custody. He is also former HM Deputy Chief Inspector of Probation for England and Wales.

Kathryn Hollingsworth is a Professor of Law at Newcastle University (UK) and has held visiting positions at the University of Otago, the University of Melbourne, the University of New South Wales and Texas Tech University. Her research focuses on children's rights especially in the context of youth justice and she has published widely in this area. She has a particular interest in the theorisation of children's rights as well as their practical application. In addition to her youth justice work, she also has an interest in judicial approaches to children's rights, including in judgement-writing and sentence delivery. She was co-director (with Professor Helen Stalford) of the AHRC-funded *Children's Rights Judgments Project*. Her work on Judgments for Children has formed the basis of judicial training in a number of jurisdictions and led to changes to judicial guidance in England and Wales. She has acted in an advisory capacity for a number of organisations including the Youth Justice Legal Centre, Children's Rights Alliance for England and the Youth Justice Board.

Ursula Kilkelly is a Professor of law at the School of Law, University College Cork where she directs the Centre for Children's Rights and Family Law. She has been researching children's rights and youth justice for over 20 years, publishing several monographs and edited collections and dozens of peer-reviewed publications over this time. Her recent books include 'Advancing Children's Rights in Detention' with Pat Bergin, published by Bristol University Press in 2022 and 'National Human Rights Institutions for Children', with Emily Logan, published by Palgrave Macmillan in 2021. She is editor with Stefaan Pleysier of Youth Justice, the leading international journal in the field of youth justice. As part of her commitment to rights-based advocacy and practice, she is a government-appointed chairperson of the Board of Management in Oberstown Children Detention Campus, Ireland's national facility for children under 18 years serving detention and remand orders.

Dr. Sue Thomas is a Senior Research Assistant with the University of South Wales. Prior to this she worked for the Youth Justice Board in Wales for eight years in a variety of roles focusing on youth offending team oversight, identifying and developing effective practice and managing a variety of projects. She also worked as a development manager for Nacro's Youth Crime Section in Wales for 17 years, responsible for planning, managing and delivering a work programme which undertook research, training and consultancy into various aspects of youth justice in Wales. Sue has a long-standing interest in Child First and what it means in policy and practice, exploring this in a professional doctorate completed in 2015.

Paula Williams is the Director of Strategy and Planning at the Youth Justice Board for England and Wales and is working with the Board to help realise their Child First ambition. She has worked within the youth justice sector for 25 years, having previously studied psychology as an undergraduate and an M.Sc.(Econ.) Criminology and Criminal Justice—undertaking research into restorative justice from the victim's perspective. She subsequently qualified as a social worker with a particular focus on youth justice and began her working career in East London in a youth justice team and experienced the transformation driven by the Crime and Disorder Act 1998. She has since worked in a range of roles spanning practice, management, performance improvement, policy and strategy and inspection.

1

Introduction

Stephen Case and Neal Hazel

This edited text explores, analyses and evaluates 'Child First'—a guiding principle and strategy for understanding children who offend and for shaping youth justice responses to this offending. Child First transcends traditional welfare and justice priorities and more contemporary risk management and hybrid models of youth justice to offer a progressive, child-friendly, non-criminalising r/evolution in youth justice. The Child First principle and its component tenets (seeing children as children, developing pro-social identity for positive outcomes, collaboration with children, diversion) have the potential to significantly develop and

---

S. Case (✉)
Department of Social Sciences,
Loughborough University, Loughborough, UK
e-mail: s.case@lboro.ac.uk

N. Hazel
School of Health and Society, University of Salford, Salford, UK
e-mail: n.hazel@salford.ac.uk

enhance understandings of, and responses to, offending by children in conceptual, theoretical, policy and practical terms. Indeed, Child First now informs and shapes all policy and practice across the Youth Justice System of England and Wales, is being formalised as the key reform principle for youth justice in Northern Ireland and is increasingly influential in the policy and practice in a host of western (youth) justice systems (e.g. Scotland, Ireland, Australia, New Zealand, Canada, states of the USA). Accordingly, Child First is the key vehicle for developing 'new' forms of youth justice systems, structures and strategies internationally, which centralise and prioritise the status, capacity and well-being of the 'child' rather than labelling and stigmatising children as 'offenders'.

This book draws together a collection of eminent, experienced authors from a range of youth justice sectors (e.g. academia, research, policy, strategy, practice) in order to trace and examine the origins, trajectory and utility of Child First as an evidence-based, innovative approach to modern youth justice. The author group constitutes a cadre of key stakeholders who have been at the forefront of the evolution of Child First, enabling detailed discussion of the rationale, benefits, limitations, challenges and opportunities inherent to this nascent approach. Critical themes are interwoven throughout the chapters, including analysis of Child First in terms of diversity (e.g. gender, ethnicity, sexuality, disability), its implications at different stages of youth justice systems (e.g. arrest-out-of-court-court-community sentence-custody-resettlement) and its potential impact on inter-relationships between different organisations (e.g. police, courts, youth offending teams, custodial institutions) and with other systems for supporting children (e.g. social care, education, health). The overarching aim of the text, therefore, is to cohere an expert discussion and evaluation of Child First as a valid, sustainable blueprint for a cutting-edge, principled and 'positive' approach to working with children—an innovative way forward for youth justice systems internationally.

The Socio-Historical Trajectory of Youth Justice Responses to Children When They Offend

The trajectory of youth justice historically and globally has been characterised by *conflict and ambivalence* regarding how to construct understandings of and responses to children when they offend. The evolution of youth justice has been shaped by an apparent desire to reconstruct and differentiate children (when they offend) from those ostensibly innocent and vulnerable children who do not (cf. the distinction between 'Devils and Angels'—Fionda, 2005). The inception and trajectory of 'youth justice' as a socially constructed set of formal responses (e.g. laws, sentences, structures, policies, strategies, principles, interventions) to offending by children have been characterised by processes of *bifurcation*. This process involves division of responses into two distinct, often contrasting pathways, for example, by responding to children as innocent and vulnerable in their everyday lives, yet somehow dangerous and threatening when they offend (cf. the 'innocent-dangerous child' dichotomy—Case, 2021).

In the socio-historic context of Great Britain, for example, the highly influential Youthful Offenders Act 1854 evidenced a nascent move away from punitive (criminal justice) custodial responses and towards differentiated (youth justice) responses to children's offending—illustrative of bifurcation of responses to offending by adults and children. Constructed youth justice responses to children were themselves bifurcated (e.g. simultaneously supportive and controlling), focused on reform and correction (e.g. creation of Reformatory Schools for the 'perishing classes'—Carpenter, 2013) and focused on education and training for those perceived as neglected, in need and 'pre-criminal' (e.g. creation of Industrial Schools for the 'dangerous classes'—Carpenter, 2013). The first half of the twentieth century extrapolated the conflict and ambivalence of the innocent-dangerous child dichotomy to the exponential legislative creation of justice-based structures (e.g. the formalisation of juvenile courts and borstals by the Children Act 1908) alongside the introduction of further welfare-based provision (e.g. the first professional social work departments for troubled children—Children and Young Persons Act/CYPA 1948)—with each structure pursuing simultaneous welfare and justice objectives (e.g. education and correction). The latter half of the twentieth century (certainly until the 1990s) epitomised the conflict and ambivalence of bifurcated welfare-justice responses through contradictory youth justice legislation, strategies and practices designed and implemented in ambiguous ways. For example, the 1960s was a period characterised by progressive, welfare-orientated youth justice, such as social work-based therapeutic relationship building (CYPA 1963) and the allocation of more practice discretion to social services over criminal justice agencies (CYPA 1969). However, the CYPA 1970 marked a return to justice by reallocating the main responsibility for dealing with children who offended to criminal justice agencies, reinstating an emphasis upon punitive custody and refusing to enact the previous recommendation to raise the age criminal responsibility to 14 (Case, 2021). Subsequently, the birth of Intermediate Treatment in the 1970s prioritised responding to children at risk of offending in a welfare-based context that was 'intermediate' between the family context and custody. This was soon followed by the popularisation of diversion and anti-custody approaches in the 1980s, guided by new orthodoxy thinking and systems management that emphasised welfarist, non-criminalising decision-making at each of the key decision-making points across the youth justice process. Therefore, the 'welfare versus justice' debate (cf. Smith, 2005) was intensified over the 1950–1990 period due to the conflict and ambivalence illustrated by different legislative changes, structural/practical developments and systemic constructions.

The Increasing Hybridity of Contemporary Youth Justice in the Western World

Since the 1990s, an emerging *hybridity* has characterised westernised youth justice, although there (arguably) remains an overriding bifurcation of responses to children. On the one hand, punitive responses to children as dangerous 'offenders' have become hegemonic (characterised as the 'punitive turn'—Muncie, 2008; see also Bateman's chapter in this text)—grounded in processes of control, correction, custody, repenalisation, neo-liberal responsibilisation and adulterisation. Concurrently, punitive-practical risk management methodologies have gained prominence (Case, 2021), notably the use of risk assessment instruments and 'actuarial' statistical probability testing, then targeting these risk factors through risk-focused intervention in order to reduce and prevent future offending (see also Case's chapter in this text). In stark contrast, a movement of 'child-friendly justice' has emerged to challenge the punitive practicality, underpinned by principles such as universalism, adherence to children's rights instruments such as the United Nations Convention on the Rights of the Child (e.g. non-discrimination, deprivation of liberty as a last resort, minimum necessary intervention) and the overarching requirement to protect vulnerable children, including those who offend (Goldson, 2014; see also Kilkelly's chapter in this text).

Whilst bifurcated objectives for youth justice are typically presented as contradictory and competing, this does not necessarily render them mutually exclusive. Indeed, there are salient examples of their messy conflation, such as mechanisms providing simultaneous support and responsibilisation as core elements of the 'new youth justice' of the Youth Justice System of England and Wales created in 1998 (Goldson, 2000). Therefore, the generalised 'models', strategies and objectives broadly characterising westernised approaches to youth justice are, in reality, often more hybrid and complex—approaches that reflect fluctuating philosophical approaches and/or cumulative patterns arising from competing socio-political, cultural and economic pressures (Cavadino & Dignan, 2006; Hazel, 2008). Accordingly, the growing complexity, diversity and hybridity of international youth justice over the past three decades has been reflected in the identification of two further evidence-based 'models' of youth justice (see Dunkel et al., 2014; Goldson, 2014; McAra, 2010; Winterdyck, 2014, 2021); models that can be understood as more modernised and (internally) hybrid than their welfare and justice predecessors:

> **Neo-correctionalism**—a neo-liberal 'third way' model emphasising individual freedom of choice and assigning primary responsibility for offending and its prevention to the individual, family and community

(a strategy of 'responsibilisation') over examining the criminogenic influence of social contexts (cf. Garland, 2001). There is an associated focus on correcting identified *deficits* in children's lives through targeted sentencing and increasing intervention by the State (a strategy of 'interventionism'), typically through prioritising risk management; **Minimum intervention**—a significantly less common/popular alternative approach challenging the potentially net-widening, disproportionate and criminalising nature of responsibilisation and interventionism strategies through an ethos of minimal (necessary) intervention, on the part of the justice system. This approach is essentially neutral, however, as to whether other systems of care, education of personal development should provide alternative means of support or guidance.

These contemporary models of youth justice demonstrate sufficient complexity and nuance to indicate conceptual progress in the field beyond the traditional 'welfare versus justice' caricature. However, the models (arguably) still perpetuate a discernibly bifurcated youth justice response in relation to intervention—with neo-correctionalism facilitating a punitive, criminalising strategy of 'interventionism', contrasting with the avowedly non-criminalising, diversionary strategy of minimum necessary intervention.

The socio-historical trajectory of westernised youth justice, notably in Great Britain, therefore, illustrates a series of recurrent binary and dichotomised/bifurcated reconstructions of both childhood and children (when they offend)—from vulnerable to threatening, immature to adulterised/responsible, deprived to depraved and being 'in need' to presenting 'risk' (Case, 2021). Consistent, recurring processes of 'othering' children when they offend have precluded more nuanced and sensitive understandings of children as sharing common characteristics or, for example, as being both offenders and victims at the same time. This is indicative of 'cognitive dissonance'—pursuing apparently contrasting and contradictory, response pathways and strategies simultaneously (e.g. care-control, welfare-justice, interventionism-minimum necessary intervention), based on similarly conflicting understandings/constructions of children who offend. Sustained bifurcation and cognitive dissonance have been fostered at a systemic level because youth justice internationally has typically cohered around two polarised strategic objectives (McAra, 2010: 288):

> to help troubled young people to change, develop and overcome their problems; to deliver a firm, prompt and appropriate response to youth offending that protects the public.

Therefore, it remains possible in the twenty-first century to discern a persistent *conflict and ambivalence* in the trajectory of youth justice. This cognitive dissonance has been reflected in bifurcation and animated through punitive practicality in responses to offending by children and the principled positivity that has emerged to challenge this 'dystopian punitiveness' (Goldson, 2014), in the form of rights-based, child-friendly justice (cf. Dunkel, 2014)—an approach encapsulated and evidenced by the Child First principle and strategy (cf. Case, 2021).

From 'Children First, Offenders Second' to 'Child First'

The Child First 2014 strategic objective has its origins in Wales in the principle of 'Children First, Offenders Second', which was first articulated by academic researchers Kevin Haines and Mark Drakeford in their ground-breaking text 'Young People and Youth Justice' (Haines & Drakeford, 1998; see also Haines and Thomas's chapter in this text). The original 'Children First, Offenders Second' (CFOS) principle challenged what the authors perceived to be the anti-child elements of the 'new youth justice' (Goldson, 2000) strategies contained within the 'Crime and Disorder Act 1998', particularly those that:

- *criminalised children* through the application of 'youth offender' labels (i.e. ignoring their 'child' status);
- **prioritised** *offence- and offender-based* interventions;
- assigned too much *responsibility to children* for causing and desisting from offending;

- *breached children's rights* under the United Nations Convention on the Rights of Child (UNCRC);
- mobilised non-child-friendly strategies using *punitive* (punishing) and *risk-based approaches* to delivering youth justice.

The CFOS principle was subsequently integrated into the Welsh national youth inclusion strategy 'Extending Entitlement' (National Assembly Policy Unit, 2000, 2002). It subsequently became the foundation of the 'All Wales Youth Offending Strategy' (Welsh Assembly Government & the YJB, 2004), now the 'Children and Young People First' strategy (Welsh Government & YJB, 2014; see also 'Youth Justice Blueprint for Wales'—MoJ & Welsh Government, 2019). Alongside these strategic developments in Wales, a long-term body of academic research was being conducted with children, parents, Youth Offending Team (YOT) staff, police, schools, third sector organisations and national policy-makers (e.g. YJB Cymru; Welsh Government) to unpack, expand and evaluate CFOS practice (see also Thomas, 2015). This research developed the CFOS principle into an evidence-based model of practice entitled 'Positive Youth Justice' (Haines & Case, 2015), which consisted of inter-related, 'effective' components of practice in the Youth Justice System (YJS), notably:

- *child-friendly, child-appropriate* treatment of older children who offend in accordance with 'child' status and capacities;
- *promotion of positive behaviours and outcomes* for children (e.g. access to universal entitlements and rights);
- *diversion* from the formal YJS, including child-friendly decision-making at all stages of the YJS;
- more meaningful *engagement and participation* of children in youth justice processes such as decision-making and intervention planning;
- *making adult professionals responsible* for ensuring that children in the YJS achieve positive outcomes and access support and guidance.

Throughout its policy-based and strategic development in Wales, a succession of multi-agency, interventions and programmes provided empirical evidence of the effectiveness of CFOS (see Case & Browning

2021; Haines & Case, 2015) in reducing negative behaviours and outcomes such as the numbers of children receiving school exclusions, reporting substance use, subject to anti-social behaviour management, offending annually, entering the YJS for the first time, reoffending and receiving custodial sentences (see Case & Haines, 2003, 2004, 2009; Haines & Case, 2005). These programmes have also provided evidence of positive (i.e. not simply preventative) outcomes, for example, increases in the annual numbers of children diverted from the formal YJS and into appropriate support services (Haines et al., 2013), improvements in children's perceptions that they can access their universal rights (Case et al., 2005) and children's increased engagement with positive, pro-social opportunities and services in their community (Case & Haines, 2018; Case et al., 2012a, b; Haines & Case, 2015).

Principled Positivity Takes Root: CFOS Finally Comes to England (2015 to Present Day)

In September 2015, Justice Secretary Michael Gove commissioned a full-scale 'Review of the Youth Justice System in England and Wales' (Taylor, 2016). The author acknowledged that 'this review … presents an opportunity to build on considerable success' (Taylor Interim Report, 2016: 2), notably long-term downward trajectories in annual arrests, first-time entrants into the YJS (FTEs) and disposals (cautions and convictions), reoffending numbers and custody rates. The Government rationale for the review was that reoffending *rates* remained a persistent problem, as did annual statistical increases in the proportion of children with multiple complex needs and personal/social problems entering the YJS. Following secondary data analysis and consultation with the sector, Taylor established a set of recommendations for improving youth justice in England and Wales by centralising the role of education, pursuing more integrated delivery approaches (e.g. multi-agency partnerships) and promoting more local devolution and practitioner discretion in decision-making, assessment, planning and delivery of youth justice interventions. The most notable recommendation was for a reorientated system of youth justice where 'we see the child first and the offender second' (Taylor, 2016: 3), echoing ongoing strategic developments in Welsh youth justice.

Soon after being appointed Chair of the YJB (2016–2020), Taylor oversaw a wholesale change of membership, recruiting a cadre of fresh, innovative professionals with extensive practice experience and CFOS credentials, including a former Children's Commissioner, former chief police officer, a YOT manager and practice-facing academic researchers. This change of personnel (alongside the recent review recommendations) catalysed a formal and deliberate culture shift for YJB strategic planning, moving away from adherence to risk management criteria and towards CFOS-based principles for youth justice. These structural and cultural changes were augmented by a series of contextual, philosophical, political and strategic developments challenging the status quo of dominant neo-correctionalist, risk management thinking (Case & Browning, 2021), most notably relating to:

Evidence: Evolving academic and empirical insights regarding successful and appropriate components of youth justice strategies and models of practice internationally, alongside evidence-based critiques of the weaknesses and limitations or previous models and approaches, we are expanding knowledge and understanding of the influences on children's offending behaviour and how best to respond to it (cf. Baker for YJB, 2014);

Principled debates: The 'principled youth justice' model of Goldson and Muncie (2006) argued that youth justice should address socio-economic inequalities, prioritise diversion from the formal YJS and promote child-appropriate justice (see also Harding & Becroft, 2013). An associated 'child-friendly justice' movement emerged seeking to protect the rights, inherent child status and best interests of children when they offend, so viewing them as 'vulnerable becomings in need of protection, help, guidance and support' (Goldson & Muncie, 2015: vii);

Socio-economic change: Sweeping economic austerity internationally had precipitated the enforced downsising of vital children's support services. However, these 'crises' (in combination with the developments above) have motivated key to explore new understandings of

and responses to children's offending behaviour that are founded in broader (yet also more localised) evidence-bases and that may be more innovative and cost effective than previous approaches;
Political dynamism: Governmental instability and insecurity (e.g. resulting from austerity, Brexit, differences between UK nation states, internal party changes) catalysed frequent changes in key stakeholder personnel and in the visibility and priority of youth justice as a political issue. Indeed, a significant consequence of this dynamism was the commissioning of the Youth Justice Review (Taylor, 2016);
Strategic developments in related policy areas: The National Police Chiefs' Council (NPCC) 'Child Centred Policing' national strategy document stated that 'It is crucial that in all encounters with the police those below the age of 18 should be treated as children first' (NPCC, 2015: 9); a philosophy reiterated by the Youth Justice Review. Subsequently, the Sentencing Council produced their 'Sentencing Children and Young People' guidelines and principles, which stated that 'the approach to sentencing should be individualistic and focused on the child or young person, as opposed to offence focused' (Sentencing Council, 2017: 4), thus Child First, not offence or offender first.

Consequently, CFOS was reconstructed into the 'Child First' principle by the YJB and operationalised as a fusion of the central evidence-based tenets of the aforementioned 'Positive Youth Justice' model (Haines & Case, 2015; see also Case & Browning, 2021) and 'Constructive Resettlement' approach (Hazel & Bateman, 2020; YJB, 2018)—constructive (strengths based, future-focused, empowering), co-created (with the child), customised (for the child), consistent (shared objectives) and co-ordinated (through multi-agency partnership). Soon after its initial operationalisation in a 'Board information paper' (YJB, 2018), Child First, as the central principle for and animator of youth justice *practice* in England, was officially articulated in 'Standards for children in the justice system' document (MoJ/YJB, 2019), which provided a 'framework for youth justice practice' and the 'minimum expectations for all agencies' to ensure that positive outcomes for children align with the new Child First principle (YJB, 2019: 4). These revised 'National Standards' for practitioners were, therefore, 'indicative of a clear distinction between the philosophy now espoused by the YJB [Child First] and that which informed the previous iteration of the standards [risk management]' (Bateman, 2020: 4). The new expectations for Child First practice were consolidated in the YJB 'Case Management Guidance' for practitioners, separate guidance documents outlining how practitioners and managers should work with children at different stages of the YJS: out-of-court, in-court working, bail and remand, using reports, assessment, community interventions, custody and resettlement, and supporting parents (YJB, 2019). The strategic prioritisation of Child First was reflected in the Vision Statement of the YJB Strategic Plan 2021–2024, which committed to Child First as the 'strategic approach and central guiding principle' for youth justice (YJB, 2021: 3), consolidating Taylor by asserting that:

> We see children first and offenders second. We make every effort to champion the needs of children wherever they are in the youth justice system and ensure we give them a voice; We strongly believe that children can and should be given every opportunity to make positive changes. (YJB, 2021: 7)

The Strategic Plan operationalised Child First into four inter-related 'tenets' (YJB, 2021: 10–11):

- *See children as children*: Prioritise the best interests of children, recognising their particular needs, capacities, rights and potential. All work is child-focused, developmentally informed, acknowledges structural barriers and meets responsibilities towards children;
- *Develop pro-social identity for positive child outcomes*: Promote children's individual strengths and capacities to develop their pro-social identity for sustainable desistance, leading to safer communities and fewer victims. All work is constructive and future-focused, built on supportive relationships that empower children to fulfil their potential and make positive contributions to society;
- *Collaborate with children*: Encourage children's active participation, engagement and wider social inclusion. All work is a meaningful collaboration with children and their carers;

- *Promote diversion*: Promote a childhood removed from the justice system, using pre-emptive prevention, diversion and minimal intervention. All work minimises criminogenic stigma from contact with the system.

Child First as a Principled Philosophy, Not a Reductionist Model

'Child First' is now (at the time of writing in 2022) the official 'strategic approach and central guiding principle' for youth justice policy and practice in England and Wales, underpinning 'a vision for a youth justice system that treats children as children', cohered by its four central tenets. As stated, the Child First principle explicitly questions and challenges established adult-centric, adulterising and interventionist/labelling/criminalising constructions of children (when they offend) as risky and threatening 'offenders' (cf. Case, 2021), encompassing a range of theoretical, ideological and principled assumptions about the nature of childhood and children's evolving capacity (cf. Smith, 2010). Therefore, Child First offers more than simply a new 'model' of youth justice[1] in the sense of a prescriptive delivery framework constituted by key features, practices, strategies and interventions, superseding traditionally bifurcated (e.g. polarised, dichotomised) models of youth justice (e.g. welfare-justice), whilst actively challenging and rejecting the hegemonic, reductionist and adult-centric neo-correctionalist risk management paradigm that is anchored in pathologising, individualising and deficit-based notions of the problem child (see the detailed critique of Case, 2021). As will be explored across this text, Child First has the potential to offer a guiding principle for reconstructing understandings of 'youth offending' (children who offend) and for shaping a youth justice that can become the beating heart of practice—a relational, dynamic and contextual force for change in how children are

---

[1] Understood here as a complex social construction that can be broadly operationalised as the structures, systems, processes, frameworks, strategies, policies, organisations, principles and theories underpinning responses to offending by 'children' and 'young people' in particular jurisdictions at a given point in time (cf. Case, 2021).

responded to when they offend and how they experience youth justice[2] (Greenhalgh & Mazano, 2021). It will be asserted that Child First constitutes a radical, expansionist cultural and practical shift for youth justice, presenting a progressive *philosophy*, in terms of a methodical and reasoned way of thinking, an attitude and a guiding principle, that moves above and beyond conventional bifurcated constructions of children's offending beset by conceptual, systemic and practical reductionism. Ironically, yet in this case helpfully/positively, Child First is itself bifurcated in the sense of being simultaneously reactionary and progressive:

- **Reactionary**—critical of the othering of children who offend through punitive, controlling, stigmatising and harmful constructions and responses promoted by traditional and contemporary models of youth justice;
- **Progressive**—responses to children first and foremost at the touchstone and foundation for practice, deemphasising and eliminating punitiveness harm and criminalisation—child friendly and child appropriate, children's rights as a progressive social norm, does not require more spending (i.e. economic-normative—see Haines & Case, 2015).

The exponential prominence of Child First at multiple levels of youth justice construction (e.g. strategic development, practice guidance, practice approaches) strongly implies that it presents as a *principle* transcending the traditionally bifurcated 'models' and frameworks that have resulted from binary thinking regarding children who offend and notions of childhood for these children; binary thinking that has characterised the bifurcated trajectory and evolution of youth justice over the past century. The Child First principle offers an holistic, expansionist *evolution* (rather than alternative model) of previously reductionist youth justice approaches, progress in the field beyond narrowly-framed, youth justice context-dependent responses to offending. Child First necessitates broader considerations of social policy that recommend responses to the

---

[2] Indeed, this progressive philosophy could be applied equally to the treatment of children in trouble by related support systems including policing, social care, education, health and youth work.

status, problems, experiences and perspectives of the 'child' in localised, discretionary and non-prescriptive ways (e.g. multi-systemic practice). It can also be asserted that Child First not only transcends the traditional binary thinking that has beset youth justice, but also transcends representation as a stand-alone 'strategic objective' for youth justice (cf. Bateman, 2020), despite its representation as such by the YJB for England and Wales. Moreover, Child First should be conceptualised as a *philosophy*—a guiding set of principles, objectives, understandings and experiences that frame and animate professional knowledge, skills and practice (Haines & Case, 2020). Child First is at once a 'philosophy of positive youth justice' (Haines & Case, 2015: 1), a 'philosophical stance' (Bateman, 2020) and the 'philosophical foundations' (Goldson & Briggs, 2021: 1) upon which the abolition of youth justice rests and grows. Child First as a philosophy can be constructed and operationalised as a series of relational and dynamic features, contexts and even forces that shape and guide youth justice mechanisms and changes at the individual, systemic and structural levels (after Greenhalgh & Manzano, 2021; see also Case, 2021). Consequently, our central analytical framework is an interrogation of the role and influence of Child First in the evolution (progression, expansion) and revolution (revisiting, repurposing) of contemporary youth justice as a blueprint for new thinking and progressive models of practice in England and Wales and further afield.

Structure of the Book

Part I of this text is entitled 'Child First: Challenging Youth Justice Systems'. This section of chapters situates and contextualises the emergence of Child First justice within the socio-historical trajectory of youth justice 'models' and strategies in the industrialised Western world. In Chapter 2, Tim Bateman explores the historical reliance of Western youth justice systems, policies and practices upon assumptions that derive primarily from punitive arrangements for dealing with adult offenders, which sharply contrast with the requirements of Child First precepts. He argues that the persistence of the punitive expectations and conflicting, ambivalent perceptions of children that emerge once they offend (e.g. their reconstruction from innocent to dangerous and from vulnerable to culpable) will inevitably constrain the ambitions of Child First until they are successfully challenged and addressed. In Chapter 3, Stephen Case extends these arguments through a detailed examination of the emergence of Child First as a policy and practice principle to explicitly and directly challenge the perceived negative excesses of the 'new youth justice' in England and Wales, notably the adult-centric, risk-led strategies of adulterisation, punishment/justice, preventing negative behaviours/outcomes, responsibilising children and programme fetishism. Case illustrates these arguments through a detailed focus on the rise to prominence of neo-correctionalist risk management, animated by the Risk Factor Prevention Paradigm. He concludes by outlining and evaluating the central tenets of the 'Positive Youth Justice' practice 'model' (underpinned by the 'Children First, Offenders Second' principle) in terms of the nature of its explicit challenge to the key features of risk management and its empirical bases as a progressive form of 'evidence-based' youth justice. In Chapter 4, Kevin Haines and Sue Thomas outline the evolution of the 'Children First, Offenders Second' (CFOS) principle (the precursor to Child First) in Wales as a deliberate, principled challenge to historical populism (see also Bateman's chapter) and the regressive, repressive and anti-child movement of the Labour Government that took office in 1997 to oversee the newly-created Youth Justice System of England and Wales. Paying particular attention to the links between academia, policy development and implementation in the evolution of CFOS, Haines and Thomas trace policy, strategy and practice developments in Wales and draw parallels and contrasts with those in England, concluding with the adoption of CFOS as the official policy of the Youth Justice Board for England and Wales. Part I ends with Chapter 5, in which Ursula Kilkelly offers an expert critical commentary on the developing relationship between Child First and the international children's rights movement, itself underpinned by the United Nations Convention on the Rights of the Child 1989. Kilkelly argues from a children's rights-based, Child First perspective that children in conflict with the law have a right to treatment that is age appropriate, meets their needs and enhances the support of family relationships, whilst the principles of diversion and detention as a last resort should be emphasised as means of minimising children's contact with youth justice systems. She asserts that although children's rights are one element of Child First, the latter approach is not explicitly or exclusively rights-based, which is arguably a missed opportunity to leverage the strengths of the rights approach, with which Child First shares common values and principles. Kilkelly concludes that considering the Child First approach from a children's rights perspective helps to identify how a rights-basis would strengthen both the case for and the substance of a Child First approach, as a progressive path towards protecting the rights of all children in conflict with the law.

Part II moves beyond the largely theoretical and conceptual concerns of Part I to focus in more depth on the role of Child First in developing youth justice *policy*. In Chapter 6, John Drew explores the development of youth justice policy, using an insider's perspective gained from his experiences as the Chief Executive of the Youth Justice Board between 2009 and 2013 as well as a front-line youth justice social worker in the 1970s and 1980s. He concentrates on the slow emergence of elements of more 'child-focused' youth justice policy from 2004 to 2013, arguing that these fell short of creating a 'Child First' policy, but played a part in preparing the ground for the emergence of 'Child First' youth justice in 2019. He asserts that the creation of the Youth Justice Board was central to this process by, in turn, creating space within which a child-focus could develop. In Chapter 7, Neal Hazel and Paula Williams discuss 'Developing principled youth justice standards' in the context of Child First. The authors chart the development of 'Child First' as a distinct policy initiative in England and Wales over a three-year period from 2018 to 2021, specifically considering the progress made by the Youth Justice Board since formally adopting the concept as the primary principle to guide policy and practice standards for the sector. In examining the opportunities and barriers faced in its adoption journey, the chapter presents lessons for similar youth justice policy development in other jurisdictions, for its future operationalisation by practitioners, and for the nexus between academic concept and real-world impact more generally. Chapter 8 from Kathryn Hollingsworth examines Child First in the crucial context of court sentencing, asserting that translating Child First principles into sentencing practice is arguably most difficult for children accused and convicted of serious offending, who are most often tried and sentenced in the 'adult' Crown Court and subjected to adulterising, punitive treatment as a result. Hollingsworth advocates for the adoption of a Child First approach within the current system of Crown Court sentencing, focusing in particular on the responsibilities of the adults involved—including the sentencing judge, the lawyers, and the youth justice practitioners—and the potential *they* have to bring very real differences to how children convicted of serious offences experience the justice system now and in the future.

Part III moves consideration of Child First into the field of *practice* development. In Chapter 9, Ben Byrne discusses the implications of Child First for policy and practice, paying particular attention to the fundamental challenge posed by Child First to the current practical arrangements for responding to children in conflict with the law. His chapter analyses the implications of the Child First principle/strategic objective for a range of stakeholders nationally and locally, assessing the role of partners in the delivery of Child First services. Byrne shares examples of promising Child First practice as a catalyst for further reform, drawing on his experience of leading reforms locally and nationally as a YJB board member with responsibility for developing the Child First agenda. Chapter 10 by Anne-Marie Day is an evidence-based exploration of the place of risk within Child First justice through the perspectives of youth justice practitioners. Day outlines the challenges facing frontline practitioners and managers in their implementation of Child First in practice, which have been variously conceptualised as resistance and reticence, contradiction and bifurcation and confusion about competing narratives emerging from different UK Government departments about how to meet the statutory requirement to 'prevent' youth offending. The chapter concludes with an emphasis on the importance of meaningfully engaging with youth justice practitioners in debates about how to operationalise and resolve the 'hard balance' between the Risk Factor Prevention Paradigm (see also Case's chapter in Part I) and Child First justice. In Chapter 11, Kathy Hampson interrogates the cementing of Child First in practice in terms of the extent and nature of the principle's embeddedness within youth justice policy in England and Wales and how this impacts upon the delivery of youth justice services on the ground. Hampson identifies the barriers to, challenges with, and enablers of implementing Child First policy into practice, looking at the day-to-day realities for youth justice practitioners, which ultimately affects the experiences of the children they reach. She cautions that a risk-focus remains evident in youth justice practice, which requires more than Child First as merely a 're-branding' exercise to overturn. Hampson concludes by observing a 'new dawn' of Child First youth justice that offers opportunities for the sector to truly change its focus towards positively changing children's lives by leaving behind outdated models and turning towards a more positive youth justice (see also Case's chapter in Part I). The final chapter by Samantha Burns and Sean Creaney introduces the critical and much-neglected practice of embracing children's voices to facilitate the transformation of youth justice practice through co-production and Child First participation. The authors review the extent and nature of children's participation in decision-making in youth justice and present opportunities for promoting Child First ways of working with children. The chapter's core themes include, but are not limited to: children's experiences of supervision and shared decision-making, peer-led approaches, children's 'untapped' potential as 'knowers' or 'experts', and non-hierarchical empathic relationship building. Burns and Creaney critically reflect upon the enablers and constraints to Child First participation including potential resistance to change amongst the youth justice workforce, the perception that children pose a 'threat' to society, the credibility of children's knowledge and capabilities, the continuation of a 'risk' led deficit-based practice and the urgent need to disrupt disempowering adult-led practices. The chapter concludes by reiterating children's participatory right to influence the decision-making process, their ability to exercise agency and meaningfully contribute to policy and practice developments and transformation of youth justice services.

In the final chapter, 'Postscript—Progress and Challenges for Progressing Progressive Child First Youth Justice', the editors reflect on the progress of Child First through a critical analysis and evaluation of the multi-faceted and multi-levelled challenges to embedding the guiding principle in youth justice policy and practice—challenges faced by academics, policy-makers, practitioners and the broader Youth Justice System. The postscript concludes with final thoughts on protecting the progress made by Child First thus far and preparing for the next set of emergent opportunities to further embed Child First within youth justice systems internationally.

References

Bateman, T. (2020). *The state of youth justice 2020*. NAYJ.

Carpenter, M. (2013). *Reformatory schools for the children of the perishing and dangerous classes, and for juvenile offenders*. CUP.

Case, S. P. (2021). *Youth justice: A critical introduction*. Routledge.

Case, S. P., & Browning, A. (2021). *Child first: The evidence-base*. https://repository.lboro.ac.uk/articles/report/Child_First_Justice_the_research_evidence-base_Full_report_/14152040

Case, S. P., & Haines, K. R. (2003). Promoting prevention: Preventing youth drug use in Swansea by targeting risk and protective factors. *Journal of Substance Use, 8*(4), 243–251.

Case, S. P., & Haines, K. R. (2004). Promoting prevention: Evaluating a multi-agency initiative of youth consultation and crime prevention in Swansea. *Children and Society, 18*(5), 355–370.

Case, S. P., & Haines, K. R. (2009). *Understanding youth offending: Risk factor research, Policy and practice*. Willan.

Case, S. P., & Haines, K. R. (2012). Supporting an evolving and devolving youth justice board. *Criminal Justice Matters, 88*(1), 38–40.

Case, S. P., & Haines, K. R. (2018). Transatlantic 'positive youth justice': Coherent movement or disparate critique? *Crime Prevention and Community Safety, 20*(3), 208–222.

Case, S. P., Clutton, S., & Haines, K. R. (2005). Extending entitlement: A Welsh policy for children. *Wales Journal of Law and Policy, 4*(2), 187–202.

Cavadino, M., & Dignan, J. (2006). *Penal systems: A comparative approach*. Sage Publications.

Dunkel, F. (2014). Juvenile justice systems in Europe—Reform developments between justice, welfare and 'new punitiveness'. *Criminological Studies, 1*.

Garland, D. (2001). *The culture of control*. OUP.

Goldson, B. (2000). *The new youth justice*. Russell House.

Goldson, B., & Briggs, D. (2021). *Making youth justice*. Howard League.
Goldson, B., & Muncie, J. (2006). Rethinking youth justice: Comparative analysis, international human rights and research evidence. *Youth Justice, 6*(2), 91–106.
Goldson, B., & Muncie, J. (2015). *Youth crime and justice*. Sage.
Greenhalgh, J., & Manzano, A. (2021). Understanding 'context' in realist synthesis and evaluation. *International Journal of Social Research Methodology*.
Haines, K. R., & Case, S. P. (2015). *Positive youth justice: Children first, offenders second*. Policy Press.
Haines, K. R., & Drakeford, M. (1998). *Young people and youth justice*. Macmillan.
Harding, C. J., & Beecroft, A. J. (2013). *10 characteristics of a good youth justice system*. A Paper for the Pacific Judicial Development Programme Family Violence and Youth Justice Workshop. Port Vila, Vanuatu.
Hazel, N. (2008). *Cross-national comparison of youth justice*. Youth Justice Board.
McAra, L. (2010). 'Models of youth justice'. In D. J. Smith (Ed.), *A new response to youth crime*. Willan.
Ministry of justice and youth justice board. (2019). *Standards for children in the justice system*. Ministry of Justice.
Muncie, J. (2008). The 'punitive' turn in juvenile justice: Cultures of control and rights compliance in Western Europe and the USA. *Youth Justice, 8*(2), 107–121.
National Police Chiefs' Council. (2015). *Child-centred policing—National strategy for the policing of children and young people*.
Sentencing Council. (2017). *Sentencing children and young people*. Overarching principles and offence specific guidelines for sexual offences and robbery definitive guidelines.
Smith, R. (2005). Welfare versus justice—Again! *Youth Justice, 5*(1), 3–16.
Smith, R. (2010). *Doing justice to young people: Youth crime and social justice*. Willan.
Taylor, C. (2016). *Review of the youth justice system in England and Wales*. Ministry of Justice.
Welsh Assembly Government and Youth Justice Board. (2004). *All Wales youth offending strategy*.
Welsh Government and Youth Justice Board. (2014). *Children and young people first*.
Youth Justice Board. (2014). *AssetPlus Rationale*.

Youth Justice Board. (2018). *Board information paper.*

Youth Justice Board. (2019). *Youth justice board for England and Wales strategic plan 2019–2022.*

Youth Justice Board. (2021). *Youth justice board for England and Wales strategic plan 2021–2024.*

Part I

Child First: Challenging Youth Justice Systems

2

Challenging Punitive Youth Justice

Tim Bateman

A Site of Unresolved Tension

Youth justice policy and practice in England and Wales has, since its inception, been characterised by a fundamental tension. That tension is thrown into sharper relief by the aspiration that children in conflict with the law should be treated as children first, but the range of initiatives intended to move towards adoption of a Child First approach has, to date, failed to trigger any thoroughgoing attempt to resolve the dilemma. Indeed, for the most part, the tension goes unrecognised, but its persistence poses one of the principal challenges to the consistent realisation of a Child First vision.

Youth justice jurisdiction encompasses individuals aged 10–17 years who are processed for behaviour that transgresses the criminal law. Those below that age range are deemed insufficiently competent to be held

T. Bateman (✉)
London, UK
e-mail: tim.bateman@ntlworld.com

© The Author(s), under exclusive license to Springer Nature
Switzerland AG 2023
S. Case and N. Hazel (eds.), *Child First*,
https://doi.org/10.1007/978-3-031-19272-2_2

criminally liable; those above it, are adults for criminal justice purposes (Bateman, 2020a). Accordingly, youth justice provisions deal with a population who are unequivocally children. That childhood status is confirmed by the UK's ratification of the UN Convention on the Rights of the Child in 1991 which commits states to recognising '*every human being below the age of 18 years*' as being a child (United Nations, 1990: Article 1) and replicated in domestic legislation by the Children Act 1989 (White et al., 1990).

Yet, the treatment of children who offend is divorced—operationally and philosophically—from other mainstream and specialist services for children. Youth justice arrangements mirror—albeit with some modification—those for dealing with adults who offend (Taylor, 2016). Government declarations provide assurances that the Youth Justice System (YJS) '*is different to the adult system and is structured to address the needs of children*' (Youth Justice Board/Ministry of Justice, 2021: 2), pointing in justification to the existence of separate courts for children and a distinct workforce, in the form of youth offending teams (YOTs), responsible for supervising children who offend. Nevertheless, the YJS remains fundamentally in *vertical* alignment with the adult criminal justice system, rather than having a horizontal orientation to other elements of service provision for children who require state intervention (Bateman, 2021a). Thus, whereas children's social care and education falls within the purview of the Department of Education, youth justice is the responsibility of the Ministry of Justice. Similarly, criminal justice legislation applies by default to children unless they are explicitly excluded from the provisions.

Herein lies the tension: arrangements for dealing with vulnerable children in conflict with the law rely on the imputation, to those children, of responsibility for their behaviour that is analogous to that ascribed to adult defendants. In particular, the adult sentencing framework, introduced by the Criminal Justice Act 1991, is based on the infliction of punishment appropriate to the crime. It extends to the treatment of children who offend. The Sentencing Council (2017: 4) confirms that '*the seriousness of the offence*', rather than the needs of the child, is '*the starting point*' for determining sentence. In its response to a review of the YJS, the government ignored the call to develop an approach '*in which young people are treated as children first and offenders second*' (Taylor, 2016: 48), but confirmed that improvements were needed to '*punish crime*' (Ministry of Justice, 2016: 3).

The Youth Justice Board (YJB), which has promoted Child First aspirations since 2018, originally saw one of its objectives as being to:

> ensure that young people who do offend are identified and dealt with without delay with punishment proportionate to the seriousness and frequency of offending. (Youth Justice Board, 2002: 36)

As recently as 2014, the Board's vision included '*achieving a youth justice system where ... more offenders are held to account for their actions*' (Youth Justice Board, 2014: 4).

This is not to suggest that agencies cannot change their philosophical base; indeed, the YJB should be commended for shifting its stance. It is rather to highlight the context in which Child First tenets are being promoted and the profound nature of the adaptation required. Inevitably, Child First principles will have to overcome what Williams (1977: 121) calls '*residual*' culture; assumptions, working practices; and traditions that have become deeply embedded over time. The strength of such residues should not be underestimated. Perhaps more importantly, from the current perspective, the punitive adult precepts around which youth justice policy and practice have cohered, retain their hold. As noted, the youth justice framework continues to have punishment as a core rationale. Neither the latest edition of youth justice National Standards (Ministry of Justice/Youth Justice Board, 2019) nor the Board's latest Strategic Plan (Youth Justice Board, 2021) mention punishment but neither document explicitly challenges it. Failing to acknowledge the tension does not however necessarily alleviate it. Although shifts of this nature inevitably take time to bed in, it is nonetheless worrying that the Ministerial foreword for the former document refers, on one occasion, to children as '*offenders*' and prioritises '*breaking the cycle offending*' rather than children's longer-term well-being (Ministry of Justice/Youth Justice Board, 2019: 2).

As Case and Browning (2021: 11) have made clear, Child First principles will be '*explicitly opposed to the 'negative', punitive features of risk-based youth justice*'. To the extent that youth justice policy and practice continues to be determined, in large part, by its close relationship with the adult criminal justice system, and the punitive overtones which such a relationship imparts, Child First ambitions are inevitably constrained. A thoroughgoing Child First philosophy implies a radical rupture from adult precepts and an unambiguous rejection of punishment of children. The remainder of the chapter delineates how punitive values impinge on the treatment of children at different stages of the youth justice process, to demarcate the nature of the challenge posed.

The Social Construction of Youth Crime and the Child to 'Offender' Transition

It is commonly observed that youth crime is a social construction; what counts as an offence and who constitutes a 'youth' for these purposes are not objective categories but are socially defined (Case, 2021). Such definitions provide frames of reference for determining how children in conflict with the law are treated. Further, the construction of youth offending differs from one jurisdiction to another and shifts over time, resulting in variations in the arrangements for dealing with children in conflict with the law and forms of interventions to which they are subject. Differences in the minimum age of criminal responsibility between jurisdictions, for instance, can be understood as reflecting divergent constructions of children who offend (Bateman, 2021a).

From this perspective, 'juvenile delinquency' is a recent 'discovery' in that, until the mid-nineteenth century, children's criminal behaviour was not distinguished from that of adults, and available responses to lawbreaking for those deemed sufficiently mature to be criminally liable, were the same irrespective of age (Muncie, 2021: 50). The emergence of a separate YJS thus represented a substantial reconstruction of how children who committed crime were socially located. The introduction of the juvenile court as a distinct venue for children, through the Children Act 1908, was the culmination of a cluster of pre-ceding developments, including separate custodial facilities and an increasingly specialist workforce, that in combination constituted the creation of a separate YJS. The new court had jurisdiction over children who were charged with an offence, but also dealt with care cases and other proceedings regarding children's welfare (Bateman, 2020b), demonstrating that childhood status, at this time understood as applying to those below the age of 17 years, was increasingly distinguished from adulthood. These developments accordingly reflected a new understanding of children's offending, but they also served to stimulate further reconceptualisation over the course of the next century, up to the present (Case, 2021).

While the creation of a separate system for children represented progress by comparison with their previous treatment as adults, it did not signal a clear move towards the adoption of, what would today be recognised as, Child First principles. During the Parliamentary debate that accompanied the passage of the Children Act 1908, it was clarified that the new courts '*should be agencies for the rescue as well as punishment of child*ren', emphasising that those who offended would follow a different (explicitly punitive) pathway from those in need of care and protection, despite cases being heard in the same venue (cited in Curtis, 2005: 53). As Harris and Webb (1987: 9) were later to observe, '*conflict and confusion*' were inevitable by-products. Tensions revolved around the crystallisation of a divide between children as vulnerable beings whom society has a responsibility to protect and those who, because they have offended, are deemed to have forfeited their childhood status, and those associated rights and safeguards (Fionda, 2005). The fact that this process served to delineate a particular group—namely the children of the poor and disadvantaged—who were frequently framed as underserving in dominant narratives, no doubt made this distinction appear less arbitrary than it might otherwise have seemed (Kingston & Webster, 2016; Yates, 2010).

This artificial dichotomy, whereby children who break the law undergo a transition from innocent 'child' to culpable 'offender', has been a central feature of subsequent youth justice history. While the transition has taken varying forms at different periods, the assumption that children recast as offenders, are deserving of punishment is a consistent defining quality (Case & Bateman, 2020). The endurance of these different constructions of children according to whether they engage in lawbreaking activities, is no doubt buttressed by media accounts that are replete with negative imagery of children in trouble. As Gordon (2018) has demonstrated, such accounts typically dehumanise children who offend, bemoan a lack of effective police action, castigate liberal tolerance and endorse perceived public demands for tougher sentencing. In reaffirming such constructions, policymakers thereby are reflecting, and simultaneously strengthening, a dominant discourse.

Welfare and Justice—Or Punishment?

It is customary to describe shifts in the development of youth justice in terms of oscillations between 'welfare' and 'justice' (Muncie, 2021). These two philosophical models provide radically different conceptions of the rationale for, and purpose of, work with children in trouble. The former emphasises the similar backgrounds, and overlapping characteristics, of children who transgress the law and those in need of care and protection. It understands youth crime as a manifestation of underlying need and, correspondingly, endorses treatment to address the causes of delinquency rather than responding to the symptoms. 'Justice', by contrast, starts from the fact that children's contact with the YJS occurs where they have broken the law and that it is this feature which distinguishes them from other children in need. Compulsory intervention is accordingly only justified to the extent that it is a proportionate response to the child's offending, suitably tempered to allow for reduced culpability. Welfare need, according to justice tenets, should be addressed outside the criminal arena (Hazel, 2008).

It has been suggested recently that the binary distinction between welfare and justice may be insufficient to encompass the full range of youth justice arrangements. McAra and McVie (2015: 221), for example, distinguish three additional '*paradigms*': restorative; diversionary; and actuarial (or risk based). Moreover, while the welfare-justice dichotomy may be analytically valuable in other contexts, it is not particularly helpful in determining the extent to which policy and practice is compatible with a Child First ethos. This is not just because the welfare-justice divide is a continuum wherein the nature of rehabilitative work with children at any given period will manifest elements of both approaches;

it is rather that there is no necessary correspondence between reliance on welfare and justice precepts at any given juncture and the extent to which outcomes are child-friendly (Hazel, 2008).

One might anticipate that welfarist inclinations would be associated with a more progressive treatment of children in trouble, whereas a justice-informed approach would engender increasingly punitive outcomes. If that were true, the realisation of a Child First system might be achieved by a consistent implementation of the former model, but such correlations are not evident in the historical record. The Children and Young Persons Act 1969 represented the highpoint of welfarism for youth justice. The legislation introduced welfare-type disposals, in the form of care and supervision orders, as sentences available to the juvenile court in criminal cases in the expectation that these would supplant custody and other correctional penalties (Bateman, 2021a). Such expectations proved overly optimistic, however, as the new orders were simply grafted onto existing arrangements, leading to a sharp growth in the use of child incarceration over the next decade (Thorpe et al., 1980). The 'back to justice movement' that emerged during the late 1970s in response to the perceived failure of welfarist pretentions, dominated youth justice discourse throughout the 1980s. It rejected rehabilitative treatment through the YJS in favour of increased diversion, minimum intervention and decarceration, relying on the natural process of maturation to enable children to '*grow out of crime*' (Rutherford, 1992). Although justice precepts invoked notions of proportionate punishment, outcomes for children became demonstrably more lenient and custodial sentences declined by 80% between 1980 and 1990 (Bateman, 2014a). The ascendancy of the justice paradigm was subsequently reflected in legislative form when the Children Act 1989 established the new family proceedings court, formally severing the organisational ties between care and youth justice proceedings by removing the former from the juvenile court's jurisdiction. Three years later, the Criminal Justice Act 1991 enshrined justice principles into the statutory sentencing framework (for children and adults) based on notions of 'just deserts' (Bateman, 2021b).

The formal adoption of a justice model was, however, no guarantee of increased tolerance towards children who offended. The onset of a 'punitive turn' in the wake of a moral panic triggered by the 1992 murder of two-year-old James Bulger, by two boys themselves barely over the age of criminal responsibility, fostered a more hostile climate to those who made the transition from child to offender. A lower use of diversionary measures and a rapidly expanding use of child imprisonment of over 90% by the end of the millennium ensued (Nacro, 2003). Such outcomes demonstrated that justice was compatible with both harsher and more lenient treatment.

The Labour administration which took power, in 1997, made good on its promise to be tough on youth crime by ensuring that there would be '*no more excuses*' (Home Office, 1997). The flagship Crime and Disorder Act 1998 introduced a range of measures designed to hold children to account for their behaviour, limit pre-court diversion, and make custody more easily available in the youth court (Goldson, 2000). In many respects, the Act simply built on existing punitive overtones, leading one contemporary commentator to call it '*old hat*' (Fionda, 1999: 36). However, a significant innovation of the '*new youth justice*' (Goldson, 2000) was the wholesale espousal of the 'risk factor prevention paradigm' (Haines & Case, 2008), whose adoption by practitioners was assured through the national roll-out of a mandatory assessment framework (ASSET) that purported to identify, and quantify, children's risk of offending (Baker, 2004). This intensified focus on risk is most frequently characterised as an example of 'actuarialism', but it might equally be understood as form of '*repressive welfarism*' (Phoenix, 2009: 113) since the risk-factor model seeks to address children's 'criminogenic' needs, thus conflating the consequences of material and social deprivation with the risk that children pose to others. This latter characterisation provides further confirmation of the lack of an automatic correspondence between welfare and child-friendly outcomes.

More recently, youth justice has taken another sharp turn: from 2008, coinciding with the introduction of a government target to reduce the number of children entering the YJS for the first time, so-called first-time entrants (FTEs), there has been a sharp decline, of around 80%, in the number of children receiving cautions or convictions and a corresponding contraction in child imprisonment (Bateman, 2020a). This fall is, largely, a consequence of an increased use of informal diversion, facilitated by a growth in the range of disposals available to the police that do not constitute a formal youth justice sanction (Bateman, 2014a). While maximum diversion and a reduced child incarceration are hallmarks of a Child First orientation (Case & Browning, 2021), recent trends cannot be attributed to the adoption of Child First principles, since they pre-date the philosophical shift by more than a decade (Bateman, 2020a). Since that shift, however, the more lenient treatment of children has been reinforced by a renewed policy emphasis that youth justice interventions should seek to address the welfare needs of children who come to the attention of criminal justice agencies. Charlie Taylor, for instance, in his review of the YJS, contended that:

> the focus must be on improving their welfare, health and education – their life prospects – rather than simply imposing punishment. (Taylor, 2016: 3)

This latest iteration of welfarism, unlike the earlier instantiations described above, is thus associated with more child-friendly outcomes. Once again, we are drawn to conclude that the relationship between welfare/justice and the extent to which the treatment of children tends in a progressive or regressive direction is relatively contingent. Welfare and justice are themselves amenable to different constructions depending upon the wider context. In assessing the challenge to implanting Child First principles into the YJS, a focus on the extent to which intervention is motivated by punitiveness and outcomes are indicative of punishment, are, therefore, better yardsticks than whether welfare or justice is ascendant. Let us now turn to examine different stages of the youth justice process to explore the role of punishment at each juncture.

The Minimum Age of Criminal Responsibility—And Punishment

The minimum age of criminal responsibility (MACR) determines the threshold at which children become eligible for entry into the YJS and opens the gate to the pathway along which children are ascribed offender status. The current MACR in England and Wales was set at ten years almost 60 years ago, by the Children and Young Persons Act 1963 (Crofts, 2009), at a time when childhood was constructed very differently. One indication of the alteration in how children are understood is reflected in progressive rises in the school leaving age: from 15 to 16 years in 1972; to 17 years in 2013; and 18 years in 2015 (Gillard, 2018); another is the increase in the age at which children can purchase tobacco, from 16 to 18 years in 2007, following an analogous modification in the age at which children could buy alcohol (Wintour, 2007). There have been no corresponding amendments to the MACR.

The low MACR has drawn criticism from the United Nations Committee on the Rights of the Child (UNCRC), who have repeatedly expressed concern that the current threshold is inconsistent with the Convention on the Rights of the Child (see, for instance, UNCRC, 2016) but the criticisms have fallen on deaf political ears (Bateman, 2012). The Committee's own view as to the lowest acceptable MACR has, moreover, altered from 12 years in 2007 to 14 years in 2019, in line with changing understandings of '*the facts of emotional, mental and intellectual maturity*' (UNCRC, 2019: 9). The availability of criminalisation for children of primary school age is, in addition to infringing rights, out of step with international norms. A 2008 survey of 90 countries confirmed that the most common MACR was 14 years (Hazel, 2008); within Europe, outside the UK, only Switzerland has a MACR as low as ten (Child Rights International Network, n.d.).

This evident outlier status is exacerbated by the fact that, although formally the MACR has remained static since 1963, there has, for practical purposes, been a lowering of the age at which children are subject to criminal proceedings. Until 1998 a measure of protection was afforded by the doctrine of *doli incapax*, a common law presumption, of more than 700 years standing, that children under 14 years were not criminally liable for offending unless the prosecution could demonstrate that they knew that the behaviour in question was seriously wrong, as opposed to naughty or mischievous. It thus constituted a filter ensuring that issues of maturity, capacity and culpability were considered before children aged 10–13 years were criminalised (Bandalli, 2000). The Crime and Disorder Act 1998 abolished *doli incapax*, thereby rendering children '*unequivocally responsible and accountable for choices made and harm caused*' from the age of ten (Bandalli, 2000: 86–87). The change had an immediate negative impact: in the year after implementation the number of 10–14-year-olds receiving a caution or conviction, for an indictable offence, rose by 29% compared with the twelve months prior to abolition. Equivalent figures for children aged 15–17 years showed a decline over the same period (Bateman, 2012).

The government has pointed out that the recent decline in the cohort of younger children entering the YJS has been particularly sharp. In the year ending March 2020, 1,872 children received a formal sanction compared to 16,160 a decade earlier, a fall of 88% (Youth Justice Board/Ministry of Justice, 2021). But this remains a significant number. As Lord Dholakia (2017: column 2189) argued, when introducing a private members bill to raise the MACR to 12, what happens to such a group of '*vulnerable children can hardly be regarded as unimportant*'. One might add that the reluctance to countenance any reform of the MACR appears irrational given the government target to reduce FTEs; excluding younger children from system entry would inevitably assist that target.

Perhaps more significantly for current purposes, a low MACR poses a challenge to a Child First youth justice for two related reasons. First, it makes available punishment, in the form of criminal justice intervention, to very young children despite clear evidence that criminalisation '*does not reduce reoffending and can be harmful*' (Brown & Bunn, 2018: 4). Second, the rationale for retaining the current age threshold betrays patently punitive undertones.

In arguing for the abolition of *doli incapax*, rather than adducing considerations of effectiveness, the government simply declared: '*we must stop making excuses for children who offend. … As they develop, children must bear an increasing responsibility for their actions*' (Home Office, 1997: paragraph 4.1). The idea that 10-year-olds should not be held criminally liable for their conduct was dismissed as '*contrary to common sense*' (Home Office, 1997: paragraph 4.4). Similarly, in justifying a low MACR, administrations of both political hues have resorted to a remarkably consistent rhetoric, that simply casts children at that age as being capable of recognising the difference between right and wrong and concluding that it is thereby appropriate that they should be held culpable for their behaviour. A recent, representative, example is provided by evidence given in 2020 to the Justice Committee (2020: paragraph 62), outlining the government's belief that:

> children aged 10 and over are able to differentiate between bad behaviour and serious wrongdoing, and it is right that they can be held accountable for their actions.

This rationale closely echoes that offered eight years earlier by Damian Green (2012), then Minister for Policing, who exposed the punitive underpinnings of this logic:

> [it is] entirely appropriate to hold children aged 10 and over to account for their actions, and to allow the criminal courts to decide on an effective punishment when an offence has been committed.

A further signal of the punitiveness implicit in maintaining the current MACR is apparent in what Goldson (2009: 152) calls the problem of '*intra-jurisdictional integrity*'; the tension between the age at which children are deemed capable of criminal intent and the thresholds at which other rights and safeguards are applied. As noted above, children cannot leave school until they reach their eighteenth birthday; nor can they vote, sit on a jury, buy alcohol or tobacco before attaining that age. Children cannot consent to sex until they are 16 and they cannot enter paid employment prior to age 13. Goldson argues that these thresholds pose an obvious conceptual strain with attribution of adult-type responsibility from age ten to children who infringe the criminal law.

That strain is resolved once it is recognised that government policy tends to embody constructions of children who offend as different from those who do not. The former are thereby deemed to have relinquished the safeguards and protections that are typically available to other children who demonstrate the requisite compliance with adult expectations of innocence. In the process, those making the transition to offender status come to merit punishment (Bateman, 2014b).

Youth Justice Sanctions—And Punishment

The number of children subject to youth justice sanctions has fallen abruptly over the past decade and a half, with a corresponding expansion in the use of informal mechanisms that serve to divert children from the YJS. While this dramatic contraction is welcome, it should not be assumed that informal diversionary measures are necessarily unproblematic from a Child First perspective.

Relatively little is known about the nature or extent of interventions with children who are diverted. Published data on community resolutions, the most common form of informal disposal, do not distinguish children from adults; nor is the quality and effectiveness of such intervention monitored locally (Criminal Justice Joint Inspections, 2018). Any analysis must, therefore, be tentative, but it is possible to identify a range of potential concerns which suggest that, in at least some cases, decriminalisation does not imply the abandonment of punitiveness.

In the year ending March 2021, preventative and diversionary work accounted for more than half of YOT caseloads (Youth Justice Board, 2021). While youth justice provision has been integrated with wider children's services in some areas, the high proportion of YOT intervention involving non-statutory work suggests that diversion from the criminal justice system does not always result in reallocation to mainstream provision as the adoption of Child First principles might imply. It is perhaps unsurprising therefore that diversionary interventions draw heavily on those available for children post-court (Criminal Justice Joint Inspections, 2018) and that there has been an extension of 'offence-focused' work to the pre-court sphere (Kelly & Armitage, 2015).

Roger Smith (2021: 27) has persuasively argued that decriminalising impulses can be seen '*as establishing a relatively limited frame of legitimacy for diversion*' since eligibility continues to be based on offence gravity and previous offending (Ministry of Justice/Youth Justice Board, 2013). They do not allow multiple diversionary options thereby endorsing criminalisation of children whose offending is more serious or persistent. The process continues to embody the ascription of individual responsibility to (and by implication the appropriateness of punishment for) offending, rather than providing non-stigmatising support to disadvantaged children as a matter of right and social justice (Smith, 2021). It might be noted too that the expansion of diversion has contributed to an increased overrepresentation of minority ethnic children within the YJS. Between 2008 and 2019, the number of white FTEs fell by 91%; the equivalent figure for black children was 78% (Youth Justice Board/Ministry of Justice, 2021). Whatever the explanation for this disparity, it is evident that increased decriminalisation has tended to benefit white children to a considerably greater extent than their minority ethnic peers, suggesting that eligibility for diversion is not equally available to all and that some children are more likely to attract punishment than others.

The most punitive responses are unsurprisingly reserved for those children who do enter the formal reaches of the YJS. As noted above, the principal determinant of sentencing is offence seriousness, tying the disposal to the extent of punishment merited by the child's lawbreaking, just as for adults. This approach is extended to cautions by 2013 guidance issued by the Ministry of Justice/Youth Justice Board (2013) which, despite its age, still applies at the time of writing. Whether children receive an out-of-court disposal or are prosecuted is, in large part, dictated by offence gravity rather than the best interests of the child, their needs, capacities and potential as would be required by a Child First approach (Case & Browning, 2021). In determining the nature of interventions, YOTs are enjoined to ensure that they are '*proportionate to the offence committed*' (Ministry of Justice/Youth Justice Board, 2013: paragraph 8.7). Current YJB case management guidance for out-of-court disposals (being revised at the time of writing to better comply with Child First principles) betrays cultural residues associated with risk management, a focus on offending rather than the child's well-being and making children responsible for repairing harm. Interventions for youth conditional cautions should, according to the guidance, typically include:

> community reparation activity to make good the damage caused by the offence direct reparation to any victim or victims…brief cognitive behavioural work to address the thinking and attitudes behind the decision to offend interventions to address specific offences.… (Youth Justice Board, 2019: 6)

Cautions constitute records of offending, which can, in the event of further criminal proceedings, aggravate the seriousness of the later offending and the extent of punishment that may be meted out (Sentencing Council, 2017). Formal out-of-court sanctions may also be considered in the determination of whether a child is a 'persistent offender', a requirement of imposing custody in the youth court on a child aged 12–14 years (Nacro, 2007a). Diversion from court to cautioning does not sever links to punitive outcomes.

Despite such reservations, a Child First approach would seek to minimise the use of prosecution, since court appearances entail higher levels of stigmatisation and more explicitly punitive interventions. In this context, it is concerning that the proportionate use of cautioning has fallen considerably in recent years. In 2009, 89% of children entering the system for the first time received a caution; by 2019, that proportion had fallen to just over half (54%) (Youth Justice Board/Ministry of Justice, 2021). Children with no prior contact with the YJS have accordingly been progressively subject to increasing levels of punishment. A similar, uptariffing, dynamic also appears evident in data for children sentenced at court. In 2011, just 2% of youth rehabilitation orders had five or more requirements attached to them; by 2020, that proportion had risen to 14% (Youth Justice Board/Ministry of Justice, 2021), suggesting a substantial increase in intensity of intervention for children subject to such disposals.

While punishment is a defining feature of all court decision-making, it takes on an additional significance for children deemed to have committed more serious offences. In such cases, the principal aim of the YJS—to prevent offending—can justify deterrent sentencing, invoking a more punitive outcome than the offence would ordinarily warrant (Sentencing Council, 2017). If a child is charged with a 'grave' crime, the case may be committed to crown court, where adult sentencing powers become available (Nacro, 2007b). Although these provisions should be used rarely (Youth Justice Legal Centre, 2020), during 2020, 665 children were dealt with in the higher court, of whom 252 were sentenced to custody (Bateman, 2021b). It is to the use of child imprisonment that we now turn.

Child Incarceration—And Punishment

A Child First approach would not deny that it may be necessary to deprive children of their liberty but only where they:

> pose a serious risk to others and there are genuinely no alternative options for mitigating that risk in the community. (End Child Imprisonment, 2020: 7)

Deprivation of liberty should thus be used only '*as a measure of last resort and for the shortest appropriate period of time*' in accordance with the Convention on the Rights of the Child (United Nations, 1990: Article 37b). The government contends that the principle of last resort is ensured by the current sentencing framework. In making this claim, they point to statutory provisions (equally applicable to adults) that restrict the imposition of custody to offending '*so serious that no other sanction is appropriate*' (Justice Committee, 2020: paragraph 87).

The use of child imprisonment has reduced markedly in recent years. The population of the children's secure estate was routinely higher than 3,000 during 2008, but by June 2021 was 554 (Youth Custody Service, 2021). But the sentencing framework has not changed over that period, suggesting that it is compatible with higher and lower uses of child imprisonment; the government's contention that it guarantees that deprivation is a last resort is accordingly untenable. Moreover, it is evident that children continue to be incarcerated for minor offences: during 2020, 18 children were imprisoned for common assault; ten for handling stolen goods; six for possession of cannabis; six for breach of a criminal behaviour order (the replacement for the notorious ASBO); and four for shoplifting (Ministry of Justice, 2021a). The statutory provisions allow such outcomes because persistence is an aggravating factor in determining the extent of punishment that is proportionate. The Standing Committee for Youth Justice (2020) has argued that ensuring child imprisonment is a last resort requires much tighter legislative restrictions on the use of child imprisonment than currently pertain. Such restrictions would preclude custody except for offences with a maximum penalty of life imprisonment where a community-based sentence would not be adequate to address the risk of serious harm posed by the child through the commission of further offences.

It is moreover apparent that existing arrangements do not guarantee short periods of detention. The maximum sentence available in the youth court for a single offence is two years, compared six months in the adult magistrates' court (Nacro, 2007a). As noted above, where children are tried in the crown court the adult maximum sentence applies, including life imprisonment (Sentencing Council, 2017). Where a child is convicted of murder, a life sentence is mandatory. The 'starting point' for the minimum term to be served in custody is currently 12 years, but there are provisions in the Police, Crime, Sentencing and Courts Bill (HM Government, 2021), before Parliament at the time of writing, to introduce a sliding scale which would increase this term for all children except those below 14 years of age where the offence has no aggravating features and did not involve the use of a weapon. The UNCRC (2019: 13) has been critical of life sentences for children, arguing that such disposals are '*cruel, inhuman or degrading*'.

Periods of confinement for children in England and Wales are out of alignment with international norms. Whereas adult sentences are available in the former to children for 'grave' crimes, other jurisdictions commonly set an upper limit to child imprisonment well below the adult maximum: three years in Uganda, Brazil, Bolivia and Peru; four in Switzerland; and ten in most Eastern European counties. The availability of life sentences for children similarly contrasts sharply with the rest of Europe. Outside of the UK, just two states—France and Cyprus—have legislation permitting life imprisonment of a child and those provisions are rarely, if ever, used (Bateman, 2020a). In England and Wales, by contrast, 1,528 children were given life sentences between 2015 and 2020 (Ministry of Justice, 2021a).

The punitive undercurrent of child imprisonment is perhaps best evidenced in the treatment of those deprived of their liberty. The secure estate consists of three types of establishment: secure children's homes (SCHs); secure training centres (STCs); and young offender institutions (YOIs) which differ in terms of ethos, regulative framework and staffing. YOIs accommodate boys aged 15–17 years. They are staffed by prison officers, bear a marked resemblance to adult prisons and are commonly located in premises that have fulfilled that function in the past. They are considerably larger than other secure facilities for children, ranging from a capacity of well over 300 at Wetherby to 64 at Parc in Wales. STCs are privately operated custodial facilities for children aged 12–17, including boys aged 15–17 who are deemed too vulnerable to be placed in YOIs. They are considerably smaller than YOIs, with a capacity for up to 80 children.

SCHs, by contrast with the other two forms of provision, are childcare establishments that can also accommodate children detained on welfare grounds, under section 25 of the Children Act 1989. They cater for children aged 10–17 who are assessed as being particularly vulnerable and are staffed by qualified child welfare professionals. SCHs are substantially smaller than other forms of provision: the largest has capacity for 42 children while none of the others accommodates more than 24 (Bateman, 2016; End Child Imprisonment, 2020). Staffing levels within custodial facilities have an impact on children's experiences and might also be seen as reflective of the value placed on provision of high-quality care to children deprived of their liberty. Staff-to-child ratios are more than three times higher in SCHs than in YOIs and are also substantially above those in STCs (Warner et al., 2018).

Child First principles would imply that where children are deprived of their liberty, they should be placed in '*a safe, welfare-based setting which is purposely designed to care for children with extensive needs, rather than to inflict punishment*' (End Child Imprisonment, 2020). There is a clear consensus that of existing forms of secure provision, SCHs '*are the most child focused type … having a more informal, family atmosphere*' (Independent Inquiry into Child Sexual Abuse, 2018: 13). Even the government acknowledges that SCHs

> come closest to delivering the principles of best practice … and designed to provide a therapeutic environment. (Ministry of Justice, 2020a)

While not all SCHs would necessarily meet the stringent minimum expectations that some commentators have argued should apply when children are deprived of their liberty (End Child Imprisonment, 2019), it is nonetheless evident that '*at their best*', they demonstrate that a model of secure accommodation based on a childcare ethos can provide a safe environment that has the potential to minimise the damage caused by custody (Bateman, 2016: 12).

Conversely, there is widespread agreement that YOIs and STCs are not fit for purpose (Wood et al., 2017), and in 2017, HM Chief Inspector of Prisons (2017) reported that no such establishments were safe places to detain children. Yet most incarcerated children continue to be held in these two forms of provision. In July 2021, three quarters of the detained child population were detained in YOIs; just 14% were accommodated in SCHs (Youth Custody Service, 2021). The latter figure would have been lower had it not been for the closure of Medway STC in March 2020 (End Child Imprisonment, 2020). All children were also removed from Rainsbrook STC in June 2021 '*following serious safety concerns*' (Ministry of Justice, 2021b), leaving just one STC open for placement.

How might this distribution of children across the secure estate be understood? Staffing ratios and quality of care are inevitably reflected in per capita costs which range from: £99,000 per annum in a YOI; £211,000 in an STC; and £251,000 in an SCH (Ministry of Justice, 2020b). Given that no other rationale has been given, one is left to surmise that cost, rather than children's well-being, '*is a dominant driving force*' (Little, 2020: 1). It might also be interpreted as an instance of 'less eligibility', the doctrine that, if imprisonment is to deter, those subject to it should not receive treatment preferential to that of their most deprived peers in the community (Sparks, 1996). Such an account would be consistent with the argument presented above, that in popular discourse children who offend are deemed less deserving of their childhood status than their 'innocent' peers. Punishment by another name. As at other stages of the YJS, the large majority of children subject to this highest form of punishment have backgrounds characterised by poverty and disadvantage (Jacobson et al., 2010). Minority ethnic children are more likely to come from deprived communities and are increasingly over-represented among those experiencing such punitive outcomes. In June 2021, more than half of children in custody were from a minority ethnic background (Youth Custody Service, 2021).

The government has committed to the phasing out of YOIs and STCs and their replacement by a network of secure schools (Ministry of Justice,

2016) but progress towards that aspiration has been astonishingly slow. To date, one pilot has been confirmed, on the site of Medway STC, but the planned opening has been subject to considerable delay and will not now occur before 2022, six years after abolition was agreed (Bateman, 2020a). At this speed, it would take 60 years to relocate all those currently held YOIs and STCs, suggesting that this achievement has a low priority. The new form of provision may prove an improvement over those it will (eventually) replace, but no justification has been provided for not taking the obvious alternative of investing in additional SCH capacity, rather than '*reinventing the wheel*' (Bateman, 2016: 12). Secure schools will have dual status as SCHs and 'secure academies', but local authorities, who manage all current SCHs bar one, will be precluded from running them. This crucial difference will retain the divide between provision for most children in custody and other services for vulnerable children, reinforcing the potential for maintenance of the child to offender transition (End Child Imprisonment, 2020).

Conclusion

This chapter argues that a deep rooted, rarely contested, commitment to punishment pervades youth justice policy and practice. It might, with some legitimacy, be objected that by focusing on this sole aspect of the YJS, significant advances of recent years have been underplayed. It is important to acknowledge where progress has been made. The benefits to vulnerable children of expanding diversion, reducing court throughput and the contraction in the use of child imprisonment should not be underestimated. There has been a welcome, albeit partial, abandonment of risk-based practice in favour of relationship-based work predicated on principles associated with desistance (Wigzell, 2021). Such trends are evidently compatible with Child First precepts. The formal adoption of Child First aspirations by the YJB is, itself, a seismic shift that deserves to be applauded. At the same time, the success of the Child First endeavour is contingent on a recognition that punishment is antithetical to child-friendly outcomes. A consistent Child First vision must both acknowledge that tension and mount a challenge to punitiveness wherever it continues to hold sway.

References

Baker, K. (2004). Is ASSET really an asset? Assessment of young offenders in practice. In R. Burnett & C. Roberts (Eds.), *What works in probation and youth justice* (pp. 70–87). Willan.
Bandalli, S. (2000). Children, responsibility and the new youth justice. In B. Goldson (Ed.), *The new youth justice* (pp. 81–95). Russell House Publishing.
Bateman, T. (2012). *Criminalising children for no good purpose: The age of criminal responsibility in England and Wales*. National Association for Youth Justice.
Bateman, T. (2014a). Where has all the youth crime gone? Youth justice in an age of austerity. *Children and Society, 28*(5), 416–424.
Bateman, T. (2014b). Catching them young—Some reflections on the meaning of the age of criminal responsibility in England and Wales. *Safer Communities, 13*(3), 133–142.
Bateman, T. (2016). *The state of youth custody*. National Association for Youth Justice.
Bateman, T. (2020a). *The state of youth justice 2020: An overview of trends and developments*. National Association for Youth Justice.
Bateman, T. (2020b). Responding to youth offending: Historical and current developments in practice. In P. Ugwudike, H. Graham, F. McNeill, P. Raynor, F. Taxman, & C. Trotter (Eds.), *The Routledge companion to rehabilitative work in criminal justice* (pp. 715–728). Routledge.
Bateman, T. (2021a). Youth crime and youth justice. In P. Davies & N. Rowe (Eds.), *An introduction to criminology*. Sage.
Bateman, T. (2021b). *Bridging the care-crime gap: Reforming the youth court?* National Association for Youth Justice.
Brown, P., & Bunn, S. (2018). *Age of criminal responsibility* (Postnote number 577). Parliamentary Office for Science and Technology.
Case, S. (2021). *Youth justice: A critical introduction* (2nd ed.). Routledge.
Case, S., & Bateman, T. (2020). The punitive transition in youth justice: Reconstructing the child as offender. *Children and Society, 34*(6), 475–491.

Case, S., & Browning, A. (2021). *Child first justice: The research evidence-base.* University of Loughborough.

Child Rights International Network. (n.d.). *Minimum ages of criminal responsibility in Europe.* CRIN.

Criminal Justice Joint Inspections. (2018). *Out-of-court disposal work in youth offending teams.* HM Inspectorate of Probation.

Crofts, T. (2009). Catching up with Europe: Taking the age of criminal responsibility seriously in England. *European Journal of Crime Criminal Law and Criminal Justice, 17*, 267–292.

Curtis, S. (2005). The welfare principle. In T. Bateman & J. Pitts (Eds.), *The RHP companion to youth justice* (pp. 53–57). Russell House Publishing.

End Child Imprisonment. (2019). *Principles and minimum expectations for children deprived of their liberty.* End Child Imprisonment.

End Child Imprisonment. (2020). *The case for ending child imprisonment: Questions & answers.* End Child Imprisonment.

Fionda, J. (1999). Crime and Disorder Act 1998: New labour, old hat: Youth justice and the Crime and Disorder Act 1998. *Criminal Law Review*, 36–47.

Fionda, J. (2005). *Devils and angels: Youth policy and crime.* Hart.

Gillard, D. (2018). *Education in England: A history.* EducationEngland.org.

Goldson, B. (2000). *The new youth justice.* Russell House Publishing.

Goldson, B. (2009). Difficult to understand or defend a reasoned case for raising the age of criminal responsibility. *Howard Journal of Criminal Justice, 48*(5), 514–521.

Gordon, F. (2018). *Children, young people and the press in a transitioning society: Representations, reactions and criminalisation.* Palgrave Macmillan.

Green, D. (2012, December 18). Age of criminal responsibility. In *Hansard* (column 686). UK Parliament.

Haines, K., & Case, S. (2008). The rhetoric and reality of the 'Risk Factor Prevention Paradigm' approach to preventing and reducing youth offending. *Youth Justice, 8*(1), 5–20.

Harris, R., & Webb, D. (1987). *Welfare, power and juvenile justice.* Tavistock.

Hazel, N. (2008). *Cross-national comparison of youth justice.* Youth Justice Board.

HM Chief Inspector of Prisons. (2017). *Annual report 2016–17.* HMIP.

HM Government. (2021). *Police, crime, sentencing and courts bill.* UK Parliament.

Home Office. (1997). *No more excuses: A new approach to tackling youth crime in England and Wales.* Home Office.

Independent Inquiry into Child Sexual Abuse. (2018). *Child sexual abuse in custodial institutions: A rapid evidence assessment.* IICSA.

Jacobson, J., Bhardwa, B., Gyateng, T., Hunter, G., & Hough, M. (2010). *Punishing disadvantage: A profile of children in custody.* Prison Reform Trust.

Justice Committee. (2020). *Children and young people in custody (Part 1): Entry into the youth justice system.* UK Parliament.

Kelly, L., & Armitage, V. (2015). Diverse diversions: Youth justice reform, localised practice and a 'new interventionist diversion'. *Youth Justice, 15*(2), 117–133.

Kingston, S., & Webster, C. (2016). The most 'undeserving' of all? How poverty drives young men to victimisation and crime. *Journal of Poverty and Social Justice, 23*(3), 215–222.

Little, R. (2020). Paying the price: Consequences for children's education in prison in a market society. *International Journal of Educational Development, 77*, 102212.

Lord Dholakia. (2017, September 8). Age of Criminal Responsibility Bill, House of Lords, 2nd reading. In *Hansard* (Vol. 783). UK Parliament.

McAra, L., & McVie, S. (2015). The case for diversion and minimum necessary intervention. In B. Goldson & J. Muncie (Eds.), *Youth crime and justice* (pp. 119–136). Sage.

Ministry of Justice. (2016). *The government response to Charlie Taylor's Review of the Youth Justice System.* MoJ.

Ministry of Justice. (2020a). *A smarter approach to sentencing.* MoJ.

Ministry of Justice. (2020b). *Freedom of Information Act (FOIA) Request—191210003.* MoJ.

Ministry of Justice. (2021a). *Criminal Justice Statistics quarterly, England and Wales, year ending December 2020.* MoJ.

Ministry of Justice. (2021b, June 16). *Lord Chancellor takes immediate action to move children from Rainsbrook.* Press release. MoJ.

Ministry of Justice/Youth Justice Board. (2013). *Youth out-of-court disposals: Guide for police and Youth Offending Services.* YJB.

Ministry of Justice/Youth Justice Board. (2019). *Standards for children in the youth justice system 2019.* MoJ.

Muncie, J. (2021). *Youth and crime* (5th ed.). Sage.

Nacro. (2003). *A failure of justice: Ending child imprisonment.* Nacro.

Nacro. (2007a). *The detention and training order: Current position and future developments.* Nacro.

Nacro. (2007b). *'Grave crimes', mode of trial, and long term detention.* Nacro.

Phoenix, J. (2009). Beyond risk assessment: The return of repressive welfarism. In M. Barry & F. McNeill (Eds.), *Youth offending and youth justice* (pp. 113–131). Jessica Kingsley.

Rutherford, A. (1992). *Growing out of crime: The new era* (2nd ed.). Waterside Press.

Sentencing Council. (2017). *Sentencing children and young people: Overarching principles and offence specific guidelines for sexual offences and robbery. Definitive guideline.* Sentencing Council.

Smith, R. (2021). Diversion, rights and social justice. *Youth Justice, 21*(1), 18–22.

Sparks, R. (1996). Penal austerity: The doctrine of less eligibility reborn? In R. Matthews & P. Francis (Eds.), *Prisons 2000. An international perspective on the current state and future of imprisonment* (pp. 74–93). Macmillan.

Standing Committee for Youth Justice. (2020). *Ensuring custody is the last resort for children in England and Wales.* SCYJ.

Taylor, C. (2016). *Review of the youth justice system in England and Wales.* MOJ.

Thorpe, D. H., Smith, D., Green, C. J., & Paley, J. H. (1980). *Out of care: The community support of juvenile offenders.* George Allen and Unwin.

United Nations. (1990). *Convention on the Rights of the Child.* UN.

United Nations Committee on the Rights of the Child. (2016). *Concluding observations on the fifth periodic report of the United Kingdom of Great Britain and Northern Ireland.* UN.

United Nations Committee on the Rights of the Child. (2019). *General Comment No. 24 replacing General Comment No. 10. Children's rights in juvenile justice.* UN.

Warner, L., Hales, H., Smith, J., & Bartlett, A. (2018). *Secure settings for young people: A national scoping exercise.* University of London.

White, R., Carr, P., & Lowe, N. (1990). *A guide to the Children Act 1989.* Butterworths.

Wigzell, A. (2021). *Explaining desistance: Looking forward, not backwards.* National Association for Youth Justice.

Williams, R. (1997). *Marxism and literature.* Oxford University Press.

Wintour, P. (2007, January 1). Legal age for buying tobacco raised to 18 from October 1. *The Guardian.*

Wood, A., Bailey, S., & Butler, R. (2017). *Findings and recommendations of the Youth Custody Improvement Board.* Youth Custody Improvement Board.

Yates, J. (2010). Structural disadvantage, youth, class, crime and poverty. In W. Taylor, R. Earle, & R. Hester (Eds.), *Youth justice handbook: Theory, policy and practice* (pp. 5–22). Willan.

Youth Custody Service. (2021). *Monthly youth custody report—June 2021: England and Wales*. MOJ.
Youth Justice Board. (2002). *Corporate plan 2002–3 to 2004–5 and business plan 2002–03*. YJB.
Youth Justice Board. (2014). *YJB corporate plan 2014–17 and business plan 2014/15*. YJB.
Youth Justice Board. (2019). *How to use out-of-court disposals: Section 1 case management guidance*. YJB.
Youth Justice Board. (2021). *Strategic plan 2021–2024*. YJB.
Youth Justice Board/Ministry of Justice. (2021). *Youth justice statistics 2019/20: England and Wales*. MoJ.
Youth Justice Legal Centre. (2020). *High Court judgment—Sending children to the Crown Court should be rare*. YJLC.

3

Challenging the Risk Paradigm: Children First, Positive Youth Justice

Stephen Case

The Emergence of 'Evidence-Based' Risk Management as Youth Justice

Towards the end of the twentieth century, a period of globalisation swept across the Western world, one animated by rapid socio-economic, political, geographical and technological transformations. The resultant public insecurities, uncertainties and anxieties coalesced into perceptions of these rapid and sweeping transformations as 'risks' and threats needing to be predicted, controlled and managed (cf. the 'risk society' thesis—Beck, 1992). A socio-political climate of *neo-liberalism* emerged, which subsumed concerns with the social contexts of crime within modernising

---

S. Case (✉)
Criminology, Sociology and Social Policy, Loughborough University, Loughborough, UK
e-mail: s.case@lboro.ac.uk

emphases on prescriptions of individual, family and community responsibility, freedom of choice and governance at a distance (Dunkel, 2014; Garland, 2002). A concomitant 'punitive turn' was evidenced in the youth justice field—a movement towards managing the risks presented to the public by allegedly dangerous, threatening children (Case, 2021a) through the increased use of strategies of punishment, control, surveillance and restriction (Muncie, 2015).

Globalised, neo-liberal and punitive pressures catalysed the *modernisation* of methods and practices for generating evidence to explain and respond to 'youth offending',[1] emphasising the role of evidence-based policy as a strategic driver of youth justice responses (Stephenson & Allen, 2013). Evidence-based policy was to be translated into 'evidence-based practice', a modernising, ostensibly 'scientific' criminal justice approach adopted from the field of medicine (Sackett, 1997) that sought to ensure that all practice responses to offending behaviour were accountable, transparent and defensible. As such, evidence-based practice was introduced and utilised as a tool of *managerialism*[2] to guide for practice and resource allocation, signifying a move away from the purportedly overly-discretionary, less consistent, uncoordinated and expensive systemic responses of youth Justice past (Beck, 1992; Wilcox, 2003; YJB, 2013).

The application of evidenced-based practice in the Youth Justice System (YJS) of England and Wales allegedly represented 'the conscientious, explicit and judicious use of current best evidence in making and decisions regarding the prevention of offending by individual young people … in a systematic and objective manner' (Stephenson et al., 2011: 7). However, it soon became clear that the UK Government

---

[1] A pejorative construction resulting from modernising processes of categorisation and 'othering' of younger populations and the perceived need to control, managed and punish these populations in order to protect the public (Muncie, 2015).

[2] A neo-liberal strategy of centralised (government) control, management and prescription over the interpretation and implementation of national policy in localised (evidence-based) practice often animated by regular auditing and monitoring processes, data collection, performance indicators, guidelines, checklists and prescribed procedures (Kemshall, 2008; Turnbull & Spence, 2011).

and the Youth Justice Board[3] (YJB) were selectively commissioning and disseminating youth justice research that provided evidence-based practice evidence to support their preformed neo-liberal policy position on youth justice (see McAra, 2017). Consequently, a particular research evidence-base was privileged to explain offending by children/young people and to inform youth justice responses in England and Wales, which perpetuated and self-fulfilled two specific, inter-related neo-liberal strategies (see Case, 2021a; Hazel, 2008):

> **Responsibilisation**—assigning primary responsibility to children/young people (also to families and communities) for their own exposure to criminogenic influences, for the offending behaviour that resulted and for their inability to desist from it;
> **Correctionalism**—conceptualising and explaining offending by children/young people as the product of identifiable, quantifiable 'deficits' and flaws within the individual that can be targeted, treated and allegedly corrected through youth justice sentences and interventions.

These mutually-reinforcing, neo-liberal strategies of responsibilisation and correctionalism were indicative of a self-fulfilling strategy of generating 'policy-based evidence' (see Goldson & Hughes, 2010). They characterised a reconstructed 'new youth justice' (Goldson, 2000) approach in England and Wales, underpinned by a 'new' (non-welfare, non-justice) set of modernising, managerialist strategies that pursued prevention as the 'new' primary objective of the YJS, animated by the 'new' prioritisation of risk-based early intervention practice. The 'new youth justice' enabled the UK government to rationalise the privileging of a reductionist, risk-led 'evidence-base' produced by developmental criminologists/psychologists (see Case, 2021b), which served to simultaneously blame children/young people (often disproportionately) for their own exposure to criminogenic influences and to restrict the empirical lens of evidence generation to individualised factors. The corollary of this deliberate reduction of the explanatory evidence-base

---

[3] A non-departmental public body created to advise government on youth justice strategy and objectives and to guide practitioners with their implementation (YJB, 2000).

was deemed to *decontextualisation*—the downplaying of the complexity involved in exploring the impact of a broader range of *contextual* criminogenic factors—structural, political, economic,[4] cultural, historical, interactional and situational influences (Myers et al., 2020; Ward, 2020).

The Emergence of Neo-correctionalist Risk Management

Across westernised youth justice systems in the twenty-first century, perhaps most notably the YJS of England and Wales, 'risk' became the main conceptual lens through which evidence was generated to fulfil neo-liberal responsibilising and correctionalist objectives, with 'risk factors' becoming the central 'explanatory' concept for the hegemonic, risk-focused youth justice evidence-base. Risk factors constitute quantified representations of problematic and criminogenic experiences, characteristics and 'deficits', primarily located in the *psychosocial* domains of a child's life (Ashton et al., 2020)—the psychological (e.g. emotional, cognitive, attitudinal) and the immediate social (e.g. family, education, neighbourhood/community, peer group). The body of Risk Factor Research (RFR) that constituted the most significant and prolific evidential basis for these explanations typically utilised 'quantitative scientific methods that can identify potential offenders and reduce recidivism by predicting future behavior' (Kehl et al., 2017: 7–8). The data/evidence generation methodologies of RFR focus on quantified (often binary), aggregated measurements of risk and offending, which are then related through statistical analyses (Case & Haines, 2009). Accordingly, the explanatory theories that have emerged from the hegemonic quantitative, 'artefactual' form of RFR (Kemshall, 2008) have been predominantly developmental, deterministic and neo-positivist—identifying risk factors in early life that are (statistically) predictive (rather than causal) of later offending. The predilection here is for abstracted empiricism and

---

[4] As if to compound matters, there is also a history in criminological research and its associated 'evidence-based' risk assessment tools of reconstructing macro-level influences such as socio-economic deprivation and social marginalisation as individualised risk factors (cf. Harcourt, 2007; see also Tonry, 2019).

reductionism (Case, 2021b), prioritising psychosocial deficits expressed through probabilistic laws and statistical symbolism that serve to uncritically detach and disembed the individual (child) from their structural influences (e.g. family, neighbourhood, demographic characteristics) on their formations of identity and self (cf. Young's, 2016 notion of 'voodoo criminology').

The Risk Factor Prevention Paradigm: Risk Management in Practice

The implementation and application of artefactual RFR evidence in youth justice practice have been pursued through the 'Risk Factor Prevention Paradigm' (Farrington, 2000; Hawkins & Catalano, 1992), which has provided Western governments with a fit-for-purpose, common sense, modernising approach in the service of risk management objectives in the twenty-first century (Case, 2021a, 2021b; Hopkins-Burke, 2016). The Risk Factor Prevention Paradigm (RFPP) rests on an evidence-based central preventative premise to 'identify the risk factors for offending and implement prevention methods designed to counteract them' (Farrington, 2007: 606). The RFPP purportedly offered significant practical advantages over the less 'effective' youth justice practices of the past (e.g. welfare- and justice-based models) by providing a framework that 'links explanation and prevention .... is readily accepted by policy makers, practitioners, and the general public....[and is] based on empirical research' (Farrington, 2000: 7). Taken together, artefactual RFR and the RFPP, therefore, coalesce into an evidenced framework (i.e. 'paradigm') and 'foundational scientific body of knowledge' for governing the work of youth justice practitioners—a set of theories, assumptions and ideas about why children offend and what the purpose and content of youth justice professional practice should be (cf. Haines & Case, 2015; see also Kuhn, 1996). This evidence-base has proven very attractive to youth justice stakeholders (e.g. certain policy-raters), who have readily and uncritically accepted the deterministic explanations of artefactual RFR as 'universal truths that are stable and reliable' (Smith, 2016: 83) and have embraced the RFPP as offering 'clear, unambiguous guidance on how to solve a problem as complex as offending by children' (Smith, 2016: 86).

Following the Crime and Disorder Act 1998, the newly created YJB produced a series of Key Elements of Effective Practice (KEEP) documents outlined the 'essential elements of practice with all children at all stages of the YJS' (YJB, 2003: 6) for youth justice practitioners working in England and Wales. Indicative of a government with a preformed risk management agenda to service their 'new youth justice' approach, the KEEPs were alarmingly reductionist, privileging findings from artefactual RFR and RFPP-led practice (Smith, 2016) as evidence of 'effective' youth justice policy and practice. Indeed, the YJB placed an expectation on KEEP authors to conduct systematic reviews of evidence using the Campbell Collaboration guidelines (Prior & Mason, 2010; see also Strang et al., 2017; Weisburd et al., 2017); guidelines that are inherently reductionist due to their elevation of quasi/experimental methodologies (e.g. Randomised Controlled Trials) as their gold standard, which therefore privilege 'what works' interventions emphasising the targeting of psychosocial risk factors (France & Utting, 2005; Sherman et al., 1998; Sutton et al., 2021). The predominance of artefactual RFR evidence across the KEEP documents rendered 'certain research questions… "unaskable" because they cannot be addressed using experimental methods' (Prior & Mason, 2010: 219); thus negating any potential for the production of 'inconvenient evidence' (Goldson & Muncie, 2015; see also the 'Political Model' of research utilisation—Weiss, 1979); concurrently depersonalising and deprofessionalising the recommended practice of youth justice staff through a prescribed adherence to the risk lens (Turnbull & Spence, 2011).

The central, pivotal KEEP was avowedly risk-based. In 'Assessment, Planning Interventions and Supervision' (APIS), the YJB established the 'foundation activities which guide and shape all work with young people who offend' (YJB, 2003: 6). APIS prescribed 'a consistent risk management methodology resting on a platform of knowledge' (Stephenson et al., 2011: 4), with the mooted benefits for enabling objective, standardised and evidence-based (risk) assessment previously not possible through clinical, discretionary models (Baker, 2005). The 'dependable methods' prescribed by APIS centred on the application of the newly-created 'Asset' structured risk assessment instrument (YJB, 2000), which offered a 'rigorous evidence-based assessment' (YJB, 2003: 20) or exposure to risk factors. Whilst the guidance for conducting this 'rigorous' assessment cautioned against 'relying on a favourite or fashionable theory' (YJB, 2003: 103–104) to explain offending, it also counterintuitively dictated that assessments be informed by a restricted group of developmental, artefactual RFR theories.[5] Consequently, the Asset was overwhelmingly populated by the 'risk factors associated with offending behaviour' (YJB, 2003: 27) that had been widely-replicated in artefactual RFR, all of which were situated within psychosocial risk categories/domains, thus associated planning, judgements and decisions were inevitably framed by psychosocial risk evidence and explanations.

A thorough-going conceptual, methodological and practical reductionism in youth justice has been mobilised by over two decades of risk-dominated conceptions of 'evidence-based practice' and 'effective practice' guidance and assessment tool over-simplification of complex and dynamic aspects of children's lives (e.g. experiences, interactions, perceptions, thoughts) into readily quantifiable. 'dynamic' (i.e. targetable, malleable) and restricted psychosocial 'risk factors' cannot possibly offer a valid representation of the 'lived realities' of those children (France, 2008) nor encompass the full range of criminogenic influences on those children's lives, such as 'needs, motives, knowledge, social deficits…. [and] social and physical contextual factors' (Ward, 2020: 2). In particular, risk assessment in the YJS of England and Wales has embodied a staged process of reductionism that has rendered risk more of a generalised and dehumanised artefact than a practical explanatory concept (Cox, 2020; O'Mahony, 2009; Phoenix, 2016). The economic and practical sustainability of RFR and the RFPP (e.g. Asset risk assessment, APIS), therefore, can be attributed to the self-fulfilling reductionism of evidence generation in research and practice, which has self-perpetuated a restricted psychosocial evidence-base by exclusively employing a risk lens to examine and explain offending by children.

---

[5] Criminal Careers (Farrington, 2000), the Age-Graded Informal Social Control Theory (Sampson & Laub, 1993) and Interactional Theory (Thornberry et al., 2003).

Notwithstanding these reductionist limitations, application of the RFPP peaked in November 2009 with the inception of the 'Scaled Approach' assessment and intervention framework, which dictated that formal youth justice intervention must be proportionate in frequency, intensity and nature to a child assessed level of risk of reoffending, producing a typology of low risk/standard intervention, medium risk/enhanced intervention, high risk/intensive intervention (YJB, 2010; see also Sutherland, 2009). The Scaled Approach effectively formalised widespread utilisation of the RFPP in the YJS by consolidating risk (factors) as the primary conceptual and explanatory animator of youth justice policy and practice, as opposed to, for example, designing youth justice with a robust theoretical, philosophical or principled core. The framework was immediately criticised for its perpetuating the limitations of risk-based youth justice, notably its uncritical use of aggregation, which 'inevitably imposes limits on the accuracy' of these predictions (Bateman, 2011: 175), reduces understanding of the risk profiles and life experiences of individual children (the 'ecological fallacy') and potentially invalidates any proposed intervention (Haines & Case, 2018). Intervention validity was further reduced by the Scaled Approach's inherent partiality—privileging individualised, psychosocial interventions as responses to assessed psychosocial risk factors (the focus of Asset assessment), so 'attention is drawn away from structural, social inequalities for which government itself has some responsibility' (Case & Haines, 2009: 23). Consequently, the Scaled Approach was criticised on the same methodological grounds as its central Asset component, moreover, extending processes of risk-based reductionism and invalidity into the sphere of intervention. Nevertheless, the YJB proselytised of the benefits of the Scaled Approach on the basis of a partial (limited and biased) and highly problematic 'evidence-base' exemplifying how the risk management approach had been over-sold, misrepresented and invalidated by a body of naïve, over-zealous and unreflective stakeholder proponents of developmental and artefactual RFR (see Haines & Case, 2012).

In the same year as the Scaled Approach was introduced, the publication of the evidence-based polemic text 'Understanding Youth Offending: Risk Factor Research, Policy and Practice' (Case & Haines,

2009) was to radically alter the critical policy and practice landscape[6] with its through-going evaluation of the conceptual, evidential, methodological and ethical weaknesses of artefactual RFR and the RFPP. Following a comprehensive review of the most important studies in the evolution of the risk evidence-based, the authors offered a damning evaluation of RFR/RFPP through a series of stringent, hard-hitting criticisms regarding:

> **Reductionism**—artefactual RFR studies, rather than the qualitative, 'constructivist' RFR exploring how children understand, perceive, experience, resist and negotiate risk in their everyday lives (see Kemshall, 2008) conceptualise 'risk' as a quantifiable, numerical, statistical 'factor'. This methodology serves to dumb down a potentially complex and multi-faceted element of children's lives that they experience, perceive and negotiate in individualised ways. Artefactual RFR has utilised the 'factorisation' of risk as a reductionist tool (Case, 2021b) to facilitate statistical analyses (e.g. associating aggregated risk 'scores' with the presence/absence of offending) that produce deterministic and developmental (often imputed, adult-centric and invalid) conclusions regarding the existence and nature of the risk factor-offending relationship—typically the assumption that exposure to risk factors predicts later offending;
>
> **Partiality**—the dominant artefactual form of RFR privileges the examination of risk factors situated within psychological/individual and immediate social (family, education, neighbourhood, lifestyle) domains of a child's life, whilst marginalising contextual influences such as broader socio-structural issues (e.g. poverty, unemployment, neighbourhood disorganisation, changes in law and criminal justice practices) and social interactions/relationships with significant adults within and outside of the YJS. This pervading 'psychosocial bias' has created a partial, reductionist evidence-base of individualised psychosocial explanations of youth offending and equivalent recommendations for responsive intervention;

---

[6] For example, the Chief Executive of the YJB at that time, Professor John Drew, was motivated to initiate a consultation process focused on abolishing the Scaled Approach framework following his reading of the text (see Drew, in Case, 2021a).

Invalidity—the RFR/RFPP evidence-base is characterised by measures of risk that have been rendered invalid due to their over-simplification, partiality, ambiguity, inconsistency (unreliability) and reliance on probabilistic invalid analyses (i.e. privileging statistical tests that require 'samples' of children and 'normal distributions'—neither of which is common in the YJS). The consequences are invalid conclusions regarding the existence and nature of the risk factor-offending relationship (based on imputation and inappropriate extrapolation of statistical results) and the purported homogeneity of RFR studies (which vary greatly in design and methodology). These invalidities are compounded by the planning of interventions on the basis of imputed relationships, the application of aggregated risk profiles to individual children and the 'scaled', potentially disproportionate use of intervention based on prospective and subjective risk measures, rather than substantive, actual need;

Negative perceptions of children who offend—pursuing risk management objectives through the RFPP reinforces a prevention agenda for youth justice systems and practitioners, prioritising the prevention of negative behaviours (e.g. re/offending, substance use) and negative outcomes (e.g. exposure to risk factors, reconviction). This agenda simultaneously (and ironically) promotes negative perceptions (and treatment) of children who offend as bundles of individualised risks and deficits to be managed, corrected and controlled by adults (Case, 2021a). Consequently, children who offend are portrayed as dangerous, threatening and flawed, rather than as agentic experiences and negotiators of their exposure to risk, problems and unmet needs;

Adult-centrism—the RFPP was not developed through research consultation or practice with the people who possess the deepest and most meaningful understanding of the target behaviour: children! Youth justice practitioners could be added as a woefully-neglected key stakeholder group in the evolution of RFPP evidence—representing the very adults tasked to make sense of and mobilise the RFPP on a daily basis. Developing an explanatory and preventative practice paradigm without the full participation of the two most important stakeholder groups in the youth justice field—those who commit the target behaviour and those who respond to it—inherently restricts and arguably invalidates the explanations produced and responses recommended. Due to this adult-centrism and the other negative and invalidating evidential grounds cited, risk-based youth justice (risk management) is anathema to any conception of 'child-friendly' youth justice.

From Risk Management to 'Children First, Offenders Second'

During the second decade of the twenty-first century, the principle of 'children first, offenders second' (CFOS) rose to prominence as the foundation of an alternative positive, progressive approach to youth justice that contrasted starkly and deliberately with the negative, poorly-evidenced, methodologically flawed, unethical and anti-child model of RFPP-led risk management underpinned by artefactual RFR and animated by the RFPP. The CFOS principle constitutes the genesis of the foundational 'Child First' strategic objective for contemporary youth justice policy and practice in England and Wales (YJB, 2021; see also Case & Browning, 2021). CFOS has its origins in research-informed practice in Wales and was first articulated (created) by academic researchers Kevin Haines and Mark Drakeford[7] in their ground-breaking text 'Young People and Youth Justice' (Haines & Drakeford, 1998). The CFOS principle challenged what the authors perceived to be the anti-child elements of the 'new youth justice' (Goldson, 2000) strategies contained within the Crime and Disorder Act 1998, particularly those that:

- *criminalised children* through the application of 'youth offender' labels (i.e. ignoring their 'child' status);
- prioritised *offence- and offender-based* interventions;
- assigned too much *responsibility to children* for causing and desisting from offending;

---

[7] First Minister of Wales since 2018.

- *breached children's rights* under the United Nations Convention on the Rights of Child (UNCRC);
- mobilised non-child-friendly strategies using *punitive* (punishing) and *risk-based approaches* to delivering youth justice.

(after Haines & Case, 2015)

The CFOS principle was readily integrated into the Welsh national youth inclusion strategy 'Extending Entitlement' (National Assembly Policy Unit, 2002) and subsequently became the foundation of the 'All Wales Youth Offending Strategy' (Welsh Assembly Government & YJB, 2004), which evolved into the 'Children and Young People First' strategy (Welsh Government & YJB, 2014). These strategic developments in Wales were complemented and informed by a long-term body of academic research conducted with children, parents, Youth Offending Team (YOT) staff, police, schools, third sector organisations and national policy-makers (e.g. YJB Cymru, Welsh Government) to unpack, expand and evaluate CFOS practice (e.g. Case & Haines, 2003, 2004, 2007, 2008, 2015, 2018, 2020; Haines & Case, 2005, 2015, 2018). This research developed the CFOS principle into an evidence-based model of practice entitled 'Positive Youth Justice' (Haines & Case, 2015), which consisted of inter-related, demonstrably 'effective' component principles for youth justice practice, notably:

- *child-friendly/appropriate* treatment of young people who offend in accordance with the status and cognitive, emotional, developmental capacity of the 'child' (as defined under the UNCRC);
- *promotion of positive behaviours and outcomes* for children, including access to universal entitlements/rights and engagement with support;
- *diversion* from and *minimal necessary intervention* through formal youth justice processes and systems, including child-friendly decision-making at all stages of the YJS;
- *evidence-based partnership* through the meaningful engagement and participation of children in youth justice processes such as decision-making and intervention planning;
- *making adult professionals responsible* for ensuring that children in the YJS achieve positive outcomes and access support and guidance.

The Evolution of Positive Youth Justice: Challenging Risk-Based 'Negative' Youth Justice

The PYJ model (Haines & Case, 2015) constructs children who offend as 'part of the solution' to youth offending, not part of the problem, and pursues this solution by embedding a set of positive principles within youth justice practice that are based on notions of normalisation, inclusion and children's rights, whilst disavowing the unprincipled, negative excesses of hegemonic risk management as the driver of the 'new youth justice'. Accordingly, CFOS-led Positive Youth Justice:

> has a coherent *philosophy* (children first), an explicit sense of *purpose* (prevention is better than cure, children are part of the solution, not part of the problem), clear *goals* (responsibilising adults, evidence-based partnership working) and clearly articulated, desirable *outcomes* for children (positive behaviour, access to rights/entitlements). (Case & Haines, in Goldson & Muncie, 2015: 113)

The mutually-reinforcing component principles of the PYJ model will now be unpacked and interrogated further in terms of their philosophical and evidential bases in CFOS-based and anti-risk youth justice.

Child-Friendly/Appropriate (Not Adulterised)

The essence of the PYJ model is that responses to young people who offend should be constructed with the recipient's status as a 'child' at the forefront (i.e. children first), thus youth justice works with 'children', not 'young people'. This principle underpins the central tenet of the YJB's Child First guiding principle/strategic objective 'seeing children as children' (YJB, 2021; see also Case & Browning, 2021). The PYJ rationale is that 'new youth justice' strategies of responsibilisation and risk-focused prevention (risk management) have adulterised children—treating them like little adults, rather than recognising their status and relative (lack of) development and capacity as a child in legal, (other) policy, cultural, social and psychological terms (see Arthur, 2016; Sentencing Council, 2017; Taylor, 2016). The children first nature of PYJ, therefore, deliberately rejects the 'new youth justice' practice of treating children who offend as mini-adults (i.e. 'adulterisation') in a mini-criminal justice system (see also Muncie, 2008), because such 'adulterisation' overlooks children's inherent vulnerability and need for protection—contradictory to 'good youth justice' (Harding & Beecroft, 2013) and 'child-friendly justice' (Goldson & Muncie, 2015). The co-creator of CFOS, Professor Mark Drakeford (see Haines & Drakeford, 1998), has asserted that offending by children is 'only one element of a much wider and more complex identity' (2009: 8) and so should be responded to through a children-first approach that is 'embedded in a wider and more generic set of policy-making responses' (2010: 143). The CFOS principle and PYJ model avoid using the term 'offender' (Haines & Case, 2015 opt for 'children in conflict with the law and the YJS') due to its potentially labelling and stigmatising effects on the recipient. CFOS and PYJ place the 'child' at the centre of understandings and responses to youth offending (i.e. child-friendly); designing services and interventions that are fit for children (not targeted on 'offenders') and are child-appropriate in the sense of being meaningful, understood, appreciated by and developed in participation with children.

Child-friendly/appropriate youth justice engages with children in child-sensitive ways and responds to needs, problems and rights/entitlements in all aspects of their lives in a holistic, whole child manner. The PYJ evidence-base (see Case & Browning, 2021) indicates that all other component principles should be informed and underpinned by this central CFOS principle of child-friendly/appropriate youth justice. For example, formal and diversionary interventions for children who offend should be child-friendly/appropriate. Interventions that are punitive, retributive (or at least experienced in that way by children) and disproportionate can have unintended consequences that exacerbate existing problems and offending trajectories (Kelly, 2012), so are anathema to children first, positive approaches to delivering youth justice. Similarly, justice-based strategies of proportionality (matching the punishment to the seriousness of the offence) are inherently malleable and subject to a range of criminalising influences (e.g. political agenda, public opinion, practitioner discretion) that can encourage punitive responses (Haines & Case, 2012; Muncie, 2008) such as increased accountability for children who offend (Hazel & Bateman, 2020), adulterised sentencing (Cavadino & Dignan, 2006) and repressive crime control initiatives (Jepsen, 2006). Even some restorative justice has adopted these negative characteristics when applied to children who offend, prioritising the needs of the victim and the need for the 'offender' to restore and repair harm caused over the needs and status of the child (cf. Sherman & Strang, 2007). Further, the needs-led, safety net focus of welfare-based youth justice can be wedded to notions of treatment and correctionalism (as opposed to the promotion of positive behaviours/outcomes)—encouraging adult-centrism, interventionism, net-widening and indeterminism in the YJS. The children first focus of PYJ addresses the adult-centrism and interventionism—none of which are child-friendly/appropriate strategies or outcomes.

Diversion and Minimum Necessary Intervention (Not Punishment- or Welfare-Based)

The PYJ model supports the ethos of 'normalisation'—understanding offending as an everyday, 'normal' aspect of childhood that children will most likely grow out of through 'maturation' (see Glueck and Glueck 1930, in Case & Haines, 2009) and that should be responded to accordingly through diversion and minimum necessary intervention. Therefore, this principle is the explicit predecessor of the YJB Child First tenet of 'promote diversion' (Case & Browning, 2021; YJB, 2021). The model supports an approach to responding to children's offending (related) behaviour where possible (and necessary) through normal child-rearing practices in the context of the family (see also Harding & Beecroft, 2013). Where normalisation processes do not or cannot occur and professional intervention is required, then its focus should be on promoting positive behaviours and outcomes for children (e.g. enabling their access to universal entitlements to services, activities, support and information) and children should be *worked with* in participatory ways to achieve these aims (Case & Haines, 2015). This approach directly contrasts with the 'new youth justice' tendency to *do to* children by prioritising the prevention of negative behaviours and outcomes using correctionalist, punitive and interventionist methods. In this way, PYJ is not anti-intervention, but more opposed to intervention that is unnecessary and disproportionately formal and frequent/intensive (interventionism)—negative excesses that have been encouraged and engendered by risk management and adherence to the RFPP.

The diversionary objectives of PYJ are animated by the strategy of systems management (see Tutt & Giller, 1987), which holds that 'outcomes for individual children and the way in which the YJS works can be changed by managing processes and targeting specific decision-making points within the system itself' (Haines, in Goldson, 2008: 349). By adopting a systems management perspective, the YJS can be understood and operationalised as an inter-connected, mutually-reinforcing series of decision-making points about children, such as decisions to arrest, bail, remand, divert, punish, sentence/prosecute, imprison and release—with each decision encouraging children first, diversionary and promotional practice (Haines & Case, 2015; Haines et al., 2013). Consequently, systems management is a principle with a clear philosophy (children first) and an explicit purpose (children as part of the solution to the problem, prevention is better than cure); challenging the unprincipled net-widening potential of the 'new youth justice' grounded in risk management.

Promoting Positive Behaviours and Outcomes (Not Prioritising Preventing Negatives)

Risk management and the RFPP encourage an exclusive, reductionist focus on prevention—preventing negative behaviours/outcomes. However, this negative, retrospective focus on identifying and addressing risk influences can be criticised for fostering punitive and criminalising youth justice responses that problematise (rather than normalise) offending by children and that socially exclude (rather than include) children when they offend by labelling and constructing them as 'young offenders' (Case & Haines, 2009). Most prevention work is inevitably targeted (not universal) and takes place with identified offenders or children considered to be 'at risk' of offending, which tends to draw these children further into the YJS (Case & Haines, 2015; Hazel & Bateman, 2020). PYJ argues for a children first response where intervention prioritises social inclusion, participation and engagement as drivers of youth justice processes and vehicles to promote positive behaviours and outcomes (e.g. access to universal services, rights and entitlements, diversion into child-focused services outside of the YJS, engagement with education, family cohesion, citizenship). As such, the principle is the precursor to the YJB's Child First tenet of 'develop pro-social identity for positive child outcomes' (YJB, 2021; see also Case & Browning, 2021). This promotional approach is a central animator of PYJ—a progressive, normalising, valid and child-friendly/appropriate method of conceptualising and responding to children who offend and/or demonstrate associated problems (Case & Haines, 2015) whilst avoiding the concurrent exclusionary potential of prevention-obsessed, offender-first, risk-based strategies of the 'new youth justice' (see Case & Haines, 2009, 2020).

A pivotal positive outcome (arguably also a positive, enabling *process*) for CFOS-led youth justice practice is children's *engagement*, which overarches other positive principles such as participation, legitimacy and relationship-building, thus underpinning the YJB Child First tenet of 'collaboration with children' (YJB, 2021; see also Case & Browning, 2021). Engagement encompasses children's meaningful involvement in and commitment to the decisions and outcomes at every stage of the youth justice process (e.g. assessment, sentencing, intervention planning). Children's meaningful engagement is crucial to effective systems management in the pursuit of child-friendly/appropriate, diversionary and positive youth justice responses, yet has been relatively overlooked in the socio-historical construction of youth justice policy and practice guidelines. According to Williamson and Cairns (2005: 1), 'Principles are one thing; practice is another. Too often the aim of engaging young people is vitiated [made less effective] by existing structures of professional power and cultural attitudes'.

A clear barrier to effective engagement with children in the youth justice context is the underlying emphasis on enforcement and compliance, which can disengage children and hamper relationship-building between children and YOT staff (Case et al., 2020; Case & Haines, 2015). The full and complete integration of children's engagement with and participation in youth justice decision-making is a constant difficulty because YOT practitioners have a statutory obligation to enforce the non-negotiable rules and regulations and to ensure children's compliance with court orders (see CRC, 2008). The enforcement-led nature of child–practitioner relationships in the YJS can reduce children's capacity, motivation, willingness and confidence to participate and to engage with youth justice services, whilst also reducing the capacity and willingness of practitioners and organisations to fully include and engage with children (Case, 2021b). Traditionally, engagement research and guidance that exists in the youth justice field has privileged the adult perspectives and skills development for practitioners at the expense of children's perspectives, despite successive children's rights conventions advocating that children have the right to be listened to regarding all decisions that affect them (Article 12 of the UNCRC). The relative neglect of children's voices in youth justice processes and the extent of centralised practice prescriptions, according to critics, has essentially rendered children's subjective experiences 'unknowable' (Phoenix & Kelly, 2013). However, all is not lost. A host of evidence-led academics and practitioners have championed the engagement of children in positive youth justice processes, for example, through 'maximizing the discretion of youth justice workers to hear and respond to children's voices, and to 'rethink' aspects of practice that impair what can be heard and acted upon' (Drake et al., 2014: 23). Contemporary research has indicated that enabling children's engagement with decision-making processes and with the design, implementation and evaluation of youth justice services can facilitate strategic planning, can enhance the meaningful and appropriate decision-making of practitioners and services, and can improve the quality of the child–adult relationships that influence intervention effectiveness (Creaney & Smith, 2014).

A key feature of CFOS-led engagement is *legitimacy*, which directly challenges the potentially labelling and stigmatising effects of contact with the YJS. Legitimacy refers to the maintenance of social order, suggesting that individuals are more likely to adhere to social norms and to obey the law if they view state authority and the discharge of authority by agents of the State (e.g. police, magistrates, judges, YOT staff) and their interactions with these agents as moral, just and fair (see Tyler, 2006, 2007; see also Haines & Case, 2015). In contrast, if treatment by criminal/youth justice agencies and agents is perceived as illegitimate (e.g. immoral, unjust, unfair), perceptions that can be exacerbated by the adulterisation, labelling, net-widening and interventionism of risk management, then reoffending is more likely to occur. Youth justice research has identified that children's perceptions of illegitimacy focus on treatment considered punitive, coercive, controlling and disproportionate (see Case & Browning, 2021; Hawes, 2013; Jamieson, 2006; Phoenix, 2009) and these perceptions can lead to resentment, disengagement and deviancy amplification. As such, perceptions of legitimacy constitute a positive outcome for youth justice practice; the assertion being that they can be enhanced by child-friendly/appropriate, promotional, inclusive and engaging treatment within the YJS.

Evidence-Based Partnership (Not Adult-Centric Programme Fetishism)

The PYJ model requires that its child-friendly/appropriate, diversionary and positive principles be mobilised into strategies based on a broad range of *evidence* generated through meaningful *partnership* with key stakeholders in the YJS, particularly children (e.g. through their participation and engagement), families, youth justice practitioners, policymakers, politicians and civil servants (Case & Haines, 2014). Evidence-based partnership working should be integrated at strategic and practice levels and should emphasise the participation and engagement of and relationship-building with children, rather than downplaying the potential contribution by pursuing more adult-centric 'trialogues' (three-way dialogues) between policy-makers, practitioners and researchers.[8] Evidence-based partnership is, therefore, both a principle and strategy for practice development and an explicit challenge to the tendency of individual agencies to become excessively introspective and to over-rely on the simplistic, often risk-focused programmes and interventions marketed by the YJB as part of the KEEP guidance (see Case, 2021a, 2021b; Stephenson et al., 2011). Indeed, the former Chair of the YJB, Professor Rod Morgan, was highly critical of the 'programme fetishism' of Government/YJB (Morgan, 2002: 8), asserting that policy-makers privileged reductionist, pseudo-psychological, offender-and offence-focused (correctional), 'off the shelf' programmes in their guidance to youth justice practitioners. This reductionist limitation has been compounded by the YJB tendency to 'consult' with practitioners on how to effectively implement pre-formed policy/strategy (see also Edwards & Hughes, 2009), rather than how to design and populate policy/strategy in the first place, for example, during the implementation of the Scaled Approach to assessment and intervention (cf. Case, 2021a, 2021b; Haines & Case, 2012). Therefore, evidenced-based partnership between all key stakeholders in the youth justice process (including and perhaps most importantly, practitioners and children) underpins principled, progressive and evidenced children first understandings and responses to youth offending, whilst protecting against the reductionist, potentially criminalising and prescriptive programme fetishism promoted by risk management/RFPP (Haines & Case, 2015).

Responsibilising Adults (Not Responsibilising Children)

The final evidenced, animating principle of PYJ is that child-friendly, diversionary, positive and evidence-based practice must be supported

---

[8] The evidence-based 'Reflective Friend Research' model of social science research (Case & Haines, 2014) emphasises the *relational* aspects of meaningful, valid and context-specific knowledge development in the youth justice field (and beyond) through engagement with practitioner experience, expertise and discretion.

and facilitated by 'responsibilising' adults (i.e. holding them primarily responsible for successful, positive processes and outcomes), in stark contrast to the 'new youth justice' legacy of responsibilising children and their families for the success or otherwise of youth justice sentences and interventions. PYJ asserts that adults (notably youth justice professionals) should be made primarily responsible for constructing and delivering effective youth justice (although the meaningful participation and engagement of children in design and delivery remains essential) as they hold the power in the youth justice dynamic. The basis of the CFOS-led PYJ model is that youth justice should recognise the inherent status and (relative lack of) capacity of the 'child' and that children's ability/capacity to make decisions about their own behaviour and to lead independent lives is restricted by the lack of responsibility, power and voice assigned to them in adult-led societies. Indeed, as argued by critics of 'new youth justice' responsibilisation strategies, it would seem that children are not given full social responsibility over any aspect of their life or behaviour apart from their offending behaviour (the irresponsible–responsible dichotomy). Therefore, as children do not have full social responsibilities, so adult youth justice professionals must fully accept their responsibilities towards these children (Haines & Case, 2015, 2018).

PYJ prioritises the responsibility of adult professionals (e.g. youth justice staff, policy-makers, politicians, academics) in the design, delivery and evaluation of diversionary and promotional youth justice responses, working in partnership with children and families to ensure that decisions and responses at all stages of the YJS are consistently child-friendly/appropriate and evidence-based. The principle of responsibilising adults is derived from the children's rights context of the UNCRC, which promotes a series of universally-agreed, non-negotiable minimum standards for the civil, cultural, economic, political and social rights of children (Creaney & Case, 2021; UNCRC, 1989). Where children first PYJ moves beyond the UNCRC, however, is in its promotion of *maximum outcomes* for all children, rather than simply *minimum standards*—with these maximum outcomes being the responsibility of adults (Case et al., 2005; Haines & Case, 2015). This principled element of PYJ has clear links to the 'Extending Entitlement' youth inclusion strategy in Wales (National Assembly Policy Unit, 2000), which responsibilises adult service providers and policy-makers to ensure that children have unobstructed access to support, services, opportunities and information that enables them to access their universal entitlements (see 'Welsh youth justice' section). Whilst social policies for children ('Every Child Matters'—DfES, 2004) and young people ('Youth Matters'—DfES, 2005) in England have established 'a series of global objectives for children's well-being in positive terms' (Smith, 2011: 173), critics argue that English social policy for children/young people focuses more on risk reduction and making children responsible for taking advantage of the opportunities offered to them, rather than promoting unconditional, universal entitlements to support, guidance and opportunities as in Wales (Case & Haines, 2011; Hoyle, 2008). The English social policy and youth justice policy (e.g. the 'new youth justice') views children's access to their rights and opportunities as conditional on their behaviour and the primary responsibility of children in this regard was illustrated by Tony Blair's proclamation whilst in opposition that there can be 'no rights without responsibilities' (in Giddens, 1998: 65). A principled, children first approach to PYJ, therefore, challenges the responsibilising excesses of anglicised social and youth justice policy by responsibilising adult stakeholders for the nature of youth justice services and the outcomes that children in the YJS achieve as a result.

'Child First' Positive Youth Justice

The CFOS principle (reconstructed as 'Child First') and the PYJ model and evidence-base (Case & Browning, 2021) have gained significant traction in the YJS of England and Wales in recent years. In 2016, the comprehensive 'Youth Justice Review' (Taylor, 2016) recommended the creation of 'a new [youth justice] system in which young people are treated as children first and offenders second' (Taylor, 2016: 48). This radical recommendation reflected contemporary strategic developments in related policy areas, notably:

Policing: The National Police Chiefs' Council (NPCC) 'Child Centred Policing' national strategy document stated that 'It is crucial that in all encounters with the police those below the age of 18 should be treated as children first' (NPCC, 2015: 9);
Court sentencing: The Sentencing Council's 'Sentencing Children and Young People guidelines and principles' stated that 'the approach to sentencing should be individualistic and focused on the child or young person, as opposed to offence focused' (Sentencing Council, 2017: 4), thus Child First, not offence or offender first.

The Youth Justice Review, the author (Charlie Taylor) became the Chair of the YJB in March 2017; an appointment closely followed by a wholesale change in the composition of YJB membership to include numerous stakeholders with a professional history of advocacy for Child First, positive forms of youth justice locally and nationally. Soon after, the YJB developed their own operational definition of CFOS (which they entitled 'Child First') as the central and guiding principle of a new national youth justice strategy (YJB, 2019). This definition was based on the original CFOS principle (Haines & Drakeford, 1998) as it had been developed in the PYJ model of practice[9] (Haines & Case, 2015; see also Byrne & Case, 2016), supplemented by the tenets of the evidence-based 'Constructive Resettlement' approach (Hazel et al., 2017). The centrality of 'Child First' as the primary strategic objective for the YJS is reinforced in the most recent YJB Business Plan 2020/2021 which commits to 'promote the implementation of the child first guiding principle' (YJB, 2020: 5) and further reflected in the updated Vision Statement of the 'YJB Strategic Plan 2021–2024', which commits to a YJS that is child-centred, stating:

> We see children first and offenders second. We make every effort to champion the needs of children wherever they are in the youth justice system

---

[9] The YJB's definition incorporates PYJ concepts of child-focused practice, the future-focused promotion of positive behaviours and outcomes, engagement, supportive relationships and diversion from the formal YJS. However, it does not explicitly include the concepts of evidence-based partnership, legitimacy and 'responsibilising' adults for children's outcomes (see Case & Browning 2021 for more detailed discussion; see also Haines & Case 2015).

and ensure we give them a voice; We strongly believe that children can and should be given every opportunity to make positive changes. (YJB, 2021: 7)

Furthermore, the centrality of Child First (CFOS) as the primary strategic animator of youth justice *practice* has been consolidated in revised Case Management Guidance (YJB, 2019) and National Standards (YJB, 2019) provided for youth justice (YOT) staff. Consequently, the key features of CFOS-informed PYJ currently underpin both youth justice strategy/policy and practice guidance in England and Wales.

This chapter has explored why and how the principled (CFOS-based) model of PYJ was constructed as a direct, principled challenge to the perceived negative features and excesses of the 'new youth justice' and the risk management that drove it, which became dominant in the twenty-first century (Haines & Case, 2015). It has been strongly asserted that the reductionist, deficit-led strategies of risk management (e.g. risk-based assessment and early intervention) are anathema to child-friendly youth justice (Case, 2021a). In stark contrast to risk management, PYJ de-emphasises offence/offender-focused youth justice (shaped by risk assessment-intervention frameworks) through privileging the inherent 'child' status of children who offend (hence 'children first'). Indeed, the PYM evidence-base strongly indicates that 'effective' and sustainable youth justice practices (e.g. decision-making, assessment and intervention planning) must be child-friendly/appropriate—examining the full complexity of children's lives and viewing offending as one part of the child's broader social identity (Drakeford, 2010) and ensuring that any responses are appropriately 'whole child' as a consequence (Case & Browning, 2021). Despite its emphasis of *diversion and minimum necessary intervention*, however, PYJ is not a clarion call for radical non-intervention, but rather for principled diversionary responses focused on promoting positive behaviour and outcomes for children, enabling their access to universal entitlements to services, opportunities, support and information, and valuing their vital contribution to youth justice decision-making and evidence generation processes (Case, 2021b; Case & Haines, 2015). Thus, PYJ necessitates seeing children as part of the solution, not part of the problem—with practitioners and policy-makers working in partnership with children to hold their interests, needs, rights and views as paramount throughout the youth justice process. Crucially, PYJ responses *responsibilise adult practitioners*, requiring them to view themselves as working for the children they engage with, rather than as representatives of other stakeholder groups (the YJS, community, victims). The priority for adults working to a PYM approach, therefore, is to engage closely and regularly with children to ensure that they are facilitated in expressing their views on issues that affect them (cf. Article 12 of the UNCRC), that they can participate equitably in decision-making regarding their futures and that they are enabled to access their universal entitlements as set out in progressive policy statements and international conventions (Case & Haines, 2015). These central features of PYJ coalesce to produce a model of *evidence-based partnership* working that can be viewed as legitimate to children, thus increasing the likelihood of them investing in, and committing to, the success and sustainability of youth justice processes. Empirical evidence suggests that children's engagement with youth justice practitioners goes deeper than the fundamentals of voluntarism, trust, respect and fairness (although these remain essential building blocks of the engagement relationship) and moves towards more progressive notions of partnership, reciprocity, investment and legitimate participation in decision-making processes (Case & Browning, 2021).

Taken together, the central features of PYM promote an evidence-based approach to youth justice working with children that has a coherent philosophy (children first), an explicit sense of purpose (prevention is better than cure, children are part of the solution not part of the problem), clear goals (responsibilising adults, evidence-based partnership working) and clearly articulated, desirable outcomes for children (positive behaviour, engagement, access to universal rights/entitlements). Animating the tenets of PYM into a coherent model offers practitioners a principled touchstone for their work—enabling them to better understand why they come into work every day and what they are employed to do, so providing a singularity of purpose—with an essential element being freedom in selecting what methods they employ in achieving this purpose (Haines & Case, 2015). At its core, PYJ seeks to identify and animate key principles for youth justice policy and practice that establish a consistency to how practitioners and the YJS can work with children in ways that are appropriate, principled, valid and legitimate from the perspectives of children and thus can increase the chances of creating effective assessment practices and responsive, appropriate interventions.

References

Arthur, R. (2016). *The moral foundations of youth justice*. Routledge.
Ashton, S., Iaonnou, M., Hammond, L., & Synnott, J. (2020). The relationship of offending style to psychological and social risk factors in a sample of adolescent males. *Journal of Investigative Psychology and Offender Profiling, 17*, 76–92.
Baker, K. (2005). Assessment in youth justice: Professional discretion and the use of Asset. *Youth Justice, 5*, 106–122.
Bateman, T. (2011). Punishing poverty: The scaled approach and youth justice practice. *Howard Journal of Crime and Justice, 50*, 171–183.
Beck, U. (1992). *Risk society: Towards a new modernity*. Sage.
Byrne, B., & Case, S. (2016). Towards a positive youth justice. *Safer Communities, 15*(2), 69–81.
Case, S. P. (2021a). *Youth justice: A critical introduction*. Routledge.
Case, S. P. (2021b). Challenging the reductionism of 'evidence-based' youth justice. *Sustainability, 13*(4), 1735 (Online first).
Case, S. P., & Browning, A. (2021). *Child first: The research evidence-base*. Loughborough University. https://www.lboro.ac.uk/subjects/social-policy-studies/research/child-first-justice/
Case, S. P., Clutton, S., & Haines, K. R. (2005). Extending entitlement: A Welsh policy for children. *Wales Journal of Law and Policy, 4*(2), 187–202.
Case, S. P., Creaney, S., Coleman, N., Haines, K. R., Little, R., & Worrell, V. (2020). Trusting children to enhance youth justice policy: The importance and value of children's voices. *Youth Voices*. ISBN: 978-1-911634-23-2.
Case, S. P., & Haines, K. R. (2003). Promoting prevention: Preventing youth drug use in Swansea by targeting risk and protective factors. *Journal of Substance Use, 8*(4), 243–251.
Case, S. P., & Haines, K. R. (2015). Children first, offenders second positive promotion: Reframing the prevention debate. *Youth Justice Journal, 15*(3), 226–239.

Case, S. P., & Haines, K. R. (2004). Promoting prevention: Evaluating a multi-agency initiative of youth consultation and crime prevention in Swansea. *Children and Society, 18*(5), 355–370.

Case, S. P., & Haines, K. R. (2007). Offending by young people: A further risk factor analysis. *Security Journal, 20*(2), 96–110.

Case, S. P., & Haines, K. R. (2008). Factors shaping substance use by young people. *Journal of Substance Use, 13*(1), 1–15.

Case, S. P., & Haines, K. R. (2009). *Understanding youth offending: Risk Factor research, policy and practice*. Willan.

Case, S. P. & Haines, K. R. (2011). Protection, prevention and promotion: The restricted evolution of the protective factor in criminological research. *Social Work Review, 2*, 109–122.

Case, S. P., & Haines, K. R. (2014). Reflective friend research: The relational aspects of social scientific research. In K. Lumsden (Ed.), *Reflexivity in criminological research*. Palgrave.

Case, S. P., & Haines, K. R. (2018). Transatlantic 'positive youth justice': Coherent movement or disparate critique? *Crime Prevention and Community Safety, 20*(3), 208–222.

Case, S. P., & Haines, K. R. (2020). Abolishing youth justice systems: Children first, offenders nowhere. *Youth Justice Journal, 21*, 3–17.

Cavadino, M., & Dignan, J. (2006). *Penal policy and political economy*. Sage.

Creaney, S., & Case, S. (2021). Promoting social inclusion: Participatory rights alternatives to risk discourses in youth justice. *Handbook of social inclusion: Research and practices in health and social sciences*.

Creaney, S., & Smith, R. (2014). Youth justice back at the crossroads. *Safer Communities, 13*(2).

CRC. (2008). UNCRC concluding observations. UNICEF.

Cox, A. (2020). The new economy and youth justice. *Youth Justice, 21*, 107–126.

Department for Education and Skills. (2004). *Every child matters*. DfES.

Department for Education and Skills. (2005). *Youth matters*. DfES.

Drake, D. H., Fergusson, R., & Briggs, D. B. (2014). Hearing new voices: Reviewing Youth Justice Policy through practitioners relationships with young people. *Youth Justice, 4*, 22–39.

Drakeford, M. (2009). Children first, offenders second: Youth justice in a devolved Wales. *Criminal Justice Matters, 78*(1), 8–9.

Drakeford, M. (2010). Devolution and youth justice in Wales. *Criminology and Criminal Justice, 10*, 137–154.

Dunkel, F. (2014). Juvenile Justice Systems in Europe—Reform developments between justice, welfare and 'new punitiveness'. *Criminological Studies, 1*. https://doi.org/10.15388/CrimLithuan.2014.0.3676

Edwards, A., & Hughes, G. (2009). The preventive turn and the promotion of safer communities in England and Wales. In A. Crawford (Ed.), *Crime prevention policies in comparative perspective*. Willan.

Farrington, D. (2007). Childhood risk factors and risk-focused Prevention. In M. Maguire, R. Morgan & R. Reiner (Eds.), *The oxford handbook of criminology*. Oxford: Oxford University Press.

Farrington, D. P. (2000). Explaining and preventing crime: The globalization of knowledge. *Criminology, 38*(1), 1–24.

France, A. (2008). Risk factor analysis and the youth question. *Journal of Youth Studies, 11*, 1–15.

France, A., & Utting, D. (2005). The paradigm of 'risk and protection-focused prevention' and its impact on services for children and families. *Children and Society, 19*, 77–90.

Garland, D. (2002). *The culture of control*. Oxford University Press.

Giddens, A. (1998). *The third way. The renewal of social democracy*. Polity.

Goldson, B. (2000). *The new youth justice*. Russell House.

Goldson, B., & Hughes, G. (2010). Sociological criminology and youth justice: Comparative policy analysis and academic intervention. *Criminology and Criminal Justice, 10*(2), 211–230.

Goldson, B., & Muncie, J. (2015). *Youth crime and justice*. Sage.

Haines, K. R. (2008). Systems management. In B. Goldson (Ed.), *Dictionary of youth justice*. Willan.

Haines, K. R., & Case, S. P. (2005). Promoting prevention: Targeting family-based risk and protective factors for drug use and youth offending in Swansea. *British Journal of Social Work, 35*(2), 1–18.

Haines, K. R., & Case, S. P. (2012). Is the scaled approach a failed approach? *Youth Justice, 12*(3), 212–228.

Haines, K. R., & Case, S. P. (2015). *Positive youth justice: Children first, offenders second*. Policy Press.

Haines, K. R., & Case, S. P. (2018). The future of youth justice. *Youth Justice Journal, 18*(2), 131–148.

Haines, K. R., Case, S. P., Charles, A. D., & Davies, K. (2013). The Swansea Bureau: A model of diversion from the youth justice system. *International Journal of Law, Crime and Justice, 41*(2), 167–187.

Haines, K. R., & Drakeford, M. (1998). *Young people and youth justice*. Macmillan.

Harcourt, B. (2007). *Against prediction*. University of Chicago.
Harding, C. J., & Beecroft, A. J. (2013). *10 characteristics of a good youth justice system*. A Paper for The Pacific Judicial Development Programme Family Violence and Youth Justice Workshop. Port Vila, Vanuatu.
Hawes, M. (2013). *Legitimacy and social order: A young people's perspective* (Unpublished PhD thesis). Swansea University, Swansea.
Hawkins, J. D., & Catalano, R. (1992). *Communities that care*. Jossey-Bass.
Hazel, N. (2008). *Cross-national comparison of youth justice*. Youth Justice Board.
Hazel, N., & Bateman, T. (2020). Supporting children's resettlement after custody: Beyond the risk paradigm. *Youth Justice, 21*, 71–89.
Hazel, N., Goodfellow, P., Liddle, M., Bateman, T., & Pitts, J. (2017). *Now all I care about is my future: Supporting the shift—Framework for effective resettlement of young people leaving custody*. Nacro.
Hopkins-Burke, R. (2016). *Young people, crime and justice*. Routledge.
Hoyle, D. (2008). Problematizing every child matters. Available at: https://www.infed.org/socialwork/every_child_matters_a_critique.htm
Jamieson, J. (2006). New labour, youth justice and the question of respect. *Youth Justice, 5*(3), 180–193.
Jepsen, J. (2006). Juvenile justice in Denmark: From social welfare to repression. In E. Jensen & J. Jepsen (Eds.), *Juvenile law violators, human rights and the development of new juvenile justice*. Oxford: Hart Publishing.
Kehl, D., Guo, P., & Kessler, S. (2017). *Algorithms in the criminal justice system: Assessing the use of risk assessments in sentencing*. Responsive Communities Initiative, Berkman Klein Center for Internet and Society, Harvard Law School, Cambridge, MA.
Kelly, L. (2012). Representing and preventing youth crime and disorder: Intended and unintended consequences of targeted youth programmes in England. *Youth Justice, 12*(2), 101–117.
Kemshall, H. (2008). Risk, rights and justice: Understanding and responding to youth risk. *Youth Justice, 8*(1), 21–38.
Kuhn, T. S. (1996). *The structure of scientific revolutions* (3rd ed.). University of Chicago Press.
McAra, L. (2017). Youth justice. In A. Liebling, S. Maruna & L. McAra (Eds.), *Oxford handbook of criminology*. Oxford: OUP
Morgan, R. (2002). *Annual lecture of the National Centre for Public Policy*. Swansea University.

Muncie, J. (2008). The 'punitive' turn in juvenile justice: Cultures of control and rights compliance in Western Europe and the USA. *Youth Justice, 8*(2), 107–121.

Muncie, J. (2015). *Youth and crime*. Sage.

Myers, R., Goddard, T., & Davidtz, J. (2020). Reconnecting youth: Beyond individualized programs and risks. *Youth Justice, 21*, 55–70.

National Assembly Policy Unit. (2000). *Extending entitlement: Supporting young people in Wales*. NAPU. https://www.cywu.org.uk/index.php?id=11&detail=79

National Assembly Policy Unit. (2002). *Extending entitlement: Support for 11–25-year-olds in Wales. Direction and guidance*. NAPU. https://gov.wales/sites/default/files/publications/2018-02/direction-and-guidance-extending-entitlement-support-for-11-to-25-year-olds-in-wales.pdf

National Police Chiefs' Council. (2015). *Child-centred policing. National strategy for the policing of children and young people*. NPCC.

O'Mahony, P. (2009). The risk factors prevention paradigm and the causes of youth crime: A deceptively useful analysis? *Youth Justice, 9*, 99–114.

Phoenix, J. (2009). Whose account counts? Politics and research in youth justice. In W. Taylor, R. Hester, & R. Earle (Eds.), *Youth justice handbook* (pp. 73–82). Willan/Open University.

Phoenix, J. (2016). Against youth justice and youth governance. *British Journal of Criminology, 56*, 123–140.

Phoenix, J., & Kelly, L. (2013). 'You have to do it for yourself': Responsibilization in youth justice and young people's situated knowledge of youth justice practice. *British Journal of Criminology, 53*(3), 419–437.

Prior, D., & Mason, P. (2010). A different kind of evidence. Looking for 'what works' in engaging young offenders. *Youth Justice, 10*, 211–226.

Sackett, D. (1997). Evidence-based medicine and treatment choices. *The Lancet, 349*, 570.

Sampson, R. J., & Laub, J. H. (1993). *Crime in the making: Pathways and turning points through life*. Harvard University Press.

Sentencing Council. (2017). *Sentencing children and young people: Overarching principles and offence specific guidelines for sexual offences and robbery. Definitive guidelines*. Sentencing Council.

Sherman, L. W., & Strang, H. (2007). *Restorative justice: The evidence*. The Smith Institute.

Sherman, L., Gottfredson, D., MacKenzie, D., Eck, J., Reuter, P., & Bushway, S. (1998). *Preventing crime: What works, what doesn't, what's promising*. Department of Criminology and Criminal Justice, University of Maryland.

Smith, R. (2011). *Doing justice to young people: Youth crime and social justice.* Willan.
Smith, R. (2016). *Youth justice: Ideas policy practice.* Routledge.
Stephenson, M., & Allen, R. (2013). *Youth justice: Challenges to practice.* Unitas.
Stephenson, M., Giller, H., & Brown, S. (2011). *Effective practice in youth justice.* Routledge.
Strang, H., Sherman, L. W., Ariel, B., Chilton, S., Braddock, R., Rowlinson, A., Cornelius, N., Jarman, R., & Weinborn, C. (2017). Reducing the harm of intimate partner violence: A randomized controlled trial of the Hampshire Constabulary CARA experiment Cambridge. *Journal of Evidence-Based Policing, 1*, 160–173.
Sutherland, A. (2009). The 'scaled approach' in youth justice: Fools rush in. *Youth Justice, 9*, 44–60.
Sutton, C., Monaghan, M., Case, S. P., Greenhalgh, J., & Wright, J. (2021). Contextualising youth justice interventions: Making the case for Realist Synthesis. *Sustainability*, Online first.
Taylor, C. (2016). *Review of the youth justice system in England and Wales.* Ministry of Justice.
Thornberry, T. P., Lizotte, A. J., Krohn, M. D., Smith, C. A., & Porter, P. K. (2003). Causes and consequences of delinquency. Findings from the Rochester Youth Development Study. In T. P. Thornberry & M. D. Krohn (Eds.), *Taking stock of delinquency: An overview of findings from contemporary longitudinal studies.* Kluwer.
Tonry, M. (2019). Predictions of dangerousness in sentencing: Déjà vu all over again. *Crime and Justice, 48*, 439–482.
Turnbull, G., & Spence, J. (2011). What's at risk? The proliferation of risk across child and youth policy in England. *Journal of Youth Studies, 14*(8), 939–959.
Tutt, N., & Giller, H. (1987). Manifesto for management—the elimination of custody. *Justice of the Peace, 151*, 200–202.
Tyler, T. (2006). *Why people obey the law.* Princeton University Press.
Tyler, T. (2007). *Legitimacy and criminal justice: International perspectives.* Russell Sage Foundation.
Ward, T. (2020). Why theoretical literacy is essential for forensic research and practice. *Criminal Behaviour and Mental Health, 31*, 1–4.
Weisburd, D., Farrington, D., Gill, C., & Wooditch, A. (2017). What works in crime prevention and rehabilitation: An assessment of systematic reviews. *Criminology and Public Policy, 16*, 415–449.

Weiss, C. H. (1979). The many meanings of research utilization. *Public Administration Review, 39*, 426–431.

Welsh Government & YJB. (2004). *All Wales youth offending strategy*. Welsh Government. https://www.google.com/search?client=safari&rls=en&q=All+Wales+Youth+Offending+Strategy&ie=UTF-8&oe=UTF-8

Welsh Government & YJB. (2014). *Children and young people first*. Welsh Government/YJB.

Wilcox, A. (2003). *National evaluation of the Youth Justice Board's restorative justice projects*. YJB.

Williamson, B., & Cairns, L. (2005). *Working in partnership with young people: From practice to theory*. Investing in Children and Research in Practice.

Young, J. (2016). Voodoo criminology and the numbers game. In *Cultural criminology unleashed* (pp. 27–42). Routledge.

Youth Justice Board. (2000). *Asset: Explanatory notes*. YJB.

Youth Justice Board. (2003). *Assessment, planning interventions and supervision*. YJB.

Youth Justice Board. (2010). *Process. Evaluation of the pilot of a risk-based approach to interventions*. YJB.

Youth Justice Board. (2013). *Assessment and planning interventions framework—AssetPlus* (Model Document). YJB.

Youth Justice Board. (2019). *Youth Justice Board for England and Wales Strategic plan 2019–2022*. YJB.

Youth Justice Board. (2020). *YJB Business Plan 2020/2021*. YJB.

Youth Justice Board. (2021). *Youth Justice Board for England and Wales: Strategic plan 2021–2024*. YJB. https://assets.publishing.service.gov.uk/government/uploads/system/uploads/attachment_data/file/802702/YJB_Strategic_Plan_2019_to_2022.pdf

4

Challenging Historical Populism—Children First, Offenders Second: From Concept to Policy

Kevin Haines and Sue Thomas

The Emergence of the Concept of Children First, Offenders Second

CFOS first came into the public domain in 'Young People and Youth Justice' (Haines & Drakeford, 1998). Like any set of ideas, CFOS was a product of its time—born out of a desire on the part of the authors to set out their analysis of the contemporary treatment of children (particularly those that become embroiled in the youth justice system) and to articulate their vision of a way forward that was more sensitive to the particular features of childhood. We start this chapter, therefore, by locating the development of the concept of CFOS in its 'historical' context—noting,

K. Haines (✉)
University of South Wales, Swansea, Wales, UK
e-mail: profkevin22@gmail.com

S. Thomas
Porthcawl, Wales, UK

of course, that the following 20 years (until the adoption of CFOS by the YJB as the guiding principle of all work with children) were pretty negative, especially if you were poor and in trouble, for children.

There are rarely any straight lines in Youth Justice. This is reflected not just in the language used in 'Young People and Youth Justice' and the language we use today (the term 'Youth' was hardly appropriate in the 1990s and is even less appropriate today; there is no 'Justice' in a failed system), but it is also found in the complexities and nuances of Youth Justice (it seems we are stuck with this term until someone comes up with something better) where anything one writes can immediately be disputed or refuted. What follows, therefore, may transgress the deficiencies of language and expression as well as risking oversimplification. As such the views expressed here are those of the authors and we stand by them—although feel free to disagree and debate any such points as you see fit.

Having said all of the above, it is, perhaps, not surprising and in our view entirely appropriate (and in line with the joint/shared values of the authors and the aims of Young People and Youth Justice), that Chapter 1 'Youth and Society' (in fact Drakeford) expertly and with consummate skill set out clearly the contemporary way in which children were viewed by British society. The opening words of Chapter 1 being: 'Our society does not like young people'.

The analysis, setting out the basis of the book, continued:

> If young people generally are poorly regarded, then the small minority who end up being brought to the attention of the criminal justice system is the legitimised target for all the harshest and most destructive impulses directed against their contemporaries as a whole. (Haines & Drakeford, 1998: 1)

Before going on to summarise the manifestations of the 'harshest and most destructive impulses' that characterised the 1990s (and endured for the subsequent 20 years), it is necessary and instructive to briefly review the characteristics of the preceding period.

'Historical' Populism

Broadly speaking, the 1980s in youth justice in England and Wales was characterised by what was known as 'New Orthodoxy Thinking'. This was a period in the history of youth justice when policy and practice was not dominated by politicians, but led by (predominantly) a group of influential Youth Justice Managers. New Orthodoxy Thinking (and practice) emerged to correct the unintended consequences of the juvenile justice system that developed under the range of Intermediate Treatment Schemes that characterised the 1970s, namely net-widening[1] and up-tariffing.[2] The defining principles and practices of 1980s youth justice, therefore, were maximising diversion from the Youth Justice System and minimising the use of custody (both remand and sentence).

Although the above sweeps two decades of policy and practice into two sentences (readers can always go back to Haines and Drakeford [1998], or any of the other excellent accounts of youth justice that have followed, e.g. Case, 2018), it is noteworthy that the driving force behind 1970s and 1980s policy and practice was the best interests of the child. It is (simply) that different professional groups dominated the scene in these two decades and their interpretation of best interests was radically different. This is what made the 1990s such a different decade. No longer motivated by anything approximating to the positive or constructive treatment of children the two main political parties in Great Britain engaged in a race to become (and to be seen by the general public as) the toughest on crime, including crimes committed by children.

Thus, the scene was set for the Labour Government that swept to power in 1997 to usher in the most anti-child (I [Haines] would almost go as far as to say child-hating) policies and practices that have ever existed—certainly in England and Wales, probably in Europe and not far off globally. These may see like strong words, but they are fully deserved as a description of the emerging Labour Government's thinking. The November 1997 White Paper 'No More Excuses' neatly summed up the

---

[1] Practices which draw more children in the youth justice system than is warranted, rather than diverting them out of it.
[2] Practices which increase the tariff or disposal to a more punitive outcome.

approach. The Labour Government derided the culture of diversion (and avoidance of custody) as being soft on youth crime, cast 'young offenders' in a negative 'responsibilising' light and set out proposals for being 'tough on youth crime, tough on the causes of youth crime'.

Whilst we should never forget the vitriol with which politicians and some practitioners promoted the Anti-Social Behaviour Order (ASBO) (anyone today who is not disgusted by the policy and practices that characterised the ASBO should be ashamed—as should those members of the, largely print, media who set about demonising children day after day in shock journalism), fortunately it was relatively short lived (see Lewis et al., 2016 for a fuller exposition).

Emerging Themes

What *Young People and Youth Justice* foresaw as the themes likely to dominate youth justice in the future were: National Standards (although still around today, their use has become much less prescriptive and we will not expand further upon them here), restorative justice (space precludes any further discussion on his topic but Haines' views have not changed since Haines, 1998), the responsibilisation of children for their behaviour and risk assessment. Of these four themes, although all are still with us today, in one form or another, the two themes that really stuck are risk assessment and responsibilisation. Of course, much of the history of these themes occurred in the decades following the publication of Young People and Youth Justice, the prescience of the book was identifying these themes and their underlying properties.

Risk assessment and responsibilisation are, of course, inextricably intertwined. Again, space precludes a full exposition of these practices (it took Professors Case and Haines a whole book to unpack the failings of risk assessment and all that went with it, see Case & Haines, 2009) and at the risk of oversimplifying, risk assessment and responsibilisation can be boiled down to two things: henceforth, interventions into the lives of children brought into the Youth Justice System were to be offence and offender-based.

It is against this backdrop, therefore, of an anti-child policy coupled with responses to children brought into the Youth Justice System being solely based on risk assessments which led inextricably to offence and offender-based interventions that Young People and Youth Justice was written. In particular, this backdrop set the context and the raison d'etre for CFOS.

Children First, Offenders Second—A Philosophy

The concept of CFOS is set out in Chapter 3 of Young People and Youth Justice, entitled: Developing a Youth Justice Philosophy. The term philosophy was deliberately chosen for two interlinked reasons. The notion that CFOS was based on a philosophy was to draw a sharp contrast with risk assessment which was simply a technique. We also believed that no-one really gets up, goes to work and is motivated by a technique. CFOS, on the other hand, gave youth justice professionals (and others) something positive to work towards achieving. It was intended to give meaning to the actions taken in everyday interactions with children, a way of making sense of what workers do.

In a chapter of 30 pages, however, only four were given over to articulating what CFOS meant in principle and practice. It should be clear to readers that Young People and Youth Justice was written on the cusp of the changes described above (as a result of the Crime and Disorder Act 1998) and that the concept of CFOS was nascent at the time. Indeed, it was not until 2015 that the evidence was amassed to develop CFOS, that Professors Haines and Case published 'Positive Youth Justice: Children First, Offenders Second' (Haines & Case, 2015)—a comprehensive articulation of the philosophy, principles and practices of CFOS.

At the time, however, the anti-child, offence and offender focused basis of interventions conflicted with the authors' values and what we understood to be the most effective way of helping children involved in some form of criminally-labelled activity. Over the subsequent 20-year period, Haines and Case have set about deconstructing and demolishing the principles and practices of risk factor research (see Case & Haines,

2009) and the policies and practices built upon it. We also set about a programme of research designed to test the principles and practices of CFOS and, ultimately, to demonstrating its effectiveness (as a principled approach rooted in humane values and as a set of practices).

Moving into Practice: The Developing Evidence Base

To advance this agenda two fortunate events coalesced. An innovative partnership (the first of its kind in the UK) was formed in 1994 with the manager of Swansea Youth Offending Team—a likeminded individual, keen to innovate practice and to promote positive outcomes for children. Six years later, in 2000, a young psychology graduate, called Stephen Case, joined the Department of Criminology at Swansea University as a PhD student. It was from the early 2000s, therefore, that research evidencing the effectiveness of CFOS began in earnest.

In fact, the Swansea research into the effectiveness of CFOS began by evaluating prevention projects and promoting positive outcomes for children outside of the formal criminal justice system. Professor Case's PhD was focused on understanding and explaining the outcomes of school disciplinary systems and a programme known as 'Promoting Prevention' (Haines & Case, 2004). We were also the principal investigators of the Welsh Government's flagship Extending Entitlement strategy (Haines et al., 2004).

To be sure, in some of these early works Haines and Case used the concept of risk factors as part of our analysis—although we were careful to avoid the methodological flaws of mainstream risk factor research (notably the conflation of correlation with causality)—demonstrating the learning path that we have been on over the last 20 years and how our ideas have grown and developed as the research evidence has been produced. The summation of research evidencing the effectiveness of CFOS, conducted by Haines and Case and others, has been admirably and effectively documented by Case and Browning (2021) and readers are directed to this report for a full exposition.

The reasons, however, for starting by evaluating universal crime prevention and promoting positive behaviour outcomes for children are twofold. Firstly, promoting positive behaviour and outcomes is a central plank of CFOS. If such could not be evidenced through universal provision, what chance would there be of being able to implement and evidence them for children brought into the formal criminal justice system? Secondly, it was easier to innovate in the 'prevention' realm than to do so within the formal criminal justice system. The early to mid-2000s were, remember, the relatively early days of the YJB (formed in 2000) and a time in which it was flexing its muscles and extending its control over YOTs. These were not very positive or productive (from a CFOS perspective) times in the history of the YJB and the extent of its control of local practice was stifling of innovation.

To overcome these blockages, the University/YOT partnership was of crucial importance and both parties did all they could to strengthen the alliance. His, both parties also reached out, deliberately and actively, to other individuals and agencies involved with children, including: the police, schools, community safety department, various local authority departments and Heads of Services, etc. One key to building alliances through these inter-agency relationships was the research that was being producing. That research was able to demonstrate and evidence the impact of each small step, gave the partnership the confidence to take each next small step (with the assurance that it too would be evaluated). It is important to stress that each piece of research was conducted without prejudice as to the findings. If an intervention worked, it was reported it. If an intervention had negative aspects or consequences, it was reported (and reports were made honestly and openly on some fairly negative findings—ever sensitive to issues of anonymity and the ethics of 'doing no harm'). It was this approach, however, that enabled the YOT manager (to whom much credit should be given) to begin to innovate with disposals that were more inside the formal criminal justice system, viz diversion.

Bureau

The foray into diversion ultimately produced the Bureau model (Haines et al., 2013). Readers may remember that the Labour Government's policy was essentially antithetical to diversion (seeing it as children who offended getting away with things and a failure of YOTs to do anything with/to them) and, as such, they sought to structure, control and reduce the use of diversion (see Haines, 2000). The Bureau was deliberately intended to achieve the reverse of government policy and to do so in a manner which was consistent with CFOS. The Bureau, as its evaluation demonstrated, was spectacularly successful. It achieved higher and higher rates of diversion, it kept children out of the Youth Justice System entirely (thus they did not acquire a criminal record), it achieved the lowest reconviction rates of any intervention and it enjoyed widespread inter-agency support and endorsement (including from the police, up to Chief Constable level). Subsequently, the Bureau approach has been widely adopted across England and Wales and it has received official sanction from the YJB.

This is not meant to convey the impression that the Bureau went from zero to perfectly formed CFOS-based measure overnight. As part of the developing partnership between the University and the YOT, third-year undergraduate students were placed in the YOT to undertake focused pieces of research (often in fulfilment of their dissertation requirements) evaluating, feeding back and enhancing CFOS principles and practices. One such study, for example, focused on the Bureau panels and discovered that it was only after an hour of listening to adults (mostly talking in ways that your average 15-year old would have difficulty following) that the child was invited to speak. This is clearly not a practice that is consistent with CFOS and as soon as it was pointed out to YOT staff that this is what they were doing, they immediately altered their practice to ensure that it was the child that spoke first.

The above account is just one example of the dynamic that was driving innovation in Swansea YOT and the development of CFOS—as the two were engaged in a virtuous circle of mutual learning and reinforcement. This, however, was not all that was happening.

Letting Go of the Past

Whilst partnership working developed apace locally in Swansea, the then Dr (now Professor) Case and Haines were actively engaged in more academic pursuits, notably our research into risk factor research and the links it had (or did not have) with youth justice policy and practice: research which culminated in 'Understanding Youth Offending: Risk Factor Research, Policy and Practice' (Case & Haines, 2009). Whilst researching this book, Haines well remembers an encounter with John Drew (in 2010/2011), a highly respected then Chair of the YJB, during which we engaged in a spirited discussion of the limitations of the Scaled Approach (for an evaluation of the Scaled Approach vs CFOS see, Haines & Case, 2012). As a result, John Drew convened an ad hoc advisory group of academics to advise the YJB on its policy with regard to the Scaled Approach. The emerging process, although it took some time, eventually led to the YJB eschewing risk and the Scaled Approach as appropriate tools for understanding children, their behaviour and for structuring interventions.

Whilst all of the above was going on, one of the agencies Haines reached out to was YJB Cymru (the Welsh division of the YJB). Initially, our overtures were rebuffed, as the then Director of YJB Cymru was an adherent to the policy and practices that characterised the YJB under its first Chair Norman Warner—which, as readers will remember, CFOS set itself against, both philosophically and in policy and practice terms. All of this changed, however, with the move of a senior member of Swansea YOT to become the new Director of YJB Cymru circa 2012. This change opened a new chapter in the advancement of CFOS from what had been a fairly localised initiative to a new national policy in Wales (see: Haines, 2009).

The remainder of this chapter turns to explore the influence of CFOS on YJ policy development and implementation, drawing on Thomas's reflections of working in Wales and observing these changes mainly from a third sector perspective.

YJB Cymru and Child First—Introduction

The creation of the Youth Justice System in 2000 and the YJB was to set the framework for youth justice and the response to children who offended (or were regarded to be on the cusp of doing so). The YJB is an organisation which provides central advice to local authorities and their partners on how services should be delivered. Its jurisdiction covers England and Wales but as with all centralised policy-making whether from the YJB, Ministry of Justice and Home Office there should be consideration of the status of Wales and its devolved authority for most aspects of social policy although significantly not criminal justice. This tends to mean two things: firstly, there are differences in legislation and policy from England notably in social care and housing legislation meaning that the criteria and threshold for services can differ between England and Wales and secondly the Welsh Government has policies that are distinct from England notably incorporating children's right into domestic legislation and has at times indicated its disagreement with UK Government policy when it does not fit with its ethos. This had implications for youth justice which took some time to surface because for several years there was a sense from the centre that youth justice in England and Wales should look exactly the same, when clearly the domestic contexts were starting to and have continued to diverge. Part of the role of the YJB's team in Wales, known as YJB Cymru, was to ensure engagement with the Welsh Government and to provide a bridge between the devolved and non-devolved worlds.

The treatment of children in the Youth Justice System has been the subject of long debate with centrally-led approaches and initiatives changing over time and all being presented with an ethos of being the right thing to do for children and in their best interests, whether to punish, educate, focus on restitution or be control and compliance based. They have varied from offering flexible, discretionary approaches (epitomised by use of diversion and use of informal disposals) to rigid prescription, e.g. the number of hours engagement with intensive supervision and surveillance and use of breach, both of which have been past drivers of use of custody. The scope for making youthful mistakes, lack of understanding of adolescent engagement in risky behaviour (an ordinary part of growing up), understanding the impact of adverse experiences on children's behaviour which may have brought them into the justice system (sometimes a normal response to abnormal life events) and lack of emphasis on engaging children, developing a relationship with them and using evidence-based approaches to navigate them into safer lifestyles, led to a blurred and sometimes incoherent understanding of best interests and whose interests are being best served.

Influencers

One of the dynamics that also exists in youth justice is the role of other influencers and how they have shaped policy and practice which is also relevant to the development of Child First. Bateman (2010) specifically identifies academics and the practitioner movement (including the third sector and campaigning organisations) often sharing common theoretical underpinnings and combined having a powerful and influential voice. Academic activity is well understood in developing an evidence base from which to influence policy and practice and in providing commentary when new government policies and procedures arise (political priorities, expediency and reactions to high-profile events) which are not evidence-based. As has previously been highlighted Haines and Drakeford were discussing children in a very different context to the one that emerged from the Crime and Disorder Act 1998.

The role of the third sector can take different forms from being a service provider, researching and reporting on organisational and other activity and advocating and campaigning for rights and principled and evidence-based approaches to children and adults involved in the criminal justice system. Third sector organisations have their own mission and have determined their position on criminal justice issues often based on experiences in delivering services based on their core values. These ideals tend to be service user focused, drawn from experience and not political imperatives which enabled alignment to Child First or other sympathetic approaches to be dominant approach and the approach the third sector would seek to promote (albeit the Child First label was still emerging).

The traditional position is the ideals and objectives of the third sector are different to government, that the third sector offers check and challenge, seeks to influence policy direction and criticises what it regards as unacceptable, whilst treading a fine line between sometimes needing to attract government funding balanced with wanting to be seen as a critical friend and valued stakeholder who can be engaged with despite holding an opposing view. This is always difficult as government wants to drive its initiatives forward (without substantive criticism or legal challenge) and the third sector wants to remain 'inside the tent' whilst at the same time retaining its independence.

This background is relevant as the emergence of the 'new youth justice' in 2000 caused some consternation. Thomas worked in the third sector for over 20 years working for Nacro when it had a youth crime section pre, during and post the introduction of the Crime and Disorder Act 1998, creation of YOTs and the YJB. The concerns centred on what these changes might (negatively) mean for youth justice, following on from the criticism of the Audit Commission that it was ineffective and inefficient (Audit Commission, 1996), for children and their families and the extent to which the third sector might be seen as part of the past problem and not the new solution, with its voice and thinking being out of kilter with the new orthodoxy.

The third sector tends to have developed its philosophy from its years of experience, it attracts people who potentially have a vocational interest in supporting and assisting others and uses it voice to advocate for what it believes to be right based on its own evidence and practices. Whilst it is a generalisation this is a very different position to that of government officials (civil servants) who are tasked to introduce new initiatives and have to (even though they may recognise they are problematic) and whose career may take them through several government departments with no particular vested interest in criminal or youth justice, e.g. Ministry of Justice today, Transport tomorrow. The YJB as an arms-length body and not government department has been seen differently because of its efforts to recruit from the youth justice sector and employ staff who have a good knowledge and understanding of the youth justice sector (Souhami, 2011). However, despite the latter there was an emerging tension between academic commentary, third sector experience and government policy.

The Voice of Influencers

What started to emerge from the formation of the new Youth Justice System were concerns about the way children were being treated e.g. being drawn into it (intervention was better than not—despite evidence to the contrary, e.g. McAra & McVie, 2010). Children were escalated through the system through a graduated series or orders of increasing length and additional conditions (reparation, action plan and supervision orders), with no question of whether they could engage let alone comply—a one size to fit all—contrary to the evidence base. The drive to improve standards within youth justice placed significant pressure on YOTs to see children at intervals they struggled to manage (and did not guarantee quality of engagement) or struggling to find something meaningful for the child to do whilst on an order (Thomas, 2015). Children emerged as a problematic collection of risks; local authorities were criticised for not making greater use of anti-social behaviour orders, parents and single mothers were also problematised and a generally punitive atmosphere pervaded. There was a lack of focus on anything positive—weak references to protective factors were quickly outweighed by risk. Strengths-based, desistence-focused, child-centred language and approaches were absent.

Academics were openly critical of the 'new youth justice' and the potential for harm (Goldson, 2010; Gray, 2009; Pitts, 2001). Practices were propelling children into a system they could not cope with resulting in high numbers of children under YOT supervision and in custody (2000–2004/2005 a peak period). The third sector reacted in ways that it could, e.g. responses to government consultations, indicating other preferred options with evidence to support and campaigning to challenge policies and approaches regarded as damaging and advocating for more child-friendly policy and practice. From Thomas' personal experience one of the ways in which Nacro sought to influence was to produce youth crime briefings for the youth justice sector to reflect child-centred practice to help youth justice practitioners to navigate through some of the less palatable influences on their role and function.

The Position in Wales

The position in Wales regarding youth justice started to emerge within the context of the very different philosophy of the Welsh Government, e.g. inclusivity and equality-based and rights focused. There was a need for the UK Government to engage with the Welsh Government. Although it did not have devolved responsibility, the Welsh Government indicated in emerging policy documents that children in the Youth Justice System were to be considered alongside any other child (Welsh Assembly Government, 2004) and the YJB needed to find its place in Wales as a nation.

There was recognition that a joint position was necessary, which led to the creation of the All Wales Youth Offending Strategy (AWYOS) (Welsh Assembly Government & YJB, 2004) by a multi-agency group including the UK and Welsh governments, academic and the third sector. Significantly, the AWYOS explicitly stated that 'young people should be treated as children first and offenders second', which was in direct contrast to the position emerging from UK Government policy described earlier. The Welsh Government also provided around £4 million of funding to YOTs, local authorities and partnership to support implementation of the AWYOS. The Consultative Committee for Wales was formed[3] (now known as the Wales Youth Justice Advisory Panel) (one of the initial aims was to monitor the AWYOS). Scale in Wales means that key players had easy access to each other, and the same actors interacted in a variety of fora—both a strength and weakness.

NACRO was commissioned by the Welsh Government to provide youth justice policy and practice support, a unique and very different position to anything which existed in England at the time, which was in

---

[3] This also had multi-agency membership (some of which crossed over with the formation of the AWYOS).

place for approximately 18 years and within this for a significant period to provide support to YOT Managers Cymru (YMC). YOTs in Wales formed their own association YMC, 'to influence the (Welsh) Government policy and also shout out the Welsh agenda to get priority with the YJB' (ARCS UK Ltd, 2013). This added a further dynamic to the relationship in Wales and potential influence in respect of Child First. NACRO's lead worker (Thomas' role at the time) and YMC formed a close alliance, with NACRO being regarded as trusted honest broker and expert and knowledgeable partner (ARCS UK Ltd, 2013). Contributing to delivery of the AWYOS was part of the role and function and the strong commitment to this was noted in an independent evaluation of NACRO's role and function in Wales:

> They are committed to things like the All Wales Youth Offending Strategy, to entitlements, rights of the child and so on. But that actually helps us to trust them more, because those things are part of the youth justice perspective in Wales (and part of what the Government has committed to here).

The evaluation notes the contribution to informed discussion, assisting in developing a 'culture of best practice' in Wales and having a strategic impact (ARCS UK Ltd, 2013). This very much resonates with my experience at the time and the desire to bring in the values of the third sector to influence a more child-friendly focus and ethos compatible with the Child First agenda and what YOTs in Wales regarded as important.

The YJB in Wales protected its own interests and drove forward its priorities, ensuring that initiatives developed in Wales were parallel and equivalent to those in England. It successfully influenced Welsh Government thinking in relation to youth justice and what was funded through the Welsh Government's Safer Communities Fund.[4] It was clear there were agreed youth justice priorities and several joint initiatives (Thomas, 2015). YJB Cymru was increasingly developing its own identity in Wales and being recognised as a distinct entity and a key national stakeholder in engagement and influence in Wales. However, YJB Cymru's engagement

---

[4] This has changed over the years with the equivalent now being contained in the Children and Communities Grant.

with academia was initially not as strong as it was with other stakeholders as the priority was very much on developing a relationship with the Welsh Government and other key influencers on criminal justice and social policy and practice in Wales.

Child First—Finding Its Feet

Discourse around Child First emerged in Haines and Drakeford (1998), but the journey of Child First into something more tangible was not immediate or straightforward. The AWYOS was not regarded by some as providing a comfortable alignment between UK and WG policy (Haines, 2009; Williams, 2007) and its content was not well understood by YOTs and the practice community (Thomas, 2015). As the Youth Justice System developed and outcomes for children were being better understood, there was increased questioning of whether the approaches developed were helpful or harmful to children and UK Government policies and approaches emerged in opposition to the child-friendly policies of the Welsh Government.

This created a tension. YJB Cymru had to tread a fine line between implementing centralist policies and finding a way of making them work in Wales. Whilst the commitment to a Child First approach existed in the AWYOS, some of the content strictly was not. Commentators on youth justice were critical of punitive and deficit-based approaches, net-widening and high rates of child imprisonment. This was also reflected by the UN Committee in its periodic reporting on compliance with children's rights (e.g. United Nations Committee on the Rights of the Child, 2011). It was not a debate YJB Cymru prioritised engagement with and Welsh Government officials were influenced by what YJB Cymru advised (and lacked expertise in youth justice). Approaches to children were not benchmarked against what Child First might mean.

It is difficult to pinpoint when change started to occur. Likely influences are because of the momentum and perseverance of influencer criticism (academic led) and the need to be open to other possibilities, engagement with Child First provided an alternative solution; because there started to be a softening of some of the harder line, less flexible approaches (through the emergence of UK Government Coalition policies (Ministry of Justice, 2010), reduced emphasis on prescriptive YOT performance management (Local Government Association, 2008); and evidence from research was not demonstrating that some (heavily invested-in) initiatives were producing the desired results (e.g. intensive supervision and surveillance).

The culture of the YJB changing because of different leadership which brought a preparedness to engage with critics rather than re-buff them. Certainly, from the third sector perspective the door felt like it was opening as opposed to having to knock to try and get in. One of the ways this was evident, was the YJB recognising the negative connotations of the risk factor paradigm and the limitations of Asset. The consultation process for the revision of AssetPlus suggested a more openness to engage than dictate, with the YJB responding to various forms of lobbying and requests to be part of the debate and ultimately changing its position (YJB, 2014). Publicly stating that it intended to review its thinking on the risk factor paradigm might be regarded with hindsight as a potential first step towards Child First.

Child First in Wales

It was evident from what emerged in the AWYOS was that Welsh policy needed to be factored into youth justice thinking although it also highlighted tensions and importantly flagged that children in the Youth Justice System were foremost children and should be treated as such. However, Child First to some extent lay dormant in that it existed in youth justice policy but had not been animated in any way. One of the potential reasons for this is that it is a philosophy and principled approach based, underpinned by children's rights (through the UNCRC and various international instruments) and evidence of what is required to assist children to lead positive and safe lifestyles. However, a clear explanation of what it means has not emerged until recently (YJB, 2021) and it has never been transferred into detailed practice guidance—despite evidence existing of what that might look like.

The relationship with the academic community in Wales took some time to form. From Thomas's experience as an observer from the third sector, working closely with the YJB and Welsh Government, this was because the YJB was only interested in pursuing its own agenda and was not deviating from that. Whilst there was engagement with YOTs in Wales (ARCS UK Ltd, 2013) a significant element was about delivering YJB central messaging and YOT performance oversight (a statutory YJB function). Thomas observed the discourse focusing on performance, meeting objectives, targets, etc. and questioning when it did not rather than being driven from a position of operating of children being the central concern.

The shift to being open to and supporting other innovations emerged from the academic community in Wales promoting Child First. The development of the Swansea Bureau and evaluation of its effectiveness was a very clear demonstration of what Child First could look like in practice (and embodies one of the YJB's tenets of Child First—see YJB (2021) for further details). Whilst not an initiative that originated from the YJB, YJB Cymru recognised its relevance and significance, and this endorsement gave other YOTs in Wales the confidence to incorporate it in their practice and local arrangements. The Bureau is now established as a national approach to pre-court diversion across Wales—with a legacy of 13 years.

The YJB formed the Practice Development Panel (now Hwb Doeth) in 2010 with academic input, which helped to cement the relationship between the YJB and academic community. The Welsh Centre for Crime and Social Justice[5] (an alliance of seven universities in Wales) was formed to shape crime and justice policy in Wales. Both initiatives increased academic interaction with the YJB and other justice stakeholders. For example, there is academic representation on WYJAP and in several aspects of delivery of the Youth Justice Blueprint and the YJB now formally engages with a group of academics and similarly with the

---

[5] Launch of the Welsh Centre for Crime and Social Justice | WISERD. https://wiserd.ac.uk/news/launch-welsh-centre-crime-and-social-justice.

third sector to obtain their views. These combined actions have helped to bring the Child First agenda more to the fore and to inform the wider discourse in policy and practice development.

Evidence in Policy

However, despite the AWYOS (Welsh Assembly Government & YJB, 2004), several later key policy documents presented a mixed picture in terms of presentation and understanding of Child First. For example, the 2008 Youth Crime Prevention strategic guidance indicated a relationship to the AWYOS by building on the prevention and early intervention activity set out in the document, although also included guidance on dealing with anti-social behaviour (through a tiered approach to avoid the imposition of an anti-social behaviour order—the preferred approach in Wales) and highlighted the problematic nature of offences brought to justice and indicated that national work (centrally YJB-led) was underway to address concerns and amend the criteria. The 2009–2011 AWYOS delivery plan (Welsh Assembly Government & YJB, 2014) was not written within the context of how the delivery aims met the Child First commitment. The Welsh Government Green Paper (2012) which set out proposals to introduce legislation to improve services for children in actual (or potential) contact with the Youth Justice System discusses a rights-based commitment to policy-making but does not relate the proposals made in that way.

The subsequent White Paper (Welsh Government, 2014) does, however, clearly state the Prevention of Offending Bill is intended to address some of the key principles in the UNCRC regarding the use of custody, e.g. use of alternatives, last resort and shortest possible time and although not explicitly stated are Child First in orientation. The Children and Young People First Strategy (Welsh Government & YJB, 2014) does, however, set out the vision that children must be treated as children first (and offenders second), several other principles which are compatible and sympathetic to this and identifies outcomes for each of its priority areas which start to articulate what this (positively) means for children. Finally, the Youth Justice Blueprint for Wales (Welsh Government & Ministry of Justice, 2019) takes matters further by looking at the system through a child-first lens to arrive at the recommendations it did. The development of the Blueprint was also influenced by the emerging agenda within the YJB of Child First being an acceptable place to be in policy terms (Taylor, 2016) and the thinking associated with Positive Youth Justice (Haines & Case, 2015).

What these documents described above had in common was whilst making the link to the AWYOS (and the UNCRC and by proxy Child First), they did not always fully set out how the Child First commitment looked in real terms for children and YOT practice. Plus, tensions remained as not everything contained in the documents might be regarded as a Child First approach (when compared to the tenets set out by the YJB in articulation of Child First).

This suggests the clear adoption and expression of policy relating to Child First certainly in Wales has been hit and miss and at times and 'missing in action' when it came to explaining how youth justice in Wales could be framed. It could be suggested that this is one of the inevitabilities of long-term policy development which has significant cultural change at its heart, as it takes time to influence the right people, to refine and develop the approach and in the case of Child First to move from ideology to evidence-based practice. This requires a creative approach and trust between all the stakeholders who can shape the formation and direction of travel.

A further consideration is that policy development had to suit the YJB and in Wales, the Welsh Government, e.g. how far either organisation was prepared to (or could) go in conveying what Child First meant in its own context and what potentially held them back. For example, the YJB can state its commitment to Child First but may well face critics (not necessarily from the traditional sources who have moved to be somewhere inside the tent and are more actively engaged with) but other Government departments, e.g. its sponsor the Ministry of Justice in its role in developing policy and any associated legislation which could still fly in the face of Child First. HM Inspectorate of Probation (HMIP, 2020) referred to Child First as a 'mantra' in the context of discussing the management of harmful behaviours, which provides an interesting perspective on how it can be perceived. Although children's welfare and experience of trauma were recognised as valid considerations, it appeared to imply that Child First might diminish the importance of the management of risk of harm to others.

What has been potentially most helpful for moving Child First forward is the Taylor Review's commitment to youth justice being Child First as this has given the YJB the freedom for the first time to start to explore it in an in-depth and meaningful way. It should be noted the Ministry of Justice largely accepted the contents of the review (and potentially by inference Child First) and stated the need to help children to build resilience, for proportionate responses and the need to improve outcomes for children, particularly those experiencing custody (Ministry of Justice, 2016). However, a challenge remains as the YJB's key partners in justice may be driven by other imperatives and whilst there may be agreement that Childs First is a good thing, the needs of victims and community safety should also be part of the debate. UK Government ministers also need to be convinced this is the right way to go and views may alter as ministerial portfolios and Secretaries of State change, which always leads to a need to renew and revisit policy positions. Its noteworthy the position in Wales has been stable in recent years with the same Assembly Minister retaining portfolio interest in the Youth Justice Blueprint and being regularly briefed on its content and progress, so there can be confidence in the direction of travel. Further, the youth justice sector should not be alienated as good child-focused practice does exist and a concern could be that the YJB runs some risk that it might be seen to be coming to the party a bit late as others have had Child First worked out for some time. Whilst the brief critique of Child First in policy document in Wales has indicated an embryonic approach, the important thing is it has started to emerge in contrast to UK Government policy documents where it still has some way to go with its reach needing to extend beyond the YJB.

The Future for Child First

We are hesitant to write a conclusion because that suggests the Child First journey is over, whereas nothing could be further from the truth. The remaining chapters in this book set out some of the challenges and opportunities we face in developing and effective, Child First 'justice' system. That said, however, we would like to offer a few pointers as to where we think some of the challenges and opportunities lie.

It is important, if not necessary, to continue to discuss and debate CFOS. There are differences between CFOS as Professors Case and Haines set it out in their book and the YJB's version that need careful negotiating. Additionally, there is an obvious need to (continue to) explain CFOS to new colleagues, policymakers and, indeed, all stakeholders. This is not only to educate and inform, but also to prevent drift and to avoid muddying CFOS with existing or emerging 'common sense' approaches to understanding and working with children.

These discussions and debates will only bear fruit if we add to the knowledgebase of effective CFOS work with children. We know that there is a great deal of CFOS-based research currently underway—much of it being undertaken by PhD students. This work must be encouraged and, importantly, published to ensure we all continue to grow. We know from the history of youth justice that we cannot rest on our laurels. The backlash of being soft on individuals who offend will, almost inevitably, come. This can only be countered by a solid and growing evidence base.

The incarcerated population of children in England and Wales has reduced in recent times, but it remains a stubborn stump. Incarcerating children contravenes every principle of CFOS. Notwithstanding extant plans for the future of child incarceration, how we can respond to the most serious offending by children needs to be openly debated—not least because of the inherent ineffectiveness of incarceration and its contravention of CFOS principles and practices (see, e.g., Case & Haines, 2020).

As we pursue the maturation of CFOS in policy and practice we need to review the lexicon of youth justice. Justice-based language does not convey the essence of CFOS. Terms like prevention, diversion, alternatives to prosecution or custody, supervision, etc. are all justice-based terms and they are no longer fit for purpose in a CFOS world. New minds must apply themselves to developing an appropriate CFOS lexicon.

In Haines and Drakeford (1998) we were fearful, not only of an offender-based approach but also of the withdrawal of the State from the lives of children. The last 20 years has seen, due to the austerity measures of the Conservative Government, an almost total hollowing of the national and local State from the lives of children. The consequent vacuum has been filled by uncertainty, danger and incivility—none of which has been caused by or is the responsibility of children. The State needs to fill the lives of children with positive experiences if we are to truly see the maximum implementation of CFOS.

Finally and certainly not of the least importance, is the voice of the child. CFOS has always been informed by the voice of the child, but it has rarely given direct expression to the voice of the child. This needs to change. The voice of the child must be heard through research, but also in the development of policy and the implementation of practice. The insights gained from listening to the voice of the child should guide policy and practice for the next decade and beyond.

References

ARCS UK Ltd. (2013). *Evaluation of services provided by Nacro Cymru to the Welsh Government*. Welsh Assembly Government.
Audit Commission. (1996). *Misspent youth*. Audit Commission.
Bateman, T. (2010). *The systematic determinants of levels of child incarceration in England and Wales*. A thesis submitted to the University of Bedfordshire for the degree of Professional Doctorate in Youth Justice Luton, University of Bedfordshire. https://uobrep.openrepository.com/bitstream/handle/10547/134949/thesis%20timb%201.pdf?sequence=8&isAllowed=y
Case, S. (2018). *Youth justice: A critical introduction*. Routledge.
Case, S., & Browning, A. (2021). *Child first justice: The research evidence-base*. Loughborough University.
Case, S., & Haines, K. (2009). *Understanding youth offending: Risk factor research, policy and practice*. Willan.

Case, S., & Haines, K. (2020). Abolishing Youth Justice Systems: Children first, offenders nowhere. *Youth Justice, 21*(Special Issue), 3–17.

Goldson, B. (2010). The sleep of (criminological) reason: Knowledge—Policy rupture and New Labour's youth justice legacy. *Criminology and Criminal Justice, 10*(1), 155–178.

Gray, P. (2009). The political economy of risk and the new governance of youth crime. *Punishment and Society, 11*, 443.

Haines, K. (1998). Some principled objections to a restorative justice approach to working with juvenile offenders. In L. Walgrave (Ed.), *Restorative justice for juveniles: Potentialities, risks, and problems for research*. Society, Crime, and Criminal Justice. Leuven University Press.

Haines, K. (2000). Referral orders and youth offender panels: Restorative approaches and the new youth justice. In B. Goldson (Ed.), *The new youth justice*. Russell House.

Haines, K. (2009). The dragonisation of youth justice. In W. Taylor, R. Earle, & R. Hester (Eds.), *Youth justice handbook: Theory, policy and practice*. Willan.

Haines, K., & Case, S. (2004). Promoting prevention: A multi-agency initiative to prevent youth offending through consultation in Swansea schools. *Youth Justice, 4*(2), 117–132.

Haines, K., & Case, S. (2012). Is the scaled approach a failed approach? *Youth Justice, 12*(3), 212–228.

Haines, K., & Case, S. (2015). *Positive youth justice: Children first, offenders second*. Policy Press.

Haines, K., Case, S., Davies, K., & Charles, A. (2013). The Swansea Bureau: A model of diversion from the Youth Justice System. *International Journal of Law, Crime and Justice, 41*(2), 167–187.

Haines, K., Case, S., Isles, E., Rees, I., & Hancock, A. (2004). *Extending entitlement: Making it real*. Welsh Assembly Government.

Haines, K., & Drakeford, M. (1998). *Young people and youth justice*. Macmillan.

Her Majesty's Inspectorate of Probation. (2020). *Annual report: Inspection of youth offending services (2019–2020)*. Her Majesty's Inspectorate of Probation.

Lewis, S., Crawford, A., & Traynor, P. (2016). Nipping crime in the bud? The use of antisocial behaviour interventions with young people in England and Wales. *British Journal of Criminology, 57*, 1230–1248.

Local Government Association. (2008, May). *Lifting the burdens taskforce review of the Home Office and Youth Justice final report—Recommendations*. Local Government Association.

McAra, L., & McVie, S. (2010). Youth crime and justice: Key messages from the Edinburgh Study of Youth Transitions and Crime. *Criminology and Criminal Justice, 10*(2), 179–209.

Ministry of Justice. (2010). *Breaking the cycle: Effective punishment, rehabilitation and sentencing of offenders*. Ministry of Justice.

Ministry of Justice. (2016). *The government response to Charlie Taylor's Review of the Youth Justice System*. HMSO.

Pitts, J. (2001). Korrectional karaoke: New labour and the zombification of youth justice. *Youth Justice, 1*(2), 3–16.

Souhami, A. (2011). Inside the Youth Justice Board: Ambiguity and influence in New Labour's youth justice. *Safer Communities, 10*(3), 7–16.

Taylor, C. (2016). *Review of the Youth Justice System in England and Wales*. HMSO.

Thomas, S. (2015). *Children first, offenders second: An aspiration or reality for youth justice in Wales*. Thesis submitted for Professional Doctorate in Leadership in Children and Young People's Services, University of Bedfordshire, Luton.

Welsh Assembly Government. (2004). *Children and young people: Rights to action*. Welsh Assembly Government.

Welsh Assembly Government & YJB. (2004). *The All Wales Youth Offending Strategy*. Welsh Assembly Government.

Welsh Government. (2012, September). *Proposals to improve services in Wales to better meet the needs of children and young people who are at risk of entering, or are already in the Youth Justice System*. Welsh Government.

Welsh Government. (2014). *Prevention of offending by young people*. Welsh Government.

Welsh Government & Ministry of Justice. (2019). *Youth Justice Blueprint for Wales*. https://gov.wales/sites/default/files/publications/2019-05/youth-justice-blueprint_0.pdf

Welsh Government & YJB. (2014). *Children and young people first*. Welsh Government.

Williams, J. (2007, June). Incorporating children's rights: The divergence in law and policy. *Legal Studies, 27*(2), 261–287.

YJB. (2014). *AssetPlus model document*. YJB.

YJB. (2021). *Strategic plan 2021–2024*. YJB.

5

Child First and Children's Rights: An Opportunity to Advance Rights-Based Youth Justice

Ursula Kilkelly

Introduction

According to the United Nations Convention on the Rights of the Child (CRC) and associated international instruments, children in conflict with the law have a right to treatment that is age appropriate, promotes their reintegration, meets their needs and enhances the support of family relationships (Liefaard, 2020). CRC principles of diversion and detention as a last resort, key to the children's rights approach to youth justice, seek to minimise children's contact with the criminal justice system and according to the Committee on the Rights of the Child (the CRC Committee), '[e]vidence shows that the prevalence of crime committed by children tends to decrease after the adoption of systems in line with these principles' (CRC Committee, 2019, para 3). Implementation of CRC rights in youth justice requires adapted procedures and settings,

U. Kilkelly (✉)
Enforcement of Children's Rights, Leiden University, Leiden, Netherlands
e-mail: u.kilkelly@ucc.ie

specialisation and independent monitoring to ensure the highest standards are maintained (CRC Committee, 2019). As an instrument of international law, the CRC (Article 4) creates binding legal obligations on states parties to take legislative, administrative and other measures to implement children's rights and these efforts have intensified in recent years, with growing global momentum behind the approach to fully incorporate the Convention into domestic law including in the area of youth justice (Kilkelly et al. 2021). At an international level, the Convention's reporting mechanism and communications procedure mean that international systems exist to hold states to account for the realisation of children's rights.

In addition to its standing as widely applicable international law (the CRC has been ratified by all states but the United States), a children's rights approach to youth justice carries other significant advantages. Derived from international consensus, children's rights reflect evidence of good practice in the treatment of children in conflict with the law (Kilkelly, 2008). Capable of adaptation to different national youth justice systems, the children's rights approach offers a single international benchmark against which comparisons can be drawn and a framework within which lessons can be widely shared from one jurisdiction, one continent to another. At the same time, the international children's rights standards do not all apply evenly or easily to all youth justice systems and this has led to concerns about their overlapping and contradictory nature (Hespel et al., 2012).

The Child First approach (first developed by Case & Haines, 2014, 2015) shares similar principles and values to the children's rights approach and it references 'rights' as one of a number of concepts on which the approach is based (Haines & Case, 2015: 2). According to Case and Haines, the Child First approach prioritises the promotion of positive behaviours and outcomes for children, grounded in 'child-friendly principles of universalism, diversion and normalisation' (2014: 227). Viewed originally as an alternative to the regressive youth justice policies which focused on risk, punishment and a managerialist agenda, 'Children First Offender Second' emerged as a positive youth justice strategy in post-devolution Wales (Drakeford, 2009). From these 'rhetorical' beginnings (Haines & Case, 2015: 7), the approach has been further refined (Case & Haines, 2021a), and in a significant development, what is now known as 'Child First' has been adopted as the vision for youth justice by the Youth Justice Board for England and Wales (YJB, 2021).

Although there are clear parallels between the two approaches, the Child First model is not explicitly rights based or at least not exclusively so. Given the international legal standing of the rights approach, this would appear to be a missed opportunity to further strengthen the national approach to the treatment of children in conflict with the law. It is the aim of this chapter to consider the merits of this approach and to explore how this might be done. There are three sections. The first section sets out the key elements of a rights-based approach to youth justice, drawing on a wealth of international legal standards. Consideration is given to the merits of the rights-based approach while highlighting some of the challenges of its implementation in the practice of youth justice. The second section considers the Child First approach, identifying its main principles and values, viewed from a children's rights perspective. Following consideration of both models, the third section illustrates how a rights-based approach to Child First could be achieved, concluding with some reflections on what remains to be explored.

Children's Rights and Youth Justice

Early Origins of the Rights-Based Approach

International children's standards on youth justice have their basis in the earliest human rights instruments of the twentieth century. The League of Nations Declaration on the Rights of the Child 1924 (the Geneva Declaration) recognised that 'men and women of all nations, recognizing that mankind owes to the Child the best that it has to give', declared and accepted it as their duty to meet the needs and rights of the child to development, protection and welfare. Even at this time, in acceptance that children in conflict with the law deserved special attention, the Geneva Declaration explicitly refers to the 'delinquent' child as a child that 'must be reclaimed' (Liefaard, 2020: 280). This instrument was followed by the United Nations Declaration on the Rights of the Child in 1959 which recognised for the first time that children, like adults, were rights holders entitled to the protection of the state. In its Preamble, the 1959 Declaration acknowledged that 'the child, by reason of his physical and mental immaturity, needs special safeguards and care, including appropriate legal protection, before as well as after birth'. In a shift towards a rights-based approach, the 1959 Declaration recognised the rights of the child in 'Ten Principles' while calling on parents but crucially also national governments to recognise the rights in the Declaration and 'strive for their observance'. Long since considered the property and concern of their parents, the 1959 Declaration was an important recognition that no longer a private family matter, children were holders of rights in their own right, and were entitled to have those rights vindicated by the state.

The Convention on the Rights of the Child

In 1989, the CRC was adopted unanimously by the General Assembly of the United Nations and in a ground swell of international support it came into force in rapid time, becoming the most highly ratified instrument in international law, with only the United States failing to join (Doek, 2019). As a comprehensive legal instrument, the CRC sets out the rights to which children are entitled in all areas of their lives, while making specific provision for the rights of children in particular settings including children in conflict with the law (Article 40). The Committee on the Rights of the Child (the CRC Committee), established to monitor progress in the implementation of the Convention, identified four provisions as 'general principles' to guide implementation of the CRC (CRC Committee, 2003: 4). These are: the requirement that all children enjoy their rights equally without discrimination (Article 2); the best interests of the child are a primary consideration in all actions concerning children (Article 3); the child's right to life, survival and development (Article 6) and the child's right to have their views taken into account in all matters affecting the child, with those views given due weight in accordance with the child's age and maturity (Article 12). These provisions are considered to have additional weight, as a lens through which all CRC provisions are to be interpreted and applied (Peleg, 2019). While Article 3, the best interests principle, has helped to promote child-centred decision-making (CRC Committee, 2013), Article 12 has inspired a movement to bring about rights-based participation of children in decision about matters that affect them (CRC Committee, 2009) *inter alia* through Lundy's influential model of space, voice, audience and influence (Lundy, 2007).

The CRC sets out a holistic and inclusive vision of the needs of children, recognising universal rights to health care (Article 24), education (Articles 28 and 29) and an adequate standard of living (Article 27), while giving expression to children's civic rights including their freedom of expression (Article 13), freedom of religion (Article 14) and freedom of association (Article 15). Rights of particular importance to children are recognised in Article 30, which sets out the child's rights to play, rest and leisure, and the vulnerability of children is recognised in the extensive provision in the Convention for the child's right to protection and recovery from harm, abuse and exploitation (Articles 19, 32 to 36, 39). Uniquely in the CRC, children are entitled to information about their rights under Article 42 in a recognition that without knowledge of rights, their implementation will not be fully secured. The CRC recognises the important role of the family in the child's life, in the exercise of the child's rights (Article 5) and parental contact and family relationships are explicitly protected (Article 7). While parents have primary responsibility for the child's upbringing and development (Art 18(1)), the state has a duty to provide parents with appropriate assistance in this regard, including ensuring the development of 'institutions, facilities and services for the care of children' (Article 18(2)). Articles 20 and 21 have regard to children whose protection must be found outside the family and for children deprived of liberty, contact with family is an explicit right under Article 37.

The CRC takes an expansive approach to childhood, defining the child as every human being below the age of 18 years (Article 1) and although states are entitled to prescribe that majority is reached earlier, the Convention provides that children's rights and the protective status of childhood should apply from birth to 18 years. In addition, the CRC underscores the right of all children to dignity and respect as individual rights holders, equally worthy, as a matter of international law

(Kilkelly & Liefaard, 2019) and contrary to myth and misunderstanding, children's rights are not (just) about charity and pity and they cannot be reduced to child protection, participation or used interchangeably with concepts like well-being (Lundy, 2019). The Convention, as an instrument of international human rights law, requires states parties to take all measures to implement Convention rights without condition or exception and in this respect, full commitment to children's rights means upholding the rights of all children, in all circumstances (Kilkelly, 2019b: 83).

While children in conflict with the law or in the Youth Justice System are entitled, like other children, to enjoy their Convention rights, they are also entitled to special protection in acknowledgement of their vulnerability and needs. Article 40(1) sets expectations as to the national approach to youth justice, providing that states must recognise the right of every child in conflict with the law to be treated in a manner consistent with the child's sense of dignity and worth, taking into account the child's age and the desirability of promoting the child's reintegration into society. It is the duty of states parties under Article 40(2) to ensure a child enjoys the safeguards and rights of due process in the legal process, including the right to be innocent until proven guilty, informed of the charges against him/her; not to be compelled to give testimony or confess guilt and to have free access to an interpreter. Of particular importance is the right of the child, in Article 40(2)(vii), to have his/her privacy respected at all stages of the proceedings, while Article 40(3) highlights the importance of specialisation, requiring the establishment of 'laws, procedures, authorities and institutions specifically applicable to children alleged as, accused of, or recognized as having infringed the penal law'. In particular, the CRC requires the establishment of a minimum age of criminal responsibility (an international norm, set by the Committee, at 14 years) (CRC Committee, 2019, para 22) and requires states parties to put in place 'whenever appropriate and desirable, measures for dealing with such children without resorting to judicial proceedings, providing that human rights and legal safeguards are fully respected'. Article 40(4) requires states to make available a 'variety of dispositions, such as care, guidance and supervision orders; counselling; probation; foster care; education and vocational training programmes and other alternatives to institutional care' in order to ensure that children are dealt with 'in a manner appropriate to their well-being and proportionate both to their circumstances and the offence'. Article 37 provides that detention must be used 'as a measure of last resort', 'for the shortest appropriate period of time' and children deprived of liberty are entitled to respect for their dignity and age-appropriate treatment and detention (Article 37(b), CRC). Children are to be separated from adults in detention and have the right to maintain contact with family through correspondence and visits and the right to prompt access to legal and other appropriate assistance (Article 37(c) and (d), CRC).

Implementing the CRC

States parties to the Convention are required, under Article 4, to take all appropriate legislative, administrative and other measures for the implementation of Convention rights and the Committee recommends the adoption of both legal and non-legal measures in this regard (CRC Committee, 2003). This includes incorporating Convention principles and provisions into national law, including in youth justice (CRC Committee, 2003, para 22). Acknowledging that the Convention recognises only 'minimum standards', states parties are encouraged to 'enact and implement within their jurisdiction legal provisions that are more conducive to the realization of the rights of the child than those contained in the Convention', in line with Article 41 (CRC Committee, 2003, para 23). To promote domestic enforcement of children's rights, the Committee calls on states parties to put in place effective remedies to redress violations of children's rights (CRC Committee, 2003, para 24) and highlights also the important role played by non-legal measures of implementation including a comprehensive, rights-based national strategy (CRC Committee, 2003, para 28), professional training and capacity building (CRC Committee, 2003, paras 53–55) and the development of measures to document, evaluate and co-ordinate implementation of the Convention. The periodic reporting process holds states to account with respect to the duty to implement the Convention, allowing matters of concern to be raised directly with governments on the international stage (Article 44). Those states parties that have ratified the Optional Protocol on the Communications Procedure have accepted the competence of the Committee to consider complaints from children about breaches of their rights. Importantly, there has been increasing global momentum in favour of legal incorporation of the Convention at a national level and research has shown a link between strong legal protection for children's rights and the enhanced protection of those rights in practice, including in the area of youth justice (Kilkelly et al. 2021). Although England has yet to take such steps, the effects of this movement can be viewed in Scotland and Wales where measures to give legal effect to the CRC at a national level have recently strengthened the domestic legal standing of children's rights (Kilkelly et al. 2021).

The Strengths of International Standards

Building on the almost universal ratification of the legally binding Convention on the Rights of the Child, a range of detailed instruments have been adopted through an ongoing process of international dialogue and consensus building. Although the Havana Rules on Juveniles deprived of Liberty (1990) and the European Guidelines on Child-friendly Justice (2010), for instance, do not enjoy the same binding legal status as the Convention, they make an important contribution to standard setting, especially in the area of detention and the court process. A range of instruments now comprise an impressive body of international standards on the rights of children in conflict with the law and taken together, they provide important direction to national authorities on youth justice, identifying how children's rights are to be protected in all aspects of the justice system. Not susceptible to the vagaries of public opinion, these minimum standards have 'credibility' and 'a sense of timeless value' as the 'common language of youth justice' (Kilkelly, 2008: 191). The guidance is extensive in reach and detail and is applicable to the variety of national approaches to youth justice that exist around the world (Muncie, 2006). Indeed, as Liefaard remarks, 'the world has witnessed the emergence of a comprehensive international legal framework of human and children's rights standards relevant to juvenile justice' which has given rise to law reform and an increased awareness and understanding about the rights of children in justice systems (Liefaard, 2020: 283). Although the overlapping and at times contradictory nature of these instruments has caused some concern (Hespel et al., 2012), their principal value lies in the extent to which they capture 'best practice' across the Youth Justice System along with a consistent commitment to 'age-appropriate treatment, the importance of diversion and the imperative of rehabilitation' (Kilkelly, 2008: 188). Underlying these instruments is a key assumption that children in conflict with the law must be treated in a child-specific manner that is fair and respectful of their inherent dignity and rights. Liefaard observes that this requires 'a specific justice system for children', pedagogical in orientation, and specialist in approach, with key principles incorporated in law, policy and practice throughout the wider justice system (Liefaard, 2020: 284–288). These principles form the basis of a rights-based approach to youth justice and through the standard setting and monitoring work of the UN and regional bodies, children's rights in youth justice have enjoyed significant international attention. For instance, it is notable that youth justice is the only area in which the Committee on the Rights of the Child has adopted two General Comments, revising its earlier instrument in 2019 in line with emerging evidence on child development and in order to further strengthen the emphasis on prevention and early intervention and diversion and to promote improved organisation, capacity building, data collection, evaluation and research (CRC Committee, 2019, para 6). The publication of the UN Global Study on Children Deprived of Liberty has demonstrated further that the issue is indeed a priority of the world's largest international organisation (Nowak, 2019).

Gaps and Weaknesses

Although there are clear merits and strengths to the children's rights standards in the area of youth justice—most importantly, they reinforce that children in conflict with the law are children, with legal rights—there are some weaknesses and gaps in this approach. First, the CRC has been criticised for setting standards at too low a level. For instance, while the drafting parties' failure to enshrine a minimum age of criminal responsibility in the Convention has been addressed by the Committee in General Comment No 24, which it set as a recommendation of 14 years, this is not a binding standard. And similarly, while Article 40 contains important due process standards to safeguard the position of children in legal proceedings, there is nothing in the Convention to prevent a child being tried in adult court or receiving a long sentence of detention where that is considered a proportionate response. The level of discretion that states enjoy in the implementation of Convention rights can play out in negative ways for children in the justice system (Liefaard, 2020). Particular examples include the broad range of sentencing mechanisms that are tolerated within the terms of the Convention including detention up to and including life imprisonment, as long as parole is permitted (Liefaard, 2020: 294). More generally, this discretion in the interpretation and application of the Convention to youth justice permits states to pick and choose those provisions they consider most relevant or appealing. And against the ever-politicised context of youth justice, states can and do set the bar very low for those children deemed less worthy, especially those at the extreme end of the offending spectrum (Lynch & Liefaard, 2020). While the periodic monitoring mechanism requires states parties to report progress to the Committee on their implementation of the Convention, children, including those in the United Kingdom, who live in a state party that has not ratified the Optional Protocol on a Communication Procedure are unable to access this remedy for alleged breaches of their rights.

Child First

Child First is a model of youth justice that seeks to prioritise the promotion of positive behaviours and outcomes for children, recognising their needs and diverting them from the justice system so they can fulfil their potential. With its origins in Wales where it was developed in the context of a new national policy approach to children, which layered entitlements onto a rights-based approach, Drakeford explains it was used to denote an 'attitude of mind, in which offending is understood as only one element in a much wider and more complex identity' (2010: 141). The approach has continued to evolve since and has gathered support as a holistic, child-centred and principled approach to youth justice (Haines & Case, 2015). According to its proponents, the Child First, positive model of youth justice rejects the focus on negative outcomes and behaviours, on risk management and the responsibilisation of children (Case & Haines, 2014: 226). Instead, the approach is grounded in principles of 'universalism, diversion and normalisation pursued through (non-criminal justice) practice that is inclusionary, participatory, and legitimate; it is evidenced through partnership, engagement and access to universal entitlement' (Case & Haines, 2021a: 11). At the core of the Child First approach is the principle that children involved in offending behaviour must be recognised and treated as children, who are 'at the heart of the system' (Haines & Case, 2015: 79). Service delivery and the achievement of specific outcomes for children is 'the responsibility of the adults involved', the practitioners 'who must understand why they come into work every day' (Haines & Case, 2015: 79). According to Haines and Case, positive youth justice is *'child-friendly and child-appropriate*, maintaining sensitivity to the status of "child", children's universal entitlements and the inherent responsibilities of adults in all dealings with children' (emphasis in original) (Haines & Case, 2015: 80). Their special treatment is achieved through the *'normalisation* of everyday childhood behaviour' (emphasis in original), where children's needs are met and 'punitive justice' and adult-centric welfare responses are rejected (Haines & Case, 2015: 80). The model emphasises diversion and minimum necessary levels of intervention, discarding net-widening excesses of the punishment, justice and welfare models. The Child First approach prioritises children and family engagement, in partnership with practitioners and it eschews interventions that lead to social exclusion, stigmatisation and further offending. The model aims to place responsibilities on adults, through *'child-focused decision making'* (emphasis in original), across the Youth Justice System, 'evidence based partnership' and the promotion of children's universal entitlements, universal rights and capacities to realise positive behaviours and outcomes' (Haines & Case, 2015: 80).

The original model espoused by Drakeford, Haines and Case was presented as 'Children First Offending Second' (CFOS), in order to reorient youth justice around the child and make explicit that the status of child as child must trump their behaviour or 'offending', i.e. their status as offender. CFOS prevailed as the model developed, incorporating the important principles of diversion (Case & Haines, 2014) and engagement (Case & Haines, 2015). More recently, the reference to 'Offender Second' was dropped in favour of Children First, a 'positive youth justice' approach which has, as its essence, child-friendly and child-appropriate youth justice (Case, 2022: 289). More recently, the inclusion of 'Offender Second' has been problematised in favour of diverting children entirely into multi-professional support services in a case for a full non-criminal response to children's offending (Case & Haines, 2021a). In this respect, 'children first youth justice' is presented as an oxymoron, an attempt to 'humanise an inhuman system' in which 'the associated principles of "Children First" [are] more appropriately situated within integrated, "whole child" systems that normalise and decriminalise offending behaviour by children' (Case & Haines, 2021a, 13).

A very significant development in the implementation of the Child First approach to youth justice was its adoption by the Youth Justice Board for England and Wales (YJB), the statutory body with responsibility for youth justice, as a dynamic vision for the Youth Justice System (Case, 2022: 303). The YJB's explicit commitment to Child First as a 'strategic approach and central guiding principle' has significant transformative potential for a national Youth Justice System once associated with punitive and regressive approaches. In its iteration of Child First, the YJB Strategy frames the four elements as: prioritising the child's best interests, promoting children's individual strengths and capacities, encouraging children's active participation, engagement and wider social inclusion and promoting a childhood removed from the justice system, using pre-emptive prevention, diversion and minimal intervention (2021: 10–11). Taking account of its theoretical framework and the manner of its transposition into national policy, the next section explores the strengths and weaknesses of Child First.

Strengths and Weaknesses of Child First

The Child First approach has several strengths. First, it is a principle-based model that provides high level guidance and direction to policymakers and practitioners alike. Its philosophy is simple, and its values are easily understood for those working with children in conflict with the law in all parts of the Youth Justice System. The fact that the origins of the approach lie in and were developed through practice gives the approach a credibility that is compelling (Haines & Case, 2015) and its evidence base further supports buy-in from policymakers and the academic community (Case & Browning, 2021). The model has been continuously refined, allowing its elements to be adapted to specific contexts and settings (Case & Haines, 2021b), including areas like custody and resettlement that were not considered in the original model (Hazel & Bateman, 2021). The adoption of Child First as YJB Strategy has provided the opportunity for further adaptation as the process to embed it into national policy gets underway and in this regard, it is welcome that the Standards for Children in the Youth Justice System, which provide the governance framework for the youth justice system as a whole, align with the approach (MoJ & YJB, 2019).

What is not yet clear, however, is how Child First is to become embedded into practice, not just in those bodies under the auspices of the YJB, but in those parts of the Youth Justice System—the courts and parts of the youth custody estate, for instance—over which the Board has no direct responsibility. At the same time, if all state bodies in the youth justice field do not expressly adopt Child First, this could result in policy confusion, translating into mixed messages to practitioners. Experience has shown that it is in the context of 'hard cases', involving serious and violent crime, that support for progressive approaches to youth justice will be tested. In this regard, if public priorities like community safety and victims' rights are not to be viewed in competition with Child First, political support, beyond the Youth Justice Board, will be essential to prevent a return to more punitive responses. While the adoption of Child First by the YJB is important given its leadership of the Youth Justice System, more widespread policy adoption and indeed legislative change may be required to ensure it becomes the national approach, embedded in practice throughout the whole Youth Justice System. Incorporating the approach into all monitoring and inspection systems will also be key.

There are also some areas of substance where Child First could be considered weak, and where the credibility and impact of the approach will be tested. First, it appears relatively silent on the question of disproportionate minority contact, and although the YJB Strategy 'acknowledges structural barriers', as part of the commitment to prioritise the child's best interests, this seems a rather oblique reference to what is arguably the most pressing contemporary issue in youth justice in England and Wales (May et al., 2009) and indeed in other jurisdictions (Mallett, 2018). Second, the approach is silent on the use of detention and while diversion is an important goal, there appears no acknowledgement that in some instances, either because of the harm caused by the child's offending or the risk they pose to public safety, there will not be any safe alternative. It is similarly silent on the court process and does not address how children are to enjoy that most fundamental of rights, a fair trial, with proportionate sentencing and child-friendly procedures especially when subjected to adult proceedings. However principled the approach, failing to address the reality that adult courts and custody are used in some children's cases risks jeopardising the credibility of the Child First approach. Ways must be found to accommodate Child First within the relatively punitive aspects of youth justice, with which they seem directly at odds. To do otherwise is to ignore that children in those adult systems are entitled, too, to be treated as children. While some of these issues are teased out in this volume (see Hollingsworth and Swidenbank and McCathie), more research is required to articulate what Child First means in the context of serious youth crime, where the political priorities of public safety and punishment may at times require an approach driven by risk assessment, rather than diversion. In this respect, it is important that the Child First model can be articulated not just as the model that is best for children—while this is paramount of course—but that it is best for everyone, including the communities and individuals who are the victims of youth crime. Importantly, the YJB Strategy recognises this, in reflecting on the role that Child First can play in strengthening children's pro-social identity for sustainable desistance, 'leading to safer communities and fewer victims' (YJB, 2021: 11). This is an important point not just in strengthening the case for Child First, but in ensuring that public policy also has the desired effect of making communities safer for everyone.

At the same time, it is important to acknowledge that the Child First approach is still in its infancy and like any new policy direction, it will take time to become successfully embedded in practice. Many of the gaps identified here are already being addressed, including through this publication, which taken together will allow the momentum to build around an approach that has significant potential to transform the treatment of children in conflict with the law. In order to fully realise its potential, however, closer alignment or indeed integration of children's rights into Child First should be considered. The next section will consider the value of this approach and how it might be achieved.

Child First from a Children's Rights Perspective

This chapter began with an overview of the children's rights approach to youth justice, based on the UN Convention on the Rights of the Child and associated instruments. In summary, it explained that rights-based youth justice, grounded in international law, requires children to be treated with dignity and respect, in a manner consistent with their age and needs and in a specialist system that promotes diversion, from formal adjudication and from detention. A child's reintegration is the overriding goal. General children's rights principles emphasise the child's right to development, right to have actions taken in their best interests and right to be heard and have their views taken into account in all matters affecting the child. Family relationships are recognised in the Convention as explicitly important. Under the CRC, children are rights holders; state parties bear the duty to respect, protect and fulfil those rights without condition or exception. While the CRC is a binding international treaty, it requires states parties to take legal and other measures to implement children's rights, giving them effect in national law and policy with remedies for children whose rights have been violated. The widespread acceptance of the CRC and the proliferation of other instruments in the areas of child-friendly justice and detention, for instance, ensure a set of standards for youth justice that is comprehensive, legal standing and of comparative and wide application.

While rights are listed as one of its tenets, the Child First model is not explicitly or at least not exclusively rights based. While it makes some references to rights, as one of the elements underpinning the approach, the Child First literature refers predominantly to children's 'entitlements', reflecting its origins in the Welsh youth strategy that articulated 'Ten entitlements' as expressions of basic and universal needs, linked to positive outcomes for young people (Case et al., 2005: 189). This strategy purported to create 'a set of rights … free at the point of use; universal and unconditional' and as an approach 'Extending Entitlement' was framed as 'a pro-active approach informed by rights and entitlements…' (Case et al., 2005: 190). Regardless of language (note the language of entitlement does not appear in the YJB Strategy), both approaches share broadly similar principles and values, and they share an evidence base too, as a recent extensive mapping exercise makes clear (Case & Browning, 2021). But the YJB Strategy makes few explicit references to children's rights in its explanation of Child First. The first reference is set out in the first element of the approach, framed here as 'the prioritisation of the best interests of children' (p. 10). This is a clear use of the language of 'best interests', as recognised by Article 3(1) of the CRC, although the decision to 'prioritise' rather than require those interests to be 'a primary consideration in all actions concerning the child' might reflect a divergence in approach. The second reference comes later in this element, which recognises children's 'particular needs, capacities, *rights* and potential' (emphasis added), while explaining that all work is to be 'child-focused, developmentally informed, acknowledges structural barriers and meets responsibilities towards children' (p. 10). This general reference to 'rights' here, alongside several other factors, makes clear that it is not the only element to be considered as part of the Child First approach. References in the other elements of Child First, as set out in the YJB strategy, include the reference to 'participation' (used alongside 'engagement' to suggest taking part in a service, rather than a right to a say in decision-making as in Article 12 of the CRC) in the second element, and the reference to 'diversion' in the fourth element, which reflects the approach in Article 40 of the CRC.

A thorough analysis of the comparisons between Child First and children's rights is beyond the scope of this chapter. It is evident, however, that while the values and principles of both approaches align (Case & Browning, 2021), the language used in Child First falls short of articulating a child's individual legal right to the supports and services that will meet their needs. In this regard, use of the plural term 'children' is interesting and to be contrasted with the term 'child' used in the CRC to denote the individual status of each child as rights holder. Similarly, the YJB Strategy refers to the 'responsibilities adults have towards children', rather than using the human rights language of 'duties', encapsulated in the CRC by the use of the 'shall' to connote the legal requirement on the national authorities (not simply adults) of the obligation to protect, promote and fulfil the rights of the child.

Much of the sentiment and the intent is the same of course. Both Child First and children's rights approaches highlight the central importance of ensuring that children are treated with regard to their age and understanding, in a manner that takes account of their circumstances and needs. While Child First stresses the 'children as children' approach, children's rights represent a focus on each child as an individual worthy of respect, not an adult in waiting or, for children in conflict with the law, a child less worthy. Both approaches espouse the importance of diversion as a formal and explicit principle, keeping children out of the formal justice system and preventing children from further offending. Both approaches emphasise the need to avoid stigmatising and labelling children, protecting them from the harshness of justice and punitive responses. Both approaches, although perhaps in different ways, espouse the importance of children participating in processes and decision-making about their lives. While Child First highlights 'engagement' as an essential component of '"effective" youth justice practice' (Case & Haines, 2015: 157) and is set out in the YJB Strategy in terms of children's 'active participation, engagement and wider inclusion', the children's rights approach recognises the integral nature of children's participation in decision-making about matters that affect them. For children's rights, this is about agency, dignity and respect for children as individuals worthy in their own right, with a voice and a right to have a say. For Child First, this reflects more of a focus on engagement and on collaboration. A further illustration of common ground is in relation to children's needs. While Child First prioritises children's access to universal services—like health, education and welfare—the Convention recognises rights to health, education, development, protection and care as fundamental rights of the child to which children have an express legal entitlement. And finally, the Child First approach 'holds the status of "child" as paramount in all policy and practice', an approach which 'demands an acceptance of the child's inherent vulnerability by virtue of age, immaturity' and other factors (Case & Haines, 2014: 232). Here too, the approach aligns with the rights-based approach that views children in conflict with the law as entitled to special protection and treatment on the basis of their age, development and particular circumstances.

At the same time, it is nonetheless a missed opportunity *not* to link Child First more explicitly to the approach of children's rights, as set out in the widely applicable international legal framework. This would have many benefits. It would strengthen the argument that as children, and rights holders, children who come into conflict with the law are children too, worthy of respect, dignity, having their needs met and having a say in their lives. Using rights language would also make clear that Child First represents not only evidence-based good practice, but they come with the legal weight of an almost universally adopted set of international standards which also comes with an evidence base. Linking to the language and approach of the CRC would bring with it a wealth not just of international guidance, but active contribution to and indeed leadership of a community that shares a common goal and has approaches that can facilitate learning.

While it is clear that Child First is not exclusively rights based, given the benefits and strengths of the rights-based approach, it is not immediately clear why this is the case. It is true that rights language is not politically acceptable in some jurisdictions and England and Wales would not be the first to eschew explicit rights language in its national policy. Australia has shown clear reluctance to engage with the rights-based approach to children in law and policy (Tobin, 2021) while New Zealand has preferred to base its national children's strategy on the concept of 'well-being', reflecting a concern that rights are 'too individualistic' (Lynch, 2021). At the same time, if this opposition or reluctance can be overcome, a rights-based approach to Child First would hold even greater potential to improve the lives of children who come into conflict with the law for the reasons set out here. This final section provides some illustration as to how this might be achieved.

Giving Child First a Rights-Basis

To strengthen the rights-basis to Child First, there are two main ways this could be done—the first is by integrating the explicit language of children's rights into Child First, including adding elements not already explicit in the model. The second approach is by drawing on the general measures of implementation integral to the children's rights approach to further support the translation of Child First into practice. Some illustration of these will now follow.

First, with regard to giving Child First an explicit rights-basis, it is important to predicate the model on the status of the child as a rights holder, as a person worthy of dignity and respect with a right to treatment in line with their needs, vulnerabilities and circumstances. More specifically, then, 'seeing children as children' could be expressed as a child's right to treated with respect and dignity and with regard to the child's age and understanding, a right that applies to all children in all circumstances. Drawing on the CRC Committee's General Comment No 24 would support an emphasis here on the child's development (Art 6) and recognition for the specific vulnerabilities and needs of children in conflict with the law (Art 40). While Child First already contains a commitment to prioritise the child's best interests, a greater emphasis on 'all children', through the non-discrimination principle of Article 2 of the CRC would highlight children's fundamental right to equal treatment. This is especially important given the disproportionate involvement in the Youth Justice System of children from minority backgrounds and the importance of underscoring the right of every child to equal enjoyment of their rights, regardless of their background or status, or any 'structural barriers' to which the YJB Strategy refers.

Including reference to the child's right to be heard would strengthen the focus on the child's capacity and agency in the Child First references to collaboration and engagement. The second element—developing a pro-social identity—would be made more explicit by reliance on the child's right to education and development in line with Article 28, 29 and 6 of the CRC. More specific reference, for instance, to the child's right to health (Article 24 of the CRC) both in the early stages of life and in adolescence, as articulated in the Committee's General Comments, would give greater substance to Child First in an area of critical importance to all children, but especially those who come into conflict with the law. Regard should be had to the duty on states under Article 28 to promote regular attendance at school, to promote positive approaches to school discipline, to encourage the development of different forms of education and make vocational guidance available to all. The duty on states under Article 29 to direct education to the development of the child's talents and full potential is also relevant here. While Child First highlights the importance of supportive relationships, explicit reliance on the recognition in the Convention on the support provided to children by their family and community would be important to acknowledge (Art 5, 18, 37), along with the state's duty to provide support to family in return (Art 18). In relation to the third tenet, that of collaboration and engagement, this could be improved through an explicit reference to the right of the child to be heard, under Article 12, to reinforce the voice of the child throughout youth justice decision-making including the development and implementation of national policy relevant to the respect given to children as agents and actors in their own lives, with a right to be part of decisions made about them. While children's engagement in programmes and access to services means something quite different, there is no doubt that participation rights co-exist with concepts of engagement and collaboration in a mutually enforcing manner such that a reference to the child's right to be heard would be important here. Making reference to the European Guidelines on Child-friendly justice in this context is an important way to highlight the duty to make decision-making systems and processes accessible to children. The duty under the Guidelines to ensure children are supported, informed and guided before, during and after justice processes would add considerable strength and depth to the approach here. Finally, for element four on diversion, there is a very straight forward reference to be made to the children's rights approach, so explicitly set out in the right to diversion from formal adjudication in Article 40 (3) of the CRC and most importantly, from detention in Article 37. The importance of this latter point cannot be overstated. Although Child First clearly espouses diversion including minimal contact with the system, the inclusion of the principle of detention as a last resort is vital to support the active prioritisation of alternatives to detention, in line with the principle that detention must be a measure of last resort. This is important too to ensure the application of Child First principles to all children, including those at the 'deep end' of the justice system for whom long periods of detention are common place.

The second way in which the children's rights approach could usefully strengthen the Children First model is by drawing on the Committee's guidance on measures of implementation. As noted already, the CRC contains an express duty on states parties to take all appropriate measures to implement CRC rights and this has been interpreted by the Committee to require the incorporation of children's rights into domestic law and policy, the adoption of national strategy to guide implementation of the Convention and a range of other structures and measures including the establishment of national children's rights institutions, children's rights budgeting, attention to monitoring and enforcement mechanisms and ensuring data and research is undertaken to monitor implementation (CRC Committee, 2003). There is little doubt that these measures can play a vital part in giving effect to children's rights at a national level, embedding children's rights in national structures and legal systems that make them sustainable (Kilkelly et al. 2021). There is also evidence that these approaches can help to build momentum and consensus around further progressive reforms, in a gradual and incremental process of children's rights implementation (Kilkelly, 2020). It is equally clear from research that incorporating children's rights into law and policy on youth justice is vital to their effective implementation (Kilkelly & Bergin, 2021; Kilkelly & Logan, 2021).

Conclusion

This chapter sought to articulate the common ground that exists between Child First and the children's rights approaches to youth justice by highlighting the respective merits of each approach. While both share key principles around a positive approach to youth justice, the absence of a more explicit rights-basis to Child First should be considered a missed opportunity to strengthen an approach that already enjoys the support of policymakers and practitioners alike. In addition to the reasons articulated above, there are two further reasons why a more robust rights-based approach is important: first, it would improve the legitimacy of the Child First approach which despite its adoption as the strategy of the Youth Justice Board does not yet enjoy legal standing. The second reason to strengthen its rights-basis is to support the greater implementation of Child First. International children's rights instruments provide important guidance as to how to improve children's rights compliance in the domestic legal system and as this chapter illustrates, a growing body of research evidence suggests that the strategic use of legal and non-legal measures could support the vision of the YJB to bring about system-wide implementation of Child First.

A further point relates to the internationalisation of Child First and the opportunity for replicating the approach that would come with a more explicit alignment to children's rights. In this regard, Child First would not only be strengthened by recourse to children's rights, adopting a rights lens would also give the model international relevance and application in a way that would extend its reach far beyond current jurisdictional boundaries.

References

Case, S. (2022). *Youth justice; a critical introduction* (2nd ed.). Routledge.
Case, S., & Browning, A. (2021). *Child first justice: The research evidence-base*. Loughborough University.

Case, S., & Haines, K. (2014). Children first, offenders second, reframing the prevention debate. *Youth Justice, 15*(3), 226–239.

Case, S., & Haines, K. (2015). Children first, offenders second: The centrality of engagement in positive youth justice. *The Howard Journal, 54*(2), 157–175.

Case, S., & Haines, K. (2021a). Abolishing youth justice systems: Children First, Offenders Nowhere. *Youth Justice, 21*(1), 3–17.

Case, S., & Haines, K. (2021b). Special issue: Charting a new course for youth justice. *Youth Justice, 21*(1).

Case, S. P., Clutton, S., & Haines, K. R. (2005). Extending entitlement: A Welsh policy for children. *Wales Journal of Law and Policy, 4*(2), 187–202.

Doek, J. (2019). The human rights of children: An introduction. In U. Kilkelly & T. Liefaard (Eds.), *International human rights of children* (pp. 3–29). Springer.

Drakeford, M. (2009). Children first, offenders second: Youth justice in a devolved Wales. *Criminal Justice Matters, 78*, 8–9.

Drakeford, M. (2010). Devolution and youth justice in Wales. *Criminology and Criminal Justice, 10*(2), 137–154.

Goldson, B., & Kilkelly, U. (2013). International human rights standards and child imprisonment: Potentialities and limitations. *International Journal of Children's Rights, 21*(2), 345–371.

Haines, K., & Case, S. (2015). *Positive youth justice: Children first, offenders second*. Policy Press.

Hazel, N., & Bateman, T. (2021). Supporting children's resettlement ('reentry') after custody: Beyond the risk paradigm. *Youth Justice, 21*(1), 71–89.

Hespel, S., Put, J., & Rom, M. (2012). Navigating the maze—The interrelation of international legal norms, with illustrations from international juvenile justice standards. *Human Rights and International Legal Discourse, 6*, 329–365.

Kilkelly, U. (2008). Youth justice and children's rights: Measuring compliance with international standards. *Youth Justice, 8*(3), 187–192.

Kilkelly, U. (2019a). The UN convention on the rights of the child: incremental and transformative approaches to legal implementation. *The International Journal of Human Rights, 23*(3), 323–337.

Kilkelly, U. (2019b). All children all rights in all circumstances. In N. Lynch (Ed.), *Children's rights in Aotearoa New Zealand* (pp. 82–84).

Kilkelly, U., & Bergin, P. (2021). *Advancing children's rights in detention: A model for international reform*. Bristol University Press.

Kilkelly, U., & Liefaard, T. (2019). International children's rights: Reflections on a complex, dynamic, and relatively young area of law. In U. Kilkelly & T. Liefaard (Eds.), *International human rights of children* (pp. 617–627). Springer.

Kilkelly, U., & Logan, E. (2021). *National independent human rights institutions for children: Protecting and promoting children's rights*. Palgrave Macmillan.

Kilkelly et al. (2021). *Incorporating the UN convention on the rights of the child into national law*. Intersentia.

Liefaard, T. (2020). Juvenile justice. In J. Todres & S. King (Eds.), *The Oxford handbook of children's rights*. Oxford University Press.

Lundy, L. (2007). "Voice" is not enough: Conceptualising Article 12 of the United Nations Convention on the Rights of the Child. *British Educational Research Journal, 33*(6), 927–942.

Lundy, L. (2019). A lexicon for research on international children's rights in troubled times. *International Journal of Children's Rights, 27*, 595–601.

Lynch, N., & Liefaard, T. (2020). What is left in the "too hard basket"? Developments and challenges for the rights of children in conflict with the law. *International Journal of Children's Rights, 28*(1), 89–110.

Lynch (2021). *Incorporation of the convention on the rights of the child in New Zealand*.

Mallett, C. (2018). Disproportionate minority contact in juvenile justice: Today's, and yesterdays, problems. *Criminal Justice Studies, 31*(3), 230–248.

May, T., Gyateng, T., & Hough, M. (2009). *Differential treatment in the youth justice system*. Equality and Human Rights Commission.

Ministry of Justice and Youth Justice Board. (2019). *Standards for children in the youth justice system*.

Muncie (2006). Responsibilisation and rights: Explorations in comparative youth criminology. *Howard Journal of Criminal Justice, 45*(1), 42–70.

Nowak, M. (2019). *Global study on children deprived of liberty*. Geneva.

Peleg, N. (2019). International children's rights law: General principles. In U. Kilkelly & T. Liefaard (Eds.), *International human rights of children* (pp. 135–157). Springer.

Tobin, J. (2021). Children's rights in Australia: Still confronting the challenges. In P. Gerber & M. Castan (Eds.), *Critical perspectives on human rights law in Australia* (Vol. 1, 1st ed., pp. 279–309). Thomson Reuters.

United Nations Committee on the Rights of the Child. (2003). *General comment No 5 general measures of implementation of the convention on the rights of the child*, UN Doc CRC/C/GC 5.

United Nations Committee on the Rights of the Child. (2009). *General comment No 12, the right of the child to be heard*, UN Doc CRC/C/GC/12.

United Nations Committee on the Rights of the Child. (2013). *General comment No. 14 on the right of the child to have his or her best interests taken as a primary consideration (art. 3, para. 1)*, UN Doc CRC/C/GC/14.

United Nations Committee on the Rights of the Child. (2019). *General comment No 24 on children's rights in the child justice system*, UN Doc CRC/C/GC 24.

Youth Justice Board for England and Wales. (2021). *Strategic plan 2021–2024*. www.yjb.gov.uk

Part II

Child First: Developing Youth Justice Policy

6

Developing Child First Youth Justice Policy in England and Wales—A View from Inside the YJB and Westminster

John Drew

Foreword: 'An insider's Perspective'

There are two senses in which I think of myself as a youth justice insider. The first is that I spent my formative adult years as a volunteer and then a social worker working with children in trouble within the criminal justice and care systems. For fifteen years, from 1970, I worked with teenage and near teenage boys who were being labelled then as 'juvenile delinquents'. This provided me with repeated first-hand lessons about the importance

J. Drew (✉)
Birmingham, UK
e-mail: jjhdrew@me.com

of 'diversion' (if not 'early intervention'[1]) and the approaches of 'desistance', even if much of this was self-taught by trial and error, rather than helped by the insights of research. However, as a practitioner in north Lancashire I was inevitably exposed to the insights of the 'Lancaster school' (Thorpe et al., 1980) and remember very well the excitement of the moments when I realised that research-led theory matched my more modest instinctive insights and helped me understand a much bigger picture of how to work with children who were committing offences (or who, just as importantly, were thought to be 'at risk' of committing offences). This experience gave me an insider's understanding of what works well in social work with children in trouble.

While my career in children's services took me away from front-line practice after the mid-eighties, what we now call 'youth justice' has always remained my passion in the late nineties I was thrilled to be able to oversee the development of a Youth Offending Team in East London, hopefully applying some of this insider knowledge from hard lessons learnt in practice, to the local area where I was by then the Director of Social Services.

The second sense in which I would lay claim to the insider's perspective in the title of this chapter arose during my four years as Chief Executive of the Youth Justice Board from 2009 onwards. The role itself was a former youth justice practitioner's dream, particularly in the circumstances in which youth justice was still struggling to respond to the 'zombification of youth justice' and 'Year Zero mentality' (Pitts, 2001) that Jack Straw had brought with him as Home Secretary in 1997. There was obviously an awful lot of learning from the previous four decades that needed to be 'rediscovered' and leading the Youth Justice Board provided a perfect platform to relearn from the past.

Over these four years, I became an insider not only to the zig zag course of policy formation in central government (two very different

---

[1] Many of the exponents of 'early intervention' have always seemed to me to run the perverse risk of setting up the processes of stigmatising and labelling children in trouble that are highlighted in the work of McAra and McVie (2010). 'Early intervention' and 'diversion' are demonstrably different things and the recent definitions of 'early prevention', 'targeted prevention' and 'prevention' issued by the YJB (Partnership letter from Stephanie Roberts-Bibby, YJB, 23.11.21) should help.

governments, four Secretaries of State, rather more Youth Justice Ministers including one who lasted a week) but also to the complex worlds of nearly 160 Youth Offending Teams on the one hand, and a group of outstanding but often hostile and rivalsome University-based teachers and researchers. While I and many others worked hard to restore the lessons of the past, and to reinstall understanding about diversion and desistance in the cause of building a more 'child-focused' youth justice, what we undoubtedly lacked was the intellectual rigour that others who followed us produced in delineating the terms of the child first movement. The often and regularly maligned Youth Justice Board has played a huge role in embracing and building 'Child First', its principal achievement of the last five years.

What Do We Mean by 'Child First' Youth Justice? A Search for Origins

I first heard a reference to what would become 'child first' youth justice in a speech given by Kevin Haines on the 1st of April 2009. In his speech Haines called for a '*Children first, right based*' youth justice, which he rightly contrasted to the YJB's approach at that time, describing this as '*offence-focused and risk based*'. The truth is that I, in common with a great many other youth justice practitioners and policymakers, had been groping for decades towards the development of ideas and initiatives that we would now more easily identify as parts of the 'child first' agenda. In my case, this exploration goes back to 1974 but it is easy to go back much earlier than the seventies to trace the genealogy (Foucault, Garland, 2014) of 'child first'.

In common with the other authors in this book, I am taking my definition of 'child first' in the first instance from the four guiding elements identified by the YJB (2021a, b). These elements are described as being to:

- "Prioritise the best interests of children and recognising their particular needs, capacities, rights and potential. All work is child-focused,

developmentally informed, acknowledges structural barriers and meets responsibilities towards children".
- "Promote children's individual strengths and capacities to develop their pro-social identity for sustainable desistance, leading to safer communities and fewer victims. All work is constructive and future-focused, built on supportive relationships that empower children to fulfill their potential and make positive contributions to society".
- "Encourage children's active participation, engagement and wider social inclusion. All work is a meaningful collaboration with children and their carers".
- "Promote a childhood removed from the justice system, using pre-emptive diversion and minimal intervention. All work minimizes criminogenic stigma from contact with the system".

These elements could be distilled as *'strength based and developmentally informed – participatory – promoting diversion and minimal intervention'*.

There is no space here for a detailed genealogy but 'child first's pre-history can be traced backwards both in terms of structural reform (e.g. the creation of the first Juvenile Court in Birmingham in 1908), and legislative reform (e.g. the Children and Young Persons Act of 1933, with its avowed intent to bring together measures relating to children in one place). Other such examples would include successive raising of the age of criminal responsibility of children,[2] culminating in the unrealised ambition of the 1969 Children and Young Persons Act to raise the age to 14 and then beyond.

The genealogy of 'Child First' can also be traced back in time in terms of the evolution of justice practice in work with children in trouble. While a distinctive element of 'child first' project is that it is about how the actual business of youth justice practice is done in a much more specific way than other government policies do and have done over time, it is not true that there have not been forerunners of such practice, for example, components of the 'Intermediate Treatment' project that

---

[2] The 1907 Children Act provided for a separate juvenile court for children aged seven years and above. Subsequent amendments increased it to eight (1933 Children and Young Persons Act) and then its current age of 10(1963 Children and Young Persons Act).

evolved in the late seventies and eighties, especially the focus on diversion (Case, 2008; Sevdiren, 2011).

Lastly, the genealogy of 'Child First' can be found in the practice of individuals working with children down the years. In recognising that there is something new and wholly admirable about the 'child first project', it is important not to ignore that countless practitioners have been engaged in 'child first practice' without having the language or labels to apply to their work.

Such progress has not always been linear or consistently progressive. Judged on some measurements progress has often been backward, the failed implementation of the 1969 Children and Young Persons Act providing a good example of this.

Another such example was the explicit rejection by both the Conservatives and New Labour of the lessons of the eighties and early nineties. Drawing the wrong conclusions from the at times chaotic organisation of juvenile justice in that period, the two main parties came together to create the *punitive turn* for youth justice that is well described elsewhere (Case, 2018; Muncie, 2008). This led to the growth in the use of child imprisonment from 1991, rising from an estimated 1,500 in 1991 (Hagell, 2005)[3] to over 3,000 in first half of 2008 (YCS, 2022).

New Labour's focus from 1997 on 'responsibilisation' (assuming children in trouble were fully conscious and therefore fully responsible for their action) and *'popular punitivism'* (one eye kept firmly on how any policy might be seen by the electorate) was very clear, and in its extreme expositions the core New Labour policies came to be seen as very hostile to the whole idea of childhood (a period of innocence, vulnerability, experimentation, and development). This orientation was signalled nowhere more clearly that in the government's subsequent abolition of the long-standing principle of *doli incapax*, the presumption that children aged 10–13 were, literally, *'incapable of evil'* or more practically *'incapable of forming the intent to commit a crime'*, unless this could be

---

[3] Hagell does not explain how she reached this figure but appears to have based it on an extrapolation from the total number of children sentenced to custody in prison service accommodation at any one time (3,344) together with separate counts of numbers of children remanded to custody and those children in secure children's homes at any one time in 1992. This calculation needs to be treated with caution.

proven in court. This sets the text for much of the core script about children and offending for the next several years and is very different in tone to 'Child First'.

It is important here to acknowledge that not everything was different to the tone of 'child first'. Very considerable investment was made by New Labour in initiatives described variously at the time as 'prevention' or 'early intervention'. When used well these supported the notion that children who offended need to be seen as children rather than as 'young offenders'. Furthermore, the institutional innovation of creating a Non-Departmental Public Body (aka 'quango'), the Youth Justice Board for England and Wales, to oversee the development and operation of the youth justice system both nationally and locally, created the 'space' in which this body, the YJB, could, if it chose so to do, establish policies according to values and objectives that were not necessarily directly connected to those of Ministers (Souhami, 2015b). The development of this process was not without mishaps and reversals. But I shall argue in later sections of this chapter that this 'space', the separation from government, is central, first, to the development of more 'child-focused' youth justice policy and then eventually to the emergence of 'Child First'.

A further twist in the genealogy of 'child first' began to appear with the changes most associated with New Labour's *Every Child Matters* (ECM) policy development from 2003. This was an attempt to link together and direct all aspects of children's policy under the slogans of initially four and then five '*outcomes*' for children. This approach, called '*Progressive Universalism*' (Purcell, 2020), was to begin to link up youth justice policy and practice with broader children's issues under the outcome statement of '*staying safe*' and the later sub-clause '*Every child on the pathway to success*', both of which strands were subject to central oversight. In concrete terms '*Every Child Matters*' announced the plan for a new series of non-custodial sentences for children who offended, and made a commitment, never fully implemented, to establish a *Common Assessment Framework* for all children in need including those in the youth justice system.

The origins of these ideas were with a group of middle ranking Ministers who became increasingly uncertain about the dominant and hostile narrative about some children's behaviour. For some this desire for a new narrative only went as far as the assertion that *most* children were not a problem, thereby echoing ideas about the deserving and the undeserving poor. But others went further, and in their focus on rethinking some of the approaches adopted towards children in trouble up to that point we can possibly see a revival of policy thinking that could eventually evolve into 'Child First'.

The creation of the new children's ministry, the Department for Children, Schools and Families (DCSF) in 2007, together with other machinery of government changes associated with Gordon Brown's elevation to Prime Minister, including his selection of his trusted lieutenant Ed Balls as its first Secretary of State, his dismemberment of the Home Office and his placing of the Youth Justice Board under the joint sponsorship of the DCSF and the new Ministry of Justice (MoJ), represented important steps towards a significant realignment at a national level of youth justice towards children's services and away from being purely an issue for criminal justice.

Developing a 'Child-Focused' Youth Justice Policy and Practice from 2009 to 2013

I was appointed as the third Chief Executive of the YJB and took up post in January 2009. The YJB I joined needed clear direction, having been rocked by a series of high-profile scandals linked to the death of children in custody (Willow, 2015), as well as criticism that, ten years on and after significant investment, its actual achievement was quite limited (Solomon & Garside, 2008). Technically, the Crime and Disorder Act had given the YJB only a function to '*advise*' government on the operation of the Youth Justice System, policymaking being retained firmly by the (in 2009) two Secretaries of State and their joint team of Civil Servants (the Youth Justice Policy team based in the DCSF but accountable to both teams of Ministers and senior civil servants). However, the reality was inevitably more complex (Souhami, 2015b). Ministers, then and now, were usually only concerned with a relatively small number of headline issues and setting 'red lines' (issues beyond which a Non-Departmental Public Body [NDPB] like the YJB should not pass[4]). In turn their principal advisors in the Civil Service were either rarely focused on youth justice (senior civil servants usually had what they perceived as more pressing priorities) or were constantly being reshuffled in a way that limited their ability to develop expertise in this policy area.[5] Furthermore, the dominant requirements of civil servants in this period of government were to 'satisfy' ministers, which meant that their focus was reactive and driven at times by whim or 'quackery' (Gendreau et al., 2009). As examples of this, I recall at one stage a significant amount of time being spent on the issue of whether children in custody should be allowed access to PlayStations as a reward for good behaviour that followed a prison visit by a Secretary of State, a type of discussion that was replayed when a later Secretary of State found the '*Monopoly*' board game in a Secure Training Centre, much to his disapproval.

One final factor in 2009 was the effective stalemate that existed caused by rivalries between the DCSF and the MoJ, headed although not limited by what appeared to be the mutual mistrust of the two Secretaries of State, Balls and Straw. I had only been in post a matter of months before receiving a request to produce a policy proposal for one Minister but '*whatever you do, don't tell* [the other Cabinet member or his officials]'.

Some of this reality was functional, some dysfunctional, but my point here is not to pour scorn on these arrangements but to explain how they could either stand in the way of the development of any profound rethinking of youth justice policy or could create policy space that was relatively easy for a less cautious NDPB to begin to fill. In my selection interview, I had said I thought it was vital that youth justice align itself closely with children's services and local government, a theme that I repeated in media interviews at the time. These sentiments chimed with key members of the YJB Board as well as the YJB's Chair, the excellent Frances Done.

---

[4] The exception to this general rule occurred on the relatively small number of occasions when major documents (e.g. Green or White papers) were issued.

[5] In my four years at the YJB, I was 'sponsored' by four different heads of youth justice policy, none of whom had had a relevant background before taking on this role.

Another issue in these early days was to move the dominant language of the Youth Justice System from 'young offenders' to 'children'. In a speech to senior staff in the YJB on the 13th of May 2009, I characterised the YJB as being '*at its heart a children's organisation working in the field of criminal justice*'.

The Evolution of New Labour Youth Justice Policy and the Youth Crime Action Plan, 2008–2010

New Labour Youth Justice policy in 2009 was most clearly articulated in the £ 100 m Youth Crime Action Plan (YCAP) that had been published in 2008 (HM Government, 2008) and was being updated for publication in July 2009 (HM Government, 2009). The YCAP, a product of a collaboration between the Home Office, the Ministry of Justice, and the Department for Schools and Families, was a detailed but not entirely consistent programme, this complexity perhaps being a consequence of being the product of three different Ministries as much as a reflection of some of the opposing ideas current in New Labour thinking to which I have already referred.

An attempt was made to give what might otherwise have been a raft of separate policy elements a common feel by characterising the policy as being:

> a triple-track approach across everything to we do to tackle youth crime:
> [1] Better prevention to tackle problems before they become serious or entrenched.
> [2] More support to address the underlying causes of poor behaviour including support for parents. This support will be non-negotiable where necessary.
> [3] Tough enforcement where behaviour is unacceptable or illegal. (HM Government, 2009)

The very reference to there being a triple-track approach served to draw attention to the '*uneasy hybridity of New Labour's youth justice*' (Goldson,

2010). When this policy is compared to the YJB's current statements on 'Child First' three points are particularly evident.

First, there is still a strong, even aggressively hostile, feel to the direction of policy, with repeat references to '*tougher action*' and a conscious distancing of children who offend from all other children, writing about the '*small minority* [of children] *commit crime and behave anti-socially with devastating impact for victim, families, and communities and the future of young offenders themselves*'. This is most obvious in the Ministerial Foreword to the revised document, which is peppered with aggressive and hostile language in respect of children in trouble, with talk about police '*patrolling the streets*', of the need to provide '*challenge to turn their lives around*', and of the Youth Justice System '*carrying out punishments that are tougher*' (HM Government, 2009).

Second, the policy was aimed more at the general public to demonstrate the '*major progress we have made in tackling youth offending*' than at shaping the priorities and approach of those who work with children in trouble—'*At the centre of our plan is a commitment to ensure that the public knows about our work*'.[6] This different focus is not of itself invalid; governments should be concerned with explaining their programmes to the general public. But the messaging (spin) about toughness served to obscure many of the more positive elements of the detail about early intervention and '*breaking the cycle of offending*' that took up the bulk of the body of the report.

Thirdly, YCAP did not stray, for the main part, into the realm of how youth justice practice should be carried out, reflecting no doubt the limitations of experience of the civil servants who had drafted it. What this did was to continue to leave open the policy space within which the YJB could develop more practice-oriented initiatives.

---

[6] It was made clear to the YJB in a meeting on the 3rd of March 2009 that our own publications must show a 'greater alignment' with the YCAP and should be aimed at building public confidence that the Government was 'tackling youth crime' rather than reporting on the operation of the youth justice system, the statutory function of the YJB.

The incarceration of children and the development of a distinctive approach from the YJB

As already described, in addition to the general policy set out in YCAP, the government also operated a small number of 'red lines' in 2009. The main one of these related to the issue of the numbers of children in custody. Jack Straw, the Justice Secretary, was very reluctant for anyone to speak about reducing the numbers of people in prison as a policy objective. The 2009 revision of YCAP avoided listing reducing the numbers of children in custody as one of the four aims of government policy, despite its retention more privately as one of the objectives of the YJB. This exclusion was presumedly a matter of deliberate choice.

To my chair, Frances Done, and I this might have constituted a major problem since we were both firmly committed to the priority of making major inroads into the numbers of children in custody, which were still very near the recent high mark of 3,200. Done made it clear to Straw that if the target to reduce numbers of children in custody remained official, even if understated, government policy (as it had been for ten years), she and I would want to highlight this target from every platform we occupied. Balls appeared to support this stance and Straw gave ground on the point. In my first speech as Chief Executive on the 1st of April 2009, I said '*We have danced around the issue of the number of children in custody for too long. We know there are too many and we need to make this a priority in the 2009*'. The argument that custody should only ever be used as a last resort, a principle from which we were still a long way, was an important part of a 'child-focused' agenda, owing much as it does to the United Nations Convention of the Rights of Children. So, our re-assertion of this aspect of youth justice policy became important in the development of a more 'child-focused' youth justice policy.

Policy was one thing, but practice was a very different matter. On my first day at the YJB, over 2,700 children had been in custody while 2008 had seen the highest month on month average since the passage of the Crime and Disorder Act. However, New Labour policy had begun to lay some of the groundwork for a reduction with its simultaneous investment in YOTs under the prevention and diversion labels of the YCAP, and by its repeal of the disastrous policing initiatives that led to the targeting of children such as the Home Office's policing initiative '*Offences Brough To Justice*'. Therefore, in the years from 2007 onwards there had been a steady reduction in the number of children entering the Youth Justice System for the first time.

Done and I took every opportunity to use our public platforms as well as the YJB's more private performance meetings with YOTs and the other elements of Youth Justice System to talk up the need to reduce numbers of children in custody. In this effort, we were aided greatly by the Magistrates Association under a series of inspiring chairs, as well as by the charity section and in particular the Prison Reform Trust whose 5 year programme '*Out of Trouble*', funded by the Diana, Princess of Wales Memorial Fund, played a major role between 2007 and 2012 in describing the practical steps needed to reduce incarceration as well as the policy and moral cases for reducing the use of imprisonment (Prison Reform Trust, 2021).

The result of the focus that such a broad alliance could bring to bear was that the numbers of children in custody began to fall rapidly, creating a trend that continues to this day. By the time, I left the YJB the average monthly number had halved from 2,726 to 1,263[7] in just over four years. Seven years on, in 2020, numbers had halved again to an average of just under 600, and while the precise impact on the operation of the courts of COVID-19 crisis can be debated, the long-term trajectory has consistently remained downward.

Allocating anything like precise responsibilities for this extraordinary reversal of incarceration is an impossibility. Some commentators have linked the reduction solely to the change in police targets that followed the abandonment of the '*Offences brought to justice*' initiative in 2006 and 2007, but few go on to analyse why such targets were abandoned; in other words, they record the fact of the change but not the reasons for it. Furthermore, the change to police targets can only account for the start of the process. I place greater importance on a range of factors including:

---

[7] This number itself was significant since it was below the previous low point of about 1300 children in custody reported in 1993 (Hagell, 2005).

- the rediscovery of the importance of diversion, given additional impetus by new writing on desistance;
- the growing acknowledgement in all parts of the system that imprisonment of children was not a solution to the issue of offending;
- increasing concerns about the conditions under which children were held in custody; and
- the growing confidence that built and built as numbers of children in custody reduced without any obvious rise in the amount of crime ascribed to children.

To see this huge change as simply a result of tinkering of policing targets in the Home Office is to miss the achievement of the 30,000 people who worked and volunteered in different parts of the Youth Justice System and worked hard to reduce incarceration in the name of doing better by children in trouble. Certainly, the progress was helped by the long-term reduction in most forms of offending by children and for some of this time by the reduction in the absolute numbers 10–17-year-olds in the population of England and Wales. But these trends were greatly aided by the adoption of an avowed anti-incarceration policy position by the YJB (and then picked up by the Coalition government as we shall see). When the Prison Reform Trust asked YOT Managers what the greatest influence on their practice was, they said it was the clear leadership of the YJB.

This achievement is important for the story of the emergence of 'Child First' for two reasons. The first is that bringing the English and Welsh position nearer to that promoted by the United Nations Convention on the Rights of the Child, that children should only be imprisoned as a measure of last resort (UNICEF, 1989), is an obvious 'child-focused' achievement. The second is that the achievement served to embolden not only the YJB but also the whole youth justice sector to shape further the direction of youth justice policy without simply waiting for the government of the day to signal the need for such a change. As such this undoubtedly prepared some of the ground for the eventual emergence of the 'Child First' project.

Developing a More 'Child-Focused' Youth Justice

One of the key roles of the Chief Executive of the YJB is to describe the principles that underpin youth justice policy. As I have already described the distinctive position of the YJB as an NDPB provided the intellectual space in which this was permitted. In my first months as Chief Executive, my focus was principally internal, selling to my staff the expectations I had of them in operating in a more open and collaborative way with the rest of the Youth Justice System. The government then announced a review of the YJB, to be led by Dame Sue Street, a former senior civil servant (Street, 2010). This review, which ultimately recognised the achievement of both the Youth Justice System and the YJB within this, was an inevitable distraction and required of us a further period of Whitehall-focused introspection, until its publication on the 25th of March 2010. Ten days later, Brown triggered the 2010 general election. The consequence was that no public speeches could be made on any aspect of government policy until the new government was formed. This meant that I had no opportunity to begin to describe the key elements of what I felt was a 'child-focused' agenda until June 2010. In my speeches for the next four months, I returned repeatedly to what I felt were the eight pillars of 'child focused' youth justice. These were:

> Favour informal approaches to avoid labeling and stigmatising;
> Build routes out of the Youth Justice system at every moment, both early but also later;
> Use custody sparingly;
> Recognise that personal relationships are, for most of us and at most times; the route to personal change;
> Recognise the individuality of the children with whom we work;
> Be more prepared to accept setbacks and avoid punishing out of frustration;
> Take care with our use of language; and
> Promote redemption.[8]

---

[8] Speeches on 28.6.10, 20.7.10 (the Howard League's *'Future of Youth Justice conference'*), 23.9.10 and 11.10.10.

These pillars owed something to my first-hand experience but also much to the work being published at that time by McAra and McVie (2010)[9] and McNeill and Weaver (2010). The read-across to the 'Child First' project seems clear now but it is important to acknowledge that I made far less of these pillars at the time than does the YJB now of 'Child First', and in doing so missed a great opportunity to make more of this 'child-focused' agenda.

To summarise, by the end of the New Labour period in government in May 2010, government policy had moved a limited distance away from its initial *'punitive populism'* by including elements of what could be called a 'child-focused' approach. This was reflected in the hybridity of official policy, as reflected in the *'triple track'* approach of YCAP, and in a willingness to offer cautious support for the move away from incarceration. But there was a limit to this. Policy was still dominated by the issue of facing outwards to the public and convincing them of the punitive components of youth justice, and there was little acknowledgement of the need to reset the fundamental focus of youth justice practice in the way that 'child first' has attempted to do.

The First Two Years of Youth Justice Policy Under the Coalition

The 2010 general election brought great upheaval, not just because of the swing to the right in British politics, but also because the new Coalition government inevitably meant that all policy, including youth justice policy, had to be negotiated through two political parties with very different cultures and political traditions. One immediate consequence of the creation of a Coalition was that the Conservative Party had to find a proportion of Ministerial places for Liberal Democrat leaders, meaning that some members of the opposition, who had been carefully developing policy positions while in opposition either had to move away or

---

[9] I readily acknowledge a huge debt of gratitude and appreciation to Lesley McAra and Susan McVie's entire *'Edinburgh Youth Transitions'* work, and to Rod Morgan, Chair of the YJB 2004–2007, who first drew their opus to my attention on my arrival at the YJB.

had no role at all in government. For the Conservatives David Burrows MP, a former youth court solicitor who had been producing a comprehensive and radical set of youth justice policy proposals since 2007, lost his youth justice portfolio and in fact never found a place in government before retiring from the Commons at the 2017 election. This had a considerable impact on youth justice policy, not least because neither Coalition partner had given any real thought to youth justice issues in their manifestos.

The effect of these two elements in youth justice policy terms was to make the new government more dependent on their professional advisors (including the YJB) and therefore more likely to continue with what existed prior to their election than might otherwise have been the case. The Coalition's first set of youth justice policies, articulated in the 2010 Green Paper *Breaking The Cycle*' (HM Government, 2010) did not in most ways significantly depart from the core arrangements established by New Labour, describing these as '*working well*' (YOTs). In particular, the three core outcomes for the Youth Justice System, reducing first time entrants, reducing reoffending and reducing the numbers of children in custody were restated at the end of the consultation period for the Green Paper (HM Government, 2011), something for which the YJB pressed hard behind the scenes during the drafting of the Green Paper, and which as I have already described New Labour had been reluctant to do in its last statement of Youth Justice policy, YCAP.

The Coalition government's support for reducing the imprisonment of children, undoubtedly encouraged by the savings that it generated, also found favour in the personal views of the new youth justice ministerial team of Ken Clarke, as Secretary of State, and Crispin Blunt as youth justice Minister. Clarke most obviously was long recognised as on the liberal wing of the Conservative Party, although also a fiscal hawk. A sceptic on the value of high levels of imprisonment he appeared doubly so in respect of the incarceration of children. Blunt, too, was happy to speak out on this issue. So, the Green Paper included a clear statement about the desirability of reducing child incarceration. The phrase that custody '*should be used sparingly as a last resort*' was a more confident and public statement than New Labour had managed and was no doubt both a reflection of the progress that the Youth Justice System had already made (total numbers of children in custody already down by one-third in the years 2009–2010) as well as the more liberal inclinations of Clarke. His Ministry had taken less than a month to cancel '*Operation Fosse*', a £100 million programme to build a new YOI for children in Leicestershire.

Beyond their adoption of much of New Labour's policy positions, the Coalition proposed new approaches to youth justice policy in four areas, these being:

- Support for greater localism through the devolution of policy and practice to local areas;
- Review of the youth justice assessment system, *Asset;*
- Cutting expenditure on youth justice, nationally and locally; and
- Abolition of the YJB.

There had also been a cautious statement about exploring the possibilities of applying a '*Payments by results*' (PBR) approach to the funding of youth justice. In private, I discouraged Ministers from taking this too far, pointing to the successes of the system as an argument against too much change. This essentially pragmatic case won the day although some Civil Servants continued to explore options as to how the government might adopt a PBR approach to youth justice.

Localism and Devolution

The main change ushered in by the Coalition was a strong focus on localism. In the name of '*Big Society*', the government supported greater devolution of policy to Youth Offending Teams, '*small government*' being the other side of the coin of '*Big Society*'. With this orientation came an instinctive favouring of less central direction of youth justice work championed by Blunt who appeared heavily influenced by lobbying from some YOTs including that for Surrey, his home area.

A cautious first step towards a longer-term plan to devolve budgets for custody to local areas was contained in the transfer of remand budgets and costs to local partnerships to incentivise the development of more community-based alternatives. In addition, the government announced a two-year Custody Pathfinder scheme that transferred notional budgets for all custody costs in four pilot areas, with the incentive that they could spend the money as they saw fit and retain any savings achieved by making less use of custody. Both these ideas had been first developed by the YJB and came with our enthusiastic support. The Coalition also supported a dramatic reduction in the number of YJB National Standards in the name of devolution. The Coalition government pushed the YJB hard on this and eventually we were to halve the number of National Standards.

Review of *Asset*

The broad localism agenda probably has no direct bearing on the development of a more 'child-focused' approach but the second element of the Coalition government's agenda, their support for a review of *Asset*, most certainly did. *Asset*, the principal assessment framework for youth justice, was one of the first of the YJB's contributions to the New Youth Justice when it was rolled out between January and April 2000 (Baker et al., 2003; Cadman, 2008). Steve Aos of the Washington State Institute for Public Policy was hugely influential in convincing government that a common assessment system was a central element of developing effective youth justice practice.

However, a decade later, there was growing support within the Youth Justice System for a complete overhaul of *Asset*. To that end, the YJB had announced in March 2010 its plan to review *Asset*. The case for a review of *Asset* came from two main sources. The academic critique came principally because of its reliance on risk factor theory and the consequences of this (Case & Haines, 2009). The practitioner criticisms were more about its bulky, unwieldy nature, although both sets of views found common ground in their rejection of what was largely a deficit rather than strength-based model of assessment.[10]

---

[10] A strengths-based approach will focus on child's strengths (including personal strengths and social and community networks) and not on their deficits. Strengths-based assessment leads to

The Coalition government added powerful support for this analysis and raised the profile of the planned review. Just as it had in child protection policy (Munro, 2010, 2011a, 2011b, 2012), the Coalition government favoured a much less prescriptive approach to assessment than had been the case under the *Asset* system. This would, as they saw it, free up front-line practitioners to exercise their professional judgement.

Coming fresh to this issue, I had been won over to these arguments. As a practitioner I had been alert to the dangers of the false positives of risk factor analysis, while the move towards seeking a strengths-based approach to working with children in trouble was an approach which I supported strongly, and which fitted well with my personal adoption of '*desistance theory*'.

Cutting Spending

The other big change ushered in at the same time as the election of the Coalition was the full impact of austerity on government spending in response to the global financial crisis of 2007–2008. The government's overall financial target of reducing public expenditure by more than £ 17 billion per annum translated to a possible target to reduce the YJB's spending by 30 per cent.[11] These targets led to a dramatic reduction in the headcount of the YJB (staffing levels were near to halved across three years) as well as significant reductions in central government funding for YOTs, which accounted for approximately one third of their spend. However, the numbers of children in custody continued to fall significantly in this time. A small amount of this was used to make improvements in custody, but the bulk of this saving was spent to cushion the level of cuts to YOTs. The consequence of the spending

---

practice that is more likely to be holistic and multidisciplinary and works with the child to build their desistance to offending behaviour.

[11] The figure eventually achieved across a four-year period was approximately £ 430 million, with the largest single element coming from decommissioning custodial places, principally in YOIs.

cuts was to direct our focus inward as we struggled to make cash savings, and to limit the amount of time for fresh thinking on the further development of a 'child-focused' youth justice.

Abolition of the YJB?

In addition to greater local freedom and flexibility for YOTs, the Green Paper proposed to abolish the YJB and transfer its functions into the Ministry of Justice as part of its wide '*bonfire of the quangos*' policy, designed to '*restore democracy and accountability to public life*' (Souhami, 2015b). The proposal to abolish the YJB was a close call but a well-publicised row between the Justice Secretary, Kenneth Clarke and the Home Secretary, Theresa May, in the run up to the Conservative Party's autumn conference in 2010 left Clarke needing to seek favour in Conservative Party circles and appeared to tip the balance. In October 2010, the Coalition government announced that the YJB would be added to the provisions of the Public Bodies bill and was scheduled for abolition in 2012.

This is not the place to describe the ebb and flow of the debates of the next thirteen months on the future of the YJB. What is relevant to this account is to note the huge amount of energy in Whitehall that came to be focused on this issue, at cost to the development of other pressing youth justice policy. The Coalition government eventually withdrew its proposal, largely because of skilled tactics by crossbench Peers in the House of Lords that flushed out a deep discomfort in Liberal Democrat circles in both Houses and made it unlikely that the government's will would prevail in any vote in the House of Lords. Lord McNally, who would later become the Chair of the YJB, announced in November 2011 that the YJB would not be abolished and did not appear to be very disappointed to be making this announcement.

The Coalition government's attempt to abolish the YJB amounted to a great waste of time. It also created further dysfunction amongst officials by leaving a group of civil servants with what appeared to be a now personal grievance against the YJB and its staff. This would surface at regular intervals up to, and possibly beyond, 2017. I was surprised at the time by the fact that some of civil servants with whom I worked daily appeared to take the government's defeat more personally than did their Ministers.

Despite the waste of time and energy involved in this distraction, other elements of youth justice policy continued to develop in a way to support a more 'child-focused' approach. I have already written about the continued fall in the number of children in custody. This trend was briefly tested by the reaction to the August 2011 riots in London and some other English cities. In fact, only 20% of those arrested were children but some sectors of the media were keen to present the riots as the work of lawless teenagers, and as a damning indictment of the Youth Justice System. An article in the Daily Mail by the journalist Max Hastings had the heading '*Years of liberal dogma have spawned a generation of amoral, uneducated, unparented, welfare dependent, brutalised youngsters*' (Hastings, 2011). The then Mayor of London, Boris Johnson, wrote to Clarke, calling for harsher punishments including the modification of the role of Pupil Referral Units to become modern day '*borstal-style*' units to which children could be sent by the courts as punishment.

At the YJB, we were keen to counter this narrative and were helped in this by a clear-thinking senior civil servant in the Ministry of Justice who suggested a '*big data*' exercise, linking data on arrests with data held by the Department for Education. These highlighted the levels of deprivation and disadvantage faced by children who were arrested. Two-thirds of those arrested were shown to have some form of special education need. This appeared to change some of the messaging. Initially, quite punitive sentencing of children caught up in the riots changed and within three months a more child-focused approach to sentencing had returned and numbers of children in custody continued their downward turn.

Meanwhile, we also took a strategic view to showcase the involvement of children and young adults in the development of 'child-focused' policy. In partnership with User Voice, led by the inspiring Mark Johnson, more than 1,300 children and young adults were involved in consultation leading up to the 2011 Youth Justice Convention in Brighton, creating a model for consultation that we then encouraged other parts of the youth justice system to follow many already being ahead of the YJB in this. The introduction of this level of '*co-production*' at a national level fits very precisely with the third element of the 'child first' project, as Creaney and Burns identify in their chapter, and has become a standing fixture of the YJB's approach to youth justice policy formulation.

The Second Phase of Youth Justice Policy Under the Coalition

In September 2012, Clarke and Blunt were replaced by Chris Grayling and Jeremy Wright as Secretary of State and Youth Justice minister, respectively, in a move that was widely reported as being a rejection of Clarke's '*avuncular liberalism*' and attracted an approving headline in the Daily Mail '*Human rights "Gone wrong"*' (Daily Mail, 20 September 2012). The Sun led with a reference to Grayling's '*Tough Justice Vow*'. While Blunt, when the junior Minister, had made distinctive personal contributions to youth justice policy especially around localism and professional discretion, the Grayling/Wright partnership appeared to be dominated by Grayling, a very ambitious politician who openly acknowledged to the author and others that he had his eyes on bigger roles both inside and outside of government. Wright's influence over youth justice policy was less obvious. Grayling's youth justice policy was clearly articulated in the Ministerial foreword to a new Green Paper on youth justice that he ordered at breakneck speed, '*Transforming Youth Custody*' (HM Government, 2013). As with his Coalition predecessors he (with this co-signatory Michael Gove, then the Education Secretary) acknowledged the successes of the Youth Justice System, but then focused on '*a hardcore of serious and prolific offenders, many of whom have racked up long criminal histories in their still young lives*'. These children became the central focus of his policies.

His solution was to place education at the heart of custody, and he proposed '*providing education in a period of detention, rather than detention with education as an afterthought*'. The favoured vehicle for this reform were a small number of large '*Secure College*' accommodating up 360 children at any one time (by 2017 there were only an average of 890 children in custody). As McAra and McVie have shown this focus on the impact of education on offending is not itself wrong, but the reliance on sentences of imprisonment to provide such education clearly contradicted the evidence about how to build desistance in children. Grayling prioritised issues of cost, and both he and Wright spoke of the current costs of secure accommodation as being '*far too high*' without ever really explaining how they thought these might be reduced. The old chestnut that all youth custody, including YOIs, cost more than a year's fees at Eton was roasted afresh.

One area where we could and should have made more progress was in the review of *Asset* and the creation of *AssetPlus*. The review had started well. I encouraged my staff to hold two seminars with academics, most of whom had been in the forefront of the criticism of *Asset*. I took this to be of central importance in the ambition to produce something significantly different to *Asset* and personally attended these initially rather frosty seminars. As we had with the original design of *Asset*, we also designed a process that included substantial involvement with a typical cross section of YOTs.

But I made two mistakes, the consequences of which are still apparent today. First, I underestimated the potential that wide engagement can lead to significant levels of add-on, thereby decreasing the chances of producing the slimmed down assessment system to which we all aspired. Second, I became so focused on the task of persuading the Treasury to release £ 13 million from the public purse for the new system that I did not pay enough attention to warning signs from some YOT leaders that the *AssetPlus* project was beginning to move off its intended path. In September 2012 Lee Westlake, the experienced YOT manager in Milton Keynes, told me of his reservations that we had '*overdesigned*' *AssetPlus* and were in danger of creating a new assessment tool that was too complex and had lost sight of the overall purpose of the redesign. I noted these views, took them seriously at the time, but miscalculated in not calling the pause that he sensibly suggested. So, while *AssetPlus* achieved some of the potential to produce a more strengths-based assessment system, it was not the game changer for which we originally hoped. This problem has been compounded subsequently by the YJB's apparent lack of awareness that they should always be designing the next version of the national assessment system, rather than resting on the work of earlier generations.

What Stage in the Development of a 'Child-Focused' Youth Justice Policy had Been Reached by April 2013?

I left the YJB at Easter in 2013 with a sense of some missions accomplished but, particularly on reflection ten years later, many still to be tackled in moving youth justice to becoming convincingly 'child focused', let alone to the positions now adopted by 'child first'.

On the positive side of my leaving assessment, we had achieved the big change of reversing the trend to incarcerating more and more children. Not only were numbers in 2013 below those artificially inflated by the New Youth Justice's net widening, but also, they had now gone below the all-time recorded low. There was no reason to suppose this number would not continue to fall and so, to the great credit of all involved, it has proved to be the case. The score? 1/1.

We had introduced an entirely fresh national focus on seeking the perspectives of children and young adults on youth justice policy and practice. There was probably not much more a national body could have done to create momentum and showcase the tremendous potential of active participation and co-production so, cumulatively, the score could be 2/2.

We had also launched the review of *Asset* with the ambition that its replacement, *AssetPlus,* should adopt a strength-based model, thereby creating a more 'child-focused' assessment base. But even a generous assessment would suggest this had only been partly successful, so 2.5/3.

The move to developing a new 'child-focused' way of thinking about youth justice had largely stalled at the end of 2010, overtaken by the threat to our very survival presented by the Public Bodies bill, so still 2.5/4.

And official government thinking did not move at all, indeed arguably became more punitive focused, 2.5/5.

There is not the space here to consider, alongside these 'big ticket' items, a whole series of smaller issues, some of which were undoubtedly positive (e.g. affording care status to children on remand in the Legal Aid, Sentencing and Punishment of Offenders Act of 2012), but none of these were important enough to move this crude scorecard decisively in a 'child focused' direction. So, while a start had been made there was still much to be done.

Conclusion: What Might Be Learnt from This Period for Youth Justice Policy and Practice Today?

This is not the place, and I am not the author best suited to review the shifts of youth justice policy from 2013 to 2022. It is sufficient to note that this has been a difficult time for the YJB, shorn of a large part of its power and influence by the Liz Truss reforms of 2017 that stripped the YJB of much of its budget and its responsibilities for commissioning services for children in custody. However, the Taylor Review of Youth Justice (Taylor, 2016a, 2016b) represented a ringing endorsement of the need to develop a new 'child focus'. Reading his reports again the departure that Taylor signified in his constant use of the words '*child*' and '*children*' is particularly noticeable, even if many of his actual recommendations have been discretely shelved, possibly because of Taylor's close ally Michael Gove's departure from the Ministry of Justice. Taylor's appointment to the Chair of the YJB in March 2017 combined with some strong appointments subsequently made the YJB Board, finally prepared the ground for the development of 'child first' youth justice. The question for the future is, therefore, where do we go next? I would like to contribute four main thoughts to this debate.

The first point to make is to constantly remind ourselves of the lessons of the early nineties, when the whole apparatus of progressive youth justice (investing in diversion, radical reduction in the use of custody) was swept away by a political narrative that owed less to any facts about children and crime and more to a perception that the public wanted punishment, '*popular punitivism*'. This took root in the lack of public knowledge about the way in which the Youth Justice System worked and the care and effectiveness of its work. The Youth Justice System of the eighties and early nineties had operated under the public's radar' with hindsight a very big mistake. I very much doubt that, if an assessment could be made, the public would feel that it is qualitatively better informed now than it was in 1992. Combatting this must be a first responsibility of all of us working in youth justice. The YJB needs to always keep this in the forefront of its mind.

Second, I am regularly reminded of the huge achievement of the leaders of the 'child first' project in achieving intellectual and cultural hegemony for 'child first' in large parts of the Youth Justice System. The YJB and its chair, Keith Fraser, should draw great satisfaction from this. But there remain parts of the Youth Justice System that have been exempt from this. A key element is the youth custody system. Outside of Secure Children's Homes there appears to be only limited understanding or application of what 'child first' should mean for custodial services, as the 2021 scandals in Secure Training Centres[12] amply illustrate. A 'child first' for custody is urgently needed and with it a determined effort to ensure that this is understood by all working in that sector and not just the top brass. Some will wonder whether such a change can ever be made when staff working in custody think, primarily, that they are working in a prison rather than in a childcare institution. The much anticipated first Secure School, still not opened despite a five-year gestation period, provides an opportunity to move things forward, but in all other ways the government is not making progress with its 2017 commitment to abolish all children's YOIs and STCs.

---

[12] The government terminated its contract with Rainsbrook STC (MTC Nuovo) following a series of inadequate inspection reports. Its contract with Oakhill (G4S) appears vulnerable at time of going to press following similarly '*unacceptable*' reports about safeguarding children there. The STC has been, since November 2021), the subject to a government approved improvement plan and the current youth justice Minister has issued a press release saying she is '*considering all options*' Children and Young People Now, 12.11.21.

Third, it is apparent that there is a gap between the thinking of the YJB about 'child first' and the views of the relevant inspectorates, in particular, HM Inspector of Probation (HMIP). At other times this might be less important but the last five years have seen HMIP move increasingly into its own policy space while the YJB's focus has been elsewhere. This creates confusion and tension, particularly in YOTs who must march to the drums of both the Chair of the YJB and the Chief Inspector of Probation. I share this perspective with Day (2022) who develops this point very convincingly. This gap needs to be closed. The youth justice system cannot serve any conflicting policy ambitions of two central government bodies.

Fourth, new attention needs to be paid to the question of the national assessment system. When I left the YJB in 2013 it did not occur to me that there would have been no significant change to *AssetPlus* over the next ten years. A motor manufacturer that did not produce a new model for ten years would be out of business. The YJB appears to have put such energy as it has into supporting local pilot projects on assessment (Bartasevicius et al., 2020). The profile of these is as yet low, and it is unclear what theory of change underpins this initiative. Bolder steps are needed as most YOTs, and most practitioners, continue to struggle under both the burden of *AssetPlus* but also with an assessment system that does not sit seamlessly alongside the approved model that is 'child first'. Elsewhere in this book Byrne makes a strong case for a single integrated recording and assessment system as an essential step to achieving a truly 'child first' approach to meeting the needs of adolescents.

The 'child first' movement has seized the imagination of a great many people in the Youth Justice System. In my view, the movement represents a significant step forward in improving the work that we do with children and their families, in particular, for the way in which it brings together theory and practice and moves beyond just general policy statements to show in detail how we can best work with children in trouble. While I hope I have shown how 'child first' builds on a pre-history of earlier attempts to build a child-focus into youth justice, it is a very significant step beyond what has gone before. I have every hope for the future, especially in 'Child First' can remain a fast-evolving movement, in which new 'guiding elements' are added continuously.

References

Baker, K., et al. (2003). *The evaluation of the validity and reliability of the youth justice board's assessment for young offenders*. Youth Justice Board.
Bartasevicius, V., Roberts, E., Liddar, A., Sharrock, S., Rantanen, K., & Barton-Crosby, J. (2020). *Pilots of alternative assessment to Asset Plus*. Department for Education. https://assets.publishing.service.gov.uk/government/uploads/system/uploads/attachment_data/file/932333/Asset_Plus_alternative_assessment.pdf
Blair, A. (2010). *A journey*. Hutchinson.
Bottoms, A. (1974). On the decriminalisation of English juvenile courts. In R. Hood (Ed.), *Crime, criminology and public policy* (pp. 319–346). Heinemann.
Bottoms, A. (2008). Children and Young Persons Act 1969. In B. Goldson (Ed.), *Dictionary of youth justice*. Willan Publishing.
Cadman, S. (2008). Assessment framework. In B. Goldson (Ed.), *Dictionary of youth justice*. Willan Publishing.
Case, S. P. (2008). Intermediate treatment. In B. Goldson (Ed.), *Dictionary of youth justice*. Willan Publishing.
Case, S. P., & Haines, K. (2009). *Understanding youth offending: Risk factor research, policy and practice*. Willan Publishing.
Case, S. P. (2018). *Youth justice—A critical introduction*. Routledge
Case, S. P., & Browning, A. (2021). *The child first strategy implementation policy*. lboro.ac.uk/ssh/child-first-justice. Loughborough University.
Conservative Party. (2010). *Invitation to join the government of Britain*. The Conservative Party.
Coyne, D. (2020). *On the outside looking in*. Paper delivered at a conference held by the Dartington Centre for Social Policy. Policy and Practice Papers. www.centreforsocialpolicy
Crick, M. (2005). *In search of Michael Howard*. Simon & Schuster.

Day, A.-M. (2022, February). 'It's a hard balance to find': The perspectives of youth justice practitioners in England on the place of 'risk' in an emerging 'child-first' world. *Youth Justice*.

Drew, J. (2020). *Children in custody: Lessons from the past, challenges for today*. Paper delivered at a conference held by the Dartington Centre for Social Policy. Policy and Practice Papers. www.centreforsocialpolicy

Firmin, C. (2021). *Contextual safeguarding—Introducing the idea and implications for youth justice*. https://youtu.be/oMNXHEYLt2M

Foucault, M. (2002). *The archaeology of knowledge*. Routledge.

Garland, D. (2014). What is a "history of the present"? On Foucault's genealogies and their critical preconditions *Punishment and Society, 16*(4) 365–384.

Gendreau, P., Smith, P., & Theriault, Y. L. (2009). Chaos theory and correctional treatment—Commonsense, correctional quackery, and the law of fartcatchers. *Journal of Contemporary Criminal Justice, 25*(4), 384–396.

Gramsci, A., as edited by Hoare, Q., & Nowell Smith, G. (1971). *Selections from the prison notebooks*. International Publishers.

Goldson, B. (2009a). What justice for children in conflict with the law? Some reflections and thoughts. *Crime and Justice, 76*(1), 19–21.

Goldson, B. (2009b). Rethinking youth justice. In B. Goldson & J. Muncie (Eds.), *Youth crime and juvenile justice*. Sage.

Goldson, B. (2010). The sleep of (criminological) reason: Knowledge—Policy rupture and New Labour's youth justice legacy. *Criminology and Criminal Justice, 10*(1), 155–178.

Gutting, G. (1994). *The Cambridge companion to Foucault*. Cambridge University Press.

Hagell, A. (2005). The use of custody for children and young people. In T. Bateman & J. Pitts (Eds.), *Youth justice*. Russell House Publications.

Haines, K. R., Case, S. P., Charles, A. D., & Davies, K. (2013). The Swansea Bureau: A model of diversion from the youth justice system. *International Journal of Law, Crime and Justice, 41*(2), 168–187.

Haines, K. R., & Case, S. P. (2015). *Positive youth justice: Children first*. Policy Press.

HM Government. (2008). *Youth Crime Action Plan*. HMSO.

HM Government. (2009). *Youth Crime Action Plan: One year on*. HMSO.

HM Government. (2010). *Breaking the cycle: Effective punishment, rehabilitation and sentencing of offenders*. HMSO.

HM Government. (2011). *Breaking the cycle: Government response*. HMSO.

HM Government. (2013). *Transforming youth custody—Putting education at the heart of detention.* HMSO.

Hastings, M. (2011, August 10). Years of liberal dogma have spawned a generation of amoral, uneducated, unparented, welfare dependent, brutalised youngsters. Daily Mail.

Hyland, J. (1993). *Yesterday's answers.* Whiting and Birch/Social Care Association (Education).

Hyland, J. (2020). *The history of approved schools.* Paper delivered at a conference held by the Dartington Centre for Social Policy. Policy and Practice Paper. www.centreforsocialpolicy

Kelly, P. (2008). Radical non-intervention. In B. Goldson (Ed.), *Dictionary of youth justice.* Willan Publishing.

Lane, D. (2020). *Conflicts, scandals and change.* Paper delivered at a conference held by the Dartington Centre for Social Policy. Policy and Practice Paper. www.centreforsocialpolicy

Liberal Democrats. (2010). *Change that works for you.* Liberal Democrats

McAra, L., & McVie, S. (2010). Youth crime and justice: Key messages from the Edinburgh study on youth transitions and crime. *Criminology and Criminal Justice, 10*(2), 179–209.

McNeill, F. (2006). A desistance paradigm for offender management. *Crime and Criminal Justice, 6*(1), 39–62.

McNeill, F., & Weaver, B. (2010). *Changing lives? Desistance research and offender management.* Universities of Glasgow and Strathclyde.

Muncie, J. (2008). The 'punitive turn' in juvenile justice: Cultures of control and rights compliance in Western Europe and the USA. *Youth Justice, 8*(2), 107–121.

Munro, E. (2010). *The Munro review of child protection, part one: A system's analysis.* Department for Education.

Munro, E. (2011a). *The Munro review of child protection: Interim report. The child's journey.* Department for Education.

Munro, E. (2011b). *The Munro review of child protection: Final report. A child-centred system.* Department for Education.

Munro, E. (2012). *The Munro review of child protection: Progress report: Moving towards a child-centred system.* Department for Education.

Pitts, J. (2001). Korrectional karaoke: New Labour and the zombification of youth justice. *Justice, 1*(2), 3–16.

Prison Reform Trust. (2021). *The first 40 years.* Prison Reform Trust

Purcell, C. (2020). *The politics of children's services reform.* Policy Press

Sevdiren, O. (2011). *Alternatives to imprisonment in England & Wales, Germany and Turkey.* Springer Heidelberg.
Smith, D. (2011). *Out of care* 30 years on. *Criminology and Criminal Justice, 10*(2), 119–135.
Solomon, E., & Garside, R. (2008). *Ten years of Labour's youth justice reforms: An independent audit.* Centre for Crime and Justice Studies.
Souhami, A. (2011). Inside the Youth Justice Board: Ambiguity and influence in New Labour's youth justice. *Safer Communities, 10*(3), 6–17.
Souhami, A. (2015a). The central institutions of youth justice: Government bureaucracy and the importance of the Youth Justice Board for England and Wales. *Youth Justice, 14,* 209–225.
Souhami, A. (2015b). Creating the Youth Justice Board: Policy and policy making in English and Welsh youth justice. *Criminology & Criminal Justice, 15,* 152–168.
Steinhauer, P. D. (1991). *The least detrimental alternative—A systematic guide to care planning and decision making for children in care.* University of Toronto Press.
Street, S. (2010). *Safeguarding the future.* HMSO.
Taylor, C. (2016a). *Review of the Youth Justice System—An interim report.* HMSO/Ministry of Justice.
Taylor, C. (2016b). *Review of the Youth Justice System in England and Wales: Final report.* HMSO/Ministry of Justice.
Thorpe, D. H., Smith, D., Green, C. J., & Paley, J. H. (1980). *Out of care: The community support of juvenile offenders.* George Allen and Unwin.
UNICEF. (1989). *United Nations Convention on the Rights of the Child.* UNICEF UK.
Willow, C. (2015). *Children behind bars.* Policy Press.
Youth Custody Service. (2022). *Monthly custody reports.* https://www.gov.uk/government/statistics/youth-custody-data
Youth Justice Board. (2020). *Business plan 2020–2021.* Assets Publishing Service Government UK.
Youth Justice Board for England and Wales. (2021a). *Strategic plan 2021a–2024.* Assets Publishing Service Government UK.
Youth Justice Board for England and Wales. (2021b). *Definitions for prevention and diversion* E-mail 21.11.21 to all Heads of YOT services and Chairs of Management Boards from the Head of Innovation and Engagement.

7

Developing Child First as the Guiding Principle for Youth Justice

Neal Hazel and Paula Williams

Introduction

In this chapter, we chart the creation of Child First as the new guiding principle for youth justice in England and Wales (YJB, 2021). In particular, we critically reflect on the wording of the principle and the steps taken to ensure that it gained acceptance and traction with policy and practice stakeholders as useful guidance. As a public policy case study, the development of Child First reveals the process of 'discourse framing' in a policy-level proposal in order to navigate the anticipated concerns and challenges of stakeholders. We are able to offer this insight because

---

N. Hazel (✉) · P. Williams
School of Health & Society, University of Salford, Salford, UK
e-mail: n.hazel@salford.ac.uk

P. Williams
Youth Justice Board for England and Wales, London, UK
e-mail: paula.williams@yjb.gov.uk

the authors led, with others,[1] its development at the Youth Justice Board for England and Wales (YJB) to the point of published policy-level advice and beyond. Appropriating a 'textual reflexivity' methodological approach adopted from social science in order to consider our policy-level decision-making, we are able to provide here a candid analysis of the considerations and contradictions involved in formulating and presenting the policy-level proposal for guiding the youth justice system.

For criminology, this chapter shows that initial stakeholder concerns about Child First are more diverse than a discourse of 'child' vs 'offender' dichotomy often used to critically assess the youth justice policy. For policy science, we contribute a clearer understanding of the process of discourse framing in drawing up policy-level proposals, and how this incorporates the concerns of stakeholders prior to the point of active negotiation typically presented in models of policy initiative development. Finally, we show the usefulness of policy-level actors developing the methodology of textual reflexivity in the interests of both engagement with stakeholders and academic insight.

Background: The Challenge of Navigating a Child First Policy

The aim of developing Child First as a policy-level initiative was to collate contemporary research understanding of what is important in effective youth justice in a single principle that is useful to guide decision-making in the youth justice system. Much of this contemporary research has been critical of existing policy and practice, arguing for reform, most notably in texts that can be aligned (some closely, some more loosely) with the idea that youth justice should treat children as 'children first, offenders second' (CFOS) (see Case & Browning, 2021 for a review of this research). The idea and phrase had made their way into youth justice parlance, but this was a chance to define them in a way

---

[1] While we led the formulation of the Child First proposal, it was written with Board members Ben Byrne, Sharon Gray and developed collectively by the YJB Board and staff. From 2021, its ongoing development is led by Board member Louise Shorter.

that would ensure their applicability and usefulness within the context of policy and practice. The development of Child First as a policy-level proposal would mean framing the messages from academic discourses that have been critical, both in the sense of academic inquiry and judgement of policy sometimes to the point of abolitionism (cf. Haines & Case, 2015, Case & Haines 2021), into discourses that can be accepted and operationally constructive to youth justice stakeholders.

We must be clear at the outset that Child First is certainly not a 'policy' or 'policy product' in the civil service sense of a government product (Civil Service Learning, 2013). Neither is the YJB an organisation that makes such polices for youth justice—the Ministry of Justice (MoJ) does that. Instead, it is the YJB's statutory duty both to advise the Secretary of State and to 'make known and…promote good practice' to the sector (Crime and Disorder Act s41). The Child First guiding principle falls primarily into the latter category. We are describing policy-making and policymakers in this chapter in the broadest academic sense of producing a product at the level of policy (as opposed to practice) and in the disciplinary sense because it is within the remit of policy science.

Introducing reforming ideas at both policy and practice levels in youth justice, and indeed in wider public policy, is challenging (see Drew in this book). It was very clear that assuming that Child First and its constituent concepts would be accepted by other stakeholders simply because they reflect contemporary evidence would be a naïve view of the policymaking process. Even in the 2000s, when there was a government narrative of 'evidence-based policy making' (cf. Blunkett, 2000), there was a healthy cynicism about the relative powerlessness of research messages in the face of political processes both within (cf. Hope & Walters, 2008; Naughton, 2005) and beyond criminal justice (Pawson, 2006). It is clear thought that research evidence can be used to successfully reform criminal justice policies (S. Taylor, 2016). Indeed, the prevailing risk paradigm in youth justice policy and practice criticised by texts aligned to CFOS (Haines & Case, 2008) was informed by positivist 'what works' literature in the 1990s–2000s (cf. Stephenson et al., 2011).

However, if a policy-level initiative, let alone a reforming one, is to be sustainable and have traction, the key challenge is navigating how problem-solving models 'interact with the complexities of real life and politics' (Civil Service Learning, 2013: 7). Those developing policy-level proposals need to understand and manage the political context. A particular challenge for progressive evidence-led reform like Child First is navigating the reported 'powerful forces' acting in favour the status quo, including within the civil service (Hallsworth et al., 2011: 39; Pollitt, 2003). This is even more challenging with the need to involve large numbers of stakeholders, or 'myriad of actors and factors' (Cairney & Weible, 2017), with the result that such innovative new models run into difficulties and are not engaged with or do not deliver (Hallsworth et al., 2011: 59). The fact that the reforming policy-level proposal would come in the form of advice from the YJB as an arms-length body sponsored by the MoJ adds another layer of complexity to ensuring its traction. The YJB's role historically in presenting such proposals in its formation and presentation of advice to ministers has been described as a 'contingent position' (Souhami, 2014: 147), requiring 'delicate balance' (Souhami et al., 2012: 38) to gain and maintain political legitimacy.

There is developing interest but still limited understanding of *how* such political legitimacy is created and maintained as such policy-level initiatives are formulated and developed towards implementation (Hallsworth et al., 2011; Miller, 2020a). Traditional theories of policy-making, which presented the process as a series of stages (cf. Hogwood and Gun 1984) or a cycle (cf. Bridgman & Davis, 2003) solving a prescribed policy problem, have been criticised for being 'naïve', failing to reflect reality (Hallsworth et al., 2011: 45; Otieno, 2019). Contemporary critical and mainstream policy scientists have increasingly recognised that 'policy making' is more of a negotiated or deliberative process in which voices are heard and concerns are addressed (Sanderson, 2009; Toulmin, 2001). Within this field, it is now well established that support for, and traction of, a policy agenda can be affected by the framing or presentation of the problem (Druckman, 2001) or proposed solution (Kingdon, 1995). Furthermore, research has identified the challenges of finding politically acceptable framing when promoting an unpopular policy, noting the importance of narratives adopted (Cohen-Blankshtain, 2008) and of a persuasive 'storyline' about the initiative emerging (Annison, 2021). Indeed, it is acknowledged how such a frame would need to negotiate the concerns and values in various narratives from stakeholders (Lofaro & Miller, 2021), sometimes leading a positive advocacy coalition (Sabatier, 1998), sometimes leading to the policy proposal adapting narratives (Dodge & Lee, 2017) and other times suffering gridlock competing narratives (Miller, 2020b). The development of Child First in youth justice provides a case study that allows us to analyse the discourse-framing processes (Hardy et al., 2000) involved in turning a research evidence base, including critical research, advocating reform into a policy-level proposal acceptable and useful to stakeholders.

In youth justice, it has been recognised that there are competing pressures internal and external to a country that shape each youth justice system over time in a piecemeal way (Goldson et al., 2021; Hazel, 2008) and cycles of youth justice policies over time in any one jurisdiction (cf. Bernard & Kurlychek, 2010; Hagell & Hazel, 2001). However, there has been little analysis of the competing pressures on the initial development of a particular policy-level initiative (Case et al., 2020). Where such analysis has taken place, it has generally been historic and focused on the story of development and role of key players (cf. Carlebach, 1970; Case, 2018) rather than an analysis of the competing pressures how they are considered and navigated. Academics have long called for a more nuanced analysis of the policy process beyond the identification of dominant discourses (such as the risk paradigm or Child First) and stages or actors in that process (cf. Fergusson, 2007). Souhami's ethnography of the YJB in the mid-2000s perhaps came closest, considering the processes of policymaking and the nature of policy itself (Souhami, 2014). As part of their critical analysis, academics in qualitative interviews have asked policymakers to reflect back on their involvement in criminal justice policymaking, generally retrospectively (cf. Annison, 2017; Case et al., 2020). However, it is unusual for those involved at the policy-level themselves to consider, record and write in a reflexive way about how they developed (let alone recently or contemporaneously) a specific initiative[2] (Annison, 2017).

For Child First, our situation meant that we are both able to adopt a position of reflexivity in relation to our roles leading the development of a contemporary policy-level proposal. This chapter's first author is an

---

[2] A notable exception considered school curriculum development in Canada (Orpwood, 1985).

academic who had a long-standing interest in reflexivity in research (cf. Hazel, 1996; Hazel & Clark, 2013) and who, since being appointed as a Youth Justice Board member, was engaging directly with policy-level initiatives for the first time. The second author was a YJB staff member with responsibility for organisational strategic objectives, who also was also conducting academic research on the influence of 'child first, offender second' ideas in practice. To help us explore the process of our own narrative or 'discourse framing', we have appropriated and applied a social science methodological concept of 'textual reflexivity' (Atkinson & Whitaker, 2019) to policy-level proposal development. In social science, this refers to how the researcher can consider their own use of language as a constitutive function, including textual strategies deployed to persuade readers of the veracity of their texts (Atkinson, 1990). Here, it meant critically analysing how the writing and presentation of Child First reflects our own attempts to ensure the evidence base is accepted by stakeholders. In practical terms, we[3] chose to note down at the time the included concepts, the reasons for using particular words, and the wider policy and practice considerations for doing so. We have considered our notes together with reviewing our communication with YJB Board and staff at the time to present this frank reflexive account of the framing and development of Child First as a policy-level initiative.

Initiating the Policy-Level Development of Child First

The development of Child First as a distinct and explicit policy-level initiative (as opposed to academic or practice initiative) within the English jurisdiction can be traced back to the final report from Taylor's review of youth justice, presented to the UK Parliament in December 2016 (Taylor, 2016a). In the previous year, Taylor had been asked by the Secretary of State for Justice to lead a departmental review that attempted '*to look at the youth justice system with fresh eyes*' (Taylor,

---

[3] The use of the word 'we' in this chapter refers to the authors (or sometimes to one of us) rather than the Youth Justice Board or any other group/organisation.

2016b: 2). Taylor's final report was the first departmental paper from the Ministry of Justice to call explicitly for a new youth justice system which sees '*the child first and the offender second*' (Taylor, 2016a: 3 and 48). In doing so, Taylor adopted the phrasing used previously in critical criminological texts advocating CFOS reform (cf., Drakeford & Haines, 1998: 89; Haines & Case, 2015), and later featuring in Wales policy planning (cf., Welsh Assembly Government, 2004). Taylor's justification for this approach also reflects previous arguments, that offending should not mean children forfeit '*the right to childhood*' (or, presumably, being considered as a child) and that supporting them requires a focus on welfare '*rather than simply imposing punishment*' (Taylor, 2016a: 3). This latter argument presented CFOS primarily as simply choosing one side of the 'welfare or punishment' dichotomy for children, well established in youth justice debates worldwide (Hazel, 2008).

The concept of CFOS presented by Taylor was not immediately adopted by the MoJ in a response that discussed 'young offenders' (MoJ, 2016). Nevertheless, the Secretary of State for Justice (Liz Truss) appointed Taylor as the new Chair of the Youth Justice Board (YJB), praising his review's '*compelling vision for reform*' (Truss, 2017: 1).

At the YJB Board meeting in January 2018, Taylor brought CFOS as one of seven proposed principles for the organisation. In this meeting, we highlighted how the concept was variously understood by policymakers and practitioners, a point supported by the Head of YJB Wales, where policy had long advocated this principle with practice lagging behind (YJB, 2018a: 22). We agreed to lead on developing a definition of 'Children First, Offenders Second' for the policy and practice context across England and Wales, aware that this would also act as a useful summary of key concepts from contemporary academic research about effective youth justice.

This definition, titled Child First, <>Offender Second (later known just as Child First, as referred to in this chapter) was developed into four points (now known as Child First tenets 1–4), drawing together contemporary understanding in youth justice from a range of sources, but in particular from the content and structure of summaries provided in Byrne and Case (2016), Hazel et al. (2017), and Haines and Case (2015). The definition was presented and accepted at the June 2018

Board meeting (Hazel et al., 2018), with some small wording adjustments since. The following section of the chapter breaks down the wording of that definition (YJB, 2021: 10–11), exploring some of the considerations and decisions taken in translating academic concepts for the policy and practice context to ensure acceptance and usefulness for stakeholders.

The Formulation of the Child First Principle: Concepts, Considerations and Concerns

Preamble

The wording of the short preamble to the four tenets already includes an important conceptual statement and reflects considerations for how to ensure policy and practice level engagement:

A 'Child First, Offender Second' approach means that all youth justice services:

The usual collective phrasing of 'children first, offenders second' (cf. Haines & Case, 2015) was deliberately singularised to refer to 'child' and 'offender'. This was intended to highlight the importance of treating children as individuals, challenging diversity blindness (cf. Bateman & Hazel, 2014), and the importance of customised rather than generic support (Hazel & Bateman, 2020).

The use of the phrase 'all youth justice services' was intended to show the universality of the principle across every part of the youth justice system, and that it would be a 'common language' to encourage multi-agency working. It was also intended to counter any inference that the principle was limited to an internal or YJB-only principle; it was intended that it should be adopted by the sector. However, it was decided not to include 'should' or similar directive wording for the sector at the end of this phrase for two reasons. First, the YJB wanted the sector to own the definition rather than it being seen as a paternalistic direction from above (as with national standards), which would encourage practitioners' engagement and ownership. Second, not using 'should' felt more definite and 'matter of fact' rather than aspirational; it is an authoritative message that this is what the evidence points to being correct. A key concern for us politically was that an approach which challenges treating children as offenders should not be perceived as an ideological choice to be 'soft on criminals'; this would be unacceptable to the electorate and consequently politicians. In contrast, the 'matter of fact' language would help show the definition as objectively evidence-led about what works in lowering crime (Case & Browning, 2021), enabling politicians to support the approach as appropriate to a 'law and order' agenda that aims to have fewer victims.

The same concern not to be dismissed politically as 'soft' meant that the title kept the 'offender second' element, even though the principle's content advocates treating children as children, full stop. It was also felt that the full phrase would link more explicitly with the existing research literature that referred to 'children first, offenders second'. However, it was determined that the 'offender second' element would not be used when referring to the principle informally, and it would be dropped entirely once the principle was more widely known and accepted.

Child First Tenet 1

The first of four tenets (as they have become known) of the Child First principle highlights the importance of the criminal justice system recognising and treating children as different to adults:

1. *Prioritise the best interests of children and recognising their particular needs, capacities, rights and potential. All work is child-focused, developmentally informed, acknowledges structural barriers and meets responsibilities towards children.*

Highlighting this difference from adults upfront and clearly to stakeholders is important given that large parts of the youth justice system are essentially subsidiaries of dominant adult-focused organisations (cf. Youth Custody Service part of HM Prisons and Probation Service; youth courts part of HM Courts & Tribunals Service). We were conscious that there is a risk that children are subsumed within policies that are designed as generic to the criminal justice system, and which do not consider children's particular characteristics; with commentators since noting the example of early release schemes during the COVID-19 pandemic, which reportedly saw hundreds of adults able to meet the generic criteria and be released, but no children (Harris & Goodfellow, 2021).

Similarly, the under-18s in the youth justice system are deliberately described throughout the Child First principle as 'children' rather than as 'young people' (and obviously not the offender-framed wording of 'young offender'), which would imply just mini adult offenders rather than a separate category with peculiar vulnerabilities. The other, and perhaps even worse, phrase deliberately avoided was 'children and young people', used, for example, in the health context and in statutes, which despite their legal status implies that only some under-18s are to be considered as children with associated vulnerabilities. We felt it crucial that stakeholders understand that all under-18s share these differences from adults (indeed, with age-related capacities often more compromised for those in the system [Hales et al., 2018]), even if many have committed very 'adult-like' serious crimes. Use of the words 'capacities' and 'developmentally informed' underline the convincing and growing evidence base around maturation which distinguishes children's competency from adults (cf. Prior et al., 2011).

The word 'prioritise' at the front of the first tenet begins to underline the legal basis for children's unique status is a deliberate reminder to stakeholders that welfare of the child must be 'paramount' (Children Act 1929 s1). Moreover, 'the best interests' will be recognised by policymakers and practitioners as the precise legal wording from the United Nations Convention of the Rights of the Child (Article 3), which states that it shall be a primary consideration. However, the Convention is thus implied rather than stated, and 'rights' is noted but not the phrase 'children's rights'; this is again cognisant of the political context for 'landing' the principle, when the phrase has been known to raise a distracting reactionary response (cf. Phillips, 2008, in MailOnline).

The second sentence for each tenet was intended to help practitioners start to think about what this means for their own practice. By starting

'All work is', these sentences highlight again the universal relevancy of the principle, and also its intention to be applicable in practice now rather than as an academic aspiration.

The phrases 'acknowledges structural barriers' and 'meets responsibilities towards children' were introduced later to the Child First principle (in YJB 2021). Both phrases address criticisms of youth justice responsibilising children when the answers often lie with adults around them (Gray, 2007; Haines & Case, 2015), making a clear statement to such critiques (including academics) that this is recognised and understood. The former phrase was felt particularly important to state given the increased understanding both from the Black Lives Matter movement (from 2020) and the YJB Journey of the Child work (YJB, 2019a) highlighting racial inequality, and also politically important in the context of the Commission on Race and Ethnic Disparities (2020–2021). It is clear that a guiding principle for youth justice should not be blind to diversity and the effects of structural inequality.

Child First Tenet 2

The second tenet of the Child First principle highlights the importance of practice with children working towards positive child outcomes:

2. *Promote children's individual strengths and capacities to develop their pro-social identity for sustainable desistance, leading to safer communities and fewer victims. All work is constructive and future-focused, built on supportive relationships that empower children to fulfil their potential and make positive contributions to society*

The focus on positive outcomes for children as children rather than just managing their risks and trying to limit their deficits as potential offenders is a strong theme in contemporary academic literature in youth justice (see in particular Haines & Case, 2015). We were conscious that this is a substantial shift in thinking for a system that has focused on trying to reduce offending by directly addressing children's negative 'risk factors' (cf. YJB, 2005). Speaking to that point for both policy-makers and practitioners, this tenet separates cause and effect; if the youth justice system focuses on promoting children's strengths to develop their pro-social identity, this will result in sustainable desistance from offending that will in turn lead to inevitable indirect benefits around safer communities and fewer victims (Hazel et al., 2017).

We anticipated the criticism from progressive academics that a Child First approach should see children's positive outcomes as a goal in itself, rather than leading to desistance and less offending (cf. Wigzell, 2021). However, we were very aware that the context for Child First to be implemented is within a youth justice system that has an overall statutory aim of 'preventing offending' (Crime and Disorder Act [C&DA] 1998), under the overall governance a justice ministry. To omit the positive effect of this way of working on reducing offending would clearly have been to turn a strength of Child First into a weakness, and render it irrelevant to both the YJB's statutory role (C&DA 1998: 41[5f]) and ministerial and civil service constituencies and their concerns. The specific reference to 'fewer victims' was direct assurance to expected political concern that the principle focused on children and forgot about their victims, which was certainly not the case and would have been particularly unpalatable in a political context with a statutory Victims Code (Ministry of Justice, 2020).

The way that this Child First tenet describes how to achieve positive outcomes is very different from most of the academic literature, which is perhaps the most significant step for the principle to ensure it is operationalisable in the current youth justice system. Literature arguing that children in trouble should be just treated as children has deliberately avoided discussing a 'theory of change' and downplayed any specific work with children who offend (Haines & Case, 2015). Its inherent argument then is that youth justice specialist organisations or professionals are not needed to support development as children. However, in a system where there are such specialists, this lacked direction for their work (cf. sentence plans) or sufficient assurances to courts. We considered that this had limited the operationalisation and adoption of Child First ways of working within the sector, particularly in England. Instead, this tenet introduces the 'development of pro-social identity' as the theory of change for youth justice agencies to work to (Beyond Youth Custody research project findings, cf. Hazel et al., 2017, 2020), and enabling a common language to replace that of managing the deficit-focused 'risk of offending' (the absence of the phrase 'risk of offending' intended to underline this). This research was at the time being translated from research into YJB policy guidance around children in leaving custody as the 'Constructive Resettlement' approach (YJB, 2018b; written by this chapter's authors), the link to which was deliberately reinforced with the reference in the tenet to all work being 'constructive'. However, when incorporating it into the Child First principle, we moved away from any implication that children needed to have already offended (or admitted guilt) by changing the concept of 'shifting identity' to 'developing pro-social identity'. Most obviously, this allowed the principle's theory of change to apply to early intervention and prevention work, which some Youth Offending Teams (YOTs)[4] had already started doing (Hazel et al., 2020). It also tried to address likely criticisms from progressive youth justice reformers that the 'theory of change' had been drawn from adult-based 'desistance theory' (cf. Maruna & Farrall, 2004) rather than research involving children; although in actuality this concern has persisted (e.g. Wigzell, 2021).

The use of the phrase 'future-focused' was intended to ensure that practitioners re-evaluated their use of processes that may reinforce the child's offender identity and stigma by focusing them on what they have done in the past rather than developing their pro-social identity. For instance, we hoped that this would trigger reconsideration of unconstructive or generic reparation work that underlined the child's specific offence (and offending identity). Relatedly, it is notable that this tenet, which focuses on what work should be done with children, omits any mention of sending them to any formal offence-focused programmes, like 'knife crime awareness' courses (e.g. MOPAC, 2021). In fact, by not including it in 'all work', this was intended as a signal to the sector that ideas of 'what works' had changed and sending children on stock programmes

---

[4] Although this book uses the term statutory term of 'Youth Offending Team', the YJB now prefers 'Youth Justice Teams' or 'Youth Justice Services'. In line with Child First tenet 4, these terms are less likely to foster criminogenic stigma (or impede engagement) by underlining the child's 'offending' status.

underlining their offences was no longer seen as good practice. Instead, the tenet makes it clear that empowering relationship-based work is the cornerstone of any intervention. This signal was felt necessary because, although research presented at practitioner conferences highlighted that a positive outcome from youth justice 'depend on relationships, not set interventions' (McAra, 2018; also McAra, 2017; Hazel, 2020), parts of the sector have been slow to change tack (Smith & Gray, 2018).

Child First Tenet 3

The third tenet of the Child First principle highlights the importance of collaborating with children if youth justice is to be relevant to them and successful in its outcomes:

3. *Encourage children's active participation, engagement and wider social inclusion. All work is a meaningful collaboration with children and their carers.*

The overall tone of this tenet was intended to move away from the conception that we could expect positive outcomes by having practitioners directly manage a child and their risk of offending (Haines & Case, 2015). We cannot do youth justice *to* a child in this way, just as policymakers and professionals cannot prevent offending directly, without involving the child.

The three words 'participation', 'engagement' and 'wider social inclusion' were a direct reference to the three stages of engagement highlighted in contemporary research (Bateman & Hazel, 2013). This was in order for us to move policymakers and practitioners past the point of measuring success through participation rates in interventions or compliance, but towards focusing on ensuring that the child feels engaged and invested. The word 'active' before participation was a signal to that practitioners should be enabled to involve children through tools and processes that build-in their involvement (see Burns and Creaney in this book).

The phrase 'social inclusion' was a tricky in terms of our wording consideration. The phrase describes quite accurately what is needed to achieve a child's investment in their community and wanting to 'make positive contributions to society', as the second tenet describes. However, but we had some concerns that the phrase may have been too closely associated in England and Wales with New Labour of the 2000s and so politically dated (e.g. Social Exclusion Unit; Charity Commission, 2001), as a quick web search of the term shows. However, the term would best spotlight the problem with any practices where children were literally excluded from society, like being locked up in custody. In addition, the word 'inclusion' is now more often understood by policymakers in relation to diversity (e.g. Civil Service, 2022), with its use here also able to highlight the needs to remove structural barriers (as noted in the first tenet).

The first draft of the tenet had the word 'co-created' (from Constructive Resettlement's 5Cs [YJB, 2018b]) rather than 'a meaningful collaboration'. However, other YJB staff noted that this limited the usefulness of the Child First principle to practice, where children could play an equal role in creating their plans and intervention. The view was that using the word 'collaboration' would allow this active engagement of children, as well as then the rest of Child First principle, to guide policymaking as much as practice. The compromise in moving from a more active 'co-creation' was to guard against tokenistic involvement of children by insisting that the collaboration is 'meaningful'.

Child First Tenet 4

The fourth tenet of the Child First principle highlights the minimising criminogenic stigma from involvement with the youth justice system:

4. *Promote a childhood removed from the justice system, using pre-emptive prevention, diversion and minimal intervention. All work minimises criminogenic stigma from contact with the system.*

Although the negative effects of labelling from involvement in the criminal justice system is not a new academic idea (cf. Becker, 1963), there has recently been a renewed and deeper academic understanding of (1) the criminogenic effects of involvement (Gatti et al., 2009; McAra & McVie, 2007; Smith, 2017) and (2) the need to limit stigma from any involvement to promote positive outcomes (Deakin et al., 2020; Hazel et al., 2020). This tenet was written in a way that the two sentences reflected these two insights, with the first sentence directed more at policymakers and decision-makers, and the second more at practitioners. We thought the positive benefits of diversion from criminal justice, against the negative effects of their involvement, fairly well accepted by criminal justice policymakers in the UK and beyond (Council of Europe, 2010; cf. Welsh Government/YJB, 2014), but considered that it was important to state clearly that children were better with their childhood 'removed from the youth justice system', with a verb that suggested action was needed for this to happen.

Although the logical conclusion of treating children as children rather than as offenders has been argued to be to abolish a youth justice system altogether (Case & Haines, 2021), we were clear that this principle was for the youth justice system framework that existed, while it could 'promote' ways to remove children from it. Relatedly, we were conscious that the term 'minimal intervention', while supported by research, may be controversial in a policy landscape that had disavowed it in the 1990s following its interpretation as increasing cautioning (Bottoms & Dignan, 2004: 32). We tried to ensure that it was clearly linked with a more active 'diversion' to other support to meet the child's needs, for positive outcomes and behaviour.

The Challenge of Embedding Child First into Wider Policy

On accepting the proposed four-tenet definition of Child First, YJB Board members abandoned the idea that it should be just one of seven principles for the organisation. Instead, it was felt that (a) this Child First was the primary principle, which would lead to the other six principles being followed and (b) it would stand as the guiding principle for the sector (policy-level and practice) rather than just the YJB's operations. Since then, it has been referred to as the 'guiding principle for youth justice' (e.g. YJB, 2021).

The agreed next steps to ensure assimilation were both to consider the implications of Child First for the YJB and its own operations and guidance, and to gain buy-in from other stakeholders. Of course, these were interlinked—it was implausible to advocate Child First while advising incompatible approaches, and interaction with other stakeholders will help other guidance. This section outlines some of the most significant steps and the considerations and intent involved.

There was consensus on the Board that a simple 'awareness campaign' was not appropriate for two reasons. First, we were still unsure how Child First would land with policymakers, practitioners and the public (despite our considerations in wording). Second, there was a danger that an awareness campaign risked being superficial and tokenistic. However, it was also clear that simply making Child First a 'project' or organisational 'priority stream' risked compartmentalising it and not achieving a principled change across all work. An options paper prompted a preference for a 'soft launch' of (1) testing with strategic stakeholders (e.g. children, policy, ministers, local authorities, MoJ officials) to explore concerns and (2) internal activity consulting on the principle and embedding it in YJB work, before wider presentation. However, anticipating a move to a more public stance shortly, it was decided that the sector's Youth Justice Convention later that year would have the theme of Child First.

Internal Development of Child First

Internal consultation and discussion about the principle's tenets (prior to any public presentation) presented an insight into likely stakeholder concerns (given the YJB staff background in both policy and practice environments), and informed how to further nuance presentation and address concerns before those stakeholders were actually engaged. This was notably at an all-staff workshop in September 2018, where concerns voiced were about three issues, neither opposed to a shift from seeing children as children first per se. First, does Child First mean that the YJB is adopting an abolitionist position calling for system change that might put us in opposition to government, such as removing all custody, raising the age of criminal responsibility, etc.? Certainly we were conscious of the oppositional position adopted by the YJB Chair in the 2000s that led to a breakdown in trust with the MoJ (Souhami, 2014). This concern enabled development of the position that the principle provides guidance within the existing youth justice system legislative framework, but could then be applied to larger system-wide questions if and when they required advice.

Second was the question of how a shift away from the 'risk paradigm' is plausible when services need to assess the risk of harm to the public. We were able to refine the position (previously in YJB, 2018b) that 'risk of offending' discourse needed to be separated from 'risk of harm', with the former avoided as treating children as potential offenders and the latter necessary but less stigmatising if framed more positively as 'public protection' or safeguarding. It is a concern that has endured in practitioners, particularly that moving away from risk would not satisfy inspections (see Day in this volume), leading to a joint statement with the probation inspectorate reiterating this position on risk (HM Inspectorate of Probation/YJB, 2022).

Third, and relatedly, where does the shift from the 'risk paradigm' leave how we deal with all our knowledge-base about 'risk factors' for offending. The answer developed (with the counsel of other academics, notably Stephen Case) was that there needed to be a thorough re-evaluation of such research through a Child First lens with its theory of change (cf. Hazel & Bateman, 2020 for research on resettlement) and then, if still appropriate, reframing 'risk factors' in terms of barriers to positive child outcomes.

Public Presentation and Consultation

The first public declaration of the Child First principle was its inclusion in the draft national standards for youth justice, which were put out for consultation in October 2018 (YJB, 2018c). In addition to listing the four tenets in the front of the document, this was also the Board's first attempt to publish regulations or advice that was based on Child First, and to that extent was clearly a work in progress and tentative. The idea of a single standard measuring Child First compliance had been rejected as, again, this was felt to risk compartmentalising what should be an overarching principle. In essence, the standards incorporated phrasing from the principle fairly directly into the specifications for the various criminal justice stages, to explicitly prioritise children's best interests, encourage their active engagement, minimise potential damage from contact, etc. It also listed the aim of the standards in positive terms, such as improving child outcomes, rather than deficit-focused risk management. However, the rest of the wording of the standards had not been changed to reflect the practice implications of this wording, leading to some obvious contradictions including an emphasis on risk management informing intervention.

Positively, however, the consultation feedback received widespread support for Child First (mainly from practitioners and third-sector stakeholders), with calls for further emphasis throughout the standards (YJB, 2018d). This provided reassurance that the sector was receptive to incorporating the implications of Child First. Consequently, revisions for the final standards (MoJ/, published February 2019) included:

- Changing 'children and young people/persons' references to just 'children', which we were conscious moved away from the legal discourse used in governing statutes.
- The status of Child First tenets changing from being the YJB's aim for itself to what it will ensure agencies adhere to, and stating that the services should monitor that adherence.
- More regular emphasis on planning and interventions that promote pro-social identity and positive outcomes rather than managing risk of offending in each standard.
- More focus on opportunities for meaningful collaboration, including children's voices and understanding being assured in court.

Perhaps the most significant change from integrating Child First into the standards was dropping the requirement of practitioners to supervise orders in line with the YJB's Scaled Approach model. Introduced by the YJB in 2009 (YJB, 2009), this framework required services to scale the level of intervention according to a child's risk of offending. Arguably, it inadvertently targeted vulnerability and those disadvantaged by structural barriers, leading to disproportionality in sentences (Bateman, 2011; Haines & Case, 2012).

We were also reassured that the considered wording in Child First had gained political approval. Not only had the MoJ signed-off the standards, but the youth justice minister also added a specific statement of support for the principle inserted into his foreword. We also noted how ministerial language had shifted to 'children', showing some immediate impact of Child First (MoJ/YJB, 2019: 2). Importantly, we had also suggested to the Secretary of State (and he agreed) that the MoJ add its branding to the national standards for the first time, which enabled us to demonstrate publicly that Child First and the standards were published and endorsed by the ministry as much as by the YJB.

The YJB's strategic plan published a few months after the final national standards (YJB, 2019b), included two further statements important to Child First's developmental journey. First, the Board's vision statement was changed from one where preventing offending would allow a positive future (offender first, child second), to recognising that positive child outcomes will prevent offending (child first, offender second) in line with the principle's tenet 2. Second, the Board made a clear statement that Child First means moving beyond a focus on managing risk of offending. Language such as 'We *now* understand the criminogenic effects' (our emphasis), almost restorative in tone, was a deliberate message for practitioners to draw a line under a past where the YJB had been the strongest advocate of the risk paradigm (e.g. YJB, 2005). It was hoped that this would allow us to answer any argument or accusation that the YJB was still advocating managing risk of offending rather than constructively helping children move forward. One reason for doing this was that we were aware that YJB itself still occasionally slipped into language previously used.

A further step was our encouraging an independent academic report that collated the research evidence base for Child First in one place (Case & Browning, 2021). This was recognised as an important missing piece for meetings with policy stakeholders where the YJB was advocating a Child First decision.

Child First's journey at the policy level is ongoing, both internal and external to the YJB, with considerations around how Child First is embedded and presented. From 2020 to 2022, there have been three main mechanisms for these considerations. First, the Case Management Guidance for YOTs is being revised, with every section being rewritten to be in line with the Child First evidence base and the 2019 national standards. We have been leading a forum where stakeholders (including practitioners and academics) are considering the most difficult issues. For instance, Child First principle (tenet 1) would imply engagement and compliance as the responsibility of YOTs, with a breach of compliance prompting asking what more could be done rather than immediately returning to court because the child has not engaged. Second, the library of guidance and documentation previously issued by the YJB is being reviewed for its compliance with Child First, leading to some being revised, some archived, and some including a disclaimer about the validity of content. Third, the Board and staff are creating position statements on elements of the youth justice system (e.g. gangs, girls, custody, trauma, resettlement), based on contemporary evidence and each related explicitly to Child First. These will be used to provide clear and consistent messaging externally and provide the core of the YJB's organisational identity.

Stakeholders' Concerns About Child First

There have been very few objections or concerns expressed by stakeholders about the Child First principle, overall or in detail. We'd like to think that this was perhaps due to the anticipation and careful consideration of possible concerns taken when wording the four tenets. Certainly, we know that on reading in Board minutes that the Child First principle had been adopted, a tabloid requested and received a copy of our definition paper, so we were anticipating objections, but none were published. On the contrary, perhaps the strongest objection was that the second part of the principle's title of 'Child First, Offender Second' was 'child-damning' labelling (Crook, 2018), which we took as supporting tenet 4 on stigma (the YJB had already started to drop the 'Offender Second' element in presentation, like the YJ Convention). This section lists the few key concerns expressed.

'Child First' and the Status of Victims

We had anticipated political concern with the place of victims in Child First, stating explicitly in tenet 2 that following the theory of change found in contemporary research would lead to *'safer communities and fewer victims'*. Nevertheless, in the Commons Select Committee, Rob Butler MP (former YJB member) observed to YJB Chair, Keith Fraser, that, 'Some people would say', 'Shouldn't it be victim first?' (Justice Select Committee, 2020: Q16). This is a reasonable observation given that the victims code in England and Wales issued under statute states that service providers, including YOTs, 'must have the victim's best interests as their primary consideration' (Ministry of Justice, 2020: 3), seemingly somewhat in conflict with the Crime and Disorder Act 1998 and Children Act 1989. However, Fraser argued that these priorities should not be pitted against each other, both equally important, and reiterated that following the evidence base would bring fewer victims because of reduced offending and reoffending.

'Minimal Intervention' and Complex Needs

Although the HM Chief Inspector of Probation, Justin Russell, has declared his full support for the Child First tenets 1–3, he has stated that he is 'increasingly sceptical' about tenet 4's 'minimal intervention', concerned that children with complex needs would not be screened or be linked with other services (HMI Probation, 2022: 5). This is a helpful reminder to ensure that minimising stigmatising contact with youth justices should not be interpreted by practitioners to mean they should not assess the needs of children brought into the youth justice system. We hope national standards and case management guidance make this clear. As the second half of the tenet implies, some children will need to be on YOT caseloads; for these children, services should take steps to minimise criminogenic stigma.

'Future-Focused' and Interventions Looking Back

The key concern from practitioners has been that Child First tenet 2's statement that 'all work is constructive and future-focused' would not allow them to continue with work that draws information from the past. In particular, this has been related to using information about a child's background in assessment and trauma-informed work, and some mediation or reparation in restorative justice (RJ). It has been important to clarify that '-focused' does not prohibit drawing on the past, but is about using that information to inform how to move the child forward for positive outcomes rather than for underlining or redressing the past. We did intend that this would involve some reassessing and reframing of interventions, including some trauma-informed work (e.g. YJB, 2020). Similarly with RJ, if used at the right time and in the right way may help a child move on from a pro-offending identity, but used as a blanket approach or to reinforce crudely the child's responsibility for their crimes (as YJB RJ training at the time implied) would underline this identity and so limit positive development (Hazel et al., 2020).

'Child First' and Staff Authority

New prison officers in training relayed to us the objection (allegedly voiced among colleagues on the wings) that the Youth Custody Service adopting Child First had undermined their authority, and consequently their safety. In particular, they mistakenly attributed to Child First, changes to regulations that meant they were no longer able to use pain-inducing techniques in behaviour management (actually introduced after an independent review [Taylor, 2020]). Although this underlines the importance of communicating effectively with the sector about Child First, the first tenet does include the recognition of children's rights and needs.

Conclusion

This chapter has charted the formulation and development between 2018 and 2022 of Child First as the guiding principle for youth justice in England and Wales. From our position of leading the development of this policy-level proposal within the YJB, we have been able to use the methodological lens of 'textual reflexivity' to analyse from the inside the steps taken to ensure that a proposal based on research evidence, much of it critical, gained traction by being acceptable and useful to policymakers and practitioners. In particular, this chapter has showed the considerations taken in framing discourse to navigate the anticipated concerns and challenges of stakeholders.

The Child First initiative collated contemporary research evidence on 'what works' in youth justice into a four-tenet principle for the youth justice sector in England and Wales. At this point in its development (in 2022, four years on from its formulation), we can reflect that the aim of being accepted and useful has been successful to the point that it has already been embedded at the policy level in a number of ways. The chapter has noted how Child First now underpins strategic and business planning for the YJB, the national standards for youth justice, a revision of the case management guidance, and YJB position statements on issues across youth justice. In addition, the Youth Custody Service adopts a Child First approach in any new policy framework (e.g. Youth Custody Service, 2022), Child First is now integral to effective practice training for staff in the youth justice system, and YOTs must assess their statutory youth justice plans against the principle. Also, the cultural shift from changing wording from 'young person' or even 'young offender' to 'children', particularly when now adopted in ministerial documents, should not be underestimated. Equally, we are very aware of areas that need ongoing work to reflect the principle, including assessment tools and court reports. Given the recognition in this chapter of political considerations in the formulation of Child first, we have also been conscious all along that the politics can change quickly with events and the election cycle; the political robustness of Child First's framing will be tested further.

This chapter has demonstrated the potential for a 'textual reflexivity' methodology to be used by actors themselves at the policy-level for understanding their discourse framing, and we call for its further development in the policy-academia nexus. Within the wider call for more reflexivity in policymaking (Annison, 2017), textual reflexivity has allowed us to move beyond just reflection for self-evaluation (Schippers & Rus, 2021), to allow better appreciation of the relative power of research evidence against concerns of different stakeholders. Furthermore, the insight that reflexivity can bring can itself be used to further engagement with stakeholders; in relation to Child First, these insights gained have been shared and at both internal and external events to help stakeholders understand decisions, while perhaps reassuring them how their interests helped shape our thinking even before consultation. Overall, by applying textual reflexivity to policymaking context, we contend that we have answered the call from policy researchers to 'grow a methodology' that is able to understand the origins of [youth justice] policy-level rhetoric, recognising the premise and tensions in formulation and presentation, and to ensure that we no longer 'remain puzzled' by them or their apparent contradictions (Fergusson, 2007: 16–17).

For youth justice specifically and policy science more generally, this chapter contributed a clearer understanding of the process of narrative or discourse framing in drawing up policy-level proposals, in particular how wording is chosen to convey those messages from research including a critical discourse in order to be acceptable and useful to stakeholders. Importantly, it has revealed how, while the way that Child First was always the dominant 'storyline' (Annison, 2021), this process tries to navigate the various concerns of stakeholders in the initial considerations of drafting. Existing models of policy-level initiative formation, even those more recent realist ones, tend to frame the formation of policies as interactive, with active negotiation between interested parties (cf. Rubin & Phelps, 2017; Sanderson, 2009; Toulmin, 2001). While that has happened with Child First, with stakeholder challenges during presentation and consultation affecting development and presentation, the influence and interests of stakeholders on policy development was present before this stage. Their anticipated concerns play a significant part in drafting ideas and wording, both substantively and in terms of influencing discourse and presentation before they are formally involved in the process. As such, we call for a reframing of the process of policy-level formation in policy science research to include the role of such anticipation of stakeholder concerns in the developing understanding of narrative or discourse framing in policy-level development. Moreover, highlighting the role of anticipation of stakeholder concern prompts a re-evaluation and inclusion of the influence of groups who may not have obviously played a part in the policy process. Policy scientists have long argued that 'policymaking' is influenced and made by a few, with consultations and other participatory arrangements are staged performances (Hajer, 2005). However, if the concerns of interested parties are understood and already 'built in' to policy-level proposals, even if this analysis of staging during formal interaction is accurate, researchers need to reconsider whether the influence of stakeholders is greater than previously understood.

For criminology, particularly for academics and others advocating Child First or similar reforming initiatives globally, lessons should be learned from the considerations in our framing and the few specific concerns raised by stakeholders. These did not speak to the discourse dichotomies usually presented in the youth justice literature as contested; of child vs offender, or welfare vs punishment (cf. Case & Bateman, 2020; Haines & Case, 2015; Hazel, 2008). These core conceptual elements of Child First were accepted relatively unchallenged by stakeholders. Instead, concerns were focused on how implications from specific elements of the principle may affect stakeholders' own interests and agenda, including: the status of victims, the complex needs of children, the professional practice of YOT workers, the authority of custodial staff. While the dichotomies may be helpful for modelling youth justice systems or assessing policies, they appear less useful for understanding policy-level discourse and explaining individual initiative development. Current critical frameworks for youth justice require a thoroughgoing reflection on the multiplicity of agendas and concerns of those involved in policy-level formation, which in themselves may or may not be about children in the justice system per se.

References

Annison, H. (2017). Interpreting influence: Towards reflexivity in penal policymaking? In S. Armstrong, J. Blaustein, A. Henry (Eds.), *Reflexivity and criminal Justice*. Palgrave Macmillan.

Annison, H. (2021). The role of storylines in penal policy change. *Punishment & Society, 24*(3), 387–409.

Atkinson, P. A. (1990). *The ethnographic imagination: Textual constructions of reality*. Routledge.

Atkinson, P., & Whitaker, E. M. (2019). Reflexivity. In *The Sage encyclopaedia of research methods*. Sage.

Audit Commission. (1996). *Misspent youth: Young people and crime*. Audit Commission for Local Authorities and the National Health Service in England and Wales.

Avis, H. H. (2018). *Engaging the incarcerated mind: An autoethnography of an educator in a juvenile justice facility*. ProQuest Dissertations Publishing.

Bateman, T. (2011). Punishing poverty: The 'scaled approach' and youth justice practice. *The Howard Journal of Crime and Justice, 50*(2), 171–183.

Bateman, T., & Hazel, N. (2013). *Engaging young people in resettlement: Research report*. Beyond Youth Custody/Nacro.

Bateman, T., & Hazel, N. (2014). *The resettlement of girls and young women: Evidence from research*. Beyond Youth Custody/Nacro.

Becker, H. (1963). *Outsiders: Studies in the sociology of deviance*. Free Press.

Bernard, T. J., & Kurlychek, M. C. (2010). *The cycle of juvenile justice* (2nd ed.). Oxford University Press.

Blunkett, D. (2000). *Influence or Irrelevance: Can social science improve Government?* Speech to the ESRC 2 February 2000.

Bottoms, A., & Dignan, J. (2004). Youth justice in Great Britain. *Crime and Justice, 31*(1), 21–183.

Bridgman, P., & Davis, G. (2003). What use is a policy cycle? Plenty, if the aim is clear. *Australian Journal of Public Administration, 62*(3), 98–102.

Byrne, B., & Case, S. (2016). Towards a positive youth justice. *Safer Communities, 15*(2), 69–81.

Cairney, P., & Weible, C. M. (2017). The new policy sciences: Combining the cognitive science of choice, multiple theories of context, and basic and applied analysis. *Policy Sciences, 50*, 619–627.

Campoy, R. W. (2005). *Case study analysis in the classroom becoming a reflective teacher*. Sage.

Carlebach, J. (1970). *Caring for children in trouble*. Routledge and Kegan Paul.
Case, S. (2018). *Youth justice: A critical introduction*. Routledge.
Case, S., & Bateman, T. (2020). The punitive transition in youth justice: Reconstructing the child as offender. *Children and Society, 34*(6), 475–491.
Case, S., & Browning, A. (2021). *Child First justice: The research evidence-base*. Loughborough University.
Case, S., & Haines, K. (2021). Abolishing youth justice systems: Children First, offenders nowhere. *Youth Justice, 21*(1), 3–17.
Case, S., Creaney, S., Deakin, J., & Haines, K. (2015, June). Youth justice: Past, present and future. *British Journal of Community Justice*.
Case, S., Drew, J., Hampson, K., Jones, G., & Kennedy, D. (2020). Professional perspectives of youth justice policy implementation: Contextual and coalface challenges. *The Howard Journal of Crime and Justice, 59*(2), 214–232.
Commission, C. (2001). *The promotion of social inclusion*. Charity Commission.
Civil Service Learning. (2013). *Policy profession skills and knowledge framework*.
Civil Service. (2022). *Civil Service diversity and inclusion strategy: 2022 to 2025*.
Cohen-Blankshtain, G. (2008). Framing transport-environmental policy: The case of company car taxation in Israel. *Transportation Research Part D, 13*, 65–74.
Council of Europe. (2010). *Guidelines of the Committee of Ministers of the Council of Europe on Child Friendly Justice*. Council of Europe.
Crook, F. (2018, December 16). Twitter. https://twitter.com/francescrook/status/1074310593870475266
Deakin, J., Fox, C., & Matos, R. (2020). Labelled as 'risky' in an era of control: How young people experience and respond to the stigma of criminalized identities. *European Journal of Criminology, 19*(4), 653–673.
Dodge, J., & Lee, J. (2017). framing dynamics and political gridlock: The curious case of hydraulic fracturing in New York. *Journal of Environmental Policy and Planning, 19*(1), 14–34.
Drakeford, M., & Haines, K. (1998). *Young people and youth justice*. Bloomsbury Publishing.
Druckman, J. M. (2001). On the limits of framing effects: Who can frame? *The Journal of Politics, 63*, 1041–1066.
Fergusson, R. (2007). Making sense of the melting pot: Multiple discourses in youth justice policy. *Youth Justice, 7*(3), 179–194. https://doi.org/10.1177/1473225407082509
Gatti, U., Tremblay, R. E., & Vitaro, F. (2009). Iatrogenic effect of juvenile justice. *The Journal of Child Psychology and Psychiatry, 50*(8), 991–998.

Goldson, B., Cunneen, C., Russell, S., Brown, D., Baldry, E., Schwartz, M., & Briggs, D. (2021). *Youth justice and penalty in comparative context*. Routledge.

Gray, P. (2007). Youth justice, social exclusion and the demise of social justice. *The Howard Journal of Crime and Justice, 46*(4), 401–416.

Hagell, A., & Hazel, N. (2001). Macro and micro patterns in the development of secure custodial institutions for serious and persistent young offenders in England and Wales. *Youth Justice, 1*(1), 3–16.

Haines, K., & Case, S. (2008). The rhetoric and reality of the 'Risk Factor Prevention Paradigm' approach to preventing and reducing youth offending. *Youth Justice, 8*(1), 15–20.

Haines, K., & Case, S. (2012). Is the scaled approach a failed approach? *Youth Justice, 12*(3), 212–228.

Haines, K., & Case, S. (2015). *Positive youth justice: Children First, Offenders Second*. Policy Press.

Hajer, M. A. (2005). Setting the stage: A dramaturgy of policy deliberation. *Administration & Society, 36*(6), 624–647.

Hales, H, Warner, L, Smith, J., & Bartlett, A. (2018). *Census of young people in secure settings on 14 September 2016: Characteristics, needs and pathways of care*. Central and North West London NHS Foundation Trust/St. Georges University of London.

Hallsworth, M., Parker, S., & Rutter, J. (2011). *Policy making in the real world: Evidence and analysis*. Institute for Government.

Hardy, C., Palmer, I., & Phillips, N. (2000). Discourse as a strategic resource. *Human Relations, 59*(9), 1227–1248.

Harris, M., & Goodfellow, P. (2021). *The youth justice system's response to the COVID-19 pandemic*. Association for Youth Justice.

Hazel, N. (1996). Elicitation techniques with young people. *Social Research Update* no.12.

Hazel, N. (2008). *Cross-national comparison of youth justice*. Youth Justice Board.

Hazel, N. (2020, November 30). *Child First concepts*. Paper to the Child First YJB Live event for the youth justice sector.

Hazel, N., & Bateman, T. (2020). Supporting children's resettlement ('reentry') after custody: Beyond the risk paradigm *Youth Justice, 21*(1), 71–89.

Hazel, N., & Clark, A. (2013). Negotiating doorstep access: Door-to-door survey researchers' strategies to obtain participation. *International Journal of Social Research Methodology, 16*(4), 307–321.

Hazel, N., with Goodfellow, P., Liddle, M., Bateman, T., & Pitts, J. (2017). *'Now all I care about is my future'. Supporting the shift: framework for the resettlement of young people leaving custody.* Nacro.

Hazel, N., Byrne, B., & Gray, S. (2018). *Proposed YJB definition of "Children First, Offenders Second".* Information paper to the YJB Board meeting, 6 June 2018.

Hazel, N., Drummond, C., Welsh, M., & Joseph, K. (2020). *Using an identity lens: Constructive working with children in the criminal justice system.* Nacro.

Hill, M., & Hupe, P. (2002). *Implementing public policy.* Sage.

HM Inspectorate of Probation. (2022). *2021 Annual report: Inspections of youth offending services.* HM Inspectorate of Probation.

HM Inspectorate of Probation/YJB. (2022). *Joint statement from HM Inspectorate of Probation and the Youth Justice Board.*

HMPPS. (2022). *Early and late release for detention and training orders policy.* MOJ/HM Prison and Probation Service.

Hogwood, B. W., & Gunn, L. A. (1984). *Policy analysis for the real world.* Oxford University Press.

Hope, T., & Walters, R. (2008). *Critical thinking about the uses of research.* Centre for Crime and Justice Studies.

Justice Select Committee. (2020, June 2). *Formal meeting (oral evidence session): Children and young people in custody.*

Kingdon, J. W. (1995). *Agendas, alternatives, and public policies.* Little Brown.

Lofaro, R. J., & Miller, H. T. (2021). Narrative politics in policy discourse: The debate over safe injection sites in Philadelphia, Pennsylvania. *Contemporary Drug Problems, 48*(1), 75–95.

Maruna, S., & Farrall, S. (2004). Desistance from crime: A theoretical reformulation. *Kolner Zeitschrift fur Soziologie und Sozialpsychologie, 43,* 171–194.

McAra L (2018, November 27). *Child friendly youth justice.* Presentation to the Youth Justice Convention. Birmingham.

McAra, L. (2017). Child-friendly youth justice? In T. Bateman, P. Goodfellow, R. Little, & A. Wigzell (Eds.), *Child-friendly youth justice?* NAYJ.

McAra, L., & McVie, S. (2007). Youth justice? The impact of agency contact on desistance from offending. *European Journal of Criminology, 4*(3), 315–345.

McAra, L., & McVie, S. (2015). The case for diversion and minimum necessary intervention. In B. Goldson & J. Muncie (Eds.), *Youth crime and justice* (pp. 119–135). Sage.

Miller, H. T. (2020a). Policy narratives: The perlocutionary agents of political discourse. *Critical Policy Studies, 14*(4), 488–501.

Miller, H. T. (2020b). *Narrative politics in public policy: Legalizing cannabis.* Palgrave Macmillan.

MoJ. (2016). *The government response to Charlie Taylor's review of the youth justice system.* Ministry of Justice.

MoJ, YJB. (2019). *Standards for children in the youth justice system 2019.* Ministry of Justice.

MoJ,. (2020). *Code of practice for victims of crime in England and Wales.* Ministry of Justice.

MOPAC. (2021). *Brave space knife crime toolkit.* London Mayors Office.

Naughton, M. (2005). 'Evidence-based policy' and the government of the criminal justice system—Only if the evidence fits! *Critical Social Policy, 25*(1), 47–69.

Orpwood, G. W. F. (1985). The reflective deliberator: A case study of curriculum policymaking. *Journal of Curriculum Studies, 17*(3), 293–304.

Otieno, J. O. (2019). The public policy process: *A conceptual framework for understanding policy processes and opportunities for influencing policy outcomes.* Leibniz Information Centre for Economics.

Pal, L. A. (2005). Case study method and policy analysis. In I. Geva-May (Ed.), *Thinking like a policy analyst.* Palgrave Macmillan.

Pawson, R. (2006). *Evidence based policy making: A realist perspective.* Sage.

Phillips, M. (2008, February 19). Children's rights? What about the rights of those who live in fear of young thugs? *MailOnline Comment column.*

Pollitt, C. (2003). *The essential public manager.* McGraw Hill.

Prior, D., Farrow, K., Hughes, N., Kelly, G., Manders, G., White, S., & Wilkinson, B. (2011). *Maturity, young adults and criminal justice: A literature review.* University of Birmingham

Rubin, A., & Phelps, M. S. (2017). Fracturing the penal state: State actors and the role of conflict in penal change. *Theoretical Criminology, 21*(4), 422–440.

Sabatier, P. A. (1998). The advocacy coalition framework: Revisions and relevance for Europe. *Journal of Public Policy, 5,* 98–130.

Sanderson, I. (2009). intelligent policy making for a complex world: Pragmatism, evidence and learning. *Political Studies, 57*(4), 699–719.

Schippers, M. C., & Rus, D. C. (2021). Optimizing decision-making processes in times of COVID-19: Using reflexivity to counteract information-processing failures. *Frontiers in Psychology, 12,* 650525.

Smith, R. (2017). *Diversion in youth justice: What can we learn from historical and contemporary practices.* Routledge.

Smith, R., & Gray, P. (2018). The changing shape of youth justice: Models of practice. *Criminology & Criminal Justice, 19*(5), 554–571.

Souhami, A. (2014). Creating the Youth Justice Board: Policy and policy making in English and Welsh youth justice. *Criminology & Criminal Justice, 15*(2), 152–168.

Souhami, A., Earle, R., Solomon, E., Case, S., & Haines, K. (2012). Was the reprieve of the Youth Justice Board a good thing? *Criminal Justice Matters, 88*(1), 38–40.

Stephenson, M., Giller, H., & Brown, S. (2011). *Effective practice in youth justice*. Routledge.

Taylor, C. (2016a). *Review of the youth justice system in England and Wales*. Ministry of Justice.

Taylor, C. (2016b). *Review of the youth justice system: An interim report of emerging findings*. Ministry of Justice.

Taylor, C. (2020). *Independent review of the use of pain-inducing techniques in the youth secure estate*. Ministry of Justice.

Taylor, S. (2016c, November). Evidence based policy? The re-medicalization of cannabis and the role of expert committees in the UK, 1972–1982. *International Journal of Drug Policy, 37*, 129–135.

Toulmin, S. (2001). *Return to reason*. Harvard University Press.

Truss, E. (2017). *Youth justice statement*. House of Commons. 24 February 2017, UIN HCWS502

Welsh Assembly Government. (2004). *All Wales youth offending strategy*. Welsh Assembly Government/Youth Justice Board.

Welsh Government/YJB. (2014). *Children and young people first*. Welsh Government/YJB.

Wigzell, A. (2021). *Explaining desistance: Looking forward, not backwards*. NAYJ.

YJB. (2005). *Risk and protective factors*. Youth Justice Board.

YJB. (2009). *Youth justice: The scaled approach*. Youth Justice Board.

YJB. (2018a). *Minutes of the 6 June 2018a Board meeting*. Youth Justice Board

YJB. (2018b). *How to make resettlement constructive*. Youth Justice Board.

YJB. (2018c). *Draft standards for children in youth justice services 2019*. Youth Justice Board.

YJB. (2018d). *Standards for children in the youth justice system 2019: Consultation response*. Youth Justice Board.

YJB. (2019a). *Journey of the child presentation*. Youth Justice Board.

YJB. (2019b). *Youth Justice Board for England and Wales Strategic Plan 2019b–2022*. Youth Justice Board.

YJB. (2020). *Enhanced case management and Child First principles*. Youth Justice Board.
YJB. (2021). *Youth Justice Board for England and Wales Strategic Plan 2021–2024*. Youth Justice Board.
Youth Custody Service. (2022). *Early and late release for detention and training orders policy framework*. Ministry of Justice.

8

Child First in the Criminal Courts

Kathryn Hollingsworth

Introduction

The chapter proceeds in four sections, each of which is linked explicitly to a Child First tenet. Section one ("Seeing Children as Children: The Fora for Determining Children's Criminal Responsibility") examines the compatibility of the court structures with tenet one (CF1) in relation to the determination of criminal responsibility; section two ("Developing Children's Pro-Social Identities for Positive Outcomes: Sentencing") focuses on tenet two (CF2), drawing on the example of sentencing practice; section three ("Collaboration with Children: Children's Participation in Trial Proceedings") looks at children's participation in trials

---

Kathryn Hollingsworth: My thanks to Kate Aubrey-Johnson for comments on an earlier draft. All errors remain my own.

K. Hollingsworth (✉)
Newcastle University, Newcastle Upon Tyne, UK
e-mail: Kathryn.hollingsworth@newcastle.ac.uk

© The Author(s), under exclusive license to Springer Nature Switzerland AG 2023
S. Case and N. Hazel (eds.), *Child First*,
https://doi.org/10.1007/978-3-031-19272-2_8

as a vehicle for exploring tenet three (CF3); and finally, section four ("Promoting Diversion and Reducing Stigma: Bail and Remand Decision-Making") considers bail and remand decision-making to examine tenet four (CF4). The very fact that children are tried and sentenced to punishment in the criminal courts is counter to the fundamental principles of Child First. In their design and in their practice, the criminal courts in England and Wales are austere and formal places that children experience as stigmatising, alienating, frightening, and confusing, and which are almost as likely than not to result in further offending. In the criminal courts therefore, children continue to be first and foremost treated as 'defendants' and their status as child is secondary at best. This chapter therefore explores the barriers, challenges, progress, and possibilities in adopting the four tenets of Child First within the existing system for holding children criminally responsible. It argues that progress towards Child First within the criminal courts has been more fragmented and more stilted than elsewhere in the Youth Justice System because of the political, constitutional and legal constraints within which the courts operate. But despite this there has been some progress; driven by a strengthening commitment to children's rights (often because of lobbying and campaigning by committed activists and professionals) and a willingness by some practitioners to use their discretion as far as possible in ways that further Child First. Although the chapter is broadly organised to map on to each of the tenets, all four have relevance to a greater or lesser degree in each of the examples used. I conclude the chapter by suggesting that progress towards Child First within the criminal courts has been more fragmented and more stilted than elsewhere in the Youth Justice System (YJS) because of the political, constitutional and legal constraints within which the courts operate. But despite this there has been some progress; driven by a strengthening commitment to children's rights (often because of lobbying and campaigning by committed activists and professionals) and a willingness by some practitioners to use their discretion as far as possible in ways that further Child First.

Tenet 1: Seeing Children as Children: The Fora for Determining Children's Criminal Responsibility

Most children charged with criminal offences in England and Wales are tried and sentenced in the youth court; a specialist branch of the magistrates' court that deals only with children's offending and which, in contrast to some other jurisdictions, is entirely separate from the courts that oversee care and protection. Protections and adaptations designed into the youth court—including more inclusive and informal courtroom processes (e.g. using children's first names), attire (e.g. no wigs or gowns), and layout (e.g. seating at the same level); the statutory requirement for parental/carer attendance (at least for under 16-year-olds); the exclusion of the public and the presumptive application of reporting restrictions— are intended to recognise and protect the particular needs, capacities and rights of children, prioritise their best interests by reducing intimidation and anxiety, facilitate participation and reduce stigma. Domestic courts and the European Court of Human Rights (ECtHR) have endorsed the youth court as a specialist tribunal capable of compatibility with children's rights (specifically the right to a fair trial: see *R (TP) v West London Youth Court* and *SC v UK*, respectively). Given the origin of Child First within children's rights as well as the child-specific jurisdiction of the youth court, it might be assumed that criminal proceedings in England and Wales also align with Child First, particularly CF1. However, as intimated in the introduction, the youth court provides only a façade of compatibility behind which lie practical shortcomings (often resource-related) and a legal and conceptual framework that places the court system fundamentally at odds with the first tenet of Child First. Moreover, a significant number of children continue to be tried and sentenced in the adult Crown Court (explored in more detail below).

Recognising Children's Particular Needs, Capacities, Rights and Potential: The Need for Child-Focused, Child-Specialist Legal Professionals

A key shortcoming of the criminal courts is that they are often unaware of the child's particular needs (which can include mental and physical health, care and protection, and educational needs) due both to the structure of the legal system, including the siloed nature of the criminal and family courts, and to resource and operational constraints which limit the dialogue between the courts and other service-providers, including children's services (Centre for Justice Innovation, 2020). Improving information flow has, therefore, been a key factor in recent calls to reform the youth court to increase its powers to compel local authorities to investigate whether children are at significant risk of serious harm (Michael Sieff Foundation, 2000), to merge the family and youth courts (Carlile, 2014; Stanley, 2021) and to enhance problem-solving practice (Bateman, 2021; Centre for Justice Innovation, 2020).

Of particular importance to the court's role in determining criminal responsibility (the focus of this section) is the recognition and understanding of the child's speech, language and communication needs (SLCN) because this goes to the child's capacity to participate in proceedings, and thus the realisation of the right to a fair trial and perceptions of procedural justice (Tyler, 2003; Wigzell et al., 2015). The communication abilities children need in court are extensive and include understanding, processing and retaining information; paying attention for long periods of time; understanding courtroom roles, proceedings and concepts; giving evidence using coherent narrative; challenging witnesses; recognising non-verbal cues; and instructing a lawyer (Grisso & Schwatz, 2000; Hopkins et al., 2018). Yet these abilities are beyond most children accused of offending due to their still-developing capacities and the high prevalence—estimated to be between 60 and 90%—of additional SLCN amongst this cohort (Anderson et al., 2016; Bryan et al., 2015; Sowerbutts et al., 2021), particularly amongst Black children (HM Inspectorate of Probation, 2021). Reduced communicative capacities are also compounded by the stress of the courtroom (Judicial College, 2021b, Appendix II): *'I was nervous. Really nervous.*

I was just looking at everyone and it was just quiet, and then there was talking, and then it was quiet, talking and then quiet and then whispering to each other. I just didn't understand it' (Interview with 14-year-old boy, on file with author).

Despite this overwhelming evidence of unmet communication needs, very little specialist or child-focused support is available to child defendants. In court, and in contrast to police detention, child defendants have no right to an appropriate adult to assist with communication or to help them understand their rights and nor do they have the same statutory entitlement to an intermediary (a communication specialist) as other child witnesses (Youth Justice and Criminal Evidence Act 1999, Part II). The court can use its inherent powers to appoint an intermediary (Criminal Practice Direction 1 (Crim PD 1); 3F.24) but this occurs rarely in practice because of an historically restrictive approach taken by the Court of Appeal, reflected in Practice Directions and Criminal Procedure Rules, and resource constraints (Centre for Justice Innovation, 2020; Lambe & Hollingsworth, 2021). Although the highly restrictive approach to intermediary provision is loosening (see *R (TI) v Bromley Youth Court* (2021)), research suggests that 92% of children with SLCN are undiagnosed before entering the YJS (Bryan et al., 2007, 2015). The availability of an intermediary, therefore, depends on pre-court SLC screening/identification of need by Youth Offending Services (YOS) and/or lawyers and judges who understand the communication needs of child defendants and when a child needs, and is entitled to, an intermediary. Legal professionals must also know how to adapt their own communication to the child's particular abilities. Children's communication needs, therefore, provides one, very important, reason why specially trained and accredited lawyers and judges are also a necessary component of CF1 (see also Council of Europe, 2010: 27; UN Committee on the Rights of the Child, 2019, para 39).

However, until 2017, there was no requirement at all for lawyers representing child defendants to be trained or accredited (Wigzell et al., 2015). Now, advocates regulated by the Bar Standards Board (BSB) who practise in youth court must declare that they meet a set of competences. The new self-accreditation scheme has both symbolic and practical importance, helping to raise the low status of youth court work (Wigzell et al., 2015) and, hopefully, the quality of advocacy children receive. However, the scheme is not comprehensive: it is not equivalent to the external accreditation that applies to those practising in children's law proceedings; it does not mandate training; it is unclear how well it is monitored; it applies only to those regulated by the BSB, thus precluding solicitors; and it does not extend to Crown Court (Centre for Justice Innovation, 2020: 17). Although only approximately 600 children per year (5%) appear is Crown Court (YJB/Ministry of Justice, 2022), the consequences for the child are most serious and adaptations necessary to facilitate the child's participation (since the default adaptations of the youth court do not apply) are unlikely to be made without a child-specialist lawyer to request them (Lambe & Hollingsworth, 2021; *R v Grant Murray and others*). Furthermore, the benefits of the scheme are undermined by legal aid fees, the level of which do not reflect the fact that youth court deals with more serious cases than the adult magistrates' court, that the law relating to children is complex and specialist, and that youth court lawyers need additional time to build rapport and understand children's specific needs (Bellamy, 2021, ch 11). In short, the legal aid scheme fails to recompense lawyers for the time and skill level necessary to represent children effectively and in ways compatible with CF1 (A'Court & Arthur, 2020). As such, there is little incentive for lawyers to specialise in child defence work. A more comprehensive scheme of external accreditation, with mandated training, which extends to all criminal defence advocates, and which attracts appropriate remuneration, is, therefore, needed.

Youth court magistrates and district judges must have two years prior experience in the adult magistrates' court and undertake specialist training before they are authorised to sit in youth court (Children and Young Persons Act 1933 (C&YPA 1933), section 45). However, they also sit in adult magistrates' courts (and increasingly so, due to reduction in youth court sittings) diminishing their youth court expertise and increasing the risk that they will 'bring adult-oriented assumptions with them when dealing with children' (Bateman, 2021: 12). A more child-specific bench would facilitate a holistic understanding of children and their backgrounds and needs (including communication needs) and could be achieved by removing the requirement for prior experience in the adult court, prohibiting magistrates from simultaneously sitting in the adult and youth court, or by a closer alignment with family magistrates through joint training or sitting in both jurisdictions (Bateman, 2021). For Crown Court judges, no mandatory training or experience is needed to sit in cases involving children, although some (optional) child rights-focused training (albeit within larger training modules where the focus is adult defendants) and resources are now available (see especially *Youth Defendants in the Crown Court Bench Book*). In the absence of specialist judges, the reduced numbers of children in the Criminal Justice System (CJS) mean a Crown Court judge is (on average) likely to encounter a child defendant only once or twice a year; making the need for a robust system of training and accreditation for *all* advocates representing children, whether in youth or Crown Court, even more vital.

Recognising the Child's Rights and Potential in Child-Focused Criminal Proceedings: The Problem with Delays

Delays in criminal proceedings have a serious detrimental impact on the child's rights (Art 40(2)(b)(iii) UNCRC and UN Committee on the Rights of the Child, 2019, paras 65 and 66) and potential, yet over the past decade delays have increased 'exponentially' (Centre for Justice Innovation, 2020: 2) with some children waiting years to be brought to court (AYJ, 2022). This condemns children to a 'holding room' (Hollingsworth & Stalford, 2022) of protracted uncertainty; negatively impacting on mental health, increasing exposure to criminogenic environments (new or on-going, particularly for those trying to escape criminal exploitation) and affecting job prospects, training and education. For children who turn 18 before the plea hearing, the consequences are even greater because they will be tried and sentenced as an adult (Just for Kids Law, 2020).

These unacceptably long delays are the combined result of pre- and post-charge processes, and the compounding impact of the COVID-19 pandemic (AYJ, 2022). Legislative changes which introduced a presumption of release without bail removed the time limits and scrutiny of bail hearings, and thus reduced the pressure on the police and CPS to bring prompt charges (Policing and Crime Act 2017), with some children 'released under investigation' and waiting years to be charged. Reduced court sitting days and closures also contribute to delays, and were considerably worsened due to the pandemic restrictions, with the time between charge, court and outcome increasing 50% between March 2020 and March 2021, and 54% between March 2021 and March 2022 (AYJ, 2022: 3; NAO, 2021). As well as creating a state of uncertainty for children, delays compound efficiency-driven measures and increase further the pressure to expedite cases. This means courts may be less likely to adjourn to receive reports about the child or (in Crown Court) to make adaptations that slow proceedings down. Clear legislative limits—like those for bail—are needed to mitigate the increased harm that delays cause to children brought to court.

Recognising Children's Rights: Tensions and Compromise

The absence of juries in youth court exemplifies a tension inherent in holding children criminally responsible in an ostensibly 'adult' system whilst making procedural adaptations to recognise their status as child; it can have a consequential impact on rights that are regarded as integral in a penal system. Unlike adults, children cannot elect trial by jury and more serious and evidentially complex cases are retained in the (youth) magistrates' court. Given that juries are less racially biased (Lammy, 2017; Thomas, 2017) and appear more likely to acquit (Crown Prosecution Service Annual Report and Accounts, 2021, charts 3 and 7)[1]—in part because there is a clear separation between the fact-finder (jury) and the judge who decides matters of law, including the admissibility of evidence—there are clear disadvantages for some children of being in

---

[1] Nb the data is not disaggregated by age/youth court.

the youth court. This exemplifies a fundamental tension in holding children criminally responsible in an essentially punitive system that has only a veneer of 'child-friendliness': it fails to adequately protect their status and rights as child; *and* fails to adequately protect their status and rights as defendant (Hollingsworth, 2020b).

Prioritising Best Interests

This halfway-house approach to children in criminal proceedings is also reflected in the status accorded to best interests in the criminal courts. In contrast to the prioritisation of best interests demanded by CF1 and the underpinning international children's rights standards, criminal courts must only 'have regard' to the child's 'welfare' (Children and Young Person's Act 1933, s 44(1)). Although closely related, the concepts of welfare and best interests are not identical. A child's best interests is—or should be—defined to capture holistically *all* the child's rights (Stalford & Hollingsworth, 2017, ch 3). 'Welfare' is vaguer, subjective, opaque and increases the likelihood of paternalistic decision-making. In contrast to family law (see Children Act, s 1(3)), there is no legislative definition of welfare in criminal proceedings (except for sentencing, see Sentencing Council (2017) discussed below) (Aubrey-Johnson et al., 2019). Its meaning and significance are, therefore, left to judicial discretion. Although the loose meaning is sometimes used in ways advantageous to children (see, e.g., *R (B) v Brent Youth Court* where the High Court interpreted the 'welfare duty' as allowing repeat bail applications in effect extending the statutory entitlement for children), an overly-narrow understanding can be adopted including in terms of its temporal reach; for example, equating only to the child's well-being during proceedings rather than extending backwards (to take account of the child's experiences in determining guilt) or forwards to any future-focused obligation (e.g. to protect beyond 18 the child's anonymity, *R (JC) v The Central Criminal Court*)). The lesser weight accorded to the child's welfare (to 'have regard', rather than to be a primary or priority consideration) reflects the (potentially) conflicting interests at stake within criminal justice: judges must balance the interests of the defendant with the interests of justice and the broader public interest. Further, if 'welfare' was prioritised, it might justify preventative detention or disproportionate responses to the offending, contrary to a child's broader rights. Replacing 'welfare' with best interests would mitigate some of that potential harm (because it is more closely associated with a rights-based approach), but without a legislative mandate prioritising the child's welfare it is, in any event, currently legally and constitutionally very difficult for the courts to do so.

Seeing Children as Children: Conceptual Limitations in Determining Criminal Responsibility

The two preceding sections point towards a fundamental conceptual problem with holding children criminal responsible in the current system. By and large, the criminal law constructs the legal subject (the defendant) as a rational, self-sufficient, atomistic and abstract agent—one who has no gender, ethnicity, class or crucially, age—who 'chooses' to offend and is held criminally responsible for that choice (Hollingsworth, 2013, 2020b). Thus, when holding people criminal responsible (as distinct from determining the *level* of culpability when sentencing), there are—bar a few specific exceptions—no conceptual differences between the adult and child legal subject. In this sense, the entire criminal system is premised upon *not* 'seeing' children *as* children. Instead, once over the minimum age of criminal responsibility (10 years), age and developmentally-related capacities (e.g. understanding of right and wrong; the ability to exercise self-control, resist peer-pressure or adult influence; to deal with trauma) are largely irrelevant to criminal responsibility *unless* capacities are so diminished that it is an abuse of process for the trial to proceed; *or* it falls within a specific defence where age is a relevant characteristic (e.g. under section 45 of the Modern Slavery Act 2015). Within this context, the statutory removal of the presumption of *doli incapax* in 1998 (which for over 500 years had required the prosecution to prove, in addition to the elements of the offence, that a child aged under 14 understood the difference between right and wrong) marked a clear regression in recognising (some) children's particular capacities and a step away from a developmentally informed system of criminal justice.

The problem of the abstract legal subject is also accompanied by narrow time-frames in criminal law, meaning that only events immediately surrounding the offence are deemed legally relevant to criminal responsibility (Chowdhury, 2020; Farmer, 2010). This means the law takes little account of life-shaping—and choice-limiting—background experiences, and their impact on the child's behaviour. Given the evidence of the correlation between childhood criminal offending and experiences of trauma, school exclusion, care-status, precarious immigration status, bereavement, neglect, poverty and so on, the criminal law is again, conceptually, ill-placed to respond to children *as* children when determining guilt. This is particularly problematic given the intersection of such life-shaping—and often criminogenic—experiences with gender and ethnicity; it means Black boys are especially likely to be disadvantaged by the law's failure to take account of child-specific contexts and experiences.

Therefore, if some children are to continue to be held criminally responsible in courts, then to be better compatible with CF1 changes are needed to how we understand who is responsible and for what, to ensure that a more contextual or relational (Hollingsworth, 2020b) approach is taken to children as legal subjects. This could be achieved through legislative or jurisprudential extensions to the circumstances in which 'age' is relevant to criminal responsibility, as with the shift to the subjective approach to the mens rea of 'recklessness' in *R v G* or the Modern Slavery Act defence, and/or through a 'developmental immaturity' defence (Wake et al., 2021). However, the Police, Crime, Sentencing and Courts Act 2020 and recent, regressive, decisions on children's rights in the Supreme Court (e.g. *R (AB) v Secretary of State for Justice*) suggest there is neither the political will nor the judicial appetite necessary to further CF1 in this way.

Given the conceptual basis underpinning the determination of children's criminal responsibility is fundamentally at odds with CF1, it is no surprise that court proceedings struggle to adequately take a child-focused approach. Various proposals for structural reform to the criminal courts have been made in recent years that could bring better alignment with CF1, including removing children from the Crown Court (although to protect adequately children's rights, jury trial in youth court would need to be available and/or merging the youth courts with the family courts (Stanley, 2021)). This latter proposal would bring together the care and criminal jurisdictions and ostensibly allow the courts to understand and respond better to children's needs (as noted above). However, as Bateman (2021) argues, lessons from overseas and from the history of the Juvenile court in England and Wales suggest that unifying the courts would not 'in and of itself, engender more positive outcomes for children in conflict with the law' because a punitive ethos, and different disposals, would remain. It would also not solve the problems of children's participation (CF3) since the family courts are no panacea in this regard. Instead, much more radical reform, one that takes children outside the criminal justice system altogether, would be needed to truly fulfil the aims of CF1 (Case & Haines, 2021).

Tenet 2: Developing Children's Pro-Social Identities for Positive Outcomes: Sentencing

As a minimum, and notwithstanding that *any* criminal sanction may be antithetical to its aims, Child First compatible sentencing must be distinct from adult sentencing, prioritise best interests (CF1), and—the focus in this section—develop children's pro-social identities for positive outcomes (CF2). These tenets of Child First have strong support from the UK's highest court:

> . . . an important aim, some would think the most important aim, of any sentence imposed should be to promote the process of maturation, the development of a sense of responsibility, and the growth of a healthy adult personality and identity. That is no doubt why the Children and Young Persons Act 1933, in section 44(1), required, and still requires, every court dealing with any juvenile offender to have regard to his or her welfare. . . (*R (Smith) v Secretary of State for the Home Department* para 25, per Lady Hale).

However, the ability of sentencing courts to meet these welfare-based obligations is constrained by the legislative framework (what sentences are available and when), binding Appellate Court decisions, and sentencing guidelines. Some sentences for children are more clearly distinct from the regime for adults, including child-specific elements focused on restorative approaches or rehabilitation (e.g. attendance at a youth offender panel as part of the Referral Order or the 'training' element of a Detention and Training Order); or even, though unusually, care (e.g. intensive fostering as an alternative to custody). Other sentences differ little from their adult equivalent, especially for serious offending. Although children are not 'imprisoned', they can nonetheless be detained for life or given an extended sentence where dangerousness conditions are met. By way of example of the difficulties facing judges within sentence *choice,* this section examines the mandatory sentence for children convicted of murder, Detention During Her Majesty's Pleasure (DDHMP).

Detention During Her Majesty's Pleasure

A life sentence for children convicted of murder is mandatory and conflicts with Child First on multiple levels: it removes the possibility of an individualised sentence that takes account of the child's best interest (CF1); the stigma of childhood offending is life-long (CF4); and the child remains on licence for life and is never legally rehabilitated (CF2). Within this context, it is impossible to see this sentence as anything other than backward-looking and contrary to CF2.

Despite this, DDHMP *is* different from the mandatory adult life sentence. First, when the court fixes the minimum custodial term, the starting point is lower than for adults and it must not be applied 'mechanistically without regard to the age and maturity of the child' (*R v Peters; R v Kyries Davies*). Instead, the court must adopt an individualistic approach which considers the child's maturity (including impulsiveness, inexperience, emotional development, negative influences) (*R v DM and SC*) and the least possible minimum term 'congruent with their welfare and rehabilitation' (*R v CN, FN, DW*, para 32). Second, until April

2022, the sentence included a 'built-in' review period of the minimum term (Emanuel et al., 2021: 205). The importance of the review was explained by Lord Bingham in *R (Smith)*:

> [t]he requirement to impose a sentence of [DDHMP] is based not on the age of the offender when sentenced but on the age of the offender when the murder was committed, and it reflects the humane principle that an offender deemed by statute to be not fully mature when committing his crime should not be punished as if he were. As he grows into maturity a more reliable judgment may be made, perhaps of what punishment he deserves and certainly of what period of detention will best promote his rehabilitation. It would in many cases subvert the object of this unique sentence if the duty of continuing review were held to terminate when the child or young person comes legally of age.

However, the Police, Crime, Sentencing and Courts Act 2022 has eschewed this principled approach in three ways. First, it increases the starting points of the minimum terms for older children (those aged 15 or 16, or 17, see section 126), bringing them progressively closer to the adult minimum term and misusing the increasing recognition of developmental maturity (Brewster, 2020) by *eroding* protections for older children rather than *extending* protections to young adults. Second, it confines review to those who were under 18 *when sentenced* rather than, as now, under 18 at *the time of the offence*. This will significantly impact older teenagers given the delays outlined above. Third, second or subsequent applications for review can only be made whilst the child is under 18, counter to the welfare and science-based evidence of children's continuing capacity to change and develop their pro-social identities into adulthood (CF2) (see section 127). It is, therefore, clear that even a sentence that is already counter to Child First is vulnerable to further erosion in a hostile political environment.

Using Discretionary Spaces for Future-Focused Sentencing: Judicial Communication of Sentencing Remarks

One of the most positive developments in sentencing children was the publication in 2017 of the Sentencing Council's second version of the *Overarching Principles for Sentencing Children and Young Persons*. The guideline, which in law must be taken into account, requires (inter alia) individualistic sentencing (para 1.2); a focus on rehabilitation and reintegration (not punishment) and consideration of the effect of the sentence on the child (para 1.2); the avoidance of 'criminalisation' and stigma (paras 1.3 and 1.6); the adoption of a developmentally-focused approach (para 1.5, 1.7, 1.8); a consideration of welfare factors (that are extensively defined); and that account be taken of the reasons why Black and other minoritised children and care-experienced children are over-represented. It is, therefore, closely aligned with children's rights, maximising the discretionary space available to sentencing judges to adopt Child First even within the current legislative framework (see Sentencing Act 2020) and statutory purposes of sentencing (which are less compatible and include general deterrence: Sentencing Council, 2017, para 1.10). However, of the few published Crown Court sentencing remarks, only about 50% make explicit reference to the Guideline and of those most do not articulate how it was used. Further, a survey by the Sentencing Council found that only half of lay magistrates said they usually or always referred to them (compared to 9 out of 10 district judges) and quantitative analysis showed the publication of the Guideline had not impacted on average sentencing severity nor addressed worse sentencing outcomes for Black and Asian boys (Sentencing Council, 2020).

However, the Guideline (if followed) is useful not only to guide the choice of sentence, but also how it is communicated (Hollingsworth, 2020a). For children, judges are the 'personification' of the legal system (Buss, 2015: 316) who have the power to 'make or break the rest of your life' (interview with young person, on file with author). How judges communicate the sentence to the child—the language, tone, the explicit and implicit messaging—can have a transformative effect (Stalford & Hollingsworth, 2020), particularly where there is a focus on *clarity* of communication (so children understand the sentence, its implications for them, and what they need to do to comply) and on *relational* communication. Preliminary findings of a small study with justice-experienced children (Hollingsworth, 2020a) suggest that sentencing remarks that convey empathy, confer recognition (e.g. by centring the child's experiences within the remarks and demonstrably taking account of various reports and the child's own views), avoid stigmatisation and convey hope and trust in the child to desist from offending, can have a profound effect on how the child feels about themselves, their future (especially where they feel empowered and supported to change) and the justice system (e.g. by breaking down hierarchies and dis-spelling concerns about non-professional or biased decision-making by judges). Sentencing is a moment in time for children, but the experience stays with them for much longer. What the judge says, and how they say it, therefore has the potential to positively shape future outcomes, as expressed by 16-year-old Grace:

> He read like he actually cared and . . . you could see he was understanding a bit more. I actually started feeling good . . . I was like, finally somebody is starting to understand why certain things happened . . . Finally it was a, it was a feeling of relief.
>
> The thing that made me want to actually prove myself was the judge because I felt like he didn't have to give me that chance. . . he's understood me a little bit, you know, he's got to know me better so . . .I just feel like it's so important to have that level of trust with people. Even though I might not see this man again . . . he gave me a chance already. . .it allows you to be a better person

Part II of the Crown Court Compendium (which provides sentencing guidance to Crown Court judges) was amended in 2021 to capture the principles above and aims to improve judicial understanding of the communication difficulties facing children (Judicial College, 2021b). The guidance also goes some way to helping judges meet their legal obligation to deliver their sentence 'in ordinary language' and in a way the *child* defendant can understand by including an Appendix on communicating with children and example sentencing remarks *for* children. This approach to sentence delivery may also impact substantive sentence outcomes as well, because it demands a shift in judicial perspective, and requires that judges demonstrably take account of all relevant information (Stalford & Hollingsworth, 2020). It is difficult to know whether and how well these principles are applied in practice (although anecdotal evidence shows some impact). Nonetheless, seen alongside initiatives such as post-sentence judicial monitoring (a central element of problem-solving practice adopted in a small number of youth courts (Bowen & Whitehead, 2016; Centre for Justice Innovation, 2020)), new approaches to sentence delivery help to demonstrate that even within a restrictive legislative framework and a negative political environment, judges can exercise their own discretionary powers in ways that promote positive, future-focused outcomes for the child.

Tenet 3: Collaboration with Children: Children's Participation in Trial Proceedings

In one regard, collaboration is built into the courtroom experience via the child's relationship with their lawyer; child defendants are deemed competent to instruct their lawyer from the age of 10. In practice, how effectively children can instruct—and thus 'collaborate' in their defence—depends, as discussed above, on the child's capacities, and on the skills and experience of the lawyer. Beyond the lawyer-client relationship, the term 'collaboration' takes on more complexity within the courtroom because it suggests a degree of agency (in terms of choice and freedom to participate) and common purpose that is difficult to reconcile with a penal system that compels a person's engagement and imposes punishment regardless of their wishes or views. Instead, it is the rights-base concept of 'effective participation' that best captures the aims of CF3.

'Effective participation' emerged as a key component of a child's right to a fair trial in *V v United Kingdom* when the UK was found to have breached Article 6 ECHR rights when two eleven-year-old boys had been unable to effectively participate during a Crown Court trial that had been held in a 'blaze of publicity'. Specifically, the ECtHR held that:

It is essential that a child charged with an offence is dealt with in a manner which takes full account of his age, level of maturity and intellectual and emotional capacities, and that steps are taken to promote his ability to understand and participate in the proceedings (para 86).

The UK responded to the ECtHR's decision by introducing a new Criminal Practice Direction (*Practice Direction Crown Court: Youth Defendants* [2001] 1 WLR 659 (CPD)). The CPD initially applied exclusively to children ('young defendants') and represented a significant step towards the aims of CF3. It stated that 'all possible steps should be taken to assist the child to understand and participate' and that the ordinary trial process 'should so far as necessary' be adapted to meet those ends, and it reminded the court of its overriding duty to have regard to the welfare of the child. It also set out the specific adaptations courts should take, including: considering whether, where there is an adult co-defendant, the child's trial should be separated; court familiarisation visits before trial; a courtroom layout that places everyone on the same level; sitting during the trial with family members or others with a like relationship (rather than in the dock) and having informal and easy access to legal representatives; using language and explanations the child can understand; a condensed timetable; removal of wigs and robes; non-uniformed court security officers; and restricted attendance in the public gallery.

Although the CPD represented a significant step forward, there are two indicators of the law's continued resistance to fully embrace the principles that underpin Child First (particularly the combined effect of CF1 and CF3) in relation to Crown Court. First, child defendants were explicitly excluded from similar, but more extensive, 'special measures' introduced for other child witnesses in the Youth Justice and Criminal Evidence Act 1999 (YJCE). This produced a bifurcated system that differentiated between children based on their status within the proceedings and not on their needs and vulnerabilities. This bifurcation continues today: amendments to the YJCE which extended live-link to child defendants come with additional conditions and limits; and amendments which provide a statutory basis for intermediaries for child defendants have yet to be brought into force. This means that child defendants must continue to rely instead on criminal procedure rules and practice directions which, though regarded as law, do not have the same status or protection of statute and are instead given effect through the court's inherent common law powers. This weaker legal basis is no doubt one reason why there continues to be an inconsistent and unfair application in practice between child defendants and other child witnesses and in its application to different defendants by different judges (Lambe & Hollingsworth, 2021). Second, although the protections afforded to child defendants in the CPD have widened (e.g. now including intermediaries), they have become less child-specific as the CPD has been extended to a broader category of 'vulnerable defendant' which also includes adults with certain types of disability. Although better protections for vulnerable adults are welcome, the consequence of absorbing 'children' into the more generic category of 'vulnerable defendant' is that age-related vulnerabilities become less visible, and the special obligations owed to children are diluted. The result is that the double vulnerability experienced by many children may be ignored: for example, if a child fails to demonstrate a vulnerability *additional* to age and developmental immaturity, such as neurodiversity, the courts may be reluctant to make special adaptations; or if the child has an additional vulnerability, any adaptations made may be insufficient to address the combined impact of age and disability (Lambe & Hollingsworth, 2021).

Furthermore, austerity measures introduced since 2010 have impacted the law and practice relating to children's effective participation; for example, under-staffed court security may prevent the child's removal from the dock; overly stretched and underpaid defence lawyers may not have time to understand their client well enough to request appropriate adjustments; and judges may be reluctant to allow adjustments that prolong delayed trials. Combined with fewer child defendants appearing in the Court, and thus less judicial familiarity with best practice on conducting trials involving children, it is not surprising that children experience criminal trials—particularly in Crown Court—as confusing, intimidating and exclusionary (Jacobsen et al., 2016).

Yet when adaptations are made, it can make a significant difference to case outcomes. It allows the child to more effectively participate and it may also influence jury decision-making by helping juries to understand

and form a more positive view of the child's behaviour in or outside of the courtroom (Maras et al., 2019). Recent changes to the pre-trial preparation process which require judges to consider explicitly which adaptations in the CPD are needed for the child's effective participation, and to give reasons if they do not, are welcome. Combined with the publication of the child-specific guidance (Judicial College, 2021a) a shift in culture and practice—where adaptations are the default rather than the exception—may slowly begin to occur.

However, even in youth court where adaptations are integral to the system, participation is 'an aspiration rather than a reality in most cases' (Centre for Justice Innovation, 2020: 3). In some courts, the adult courtroom is used without reconfiguration for children, and magistrates sit on a raised platform 'looking down on me'; some children are placed in the dock or otherwise are not close enough to their lawyer to instruct, or to benefit from their support; and not all youth courts have separate entrances and waiting rooms for children (though many do) (Centre for Justice Innovation, 2020). Children's health and communication needs continue to be missed or undiagnosed meaning the support they need—including communication support—is absent. In short, without proper resourcing, operational challenges act as a barrier to the child's effective participation, contrary to CF3, even in youth court.

A final point is that 'effective participation' in trial need not require the child to give evidence nor indeed require their physical presence in court. In this sense, the way that 'participation' is understood is different from elsewhere because the child's *effective* participation may require them to *not* physically be in court, at certain points, if (e.g.) it causes distress. Similarly, a lawyer may advise a child not to participate directly (through giving evidence) if this is harmful to their defence. In criminal proceedings, the child's effective participation may, therefore, conflict with CF3's requirement to 'encourage *active* participation' [emphasis added]. This speaks to the need to see the four tenets holistically, and contextually, and for the rights of the child to robustly underpin all elements of Child First.

Tenet 4: Promoting Diversion and Reducing Stigma: Bail and Remand Decision-Making

The decision to remand a child to custody whilst they await trial or sentence is one of the most important decisions the court will make. Children remanded to custody not only experience all the harms of incarceration—anxiety and grief caused by removal from families, friends and communities; bullying and poor conditions that harm mental and physical health (exacerbated by the COVID-19 pandemic); exposure to grooming and pro-criminogenic identity; and extended interruption to education or training—but, because of the uncertainty surrounding the length of their detention, they also miss out on the meaningful activities, support or treatment programmes which are available to sentenced children. This suspended existence is harmful to children's best interests in the immediate and longer term (CF1), is absent of any meaningful collaboration with the child (CF3), and any future focus is constructed entirely through a prism of risk rather than directed towards developing a pro-social identify and positive outcomes (CF2). Moreover, the deeper into the CJS the child gets, particularly where that involves custody, the more stigmatising their experience and the harder to desist from future offending. Ensuring the child is diverted away from custody at remand hearings is, therefore, essential to all tenets of Child First, especially CF4.

The Legal Aid, Sentencing and Punishment Act 2012 (LASPO): A Child First Framework?

In the past decade, the legal framework for remand for children has improved—on paper at least. LASPO introduced reforms that were intended to make remand to custody for children a last resort. Remand budgets were devolved to local authorities to financially incentivise them to provide feasible alternative bail packages; and where bail was not possible, Remand to Local Authority Accommodation (RLAA) was made the default option. RLAA keeps children within the community (or in secure children's homes), thus reducing stigma and enhancing the likelihood their needs will be identified and met, and that work addressing their risk of offending is commenced without delay. In turn, this can support diversion from custody at sentence by demonstrating to the sentencing judge that alternatives to custody can work for the child. Only if legislatively defined threshold criteria are met—based on age (only those aged 12 and over), legal representation, offence, possible sentence, history conditions and a strict necessity condition—can custodial remand (called 'remand to youth detention accommodation') now be used (sections 98 and 99). LASPO also removed anomalies by making the child-remand system equally applicable to boys and girls, and 17-year-olds (who were previously treated as adults). And finally, for children who *are* remanded to custody, they are now 'treated as looked after' for the purposes of the Children Act 1989 (LASPO, section 104). Looked-after status provides a gateway to local authority support, including in the longer term if the child meets the statutory criteria to qualify for care-leaver status (Hollingsworth, 2012). LASPO thus represented a symbolic shift in the law's construction of the remanded child away from the putative offender and towards a vulnerable child in the care of the state, thus helping not only to divert children from custody, but also to reduce the stigma and increase the support for those who remain.

Child First on Paper, But Not in Practice

However, the Child First ethos of LASPO has not materialised in practice in relation to court decision-making and remand. Remand to custody for children remains unacceptably high, especially for Black children. 40% of children in youth custody are on remand (the highest proportion in the past 10 years); 11% of all remand decisions resulted in remand to youth detention accommodation; and of those children who were remanded to custody, almost three-quarters did not go on to receive a custodial sentence (YJB/Ministry of Justice, 2022). The delays that are endemic in criminal justice, particularly since the COVID-19 pandemic, have also resulted in children held on remand for longer than necessary and it is clear from the response during COVID-19—where only threatened legal action prevented extensions to remand applying in the same way to children as adults (YJLC, 2021)—that there remains a failure to put children, and their rights, first.

The latest figures also show that 35% of remands to custody involved Black children and another 23% were children from other minoritised groups (Ministry of Justice, 2022). In London, the figures are worse still (Transform Justice, 2021). There are a number of explanations for the greater disproportionality during remand, including subjective risk and vulnerability assessments and less robust bail support packages (Ministry of Justice, 2022; YJB, 2021). Moving away from risk-based assessments to a Child First welfare-based approach would help address disparity in the remand of children.

Police, Crime, Sentencing and Courts Act: Diverting from Remand and Reducing Stigma?

In the light of these well-reported shortcomings, the Police, Crime, Sentencing and Courts Act 2022 aims to tighten the threshold for custodial remand further, limiting the discretion of the courts to remand children to custody and requiring reasons when they do. On the face of it, the Act brings better alignment with Child First by requiring courts to consider the 'interests and welfare' of the child before deciding whether to remand a child to youth detention accommodation (section 133(2)). However, courts already have a statutory duty to have regard to 'welfare' (Children and Young Persons Act 1933), and although the Act extends this to 'interests' it makes no reference to '*best* interests' (although it was referred to as such throughout the Parliamentary debates).[2] The utility of the provision, therefore, seems to come from an additional requirement for the court to state in open court and in writing that it has considered the 'interest and welfare' requirement *and* considered the possibility of RLAA. This acts as a strong prompt to the court but, given the absence of criteria or a definition of 'interests and welfare', judicial training is

---

[2] https://bills.parliament.uk/bills/2839/stages/12819 See especially here: https://hansard.parliament.uk/commons/2021-06-15/debates/ff9a9b8e-92cf-49aa-8b7d-2a3cbbe80643/PoliceCrimeSentencingAndCourtsBill(FourteenthSitting)).

needed to ensure this duty goes beyond a perfunctory procedural requirement to capture a more meaningful engagement with a rights-informed approach to 'welfare' (see above). This should include listening to the child's own views, as required in welfare assessments in family law, and a specific requirement for judges to *explain* what factors they took into account in considering welfare, rather than simply stating that they *have* considered it. Indeed, the Act perhaps misses an opportunity to embed a definition of welfare, similar to that in section 1(3) of the Children Act 1989, within the criminal justice context.

It is also noteworthy that the Act uses the term 'youth remand' rather than 'child remand'. Although a seemingly minor issue of nomenclature, the word 'child' would not only have reduced stigma ('youth' is more pejorative than 'child'), it also helps to remind judges—especially those less familiar with dealing with children such as remand decisions in the adult magistrates' court—that child-specific law and rights apply. The Act also leaves open the possibility of refusing bail to a child on welfare grounds; an amendment to this effect during Committee stage was withdrawn.

Holistic Decision-Making

The decision to remand is the end point of a broader social process, impacted by the prior decision-making of police, prosecution, defence lawyers, youth offending teams and children's services (Gibbs & Ratcliffe, 2018: 1; Howard League for Penal Reform, 2021) At each stage, choices are made which increase the likelihood of custodial remand. For example, where children are refused police bail (under s 38 PACE), they must appear in court at the next available sitting (usually the next morning) (PACE, section 46). In these circumstances, YOTs have little notice or time to gather relevant information, including from the child themselves, necessary to provide the court with a feasible bail package or to secure accommodation from children's services (Gibbs & Ratcliffe, 2018: 13). It also increases the likelihood that the child will appear in adult magistrates' court (given the reduced number of youth court sittings), with the decision made by a non-specialist tribunal who may be less willing to adjourn hearings to ensure alternatives to custodial remand can be arranged. And, where a child appears in court from police custody, they are usually held in court cells and appear in the secure dock, sending implicit messages to the court about the child's risk and culpability. Prosecutors are also more likely to request remand where police bail is refused. Even non-specialist defence lawyers may not adequately know the law or be able to secure from children's services a bail package that provides the basis for a robust challenge to the prosecutorial request for remand. A lack of accommodation, either to support bail or to enable RLAA, is reported as a particularly common reason for custodial remand (Howard League for Penal Reform, 2021). And, as noted above, analysis by the YJB (2021) shows that at least some of the racial disparity in remand decision-making is due to assessments of perceived risk and vulnerability by practitioners; suggesting possible bias underpinning the information provided to the court. And, even after all this is accounted for, Black children were still more likely to receive a custodial remand. Given that a child who receives a custodial remand is more likely to receive a custodial sentence, this disproportionality is also carried through to sentence. Therefore, to fully move towards Child First remand decision-making in the courts, reform and better practice is required at *all* stages and by *all* professionals, and with a focus on *all* four tenets of Child First (see further, Transform Justice, 2021).

The success of remand reforms set out in the latest Act also depend upon proper resourcing and accountability, and on systemic changes to the approach to children and their rights. Without this, courts will remain hamstrung in their decision-making. Courts—whether they are criminal or family courts—are unable to dictate to children's services the nature and type of support children receive, whether that is in a bail package or in a care plan; that is the role of children's services. Perhaps then, in a time of increasing austerity and scarce resourcing, the only way to divert children from custody in pre-trial decision-making is to legally prohibit custodial remand for *all* children, and not only 10- and 11-year-olds.

Concluding Comments

This chapter has sought to demonstrate that progress towards Child First within the criminal courts has been more fragmented, and more stilted, than elsewhere in the YJS because of the unique political, constitutional and legal position of the courts. Politically, there is little appetite for the extensive reforms necessary for true compliance with Child First. This would require removing children from the criminal courts by raising the minimum age of criminal responsibility to 18 and/or creating a wholly new system divorced from that currently used. Constitutionally, the judiciary is largely independent of the executive, its policy initiatives and decision-making, including the YJB's promotion of Child First or children's services resource-allocation. Instead, judicial decision-making operates within the constraints of law and guidance, jurisprudence, legal practice (including how lawyers strategise and frame their arguments), professional values and court culture. And legally, the treatment of child defendants within the courtroom is ordinarily grounded within the language of rights, and the vaguer, less well-established, and non-binding tenets of Child First ostensibly have less influence. Even where Child First aligns with children's rights, progress is constrained by the temporal and legal limits of those rights as well as the failures to invest the resources necessary for their meaningful realisation. However, some progress *can* be seen; driven by the children's rights agenda and by committed professionals (and NGOs) pushing for new guidance and training and exploring ways to utilise their discretion to further children's rights and Child First. But only if the commitment to Child First flows vertically (from legislation to policy to practice) and horizontally (across *all* constitutional actors) will real and consistent change for children happen; albeit within a system that is inherently *not* Child First.

Bibliography

A'Court, B., & Arthur, R. (2020). The role of lawyers in supporting young people in the criminal justice system: Balancing economic survival and children's rights. *Journal of Social Welfare and Family Law, 42*(4), 498–515.

Alliance for Youth Justice. (2022). *Policy briefing: A critical juncture for youth justice: Learning lessons and future directions for a post-pandemic youth justice system*. A+critical+juncture+for+youth+justice+26.04.22+FINAL.pdf (squarespace.com). Last visited 3 May 2022.

Anderson, S., Hawes, D., & Snow, P. (2016). Language impairments among youth offenders: A systematic review. *Children and Youth Services Review, 65*(C), 195–203.

Aubrey-Johnson, K., Lambe, S., & Twite, J. (2019). *Youth justice law and practice*. LAG/YJLC.

Bateman, T. (2021). *Bridging the care-crime gap: Reforming the youth court*. NAYJ Briefing.

Bellamy, C. (2021). *Independent review of criminal legal aid*. https://assets.publishing.service.gov.uk/government/uploads/system/uploads/attachment_data/file/1041117/clar-independent-review-report-2021.pdf. Last visited 3 May 2022.

Bowen, P., & Whitehead, S. (2016). *Problem-solving courts: An evidence review*. Centre for Justice Innovation. https://justiceinnovation.org/publications/problem-solving-courts-evidence-review. Last visited 3 May 2022.

Brewster, D. (2020). Not wired Up? The neuroscientific turn in youth to adult (Y2A) transitions policy. *Youth Justice, 20*(3), 215–234.

Bryan, K., Freer, J., & Furlong, C. (2007). Language and communication difficulties in juvenile offenders. *International Journal of Language & Communication Disorders, 42*(5), 505–520.

Bryan, K., Garvani, G., Gregory, J., & Kilner, K. (2015). Language difficulties and criminal justice: The need for earlier identification. *International Journal of Language Communication Disorder, 50*(6), 763–775.

Buss, E. (2015). The developmental stakes of youth participation in American Juvenile Court. In T. Gal & B. Duramy (Eds.), *Promoting the participation right of children across the globe: From social exclusion to child-inclusive policies*. Oxford University Press.

Case, S., & Haines, K. (2021). Abolishing youth justice systems': Children first, offenders nowhere. *Youth Justice: An International Journal, 21*(1), 3–17.

Centre for Justice Innovation. (2020). *Time to get it right: Enhancing problem-solving practice in the Youth Court.*
Chowdhury, T. (2020). *Time, temporality and legal judgment.* Routledge.
Council of Europe. (2010). *Guidelines of the Committee of Ministers of the Council of Europe on child friendly justice* (adopted by the Committee of Ministers of the Council of Europe on 17 November 2010).
Crown Prosecution Service, (2021). *Crown Prosecution Service Annual Report and Accounts 2020–21 (HC 430).*
Emanuel, D., Mawer, C., & Janes, L. (2021). The sentencing of young adults: A distinct group requiring a distinct approach. *Criminal Law Review,* (3), 203–217.
Farmer, L. (2010). Time and space in criminal law. *New Criminal Law Review: An International and Interdisciplinary Journal, 13*(2), 333–356.
Gibbs, P., & Ratcliffe, F. (2018). *Path of little resistance: Is pre-trial detention of children really a last resort?* Transform Justice.
Grisso, T., & Schwatz, R. (2000). *Youth on trial: A developmental perspective on juvenile justice.* University of Chicago Press.
HM Inspectorate of Probation. (2021). *A thematic inspection of the experiences of black and mixed heritage boys in the youth justice system.* https://www.justic einspectorates.gov.uk/hmiprobation/inspections/black-and-mixed-heritage-boys/. Last visited 3 May 2022.
Hollingsworth, K. (2012). Securing responsibility, achieving parity? The legal support for children leaving custody. *Legal Studies, 33*(1), 22–45.
Hollingsworth, K. (2013). Theorising children's rights in youth justice: The significance of autonomy and foundational rights. *Modern Law Review, 76*(6), 1046–1069.
Hollingsworth, K. (2020a). Sentencing remarks for children: Research briefing. https://www.ncl.ac.uk/law/research/impact/briefings/. Last visited 3 May 2022.
Hollingsworth, K. (2020b). Children and juvenile justice law: The possibilities of a relational-rights approach. In J. Dwyer (Ed.), *The Oxford handbook of children and the law* (pp. 775–802). Oxford University Press.
Hollingsworth, K., & Stalford, H. (2022, Forthcoming). Future-proofing children's rights protections for child foreign national offenders: Blurring the bright lines. In S. Gilmore & J. Scherpes (Eds.), *Family matters: Essays in honour of John Eekelaar.* Insentia.

Hopkins, T., Clegg, J., & Stackhouse, J. (2018). Examining the association between language, expository discourse and offending behaviour: An investigation of direction, strength and independence. *International Journal of Language & Communication Disorders, 53*(1), 113–129.

Howard League for Penal Reform. (2021). *What's wrong with remanding children to prison? Remand briefing one: Emerging themes.* https://howard league.org/publications/whats-wrong-with-remanding-children-to-prison/. Last visited 3 May 2022.

Jacobsen, J., Hunter, G., & Kirby, A. (2016). *Inside Crown Court: Personal experiences and questions of legitimacy.* Bristol University Press.

Judicial College. (2021a). *Youth defendants in the Crown Court.* https://www.judiciary.uk/wp-content/uploads/2021/03/Youth-Defendants-in-the-Crown-Court-March-2021.pdf. Last visited 3 May 2022.

Judicial College. (2021b). *Crown Court compendium: Part II sentencing.* https://www.judiciary.uk/wp-content/uploads/2020/12/Crown-Court-Com pendium-Part-II-Sentencing-August-2021b.pdf. Last visited 3 May 2022.

Just for Kids Law. (2020). *Timely justice: Turning 18. A briefing on the impact of turning 18 in the criminal justice system.* YJLCTurning18briefing(June2020)_0.pdf (justforkidslaw.org). Last visited 3 May 2022.

Lambe, S., & Hollingsworth, K. (2021). Protecting vulnerable child defendants in England and Wales: A house of cards. In G. Lansdell, B. Saunders, & A. Erikson (Eds.), *Neurodisability and the criminal justice system: Comparative and therapeutic responses.* Edward Elgar Publishing.

Lammy, D. (2017). *An independent review into the treatment of, and outcomes for, black, Asian and minority ethnic individuals in the criminal justice system.*

Lord Carlile of Berriew. (2014). *Independent Parliamentarians' Inquiry into the Operation and Effectiveness of the Youth Court.* London.

Maras, K., Marshall, I., & Sands, C. (2019). Mock juror perceptions of credibility and culpability in an autistic defendant. *Journal of Autism and Developmental Disorders, 49*(3), 996–1010.

Michael Sieff Foundation. (2000). *Implementation of the recommendations of the Carlile inquiry report: Progress report.* https://www.michaelsieff-founda tion.org.uk/implementation-of-the-recommendations-of-the-carlile-inquiry-progress-report-2020/. Last visited 3 May 2022.

Ministry of Justice. (2022). *Review of custodial remand for children.* https://assets.publishing.service.gov.uk/government/uploads/system/uploads/att achment_data/file/1050218/youth-remand-review.pdf. Last visited 3 May 2022.

National Audit Office. (2021). *Reducing the backlog in the criminal courts.* https://www.nao.org.uk/wp-content/uploads/2021/10/Reducing-the-backlog-in-criminal-courts.pdf. Last visited 3 May 2022.

Sentencing Council. (2017). *Sentencing children and young people: Definitive guideline.* https://www.sentencingcouncil.org.uk/wp-content/uploads/Sentencing-Children-and-Young-People-definitive-guideline-Web.pdf. Last visited 3 May 2022.

Sentencing Council. (2020). *Assessing the impact and implementation of the sentencing council's sentencing children and young people definitive guideline.* https://www.sentencingcouncil.org.uk/wp-content/uploads/November-2020-CYP-assessment-report-FINAL.pdf. Last visited 3 May 2022.

Stanley, C. (2021). Care and Crime Together? Merging youth and Family Courts. *Magistrate* 16–17 (Feb-Mar issue) 2014 London.

Sowerbutts, A., Eaton-Rosen, E., Bryan, K., & Beeke, S. (2021). Supporting young offenders to communicate in the youth justice system: A scoping review. *Speech, Language and Hearing, 24*(2), 87–104.

Stalford, H., & Hollingsworth, K. (2017). Judging children's rights: Tendencies, tensions, constraints and opportunities. In H. Stalford, K. Hollingsworth, & S. Gilmore (Eds.), *Rewriting children's rights judgments: From academic vision to new practice* (pp. 17–52). Hart Bloomsbury.

Stalford, H., & Hollingsworth, K. (2020). "This case is about you and your future": Towards judgments for children. *Modern Law Review, 83*(5), 1030–1058.

Thomas, C. (2017). Ethnicity and the fairness of jury trials in England and Wales 2006–2014. *Criminal Law Review, 2017*(11), 860–876.

Transform Justice. (2021, November 5). *Children imprisoned on remand—The stark reality of racial bias.* https://www.transformjustice.org.uk/children-imprisoned-on-remand-the-stark-reality-of-racial-bias/. Last accessed 17 November 2021.

Tyler, T. R. (2003). Procedural justice, legitimacy and the rule of law. *Crime and Justice, 30*, 283–357.

UN Committee on the Rights of the Child. (2019, September 18). *General Comment No 24 (2019) on children's rights in child justice systems* CRC/C/GC/24.

Wake, N., Arthur, R., Crofts, T., & Lambert, S. (2021). Legislative approaches to recognising the vulnerability of young people and preventing their criminalisation. *Public Law, 2021*(January), 145–162.

Wigzell, A., Kirby, A., & Jacobsen, J. (2015). *Bar standards board youth proceedings advocacy review.* ICPR.

YJB. (2021). *Ethnic disproportionality in remand and sentencing in the youth justice system: Analysis of administrative data.* https://assets.publishing.ser vice.gov.uk/government/uploads/system/uploads/attachment_data/file/952 483/Ethnic_disproportionality_in_remand_and_sentencing_in_the_youth_ justice_system.pdf. Last visited on 3 May 2022.

YJB/Ministry of Justice, Youth Justice Statistics 2020–2021. https://assets.pub lishing.service.gov.uk/government/uploads/system/uploads/attachment_d ata/file/1054236/Youth_Justice_Statistics_2020-21.pdf. Last visited 3 May 2022.

Youth Justice Legal Centre. (2021). Children exempt from extended custody time limits in the Crown Court. https://yjlc.uk/resources/legal-updates/chi ldren-exempt-extended-custody-time-limits-crown-court. Last visited 3 May 2022.

Cases

R (AB) v Secretary of State for Justice [2021] UKSC 28.
R (B) v Brent Youth Court [2010] EWHC 1893 (Admin).
R (JC) v The Central Criminal Court [2014] EWHC 1041.
R (Smith) v SSHD [2006] 1 AC 159.
R (TI) v Bromley Youth Court [2020] EWHC 1204.
R (TP) v West London Youth Court [2005] EWHC 2583.
R v Chin Charles [2019] EWCA Crim 1140.
R v CN, FN, DW [2020] EWCA Crim 1028.
R v DM and SC [2019] EWCA Crim 1534.
R v Grant Murray and others [2017] EWCA Crim 1228.
R v Kyries Davies [2020] EWCA Crim 921.
R v Peters [2005] EWCA Crim 605.
SC v United Kingdom (2004) 40 EHRR 10.
V v United Kingdom 30 EHRR 121.

Part III

Child First: Developing Youth Justice Practice

9

Child First: Thinking Through the Implications for Policy and Practice

Ben Byrne

Introduction

This chapter provides a reflective analysis drawn from my experience of working as a youth justice social worker and subsequently leading reforms at a local level. My perspective on the challenges of delivery at a local level are specifically shaped by work to integrate youth justice with other young people's services as Head of Youth Justice, and then as Head of Early Help and Family Services in Surrey from 2010 to 2018. My view is further informed by experience as a Youth Justice Board member from 2018 to 2021 where I was the board champion with responsibility for overseeing the development of the Child First agenda.

The adoption by the Youth Justice Board for England and Wales of Child First as its guiding principle in 2018 provides the potential for a paradigm shift in our responses to children in conflict with the law. The

---

B. Byrne (✉)
London, UK
e-mail: bbyrne100@googlemail.com

© The Author(s), under exclusive license to Springer Nature Switzerland AG 2023
S. Case and N. Hazel (eds.), *Child First*,
https://doi.org/10.1007/978-3-031-19272-2_9

significance of the national body which has responsibility for oversight of the Youth Justice System replacing an 'offender first' lens (Haines & Case, 2015) with a Child First one sets in train a range of possibilities and requirements that the Youth Justice System, and broader child welfare system, will need to embrace if Child First is to become more than a rhetorical aspiration. The Youth Justice Board (YJB) has embarked on a range measures to promote the application of the Child First approach in youth justice practice (Ministry of Justice/YJB, 2019; YJB, 2021a); an approach which, while not a stated policy objective of the UK Government, nonetheless, received endorsement by the Secretary of State as underpinning National Standards for Children in the Youth Justice System in 2019 (MoJ, 2019). This chapter reflects upon the significance of this reconceptualisation of children in trouble and considers the extensive implications for national arrangements, local youth justice practice and wider responses to vulnerable adolescents.

The arguments of this chapter were first presented in a paper to the Association of Directors of Children's Services (ADCS) Families, Communities and Young People policy committee in November 2019 and subsequently contributed to the ADCS position statement *A youth justice system that works for children* (ADCS, 2021). This policy position has since been endorsed by the Independent Review of Children's Social Care (Independent Review of Children's Social Care, 2022).

Part 1: Enablers and Barriers to Realising the Child First Principle in the Current Youth Justice and Children's Services Environment

Working with Children or Dealing with Offenders?

Children who break the law have long been conceived as inhabiting a place outside of the privileged realm of childhood. 'Othering' has taken various exclusionary forms (Haines & Drakeford, 1998), including physical exclusion in custodial institutions, where until relatively recently the Children Act was not considered to apply and where the provisions of the United Nations Convention on the Rights of the Child are still not routinely observed (Unicef, 2019, see also Kilkelly in this volume). Othering is underpinned by linguistic distancing through appellations such as *juvenile delinquent, young offender*, and for extreme cases animalistic terms such as *Rat Boy* (Collier, 1998). Practical segregation of services, exclusively for offenders, further serves to detrimentally mark out children identified as in conflict with the law from their unadjudicated peers. When conceived as 'non-children' the adverse treatment of those who come to inhabit the Youth Justice System can then more easily be justified.

> Othering within the youth justice system has resulted in individual children losing their identity and becoming treated as simply members of a broader group labelled 'young offenders' and the nature of their special treatment has been largely discriminatory, negative, controlling and punitive. (Haines & Case, 2015: 14)

The movement to bring these children back into our consciousness as, first and foremost, children, rather than offenders, has profound implications for how we formally respond to their behaviour, and how we go about the business of supporting them to access the same opportunities and entitlements that we want for all children.

The Child First Challenge to the 'New Youth Justice' Orthodoxy

Formal adoption of the Child First guiding principle by the YJB is a significant milestone in an historical process which has seen high watermarks for both welfare and justice approaches. The relationship of Child First to these totems of youth justice policy is described elsewhere in this compendium. More recently, the development of a *new youth justice* paradigm (Goldson, 2000) has sought to move beyond the welfare/justice debate, through application of the risk factor prevention paradigm and its supporting managerialist framework for delivering youth justice services (Byrne & Case, 2016). The development of current youth justice policy and practice is well-described elsewhere (Case, 2021;

Smith, 2014) and for our purposes it need only be stated that the Child First guiding principle, if faithfully applied and pursued to its logical conclusion, provides a profound challenge to the post-Crime and Disorder Act apparatus and operation of youth justice in England and Wales. This challenge is captured by Bateman (2020):

> translating the philosophical aspiration into a concrete justice system that merits a *Child First* appellation, will require radical reform of the legal and structural frameworks for the delivery of services to children in conflict with the law and a reconceptualisation of operational rationales. In particular, it will necessitate confronting, and displacing the punitive, risk-orientated, and deficit-focussed, undertones whose residues continue to influence the treatment of children who break the law. (Bateman, 2020: 130)

Child First Developments Outside of the Youth Justice System

Further developments, which come as an external challenge to current youth justice arrangements, and may help to accelerate Child First responses, have included the re-framing of the problem of violence reduction as a public health challenge, rather than one purely requiring a law and order response (Children's Commissioner, 2021; Local Government Association, 2018). This supports a recognition that children who are involved in drug supply and attendant violent offending are themselves frequently exploited and can be most accurately characterised as victims (National Crime Agency, 2018).

Some of this re-framing comes as an inevitable outcome of our reconceptualisation of child sexual exploitation (as abuse rather than a 'lifestyle choice') and the necessary re-thinking this requires for our approach to children experiencing other forms of exploitation. As Wroe and Lloyd describe it:

> Responses to extra familial harm require child protection systems to respond to forms of harm that had previously been criminalized or understood as outside the remit of child safeguarding. These include forms of

youth exploitation and violence; from CSE, to serious youth violence and more recently the exploitation of children to distribute drugs via 'county lines'. (Wroe & Lloyd, 2020: 3)

There has been a resultant shift in the response of children's services to teenagers previously perceived merely as troublesome; spurred initially by the scandals involving failures to safeguard children exposed to sexual exploitation (Jay, 2014), this has subsequently informed wider responses to vulnerable adolescents (see, for instance, the addition of contextual safeguarding in relation to extra-familial harm in the statutory guidance *Working Together to Safeguard Children* and *Keeping Children Safe in Education*, HM Government, 2018a & 2018b and report of the Children's Safeguarding Practice Review Panel, 2020).

Children's services and education settings are increasingly adopting trauma-informed practices and turning to restorative and relationship-based approaches to deal with various types of conflict and harms (Harris et al., 2020; Restorative Justice Council, 2022). When appropriately applied, these approaches align with the Child First principle and undermine the distinction between 'young offenders' dealt with through the Youth Justice System and other children who experience or cause harm. These preventative and diversionary approaches in universal and specialist settings support children who would previously have been drawn into the Youth Justice System (Case & Haines, 2020; Public Health England, 2019) and have contributed to the contraction of the Youth Justice System over the last decade.

While youth justice practitioners have always known the 'choices' being made by the children with whom they worked were significantly constrained, this wider appreciation (particularly in policing and children's services) encourages a response which is 'Child First' and systemic rather than 'offender first' and individualising. This shift in practice with adolescents can most clearly be seen in the development of contextual safeguarding (Firmin, 2020), trauma-informed (Innovate Project, 2021) and participatory responses (IRIS, 2022), which are re-shaping the work of the children's services workforce but also speak directly to youth justice practice. While this reform in children's services is far from complete (Ofsted, 2021), it does in practical terms mean the safety and well-being of the children in the Youth Justice System is no longer the exclusive preserve of youth justice practitioners. The increasingly complex cohort who remain in the contracted Youth Justice System are often also part of the child welfare system, while many children who would previously have been dealt with by YOTs now receive children's welfare services instead (Association of Directors of Children's Services, 2021).

The Child First Challenge to Racial Disparities in the Youth Justice System

The Child First principle also speaks to the issues of disproportionality that beset the Youth Justice System and offers one route to address these. An appreciation of the impact of systems and structural context upon children underpins the Child First tenet: "All work is child-focused, developmentally informed, acknowledges structural barriers and meets responsibilities towards children" (YJB, 2021a, 2021b). Thus the approach that follows is one which seeks to locate responsibility for a child's circumstances with the adults and systems around the child, rather than with the child themselves (Haines & Case, 2015). This means it has a direct relationship to the experience of black, mixed heritage and other minoritised children, both in their contact with criminal justice agencies and in the responses of other services. Black and mixed heritage children are more likely than others to attract criminal justice responses to their behaviour and less likely to be offered support through early help or early intervention; either by way of diversion from the Youth Justice System or through direct access to mainstream early help services (YJB, 2021b). Child First encourages a focus upon structural inequality, racism and discrimination, rather than locating the fault with the child and is thereby likely to have benefits in reducing the racial disparities experienced by children in the Youth Justice System.

The Child First principle promotes a recognition that offending can be both a common part of growing up (Rutherford, 2002) as expressed through the "developmentally informed" aspect of the first tenet, but also as an expression of unmet need (the first tenet's "recognising their particular needs" (see YJB, 2021a). Child First, therefore, provides a contrast to responses which seek punish, exclude and separate. Such a re-framing has the potential to re-orientate our responses to black and other minoritised children's behaviour, by seeing the child rather than the behaviour, and recognising the structural forces at play which underpin racial disparities. It also provides an opportunity to shine greater light on our responses to the behaviours which are precursors to offending; behaviours typically seen in educational settings, and in families who are in need of additional support, before problems become acute (Children's Commissioner, 2020a).

The Challenge to Embedding Child First within Current Arrangements for 'Children' and 'Offenders'

To appreciate the challenges to developing Child First practice we need to look more closely at the existing youth justice practice environment. Currently, youth justice practice, as mandated in the work of youth offending teams, is separated from wider children's services responses through an adherence to an 'offender first' set of rationales and supporting practice frameworks which continue to dominate (Bateman, 2020, Haines & Case, 2015). While responses differ between local areas, with some actively challenging the offender first underpinning of the national framework (of standards, guidance and mandated tools and structures) there is, nonetheless, still a strong regulatory draw towards the offender management approach (Day, 2022; Smith & Gray, 2019).

Children in the Youth Justice System are simultaneously (or consecutively) of interest to wider children's safeguarding services. They are, therefore, often both managed as offenders and supported as vulnerable children by different practitioners within the same local authority departments. This is in part a reflection of legislation; children who offend are subject to the criminal law and the formal responses flowing from it, however, when they are deemed vulnerable they are also subject to the Children Act 1989 and the range of safeguarding protections which apply. These children, therefore, experience bifurcated responses, from services which have different, but overlapping, remits for intervening in their lives.

This inevitable tension between criminal justice and child welfare systems is exacerbated by the very low age of criminal responsibility in England and Wales and justice structures, which are poorly adapted versions of the adult system; as evidenced in court arrangements (Centre for Justice Innovation, 2020) the court orders they apply, and the custodial facilities which sit in wait for those at the apex of the system (Children's Commissioner, 2020b). Even while retaining criminal culpability within childhood, other jurisdictions have developed more child-friendly structures and systems to dispense justice (see for instance the Scottish children's hearings system and those in much of Western Europe).

The dual systems for children in England and Wales, one providing for justice, another providing for wider concerns of welfare and wellbeing, run largely in parallel, overlapping at times but too often separate, following their own policy and practice directives. The outcome for children in trouble is often an experience of being involved with a series of multiple assessments and incoherent interventions, some of which we, and no doubt they, know to be counter-productive—such as incarceration (Goldson, 2005), stigma from prolonged involvement with criminal justice system (McAra & Mcvie, 2010), and being subjected to routinised offence-focused programmes (Phoenix & Kelly, 2013). For the services and practitioners tasked with these interventions, it is similarly incoherent, with little that is undertaken reflecting their aspiration for these children or the things they know make a difference dominated, as their work is, by process-heavy accountability systems (Byrne & Brooks, 2015), which shape not only youth justice practice but are replicated across the other systems and services with which these children are involved (Independent Review of Children's Social Care, 2021; Munro, 2011).

While distinct and separate youth justice services remain a feature, to a greater or lesser degree, in all local authorities, the same children often receive parallel interventions from safeguarding services. Up until relatively recently the multi-disciplinary YOT had been a place where those who had offended received intervention (somewhat) to the exclusion of involvement by other services (Khan & Wilson, 2010). This practice has become untenable with the re-framing of criminal exploitation (as children as victims rather than offenders—see, e.g., Pitts, 2008 and subsequent investigation by the Children's Commissioner, 2021) and the contraction of the Youth Justice System to deal with a sub-set of the most complex and usually most vulnerable adolescents, who experience overlapping education, health and social care needs (YJB, 2020). The smaller Youth Justice System now spreads its net much less frequently to involve children who are not already known to a range of other welfare services.

In short, the goalposts have moved and the YOT cohort is now also children's social care's adolescent safeguarding cohort. This awakening of mainstream safeguarding services to their responsibilities to this group of vulnerable adolescents has also encouraged the movement towards Child First responses in the wider children's system. It is not just the YJB which increasingly promotes the move to see children who offend as children first: the children's welfare and safeguarding systems have also moved in this direction (Association of Directors of Children's Services, 2021).

Integrating Services: The Rationale and the Challenge

The logic of the Child First principle suggests that responses to children in conflict with the law should be located within the appropriate children's (or preferably adolescent) services, not in an adjunct established exclusively for offenders. The evidence base and rationale for integrated services which respond to multiple, overlapping needs of vulnerable adolescents, is most comprehensively laid out by Hanson and Holmes in their work *That Difficult Age: developing a more effective response to risk in adolescents* (Hanson & Holmes, 2014). The importance of continuity of relationships is at the heart of this proposed response (Bachelor & McNeil, 2005) as is a recognition that offending is a behaviour which needs to be understood in the context of the child's life experience, family and wider environment, and in this it is no different from any other behaviour which might indicate the need for help or protection through children's services.

The case for integrated children's service arrangements, which include responses when children come into conflict with the law, is further reinforced by the reality that most of these children are, in any event, already known to or actively receiving intervention from core children's services. In principle and in practice then the retention of separate services for children who offend becomes increasingly untenable and out of step with a Child First approach. As described below, this does not mean dissolving all specialist functions or ignoring public protection responsibilities, but that these could be met through a more integrated approach which has greater benefits for children and the wider community.

For many working in youth justice, or those with a memory of arrangements before the inception of specialist youth justice responses, from the development of intermediate treatment onwards, this proposition is not without its own problems. Historically, these children were ignored or treated punitively by children's services (Bateman, 2021). Evidence suggests that children have been accelerated towards the justice system from care (Day et al., 2020), that education settings have too readily excluded the children who are most in need of help, and that in the absence of youth justice services many children would not have received the support they needed (Centre for Social Justice, 2012). The specialist advocacy of youth justice practitioners in courts, with police and in custodial settings should also not be underestimated. All these are features which need to be addressed and accounted for in any reconfigured Child First response, but none undermine the logic of children who offend being treated in one children's system, alongside other children rather than separated from them.

There is undoubtedly a long way to go to make children's services a receptive and appropriate home for children who are in conflict with law. The custom and practice in relation to safeguarding and the manner in which the child protection legislation and guidance is applied (or not) to teenagers in trouble is a significant challenge (Ibbetson, 2020). Similarly, practice in regard to child criminal exploitation is still underdeveloped in many places, meaning exploitation is missed because of a continued adherence to an offender first perspective (in the police and children's services as much as in YOTs). Underpinning the challenge around practice are cultural barriers which can be described in shorthand as 'these kids are the YOT's problem'. While the existence of separate youth offending services no doubt perpetuates this perception, getting rid of discrete youth justice provision will not, in and of itself, make children's services a welcoming home for these children, nor will it obviate the need for specialist advocacy on behalf of children in contact with criminal justice system and related public protection activity. The conclusion might be, therefore, that what is required is not a 'lift and shift' of this cohort into children's services, but a re-imagining of our response to vulnerable adolescents, which embraces the Child First youth justice principle.

Challenges to Developing Child First Practice at a Local Level

Responsibility for delivering youth justice services in the community sits with local authority-led partnerships and within each local authority the Director of Children's Services has statutory accountability for outcomes for all children in their local area, including those in the Youth Justice System. The Association of Directors of Children's Services (ADCS) policy statement *A Youth Justice System that Works for Children* reflects the frustration amongst directors of children's services (DCS) that nationally prescribed youth justice requirements hamper their ability to provide effective or efficient services which give children in conflict with the law the best chance of achieving positive outcomes (ADCS, 2021).

The requirement to maintain separate youth offending team structures, sufficiently discrete that they can be inspected as standalone entities by HM Inspectorate of Probation under a bespoke youth justice inspection regime, is a structural and practical barrier to better integration of youth justice activity within wider children's arrangement. A central argument of this chapter has been that separate structures and processes for children in conflict with the law reinforce an 'othering' of these children and undermines Child First approaches. Youth offending teams (YOT) both symbolically and practically mark out their clientele as different from other children and the nature of YOTs, and the complex structures around them, make attempts at integration extremely challenging. A review of the current of the HM Inspectorate of Probation (HMIP) youth offending inspection framework and the YJB guidance for youth justice management boards provides insight into how specialist youth justice responsibilities have become and how distinct they are from wider children's services requirements and the Ofsted inspection framework (HMIP, 2022; Ofsted, 2022; YJB, 2019). Beyond the significance of the discrete YOT structure sits a range of supporting systems which serve to ensure that children who have offended are set apart from their peers. The following may assist in bringing these local challenges to life.

Practical Barriers to Integrating Youth Justice Practice

A key practical barrier to developing Child First approaches at a local level is the requirement to operate a dedicated case management system which deals with youth offending. There are four case management systems (CMS) in use by local authorities in England and Wales, which provide for recording case-level information on children and collate these data to report to the YJB. None of these systems are integrated as part of the main children's social care databases. This means there is a separate record kept within each local authority for those who offend, distinct from the local children's social care case management system. As a result all work done in YOTs is entered on to a different recording system from work done with other children or, indeed, work done with the same child which pertains to social care or early help involvement. This is not only inefficient but hampers effective information sharing and is therefore potentially dangerous (Drew, 2020; Ibbetson, 2013). Development of an integrated local authority case management system for children, which incorporates the requirements to record and report youth justice data, would appear to be better aligned with the Child First principle.

A second example of local division caused by national requirements is the separate assessment and planning framework required for children in the Youth Justice System. The YJB specifies the use of the AssetPlus assessment framework (YJB, 2019). There are well-founded criticisms of the laborious nature of undertaking the AssetPlus documentation, which means that YOT practice is largely dominated by completion and quality assurance of the AssestPlus suite, rather than more productive work directly for and with children (Rand 2019). The more significant challenge, however, from a Child First perspective, is that an assessment framework which is designed specifically for offenders and to respond to offending behaviour is entirely the wrong starting point for effectively understanding and responding to all of a child's needs.

The Child First principle asserts that children in conflict with the law are considered first and foremost as children, whose behaviour needs to be understood in relation to the context and systems which shape their behaviour. This is no different from the task of social workers and other children and families practitioners when they seek to intervene in the life of any vulnerable child. Good social work and early help assessments for children who are also known to the Youth Justice System do already consider the needs and the risks (to self and to and from others) for these children. The unwieldy AssetPlus framework adds little to our understanding or our response for these children. The needs of children who are identified as having offended, but do not have an existing social work or early help assessment, could just as well be assessed within the mainstream local authority frameworks, if there were a willingness to do so by local authorities and a mandate to do so from the YJB.

There is currently a pilot in three local areas of an integrated assessment approach as an alternative to AssetPlus (see the Child First practice example below). Despite the apparent success of the approach in North Yorkshire, Lincolnshire and three London boroughs, and its close alignment with the Child First strategic guiding principle, there is little indication that the YJB is considering building on the learning from these pilots and no indication that it has any plans beyond the current AssetPlus assessment framework (YJB, 2021a).

The challenge of incorporating youth justice into the wider work of children's services should not be underestimated, current systems make this difficult, but nor can the need to draw the offending behaviour of children into a holistic and mainstream response to their circumstances any longer be ignored. As currently constituted, children's services will respond to children's wide-ranging need for help, protection and care but when their behaviour also comes into conflict with the law a separate set of arrangements kick in. This does not appear compatible with a Child First approach, which would ask, how best do we respond to the child's needs, while fulfilling our obligations to keep them safe and to protect others? The result would not be the local arrangements or nationally prescribed frameworks we currently have.

From practice experience at regional and national levels, it has been evident that the best YOTs, whose practitioners are highly skilled at engaging with a client group who often do not want to be engaged, recognise they are in a constant workaround to fit effective practice to the requirements of the Youth Justice System and its interface with the safeguarding system. YOTs are extremely hard to integrate within wider children and young people's services because of the increasingly specialised nature of the youth justice task (stemming from the demands outlined above). From the perspective of someone who has sought to deliver the best outcomes for children in conflict with the law in a local area, it is clear that there is very little in these requirements which is integral to supporting children, or ensuring their best interests, but is rather about fulfilling the process demands stemming from residual offender-centric perspectives of the YJB and HMIP frameworks. While there will always be some aspects of the interface with courts and criminal justice processes that require a degree of specialist knowledge, this accounts for a small amount of the current youth justice task as mandated in the post-Crime and Disorder Act architecture.

The substantive barriers to local integration can be summarised as (i) separate service structures, governance and inspection (ii) separate CMS and assessment frameworks. Much of what is problematic in terms of integration is mandated by YJB and could be dispensed with to positive effect, particularly if there were an appetite to support these changes in the MoJ and DfE. Until there is reform of these nationally prescribed systems and processes, realising genuinely Child First practice at a local level is near impossible.

Part 2: The Desired Future State

The first part of this chapter considered the evidence in relation to the enablers and the barriers to Child First responses to children in conflict with the law. I have sought to establish that wherever possible separation of services and accountability for children in conflict with law from other children's services should be avoided. Such separation entrenches othering and legitimises harsher treatment. On the basis of this analysis, I will now address the actions, which my experience suggests will best support the development of Child First practice.

What Needs to be Done to Move Towards a Child First System?

The Child First objective describes approaches to children in conflict with the law as needing to: promote access to the same rights and entitlements as are accessed by other children; respond in ways which are developmentally appropriate, non-stigmatising and participatory; and enable the greatest opportunity for positive identity formation (YJB, 2021a). For the reasons outline in the first part of this chapter, this is not achievable through discrete youth justice structures, which by definition take as their starting point a response to offence and offender. Equally, designing a system based upon the Child First principle requires more than the erasing of current youth justice provision. For children in trouble to be treated first and foremost as children there needs to be a re-imagining of responses for the diverse but overlapping cohorts of adolescents who need help and protection. A reformed system would enable children in trouble to receive appropriate provision alongside their peers, through services shaped around their needs, not the system's or its constituent organisations, as currently appears to take precedence (Hanson & Holmes, 2014).

Current arrangements for undertaking youth justice look increasingly at odds with policy objectives for the children concerned (Children's Commissioner, 2021). They not only run counter to the established evidence base for working with vulnerable adolescents (Billingham &

Irwin-Rogers, 2021; Hanson & Holmes, 2014) but are so inefficient (as described in the duplicating and bifurcated responses outlined above) that they appear unsustainable. There are a series of activities that range from wholesale legislative reform, through to local re-engineering of responses, which could be pursued to further the aims of the Child First principle. Clearly central government grasping the nettle of youth justice reform would greatly enhance the prospect of success, however, change is not dependent solely on government and there are many stakeholders in the youth justice landscape who can accelerate Child First developments. These actors and their prospective actions are considered below; any of these players could show leadership in this domain and take steps towards reform.

Developing Child First Youth Justice Legislation and Policy

The very low age of criminal responsibility in England and Wales underpins the 'offender first' approach to children in conflict with the law. While relatively few children under the age of 14 years old are prosecuted, younger children are still subject to arrest and frequently embroiled in the lower end of the Youth Justice System (triage/diversion, reprimand, final warning). This is not an area any UK Government has wanted to address in the last fifty years, but it is one which marks out the jurisdiction as ignoring the clear messages from developmental psychology that ten years of age is far too young to hold a child to account on the basis of adult culpability (Unicef, 2019). Child First is not compatible with such a young age of criminal responsibility.

Beyond the question of the age of criminal responsibility is the nature of the structures of the justice system as they apply to children. Criminal courts are not well equipped to address the complex problems of the children who inhabit the contemporary Youth Justice System (Centre for Justice Innovation, 2020). The Taylor Report recommended a panel system which was oriented around problem-solving but, although not declining this recommendation, the government has done nothing as yet to act upon it. Such an approach, which also requires more effective integration of proceedings with the family court, would enable a more holistic view of a child's needs and how best to respond to them (Taylor, 2016).

The UK Government (which has responsibility for youth justice arrangement in England and Wales) has thus far proved less receptive to explicitly supporting Child First measures than the devolved administration in Wales. As outlined throughout this chapter, beyond the adoption of National Standards for Youth Justice (MoJ/YJB, 2019) the MoJ has done little to adopt policies or adapt structures to be more responsive to the Child First principle. The Youth Justice Blueprint for Wales (Welsh Government, 2020) speaks directly to the Child First measures that can be undertaken under devolved powers and links the ambition for children in the Youth Justice System to the aspiration for all children in Wales. While the Scottish Government has not explicitly adopted Child First as guiding its policy, it has, nonetheless, signalled progressive intent by raising the age of criminal responsibility to twelve yeas of age.

The fact that responsibility for youth justice in England and Wales rests with the MoJ sits uneasily with a Child First approach (Taylor, 2016). It is perhaps inevitable that as children make up less than 1% of the custodial population the MoJ's focus is primarily on adults. A logical conclusion of the Child First approach is that children in conflict with the law should be the responsibility of the government's children's department, the Department for Education (DfE) and their needs considered alongside other children. Conversely, as long as responsibility rests elsewhere there is limited need for the DfE to fully engage with the needs of children in conflict with the law and this is likely to be to the detriment of these children (as is currently the case). While the MoJ retains responsibility for youth justice, it should ensure all policy and practice developments are scrutinised through a Child First lens, and determined efforts should be made to jointly plan with the DfE and Department for Health and Social Care, while also engaging other government departments whose work impacts on vulnerable children.

Child First Secure Care

Perhaps the most lamentable feature of the current youth justice arrangements is the juvenile secure estate (HMI Prisons, 2017). Despite repeated attempts to ameliorate the worst aspects of the adult incarceration experience, the estate cannot in any regard be considered as fulfilling Child First aspirations (as successive HMI Prisons annual reports testify). The evidence from inspection reports suggests the creation of the Youth Custody Service to manage the children's secure custodial estate has made little meaningful difference to the day-to-day experiences of children in custody. Recent examples include HMI Prisons 2021 annual report on the HM Prisons and Probation Service decision in the pandemic to "to treat children in the same way as prisoners held in the adult estate" (HMIP, 2021: 70) and the Urgent Notification issued in respect of Rainsbrook secure training centre in the same year. This is unsurprising as children's provision is still intimately linked to the arrangements for adult prisoners and still largely modelled on adult incarceration. Lord Ramsbotham's statement in 1997 that, "the Prison Service is essentially an organisation for adults, neither structured nor equipped to deal with children" (HM Chief Inspector of Prison, 1997: 8) appears as applicable today as when he made it (see for example Article 39's 2022 analysis of current custodial provision).

The government has committed to pilot secure schools as an alternative to young offenders institutions and secure training centres (STC), but progress is glacial—Charlie Taylor recommended the creation of secure schools in 2016 (Taylor, 2016) and the first one is not now due to open until 2023. There have been principled objections to the secure school model as failing to reflect a Child First approach and continuing to silo children who offend in separate institutions from others whose liberty has been denied (Allen, 2018, Article 39, 2022). The secure school is the latest in a long line of models of youth custody (Hagel & Hazel, 2001) which many commentators believe has no more likelihood of succeeding than its predecessors (Allen, 2016; Bateman, 2020). Despite these reservations, the secure school model does, at least, provide for dual registration as a children's home and a 16–19 academy, which creates synergies in more closely aligning youth justice policies and oversight with the Department for Education and wider children's services policies and practices.

Beyond the secure school pilot, a principled and energetic reform of secure provision for children is required, seeking closure of YOIs and the remaining STC. Despite a policy commitment to do this in 2016 (MoJ, 2016), there has been very little progress on developing alternatives. With, at the start of 2022, fewer than 400 hundred children in YOIs and STCs, there is no excuse to continue with provision which has repeatedly, over a long period time, shown itself to be antithetical to the Child First principle (see, for instance, HMI Prison's annual reports from 1997, 2006, 2017, 2021; Ofsted, 2008). There is, additionally, the opportunity to legislate to make custodial remand and sentence a genuine last resort (Standing Committee for Youth Justice, 2020), while investing in community alternatives to further reduce the numbers who are placed in custody.

Child First Inspection

The adoption of the Child First guiding principle challenges the rationale for the inspection of services for children in conflict with the law resting with an adult and offender focused inspectorate (Taylor, 2016). The existence of a separate inspection regime for youth offending teams is one of the biggest barriers to integrating services at a local level. The fear of an adverse judgement and the increasingly vocal approach of HMI Probation (Bateman, 2021) in recent years has encouraged a focus on discrete services and local arrangements for children in conflict with the law, at the expense of more holistic and integrated approaches (Day, 2022; Smith & Gray, 2019). Indeed the Chief Inspector of Probation has been critical of attempts to integrate YOTs into children's services as leading to a perceived watering down of attention to offending and public protection (HMI Probation, 2020).

A Child First approach aligns more naturally with the services for children in conflict with the law being incorporated into the Ofsted children's services inspection framework (Taylor, 2016). A future inspection regime should draw on involvement and insight from HMI Probation, within an integrated inspection framework led by Ofsted, which includes children in the Youth Justice System and attendant public protection concerns. However, for so long as HMI Probation continues to lead on youth justice inspections, it should carefully review its activity to ensure that it is promoting a Child First agenda, rather than risk-focused and deficit-led approaches (Day, 2022).

The logic of the Child First principle also dictates that the inspection regime for secure establishments holding children should be led by the children's inspectorate. In describing this rationale it is noted that the involvement of HMI Prisons and the Care Quality Commission to inspect secure training centres threw light on unacceptable regimes, which had largely been overlooked by Ofsted; see, for example, the history of inspections of Medway and Rainsbrook secure training centre pre and post joint inspections (Ofsted, 2021). The message here is that Ofsted, just like the rest of children's services, has a journey to undertake to itself embrace a Child First ethos when it comes to children in conflict with the law.

Establishing a Child First Framework for Assessment and Case Management

The YJB has adopted the Child First guiding principle and is seeking to use its influence and authority to encourage its application in all areas of the Youth Justice System. This is a significant development in view of the YJB's statutory responsibility to advise ministers and to monitor and promote effective practice. National Standards for Children in the Justice System (MoJ/YJB, 2019) incorporated the Child First principle and Case Management Guidance has been reviewed to reflect the YJB's thinking about how Child First should be operationalised (anticipated publication in 2022).

These are important developments but not in themselves sufficient to transform practice whilst it is still undertaken within the confines of discrete youth justice services, fulfilling centrally prescribed AssetPlus assessment requirements, on a different recording system from that used for other children. So long as these systems endure, predicated as they are on the need to differentiate those who offend from their peers, it will always be a struggle to be genuinely Child First. The best that will be achieved, by the best services, will be an uncomfortable and inefficient workaround.

To help local systems move to a Child First approach the YJB needs to provide profile and attention to the alternative assessment pilots, which have thus far proved positive developments for integrating youth justice work with wider children's services (YJB, 2021a). Based on the experience of these pilots, opportunities exist to work with key stakeholders within the system, such as the Association of Directors of Children's Services, to develop an integrated assessment and planning framework, which can be applied to all children, including those within the Youth Justice System. As described above, it is not envisaged that existing social work and early help templates need major adaptation (see the London case example below) but there is significant work to ensure that these more generic assessments routinely reflect the harms associated with offending and the contextual/extra-familial dimensions which are often present. These are primarily cultural and workforce development challenges, which can be addressed in conjunction with the work to respond effectively to a range of adolescent safeguarding challenges.

Incorporation of youth justice assessment and planning into mainstream children's services frameworks would also assist with the other priority of getting all information recorded on to one system. The greatest challenge within this will be for information to be drawn off for the YJB/DfE/MoJ which is specific to offending. The starting point, however, should be that if incorporating youth justice into wider children's services recording and case management is recognised as the right thing to do for children (and all those concerned for and affected by their behaviour) then it should be for the recording and reporting systems to adapt, not vice versa, as is currently the case. It should be of concern to all those who aspire to a Child First Youth Justice System that, to date, the YJB has not undertaken any work to consider what comes after AssetPlus. The lengthy lead-in time that will be required for any replacement to this national assessment framework means this is a matter the YJB should urgently address if it is serious about leading Child First reform.

In Focus: Child First Practice—YOT Systemic Assessment as an Alternative to AssetPlus

(London Boroughs of Kensington & Chelsea, City of Westminster, Hammersmith and Fulham).

This example is provided to demonstrate how local practice has been adapted to reflect the Child First principle. It provides evidence of how alternative assessment processes for children in conflict with the law can be integrated with the wider local authority children and families assessment process.

Building on, and in line with, the wider systemic practice model in Kensington & Chelsea, Hammersmith & Fulham, and Westminster, the three Local Authorities engaged in a pilot with the DfE and YJB in 2019 to introduce an alternative assessment and planning programme for children receiving a Youth Conditional Caution or Referral Order. The new model is informed by systemic, strengths-based and Child First approaches and is an alternative to the Youth Justice Board's AssetPlus.

Why Pilot an Alternative to AssetPlus?

Our theory is that the introduction of the assessment/planning model will:

- support a systemic and strengths-based model of practice;
- allow greater involvement of the young person and their family in their assessment and planning;
- allow more opportunity for analysis and reflection;
- enable more time to be spent with the young person and relationships to be deepened through it being a shared assessment experience;
- will ultimately contribute to more effective assessment, planning, intervention and outcomes; and
- will enable the process of assessment to become an opportunity for intervention;

- embed a common practice model and language through new assessment/planning proforma's alignment with the assessment proforma used in the wider children's services.

In the two years since the alternative assessment approach has been implemented the services have seen improved engagement with children and families, practitioners prefer the approach as it promotes time with clients and strengthened relationships over unwieldy assessment tools, and service managers consider the alternative approach is more effective and more aligned to the local authorities' core practice.

(Helen Bowring—Partners in Practice Programme Lead, Royal Borough of Kensington & Chelsea and City of Westminster).

Ultimately, Child First poses a challenge to the existence of the YJB. It could be said that the YJB's retention maintains a focus on the separation of children who offend to the detriment of the development of a Child First system. On the other hand, while there remains a distinct criminal justice response for children, it is important that this has separate oversight rather than being merged into adult structures. At this point, it can be said that we are so far away from a Child First system for children in conflict with the law that the YJB can continue to play a purposeful role in promoting progressive change. However, the YJB's interface with other accountable bodies for children (beyond criminal justice system partners) clearly needs attention if it is to fulfil its Child First aspirations. Development of a system that befits the Child First title will be long-term and sequential. There may come a point when the YJB, even in its most progressive guise, cannot be a force for good, but for the moment there appears to be space for the organisation to be a catalyst for the Child First reforms it is espousing.

Developing Child First Local Responses

Many local authorities have developed innovative and integrated arrangements, which have sought to overcome the structural barriers outlined in the first part of this chapter. The variety of current arrangements are well-captured in Smith and Gray's (2019) work. What is evident from their work is that structural innovation to promote integration of youth justice is not aided by a national framework of inspection and regulation which is more sympathetic to those local authorities which maintain separate 'offender management' orientated services for children (Day, 2022; Smith & Gray, 2019).

The work at a local level to re-design services for children in the Youth Justice System can be greatly assisted by YJB's Child First re-positioning. This would be further encouraged if the YJB was to lead on the enablers of integration outlined above in relation to governance and inspection/regulation, and case management systems and assessment. Practice will, nonetheless, still ultimately rely upon local authorities and their partners embracing a new ethos and delivery mechanisms. For reformed assessment, case recording and management processes to be effective they need to be jointly developed by YJB and the children's services stakeholders, including DfE and Association of Directors of Children's Services. This will require an investment in understanding and acting upon the experiences of children who are subject to these processes and practitioners who have to deliver them (see, e.g., of promising approaches sponsored by the YJB the work in London and Lancashire reflected in the case studies above and below). This reform and re-design will also need to engage and be cognisant of the wider partnerships (notably with police and health) which interact with children in trouble to ensure practice is held within a coherent framework.

In Focus: Child First Practice—Lancashire Child and Youth Justice Service Diversion

This example is provided to demonstrate how local practice has been adapted to reflect the Child First principle. Lancashire's Child First diversion has been a YJB Pathfinder with learning from the approach shared with the sector through practice workshops. It offers an example of how Child First diversion can be developed alongside the nationally prescribed framework for youth justice and move towards practice which is better integrated with the wider children's system.

In developing Lancashire Child and Youth Justice Service's Diversion offer, it was a clear intention to adopt a Child First framework, both in the language we used and the construction of the service. The Child First evidence base was consulted, including Case and Haines as well as the Edinburgh Study on Youth Trajectories and Crime. The over-whelming evidence was that in order to encourage and sustain diversion, we needed to ensure children were able to access child-friendly, appropriate services in order to meet their health, safety and well-being needs.

The development of the service visualised a continuum of need and drew comparisons to the experiences of children when referred into Children's Social Care front doors (often referred to as Multi-Agency Safeguarding Hubs). These children would receive proportionate, timely support from a range of services, both universal and targeted. Only very few would need the specialist support required from a statutory children's social care assessment. By the same token, not every child who has become known to police for an offence needs a specialist Youth Justice assessment and package of support. Some children do—but a proportion primarily need doors opening to be able to access support in their community from services targeted to the needs of the child and their family, for example, drug and alcohol services or early help services. The CYJS Diversion service took this philosophy as an over-arching principle and made sure that children and their families were given the correct, targeted, timely support, with the CYJS offer being part of that support, rather than the only support.

Importantly, Police colleagues need a suite of services to refer into so that referrals into CYJS are ultimately for those children who do need that more specialist support. CYJS have worked alongside Lancashire Constabulary and partner agencies to identify support services for children and their families in the community. Most recently, this has involved working alongside the Divert Youth offer in Lancashire—a partnership approach incorporating 9 Football Trusts across Lancashire who can offer support and mentoring to children who have come to the attention of the police. This "pre-YOT diversion" is an important component of our partnership offer, particularly when evidence suggests this police interaction is most likely going to be short-lived and the majority of children's offending is limited to the adolescent stage of their life-course.

(Hannah Blower, Team Manager, Lancashire Child and Youth Justice Service).

Freed from the constraints of separate recording and assessment frameworks, local authorities and partners would be at liberty to decide how best to organise their services for adolescents. Some may consider that they can best meet the needs of children in conflict with the law through retaining aspects of the youth justice specialism that currently reside in YOTs, while others would no doubt consider that more radical integration of these services and practitioners within other children and young people's arrangements aligns more closely to the Child First principle. In either approach it will be important to maintain skills to advocate for children when they come into contact with police, courts and custodial settings. As described above, re-design means more than just dropping youth justice into children's services. It will require a re-imagining of responses to the range of adolescents for whom children's services provide help, protection and care.

Some YOTs are still not managed within children's services or in the DCS's direct line of accountability. It is often argued that it does not make a difference to the service children get when the YOT is part of the local authority's community safety arrangements, rather than being part of children's services. From a Child First perspective, it matters; in just the same way as it matters that the sponsoring department is the MoJ not DfE. Ensuring youth justice is held within children's services departments does not negate the significance of the community safety response, not least in respect of contextual safeguarding and public protection, but it rightly prioritises seeing a child in conflict with the law as a Child First, not an offender.

This chapter has not explored in any detail the implications of a Child First approach for local youth justice partners other than the local authority, but it is evident that the same lens could be taken to the activities of health and policing in order to promote Child First responses. There is also a wealth of opportunity in working proactively with educational settings to better support children who have experienced adversity in order to promote inclusion, positive identity formation and access to a range of developmental opportunities. Re-imagining responses for children in trouble and their peers also provides an opportunity to engage with the capacity and energy of children themselves, their supporters, the voluntary sector and the communities who have a vested interest in their positive development (see Creaney, 2020; Smithson & Jones, 2021). It is also important to note that the current youth justice arrangements do bind statutory partners into some form of provision for children in the Youth Justice System, and there is a risk that in disrupting these arrangements the resources focused on these children could be lost. Tying-in partners and resources targeted at children who are likely to come into conflict with the law is a critical dimension of any prospective reforms. The danger of a loss of focus on these children is in part offset by the position outlined above; these children are typically already known to police and health through safeguarding and child exploitation routes. Nonetheless, retaining focus and resources for children in conflict with the law clearly needs to be explicit in any compact between local authorities and their partners.

Conclusion

The YJB's adoption of the Child First principle is an important milestone in the rise of the Child First offender second movement, marking a move from what started as a critical academic discourse to what is now an officially endorsed approach. While this still falls short of formal government policy, Child First is clearly an ever more significant influence on our responses to children in conflict with the law.

This chapter has sought to identify what a systematic response to children in trouble will require from the various stakeholders who are increasingly espousing the Child First principle. Critically, this means more than using the word 'child' rather than 'young offender' or 'young person', it means more than making existing structures slightly less adult-centric. If we are serious about treating children in conflict with the law as children, then we need to fundamentally re-shape structures and services, so that these children are drawn back into the mainstream, and we respond to their holistic needs as children, not just to one particular facet of their behaviour. Adopting Child First is an important declaration by the YJB and the youth justice sector as a whole is increasingly influenced by the principle. This piece identifies some of the far-reaching implications of a genuine commitment to Child First reforms; it is questionable whether these implications, as I have outlined them, are fully understood by the YJB or would be welcomed by central government. It is, nonetheless, important that this desired end state, and the activity required to achieve it, is articulated if Child First is to be more than a rhetorical flourish.

Reconceptualising children in trouble as, first and foremost, children, is crucial in enabling children in the Youth Justice System to access the rights enjoyed by other children. However, broader systemic and structural challenges associated with poverty and racism impact upon many childhoods and go beyond the Youth Justice System. If we are serious about enabling children to access rights and opportunities, then reform needs to go to the heart of society's structural inequalities. It is notable that aspirations for children in the Youth Justice System in both Scotland and Wales (Scottish Government, 2012, Welsh Government 2015a, 2015b) are couched in broader entitlements for all children as part of a whole government/whole system approach to providing the best start to life for children. England has no equivalent strategy for children. Without a whole system view of children's experience, it is likely that attempts to move towards a Child First approach to youth justice will founder. While developing a genuinely Child First response for children in trouble is a long-term project, it needs a shared vision as its starting point, and a coalition between a range of practitioners and policymakers to become a reality. All actors, whether at an individual or organisational level, can choose to be leaders of this change and start on the path to making Child First a reality.

References

Allen, R. (2016). The youth justice review: A plumber responds to an architect. *Unlocking Potential (blog)*. https://reformingprisons.blogspot.com/2016/12/the-youth-justice-review-plumber.html

Allen, R. (2018). Here we go again: Another type of youth custody a step closer. *Unlocking Potential (blog)*. http://reformingprisons.blogspot.com/2018/06/here-we-go-again-another-type-of-youth.html

Article 39. (2022). *Briefing on secure 16 to 19 academies (secure schools) for House of Lords Committee debates on the police, crime, sentencing and courts bill, February 2022*. https://article39.org.uk/secure-16-to-19-academies-feb-22/

Association of Directors of Children's Services. (2021). *A youth justice system that works for children*. ADCS.

Batchelor, S., & McNeill, F. (2005). The young person-worker relationship. In T. Bateman & J. Pitts (Eds.), *The RHP companion to youth justice*. Russell House Publishing.

Bateman, T. (2020). *The state of youth justice*. NAYJ.

Bateman, T. (2021). *Reform of the youth court: Bridging the care-crime gap*. NAYJ.

Billingham, L., & Irwin-Rogers, K. (2021). The terrifying abyss of insignificance: Marginalisation, mattering and violence between young people. *Onati Socio-Legal Series, 11*(5), 1222–1249.

Byrne, B., & Brooks, K. (2015). *Post-YOT youth justice*. Howard League. https://howardleague.org/wp-content/uploads/2016/04/HLWP_19_2015.pdf

Byrne, B., & Case, S. (2016). Towards a positive youth justice. *Safer Communities, 15*(2), 69–81.

Case, S. (2021). *Youth justice: A critical introduction*. Routledge.

Case, S., & Haines, K. (2020). Abolishing youth justice systems: Children first, offenders nowhere. *Youth Justice*. https://journals.sagepub.com/doi/full/10.1177/1473225419898754

Centre for Social Justice. (2012). *Rules of engagement: Changing the heart of youth justice*. Centre for Social Justice. https://www.centreforsocialjustice.org.uk/wp-content/uploads/2012/01/CSJ_Youth_Justice_Full_Report.pdf

Centre for Justice Innovation. (2020). *Young people's voices on youth courts*. https://justiceinnovation.org/sites/default/files/media/documents/2020-05/20200512_young_peoples_voices_on_youth_court_final.pdf

Child Safeguarding Practice Review Panel. (2020). *It was hard to get away.* https://assets.publishing.service.gov.uk/government/uploads/system/upl oads/attachment_data/file/870035/Safeguarding_children_at_risk_from_cri minal_exploitation_review.pdf

Children's Commissioner's Office. (2020a). *Falling through the gaps.* CCO. https://www.childrenscommissioner.gov.uk/report/teenagers-falling-through-the-gaps/

Children's Commissioner's Office. (2020b). *Injustice or in justice?* CCO. https://www.childrenscommissioner.gov.uk/wp-content/uploads/2020b/12/cco-injustice-or-in-justice.pdf

Children's Commissioner's Office. (2021). *Still not safe.* CCO. https://www.childrenscommissioner.gov.uk/wp-content/uploads/2021/02/cco-still-not-safe.pdf

Collier, R. (1998). *Masculinities, crime and criminology.* Sage.

Creaney, S. (2020). "Game playing" and "docility": Youth justice in question. *Safer Communities, 19*(3), 103–118.

Day, A. (2022, February 21). "It's a hard balance to find": The perspectives of youth justice practitioners in England on the place of 'risk' in an emerging 'child-first' world. *Youth Justice.*

Day, A., Bateman, T., & Pitts, J. (2020). *Surviving incarceration: The pathways of looked after and non-looked after children into, through and out of custody.* University of Bedfordshire. https://www.beds.ac.uk/media/271272/surviving-incarceration-final-report.pdf

Department for Education. (2018a). *Working together to safeguard children, statutory framework: Legislation relevant to safeguarding and promoting the welfare of children.* HMSO.

Department for Education. (2018b). *Keeping children safe in education statutory guidance for schools and colleges.* HMSO.

Drew, J. (2020) *Serious case review child C.* Waltham Forest Safeguarding Children Partnership. https://www.walthamforest.gov.uk/sites/default/files/2021-11/WFSCB%20-%20SCR%20Child%20C%20May%20final_.pdf

Firmin, C. (2020). *Contextual safeguarding and child protection: Re-writing the rules.* Routledge.

Goldson, B. (2000). *The new youth justice.* Russell House.

Goldson, B. (2005). Child imprisonment: A case for abolition. *Youth Justice, 5*(2), 77–90.

Haines, K., & Drakeford, M. (1998). *Young people and youth justice.* Macmillan.

Hagell, A., & Hazel, N. (2001). Macro and micro patterns in the development of secure custodial institutions for serious and persistent young offenders in England and Wales. *Youth Justice, 1*(1), 3–16.

Haines, K., & Case, S. (2015). *Positive youth justice: Children first, offenders second*. Policy Press.

Hanson, E., & Holmes, D. (2014). *That difficult age: Developing a more effective response to risks in adolescence*. The Dartington Hall Trust, Totnes. www.rip.org.uk/news-and-views/latest-news/evidence-scope-risks-in-adolescence/

Harris, J., Moreblessing, T., & Ramanathan, R. (2020). *Reimagining child welfare services for the 21st century*. Department for Education. https://assets.publishing.service.gov.uk/government/uploads/system/uploads/attachment_data/file/932340/Leeds_Partners_in_Practice.pdf

HM Inspectorate of Prisons. (1997). *Young prisoners: A thematic review by HM chief inspector of prisons for England and Wales*. https://www.justiceinspectorates.gov.uk/hmiprisons/wp-content/uploads/sites/4/2014/08/young-prisoners-rps.pdf

HM Inspectorate of Probation. (2020). *Annual report: Inspection of youth offending services (2019–2020)*. HMIP.

HM Inspectorate of Probation. (2022). *Youth offending service inspection*. https://www.justiceinspectorates.gov.uk/hmiprobation/about-hmi-probation/about-our-work/documentation-area/youth-offending-services-inspection/

HM Inspectorate of Prisons. (2006). *Annual report HM chief inspector of prisons for England and Wales 2005/2006*. https://www.gov.uk/government/publications/annual-report-hm-chief-inspector-of-prisons-for-england-and-wales-20052006

HM Inspectorate of Prisons. (2017). *HM chief inspector of prisons annual report 2016/2017*. HMSO. https://www.gov.uk/government/publications/hm-chief-inspector-of-prisons-annual-report-2016-to-2017

HM Inspectorate of Prisons. (2021). *Annual report and accounts 2020–21*. HMSO.

Ibbetson, K. (2013). *Child F—Serious case review*. Tower Hamlets Safeguarding Children Board.

Ibbetson, K. (2020). *Systemic learning review on serious youth violence*. Hounslow Safeguarding Children's Board. https://www.hscb.org.uk/wp-content/uploads/2020/11/HSCP-Serious-Youth-Violence-Systemic-Review-Learning-Review-November-2020.pdf

Independent Review of Children's Social Care. (2021). The case for change. *Children's Social Care Independent Review.* https://childrenssocialcare.indepe ndent-review.uk/wp-content/uploads/2021/06/case-for-change.pdf

Independent Review of Children's Social Care. (2022). *Final report independent review of children's social care.* https://childrenssocialcare.indepe ndent-review.uk/wp-content/uploads/2022/05/The-independent-review-of-childrens-social-care-Final-report.pdf

Innovate Project. (2021). *Trauma informed practice.* https://theinnovateproject. co.uk/trauma-informed-practice/

Iris. (2022). *Frameworks for child participation in social care.* https://www.iriss. org.uk/resources/esss-outlines/frameworks-child-participation-social-care

Jay, A. (2014). *Independent review into child sexual exploitation in Rotherham* https://www.rotherham.gov.uk/downloads/file/279/independent-inquiry-into-child-sexual-exploitation-in-rotherham

Khan, L., & Wilson, J. (2010) *You just get on and do it: Models of healthcare in youth offending teams.* Centre for Mental.

Local Government Association. (2018). *A public health approach to violence reduction.* LGA. https://www.local.gov.uk/sites/default/files/documents/15. 32%20-%20Reducing%20family%20violence_03.pdf

McAra, L., & McVie, S. (2010). Youth crime and justice: Key messages from the Edinburgh study of youth transitions and crime. *Criminology and Criminal Justice, 10*(2), 179–209.

Ministry of Justice. (December 2016). *The government response to Charlie Taylor's review of the youth justice system.* MoJ.

Ministry of Justice/Youth Justice Board. (2019). *Standards for children in the youth justice system 2019.* YJB.

Ministry of Justice/Youth Justice Board. (2020). *Addressing the needs of sentenced children in the youth justice system.* YJB.

Munro, E. (2011). *The Munro review of child protection: A child centred system.* Department of Education.

National Crime Agency. (2018). *County lines, drug supply, vulnerability and harm.* https://www.nationalcrimeagency.gov.uk/who-we-are/publicati ons/257-county-lines-drug-supply-vulnerability-and-harm-2018/file

Ofsted. (2008). *Learning lessons, taking action: Ofsted's evaluations of serious case reviews 1 April 2007 to 31 March 2008 Ofsted.*

Ofsted. (2021). *Inspections of secure training centres.* Ofsted | Medway Secure Training Centre and https://reports.ofsted.gov.uk/provider/11/1027078

Ofsted. (2022). *Inspecting local authority children's services.* https://www.gov.uk/government/publications/inspecting-local-authority-childrens-services-from-2018/inspecting-local-authority-childrens-services

Pitts, J. (2008). *Reluctant Gangsters: The changing face of youth crime.* Willian, Cullumpton.

Phoenix, J., & Kelly, L. (2013). "You have to do it for yourself" responsibilisation and youth justice. *British Journal of Criminology, 53*(3), 419–437.

Public Health England. (2019). *Preventing offending and re-offending by children (CAPRICORN).* PHE. https://www.gov.uk/government/publications/preventing-offending-and-re-offending-by-children/collaborative-approaches-to-preventing-offending-and-re-offending-by-children-capricorn-summary

Rand. (2019). *A process evaluation of asset plus.* Cambridge.

Restorative Justice Council. (2022). *Restorative practice in education.* https://restorativejustice.org.uk/restorative-practice-education-0#:~:text=A%20restorative%20school%20is%20one,steps%20to%20put%20it%20right. Accessed April 2022.

Rutherford, A. (2002). *Growing out of crime: The new era.* Hook, Waterside Press.

Scottish Government. (2012). *Getting it right for every child.* https://www.gov.scot/policies/girfec/

Smith, R. (2014). *Youth justice: Ideas, policy ad practice.* Routledge.

Smith, R., & Gray, P. (2019). The changing shape of youth justice: Models of practice. *Criminology and Criminal Justice, 19*(5), 554–571.

Smithson, H., & Jones, A. (2021). Co-creating youth justice practice with young people. *Children & Society, 35*, 348–362. https://onlinelibrary.wiley.com/doi/epdf/10.1111/chso.12441

Standing Committee for Youth Justice. (2020). *Ensuring custody is the last resort for children in England and Wales.* SCYJ.

Taylor, C. (2016). *Review of the youth justice system in England and Wales.* MoJ. https://assets.publishing.service.gov.uk/government/uploads/system/uploads/attachment_data/file/577105/youth-justice-review-final-report-print.pdf

Unicef. (2019). *A rights-based analysis of youth justice in the United Kingdom.* https://www.unicef.org.uk/wpcontent/uploads/2020/12/UnicefUK_YouthJusticeReport2020_screen.pdf

Welsh Government. (2015a). *Children and young people's programme.* https://gov.wales/sites/default/files/publications/2019-06/seven-core-aims-for-children-and-young-people.pdf

Welsh Government. (2015b). *Future Generations Act 2015b*. https://www.fut uregenerations.wales/about-us/future-generations-act/

Welsh Government. (2020). *Youth justice blueprint for Wales*. https://gov.wales/ sites/default/files/publications/2019-05/youth-justice-blueprint_0.pdf

Wroe, L., & Lloyd, J. (2020). Watching over or working with? Understanding social work innovation in response to extra-familial harm. *Social Science, 9*, 37.

YJB. (2021a). *Youth Justice Board for England and Wales: Strategic Plan 2021a–2024*. YJB. https://assets.publishing.service.gov.uk/government/upl oads/system/uploads/attachment_data/file/802702/YJB_Strategic_Plan_2 019_to_2022.pdf

YJB. (2021b). *Ethnic disproportionality in remand and sentencing in the youth justice system*. YJB.

10

The Place of Risk Within Child First Justice: An Exploration of the Perspectives of Youth Justice Practitioners

Anne-Marie Day

Introduction

The Youth Justice Board recently published an updated Strategic Plan for 2021–2024 which identified Child First as its central guiding principle (YJB, 2021: 10). Notably, this marks a shift from the approach outlined in its strategic plan of 2019–2022 of 'child first, offender second' (YJB, 2019: 7), presumably in response to criticisms that the 'offender second' element continued to have a labelling effect and deficit focus (Bateman, 2020), and aligning itself more closely with Haines and Drakeford's original principle of Children First (1998). The move to Child First has, for the Youth Justice Board, been a journey of several years, which gained significant momentum following UK Government commissioned Taylor Review of the Youth Justice System (Taylor, 2016), and subsequent appointment of Charlie Taylor as Chair of the Youth Justice Board

---

A.-M. Day (✉)
Keele University, Newcastle-Under-Lyme, Staffordshire, England
e-mail: a.day@keele.ac.uk

© The Author(s), under exclusive license to Springer Nature Switzerland AG 2023
S. Case and N. Hazel (eds.), *Child First*,
https://doi.org/10.1007/978-3-031-19272-2_10

in 2017. However, despite this shift, there remains within national legislation in England and Wales the principle aim of youth offending teams to 'prevent' offending (s37 (1) The Crime and Disorder Act 1998). Risk assessment and management have become the means by which the statutory responsibility to prevent offending has been executed. As a result of this and other key pieces of legislation, a 'risk culture' (Case & Haines, 2016; Hampson, 2018) has dominated both youth justice and wider criminal justice practice for the past quarter of a century. However, as moves away from risk and towards Child First approaches emerge from central policy narratives, it is important that we gain an understanding of the perspectives of the youth justice practitioners responsible for navigating this shift, and the impact this is having on front-line practice.

This chapter is based on findings from an evaluation of the Youth Justice Board's Constructive Resettlement Pathfinder Project. Data is drawn from 14 interviews with youth justice practitioners and operational managers, which were conducted as part of the evaluation. This chapter will argue that the policy shift away from risk narratives is meeting with a number of challenges on the ground. Previous research has argued that despite attempts by the Youth Justice Board to move towards desistance-based and Child First approaches, the risk culture continues to dominate front-line practice (Case & Browning, 2021; Day, 2022; Hampson, 2018). This chapter builds on this argument by offering further insight into the potential barriers to the cultural shift on the ground and emphasises the importance of engaging with and hearing the perceptions of front-line staff about the current and future direction of youth justice policy and practice. Unless front-line practitioners are engaged with meaningfully about these barriers, the cultural shift sought by those at a central strategic level is likely to have a limited impact.

My own background as a Probation Officer who was trained in 2002 in the RFPP for working with adults, and then subsequently children from 2007 to 2012 gives me a degree of insight and empathy into the challenges currently faced by front-line practitioners. I remember receiving training in the 'Scaled Approach' and new sentencing structure for children in 2008. This caused reticence and frustration in practitioners, who could see that the youth justice system was mirroring the adult Probation system's own version of 'managing' adults. I do not remember meaningful dialogue taking place with practitioners prior to the implementation, but I do remember lots of frustration from staff when we were trained in the new techniques. I tried to take this on board when I moved to the Youth Justice Board as a Senior Development Adviser in 2012, ensuring that I firstly spoke to practitioners before developing any policy initiatives in partnership with my YJB colleagues. I wanted to ensure that we addressed the concerns of front-line staff and that they were consulted with throughout. I was told by front-line staff that my approach was the exception, rather than the rule.

Looking back, I can see that, as a practitioner, I fed the risk culture within youth justice by believing the rhetoric that swift and clear procedures to manage a child's 'risk' would be most effective in reducing their offending. I deeply regret this and believe that a fundamental error lies in how messages from the centre were communicated to staff. We were told that the only way to prevent offending was through the management of risk via the RFPP. We were not presented with alternative approaches that may be more child-friendly. I wish I had known, as I do now, so that I could have challenged this practice from my positions as a practitioner and senior policy adviser.

Setting the Scene

It is important to firstly set out what is meant by Child First, the risk factor prevention paradigm, and desistance within a youth justice context. The risk factor prevention paradigm has been the dominant discourse across criminal justice since the 1990s and emerged in tandem with a general rise in actuarialism across public services (Smith, 2006). The actuarialist perspective seeks to identify causes within the context of risk factors, without seeking to explain why the link is there or a theory of change. It also focuses firmly on preventing and controlling the crime 'problem' through risk assessment and management. Various studies such as 'The Cambridge Study' (West & Farrington, 1973) and 'The Rochester Youth Development Study' (Loeber et al, 1996) claimed to be able to identify a series of risk factors that increase the probability of a person or child committing a criminal offence. Therefore, by identifying and addressing these key risk factors, it was concluded that a person's risk of reoffending could reduce if they received the correct 'intervention' to address this (Farrington, 2002).

The risk paradigm has been heavily criticised in recent years for its flawed methodology (Case & Haines, 2009), its labelling effect (Bateman, 2020), and the adulterisation and responsibilisation of children (Haines & Case, 2015):

> Privileging a risk-based youth justice agenda allowed the government to demonise children in conflict with the law and youth justice system, using net-widening, punitive, labelling, responsibilising measures, while simultaneously controlling the central-local relationship and the practice of YOTs and their staff via prescriptive and technicised responses to restricted conceptions of offending behaviour by children. (Haines & Case, 2015: 29)

As part of their critique, Haines and Case argued that a youth justice system could prevent offending by taking a children first, offender second approach. This approach emerged in practice through child-focused research conducted by Haines and Case (2015). The more recently renamed 'Child First Justice' (Case & Browning, 2021) would involve 'the total abandonment of risk-based assessment and intervention, but not the abandonment of assessment and intervention per se' (Case & Haines, 2016: 69). Rather, a Child First system would focus on 'Positive Promotion' (Case & Haines, 2021), rather than the negative, deficit focus of risk. Positive Promotion would be based on the concepts of 'universalism, diversion and normalisation, pursued through (non-criminal justice) practice that is inclusionary, participatory and legitimate' (Case & Haines, 2021). Crucially, this approach would involve a holistic, individualistic, tailored approach based on a child's welfare needs that focuses on their strengths and future aspirations. It is envisaged that this would be delivered by universal services, recognising that children in conflict with the law are still children first and do not need to be separated, labelled, responsibilised and criminalised.

A number of 'tenets' of Child First Justice have been identified by the YJB (2021: 10):

1. See children as children: Prioritise the best interests of children, recognising their particular needs, capacities, rights and potential. All work is child-focused, developmentally informed, acknowledges structural barriers and meets responsibilities towards children.
2. Develop pro-social identity for positive child outcomes: Promote children's individual strengths and capacities to develop their pro-social identity for sustainable desistance, leading to safer communities and fewer victims. All work is constructive and future-focused, built on supportive relationships that empower children to fulfil their potential and make positive contributions to society.
3. Collaboration with children: Encourage children's active participation, engagement and wider social inclusion. All work is a meaningful collaboration with children and their careers.
4. Promote diversion: Promote a childhood removed from the justice system, using pre-emptive prevention, diversion and minimal intervention. All work minimises criminogenic stigma from contact with the system.

The Youth Justice Board (YJB) has, in recent years, embraced this approach in their strategic documentation, which will be outlined in detail below. Elements of desistance-based approaches to working with children in conflict with the law are evident within tenet two of Child First Justice, above. Wigzell (2021: 4) notes that the desistance paradigm differs from the risk paradigm in two key ways: firstly, it focuses on how people stop offending; and secondly, desistance is a process, rather than an intervention delivered 'to' children with the aim of reducing the risk of offending. Maruna and Farrell (2004) break the desistance process into two phases—primary (stopping offending) and secondary desistance (maintenance of ceasing offending by achieving a shift in identity from pro-offending to non-offending or pro-social). Elements of desistance-based approaches have emerged within youth justice policy and practice in England and Wales in the last ten years. Firstly, the YJB responded to criticisms that the main youth justice risk assessment tool, Asset, was too focused on historical deficits by replacing it with AssetPlus in 2014. The new risk assessment sought to include consideration of a child's strengths, and identification of desistance factors. Secondly, as outlined above, the YJB have adopted a Child First approach to justice that places the concept of a child's identity development from pro-offender to pro-social as the second of its key tenets. An example of this is the recent adoption of the 'Constructive Resettlement' approach to working with children on release from custody. Constructive Resettlement is defined by the YJB (YJB, 2018: 8) as 'collaborative work with a child in custody and following release that builds upon their strengths, to help them shift their identity from pro-offending to prosocial'. Within this approach, the clear overall role for all agencies is to facilitate the child's identity shift from 'offender' to 'pro-social' by focusing on the provision of individualised personal and structural support. Constructive Resettlement builds upon the work of the Beyond Youth Custody (BYC) programme in the UK (Hazel & Bateman, 2021; Hazel et al., 2017). Beyond Youth Custody was a six-year programme ending in 2018, that sought to identify best practice in helping children resettle from custody into the community. BYC identified five key characteristics of effective and sustainable resettlement, namely, that all work with children should be constructive, co-created, customised, consistent and co-ordinated.

Given the influence of desistance approaches within Child First Justice, Wigzell (2021) concludes that central policy narratives may be moving towards 'Child First Desistance'. It is, however, important to understand how this shift has occurred.

The Policy Shift from Risk to Child First Narratives

It is important that the Youth Justice Board's move away from its focus on risk to Child First is briefly outlined. This chapter does not seek to chart all historical developments within youth justice over the last 20–30 years. Indeed, there are many papers that do this extremely well, (see, e.g., Case & Hampson, 2019; Case & Bateman, 2020; Cuneen et al.,

2018; Goldson, 2020). Chapters 1–4 of this book offer a comprehensive overview of the developments within youth justice over the past 20–30 years, with Tim Bateman firstly focusing on how the development of Youth Justice Systems in the Western world have overly relied on adult-based criminal justice systems, often in sharp contrast to Child First principles. Stephen Case builds on this in Chapter 2 by considering the development of Child First as a policy and practice principle within youth justice in England and Wales. In Chapter 3, Kevin Haines and Sue Thomas consider developments specifically within Wales, and finally Ursula Kilkelly, in Chapter 4, considers the developing relationship between Child First and the international children's rights movement, underpinned by the UNCRC 1989 (United Nation Convention on the Rights of the Child). The 'new' youth justice system was created under the 1998 Crime and Disorder Act, reflecting a wider 'punitive turn' (Muncie, 2008) towards children in trouble with the law in Western Europe and the USA. The main aim of the system in England and Wales was the *prevention of offending by children* (s37 (1) CDA 1998), with the Government viewing *risk assessment-based intervention and management* as the means by which to achieve this (Haines & Case, 2015).

It has been argued that the UK Government's continued commitment to the risk factor prevention paradigm (Case & Hampson, 2019) in the face of sustained criticism from many quarters reflects, at worst, a contempt for children in trouble with the law; and, at best, a disregard for their needs. Some of the key criticisms of the risk factor prevention paradigm (RFPP) have been documented in detail elsewhere (see, e.g., Bateman & Pitts, 2010; Haines & Case, 2009; Smith, 2006); and are outlined above. When Every Child Matters was published (Department for Education, 2004), Bateman and Pitts concluded that 'every child matters unless you have broken the law' (Bateman & Pitts, 2010: 56). Successive UK governments have tended to seek reforms to the YJS that, it has been argued, have amounted to 'stochastic features of statecraft' (Case & Hampson, 2019: 27)—a tinkering around the edges, rather than seeking wholesale reform.

An opportunity for major reform presented in 2016, with Charlie Taylor's Government-commissioned review of the Youth Justice System (Taylor, 2016). Taylor, inspired by the Child First, offender second approach (Haines & Case, 2015), made a number of significant recommendations that, if acted upon, could have brought about the reform sought by many. However, the UK Government ignored the majority of recommendations, with the main commitment being to replace a large part of the children's custodial estate (Young Offender Institutions and Secure Training Centres) with Secure Schools. Despite ignoring many of Taylor's recommendations, the UK Government appointed Taylor as Chair of the YJB in 2017. A number of Child First advocates joined the Board and have commenced a work programme that has moved the YJB's central policy narrative away from the RFPP and towards Child First Justice. Revisions and updates to strategic documents, youth justice standards, pathfinder initiatives, terminology and training events all reflect this change in recent years (Bateman, 2020).

Confusion at the Macro, Meso and Micro Levels of Youth Justice

Ideological shifts in policy often seek to trigger equally sudden shifts in practice. Such policy shifts, however, can often lead to confusion amongst practitioners (Case et al., 2020; Day, 2022; Hampson, 2018). Indeed, similar patterns of confusion emerged amongst front-line practitioners following the inception of the Crime and Disorder Act 1998, which, as part of the 'punitive turn', marked a shift in practice away from welfare and towards the management of risk (Burnett & Appleton, 2004). The confusion surrounding the current policy shift is evident at the macro, meso and micro levels. For example, at the macro level, there are competing narratives about how best to 'do' youth justice amongst academics and the wider research community. Advocates of Child First (Case & Haines, 2015) have clearly influenced the direction of YJB policy, whilst others draw attention to the importance of rights-based (e.g. Goldson & Randazzo, 2021); participatory (e.g. Smithson & Jones, 2021); or trauma informed (e.g. Evans et al., 2020) approaches to working with children in conflict with the law.

Further, there is confusion and a lack of consensus between key UK Government agencies over the meaning of key criminal justice terms such as desistance (Maruna & Mann, 2019), prevention and diversion (Case & Hampson, 2019). This has resulted in different interpretations of key terms in key policy documents, assessment tools, and inspection criteria, which for reasons of political expediency or otherwise, are leading to mixed and confusing messages to those on the youth justice 'coal face' (Case & Hampson, 2019: 33). In particular, the YJB and Her Majesty's Inspectorate of Probation's (HMIP) understanding of desistance appear to be 'at odds' (Bateman, 2020) with one another, leading to further confusion and mixed messages for youth justice managers and practitioners. Moreover, although the Youth Justice Board have stated that their approach to youth justice will be on the basis of Child First Justice, features of the RFPP remain in the YJB Case Management Guidance (YJB, 2019), which is currently being updated.

The lack of consensus and confusion is also evident at the meso-level, with many different iterations and models of youth justice teams across England and Wales. Smith and Gray (2019) contend that the 'monolithic view' of youth justice presented at the centre does not reflect the application of youth justice practice on the ground. The localism agenda (the decentralisation of power away from London and into the hands of local councils) has contributed to this, reducing the influence of the centrally based YJB on local youth justice teams (Bateman, 2020), leading to multiple iterations of how best to 'do' youth justice in different local authorities. As new principles and approaches emerge, they often compete with existing principles and practices on the ground. Goodman et al. (2017) argue that penal policy and practice rarely changes from one thing to the other. Rather, established approaches blend with emerging ideas. Smith and Gray (2019), in their analysis of 34 youth justice plans, found a number of different models of practice displaying a range of different 'blends' of ideas ranging from traditional and distinct youth offending teams, that prioritised risk assessment and management of children's criminal behaviours, through to Child First models where the youth offending team has been absorbed into a wider targeted youth support provision that prioritises welfare needs over criminal behaviours. The differing models of youth justice practice across England and Wales align themselves with differing theoretical approaches including RFPP, trauma informed practice, desistance, or Child First models. Some appear to attempt a hybrid of some, or all of, the above (Smith & Gray, 2019).

Further compounding this, confused and contradictory messages are contained in HMIP youth justice inspection reports. For example, Hampson (2018) notes that the HMIP commenced a desistance-themed inspection of youth offending teams in 2016. However, subsequent inspections 'virtually ignored' desistance, seeking alternatively to focus on risk assessment and management, and offending behaviour interventions focused on reducing a child's risk of offending and harm (Hampson, 2018: 30). As Hampson notes:

> This surely gives mixed messages to YOTs regarding what is expected of them – how can they pursue a desistance-based agenda if the criteria upon which they will be judged by the inspectorate is still (for general inspections) firmly risk-focused? (Hampson, 2018: 30)

The confusion and mixed messages are having an impact on the micro-level amongst youth justice practitioners. Hampson (2018) found that, despite the YJB developing a new assessment tool, AssetPlus, with an increased focus on desistance, the risk culture continued to dominate youth justice practice. Equally, Wigzell (2021) found that the concept of 'identity shift', a core part of desistance-based approaches in youth justice, was 'irrelevant' to children subject to youth justice supervision. However, Child First Justice has moved away from the language of identity shift, focusing instead on a child's identity development, as reflected in the second tenet. This may go some way to counter Wigzell's argument, as it reflects the dynamic nature of identity development, rather than the negative focus and rather rigid concept of identity shift.

Variations in front-line practice are also influenced by individuals' diverse backgrounds, cultures, training and perspectives. For example, Weston and Mythen (2020) found that practitioners' understandings of child sexual exploitation were 'markedly influenced by their own personal experiences, moral codes and social values'. Similarly, Bovarnick (2010) found that the approach adopted by professionals impacted on their perceptions of the children. For those who adopted a child-centred approach, children were viewed as in need of protection.

The youth justice literature has suggested that there appears to be a 'resistance and reticence' amongst practitioners to move away from risk-based approaches (Case, 2020; Hampson, 2018). Lack of adequate training, mixed messages at the macro and meso levels, confusion about key terminology, investment in established forms of practice and the reducing influence of the Youth Justice Board have all been cited as possible reasons for the limited impact of changes in practice (Bateman, 2020; Case, 2020; Hampson, 2018).

It is clear from the literature that the impact of the shift in central policy narratives away from risk-based approaches and towards Child First on front-line practice is difficult to discern (Bateman, 2020: 6). This paper seeks to explore this by focusing on the perceptions of youth justice practitioners on whether, and how, these shifts are having an impact 'on the ground'.

Research Design

The study from which this particular chapter is drawn adopted a qualitative approach using 1:1 semi-structured interviews. They were conducted with 14 youth justice practitioners and operational managers from North England as part of a wider, YJB-funded, evaluation of the Constructive Resettlement pathfinder. The pathfinder aimed to embed the principles of 'Constructive Resettlement' into policy and practice over a 3-year period in South and West Yorkshire between 2019 and 2022.

Prior to conducting the research, ethical clearance was secured from Keele University, and due to COVID-19 restrictions, all interviews were conducted online via Microsoft Teams, after participants were initially asked to participate via email. The information sheet and consent form were attached to the initial email. Once participants responded positively by email, a date and time was arranged to conduct the interview.

Immediately prior to commencing the interview, the researcher checked that the participant still consented, and made it clear that the process was entirely voluntary. An interview schedule containing 'prompts' and 'probes' was used to facilitate a conversation, the pace and direction of which was largely determined by the interviewee. The aim in the interviews was for the exchange to feel like a 'conversation with a purpose' (Burgess, 1984) and less like a structured question and answer session. All interviews were recorded on Teams and deleted immediately after transcription. All interviews were anonymised at the point of transcription. Youth justice workers and managers roles are highlighted in brackets below each quote.

Adopting inductive reasoning, data analysis of the interviews highlighted several recurring themes. The approach recognises that data is produced as a result of the interaction between interviewer and interviewee (Charmaz & Bryant, 2007). It is, therefore, recognised that the nature of the interview, the relationship between the interviewer and interviewee, and the setting can all impact on the data. A number of themes were identified, which are outlined below.

On the Ground—Resistance, Contradiction and Confusion

A number of themes emerged during the interviews with youth justice practitioners and operational managers including evidence of resistance and a culture of fear; contradiction and emerging bifurcated practice; and confusion about the meaning of key terms and how to negotiate a 'balance' between competing approaches.

Resistance and a Culture of Fear

Evidence emerged that staff feel that risk should form a central part of their work with youth justice. This is synonymous with the literature that referred to the continued dominance of the risk culture (Hampson, 2018), and a perceived reticence on the part of practitioners to move away from risk-based approaches (Case, 2020). Workers and operational managers discussed striking a balance between risk assessment and management, and welfare-based approaches such as Child First:

The risk stuff, I'm not with the school of thought that says risk has no place in a child-centred system, because I think it does. Even if you look at places like Norway where it's a welfare-based rather than criminal justice system, they are still assessing risk. (YOT Team Manager 1)

Norway does not, in fact, have a system based on the risk factor prevention paradigm, but they do have a duty to protect the public. The above quote may reflect a general conflation within practice in England and Wales of risk management and public protection, and an assumption that they must go hand in hand.

Others discussed the importance of risk assessments remaining a core feature of youth justice work from the perspective of defensive practice and decision making:

If you have a risky case that comes out of custody and does a serious offence, you can have people who are going to be looking at your work and your assessments from a risk management perspective. And basically, from a hindsight knowledge perspective, where they're going to be thinking, well we know this happened. And this was terrible. And what on earth was done about it? So that never goes away, and that's always at the back of your mind. And I guess management would say, well, we've got all these risk procedures in place that will take care of risks. (YOT Worker 1)

There was a perception amongst staff that, should a serious incident occur, the risk assessment and management systems provided a degree of protection and clarity about why key decisions were made, offering a standardised scoring system to potentially explain and justify their actions. Although, this, to a certain degree may be true, risk-based approaches can also be used as evidence of 'poor' decision making and be used to responsibilise individual practitioners when a serious incident occurs. It is apparent that the 'risk culture' within youth justice practice goes beyond interactions with children, and has created a 'risk averse culture' and workforce that is fearful of 'getting it wrong' and being subject to scrutiny and sanctions:

> There are so many specialist risk assessments, that the fear is that you haven't got time to do them all, so you leave yourself exposed. (YOT Officer 3)

Despite the apparent fear of 'getting it wrong', some practitioners and managers felt that, although Child First should form a core part of their work, risk should also be a central feature.

There was also concern about how children deemed to be 'very high risk of harm' or 'dangerous' would be safely managed in the community if risk management controls were removed:

> And I think the bit for me that's really important about it is the difference between internal and external controls in risk management, because the reality is that some of our young people, whilst it may be symptomatic of lived experience, the reality is in the here and now they are dangerous, they do present a significant risk of harm to other people. The important bit for me is actually those external controls in terms of what you put around them to contain and support them whilst they develop those internal controls that keep them safe as much as other people safe. (YOT Team Manager 3)

This appears to reflect a misunderstanding amongst practitioners that a move towards Child First Justice would mean risk management of 'dangerous' children would be removed or compromised in some way. Child First Justice advocates that children's risks to others can be managed much more effectively by assessing the whole child, including their safeguarding needs, rather than assessing a much narrower, deficit-based criteria determined by the RFPP.

One worker described the value of an assessment process in being that it allows a worker to use their professional 'gut' instinct, but the assessment allows one to make sense of that instinct and ensure that nothing is 'missed':

> I'm not disputing the professional... A lot of professionals have that ability, but that process of working it out, I think, and transferring it onto paper and working it through is still a useful one, because I know that when I do that with... When I pick up cases, my thought process

can change, my hypothesis at the start can change. I will miss things, I will start seeing connections that I didn't perhaps see initially, and that's where I think the value of the assessment process is. (YOT Team Manager 1)

The value of comprehensive assessments of a child are not in question here. Rather, it is the 'risk lens' through which the assessment is conducted that has been widely critiqued. A fear of 'getting it wrong' emerged strongly from the interviews—whether it is the fear of getting an assessment wrong and 'missing something' and leaving oneself open to professional scrutiny; or a fear how the public can be protected from children labelled as 'dangerous' or a 'high risk of harm to others' if the RFPP is removed. It is apparent that fear is a significant feature of the 'risk culture' in youth justice, and, for some workers, the very suggestion that this should be replaced with Child First, exposes these fears and leads to reticence and resistance.

A number of workers felt that there was value in retaining a focus on offending behaviour work, a core part of the RFPP, even though it was referred to as the 'negative stuff' that they 'got out of the way':

I definitely think offending behaviour needs to be addressed to start with. And I think it's quite good to get it done early on, so then all the negative stuff's done and out of the way. They can focus on that and then move on to the more positive things. It's definitely something that needs doing and I think it makes them (the child) think a little bit. (YOT Education Worker)

Here, there appears to be a recognised value in completing offending behaviour work with a child, but for this practitioner, it is one of the less favourable aspects of their time together, and it is difficult to ascertain what the identified value is.

Some workers recognised that the introduction of AssetPlus in 2014 had led to an increased focus on desistance and, in particular, a child's strengths in sentence plans and work completed with children. However, supporting Hampson's (2018) findings, it was acknowledged that it takes more than new assessment frameworks to 'change people's minds':

> I think it's probably achieved a bit of a shift, but maybe not as much as it was intended to. I think the reason for that is because you can't change people's minds with a piece of paper. (YOT Worker 5)

It is apparent that there is a perception amongst front-line practitioners that tinkering with the Youth Justice System via the creation of new assessment systems, rather than seeking wholesale reform, has had limited impact. This can also be explained, in part, by the risk averse culture that was evident with some youth justice practitioners.

A number of staff discussed their efforts to bring about the cultural shift away from risk-based approaches to Child First and some of the resistance that they had met along the way:

> And I said, exactly this thing, we should be future-focused and that's how we can manage the risk. And the person responding it, it was like their mic drop moment, "I you don't want to manage risk, you should not be in youth justice". And it totally floored me, because it's like we'd had this half hour discussion and basically they'd just chucked out everything by just saying that it's all about risk. (YOT Senior Practitioner)

Evidence of a resistance and reticence to completely abandoning the risk factor prevention paradigm (RFPP) emerged strongly from the data. There appear to be several reasons for this including a fear of 'getting it wrong' and a perception that the RFPP provides a degree of protection; how to manage children who are deemed to be 'dangerous' or a 'high risk of harm'; or a perception that an inherent part of working in the youth justice system involves the assessment and management of risk. It is possible that emerging practice on the ground supports Goodman et al.'s (2017) thesis that the development of criminal justice practice should be understood as a complex blend of many competing approaches, rather than a 'pendulum swing' between risk and Child First.

Contradiction and Bifurcated Practice

Apparent contradictory messages from HMIP and the YJB about whether the focus of youth justice practice should be on risk-based or Child First approaches was causing a number of difficulties and challenges on the ground. A recent HMIP inspection of a youth justice team that had adopted a Child First model had been subject to criticism of its risk assessment and management processes, leading to a negative outcome. This had a huge impact on practice in that youth justice team, and had also been felt in neighbouring local authority areas:

> I know with *****, and it was a shock to everybody what their inspection result was. And I'm sure that anybody who knows ***** YOT would know that they're not that YOT that got rated like they did' (YOT Team Manager 2).
>
> 'But just off the back of the inspection, we've gone back down, we've totally changed our management risk processes. They're much more labour intensive for case workers now and that's only off the back of the inspection. So, for me, I see we've gone down the wrong route because we've taken workers away from being with young people. Because the process now it's much more time-consuming. That time has to come from somewhere. And the time comes from the time they could spend with the young people. (YOT Senior Practitioner)

The lengthy bureaucratic procedures and paperwork involved in the increased focus on risk assessment and management of children was also a concern for workers, as they felt it reduced the time that they could be spending with the children. The increased focus on risk also changed the nature of the relationship with children, potentially undermining elements of a Child First relationship such as co-production, future focus and individuality. It was highlighted that the increased levels of bureaucracy and paperwork following the inspection of a neighbouring area had gone 'too far' for staff:

> I think that there is a preoccupation with risk. I think there has to be a preoccupation with risk, but I get the sense that there's a feeling amongst my colleagues who are doing all those risk assessments, that it's gone a

little bit too far in terms of the paperwork right now. But I don't want to speak for them. That's just the sense that I get. (YOT Specialist Worker)

It is apparent that the contradictory messages from HMIP and the YJB appeared to be increasing workloads for staff, as they were trying to meet, what they felt, were the competing demands of two differing approaches to working with children. It was widely acknowledged that this meant increased levels of bureaucracy, less time spent with the children, a return to deficit-focused offending behaviour work and a form of bifurcated practice. Some examples of this included that a number of YOTs sought to amend their practice to focus on risk, and meet the demands of HMIP, whilst also seeking to work with a child in a way that is Child First. Some youth offending teams had created their own 'child friendly' plan, in addition to the sentence plan:

> I just think it's a bit more user friendly. It's a bit more young person friendly. And I think it focuses on the critical elements that you need to focus on, like risk, getting their views about what might reduce it, what might increase it. And I think that the intervention plan AssetPlus doesn't really do that. (YOT Worker 4)

The bifurcated practice was evident in that youth justice teams had developed their own Child First plan that they used as the basis for all their work with children, but they continued to complete the AssetPlus plan, using risk-based terminology to satisfy the requirements of HMIP:

> Yes, because the work involved in assessments is significant. Maybe we need to be better at explaining something. So, if we're putting in a plan we're going to help you join a club, but we put in our bit of the plan and that's offending behaviour work in a way, because it means that. It's just difficult, isn't it? (YOT Officer 3)
>
> But what it means to me and in terms of thinking about practice, it's thinking about how do we move away from backward facing and negative formulated plans and work that we're going to do with young people to be more future orientated and positive. And know that that's recognised, that the research that you've been part of tells us that that's the way to do it and people like HMIP need to catch up with that. (YOT Officer 5)

It was apparent in interviews that the implementation of Child First had created a tension for both front-line staff and managers: they have a tool, AssetPlus, which, although seeking to introduce elements of desistance, still requires them to assess risk and consider historical, deficit-based factors. However, the Constructive Resettlement approach (Hazel & Bateman, 2021) requires a move towards resettlement and sentence planning that is positive, future oriented and based on a child's identity shift (as outlined in tenet 2 of Child First Justice), further exacerbating the bifurcated practice:

> When I'm countersigning assessments and looking at the plans, I do think one of the hardest things to write is a plan in the positive. It's always easier to write we're going to work on this and we're going to work on that, but it's about trying to think about what do we want the end result to be…. A lot of the time you might say I'm going to work on substance misuse. Well, that doesn't mean anything, does it? What does that measure? Whereas, actually, we want a young person to live without using substance misuse. I suppose it's around language, the way that we say stuff and it is that identity shift stuff and about young people not feeling that they are a label, really. (YOT Team Manager 2)
>
> Who wants to talk about something bad that you've done repeatedly? It's thinking about how do we move away from backward facing and negative formulated plans and work that we're going to do with young people to be more future orientated and positive. (YOT Team Manager 1)

Ultimately, for some practitioners who were embracing Child First approaches, they felt that there needed to be changes to the inspection processes and criteria to reflect the values and approaches of individual youth justice teams. As highlighted by Smith and Gray (2019), there are multiple models of youth justice practice across England and Wales. If we have an inspection framework that is not flexible and adaptable to reflect the diversity of practice, it is likely that youth justice teams who do not have a model of practice based on RFPP will be at a disadvantage and may be likely to receive a lower inspection outcome:

Until we have the discussion with the inspectorate and the inspection process fits more in with our values and principles as it is now, I think we're always going to struggle with this. Because, ultimately, nobody wants to 'need improvement'. We want to be 'good' or 'outstanding'. So, whilst you've got that pull, it were almost like those dodgy salesmen back in the day, where our commission comes from getting good and outstanding. So, you can spend very little time with a young person but do all the processes and look absolutely fantastic. But with no better outcomes for young people. (YOT Senior Practitioner)

The contradictory messages, bifurcated practice and increased paperwork were all taking front-line practitioners away from spending time with children. It was perceived that the competing and contradictory demands of HMIP and the YJB were creating a sense of frustration in workers that pointed to the urgent need for a clear central narrative to emerge. The inherent warning that the demands were going 'too far' highlights the findings from Weston and Mythen (2021) and Bovarnick (2010) that contradictory messages and competing demands of different approaches can have cause frustration and stress amongst workers.

Confusion

There was confusion amongst practitioners about the meaning of key terms, and how they relate to their own practice. As stated, the interview data was taken from a wider evaluation of 'Constructive Resettlement'—which, combined with 'child first, offender second' (Haines & Case, 2015), has provided the theoretical base for tenet 2 of Child First Justice—namely that all work with children should be future focused, strengths oriented with the aim of achieving an identity shift from pro-offending to pro-social. As such, all staff were asked about their understanding of 'Constructive Resettlement'. A number of different perspectives were offered, and many were based on a practitioner's individual background and training. For example, a staff member from a Secure Children's Home felt that this approach aligned itself with the Secure Stairs Programme, a psychologically informed model of care that focuses on comprehensive, co-produced assessments of children that are individually tailored to meet all their needs:

> What I will say is that it fits in very well with the Secure Stairs Programme. Because the two things do absolutely go hand in hand, because in order to tackle some of the barriers, you've got to get to the bottom of some of the causes. The root causes for some of the behaviours. Because otherwise it just gets dressed up as kids that don't behave very well. (Education Worker, Secure Children's Home)

Staff with experience of working with children who displayed sexually harmful behaviour drew comparisons with the Good Lives Model, a strengths-based, future-oriented therapeutic programme designed to address sexually harmful behaviours:

> Okay yes, we're looking at, we introduced the Good Lives Training about five years ago, so that's pretty much the same thing. So, that's why it didn't feel like a revolution really. (Youth Offending Team Worker 6)

One Youth Offending Team Manager compared Constructive Resettlement with Trauma Informed approaches of working with children. She stated that the trauma informed approach had underpinned all their interventions and assessments with children for over 2 years:

> This was my feedback from the training that ***** did recently, is that two years ago, that training probably would have been quite interesting and informative for us, but two years on, there was nothing new for us in it, there was nothing ground-breaking or surprising, it was basically what we do. (Youth Offending Team Manager)

For staff with a background in person-centred counselling, they could see parallels between counselling and Constructive Resettlement:

> I think there's an acknowledgement that, if we work with people where they are, instead of where we want them to be, that they do better. That they're less likely to reoffend, that they're more likely to be able to move on successfully and positively. And I'm liking the idea that we're building

on strengths rather than focusing in on negatives, because I think… I've got a bit of a counselling background as well. And all of that is based in understanding people's strengths, so that they can build on that and go on, go forward rather than reminding people that they've made a mistake. (Youth Offending Team Worker 5)

The understanding of Constructive Resettlement as a strengths-based, future-oriented approach to working with children (tenet 2 of Child First Justice) and the extent to which it was viewed as a change in direction of practice for staff, therefore, varied considerably and depended on their own individual backgrounds and experiences. There was a general pattern emerging that, for staff who had worked with other therapeutic and welfare-based models of intervention, that they viewed the Constructive Resettlement approach as a useful refresher that reinforced their own individual knowledge and practice. The comparisons to other models were rather general and seemed to focus on co-production, and welfare, and suggested that there may be some confusion about what Child First and desistance approaches are, particularly the focus on guiding identity development. It is apparent that this is reflective of practitioners' broader understandings of Child First Justice: they understand it in general terms as a welfare-based approach to working with children, but the specifics and details of this appear to be filled by their own background, knowledge and experiences, rather than by the specifics of the approach, as outlined in Child First documentation.

Confusion about how to work in Child First approaches with children was also evident. Interestingly, staff wanted more practical guidance, training and a toolkit of resources that they could use with children:

Obviously, I've got the slides, but it would've just been nice to have had a bit of guidance or some work that we could use with our young people. (Youth Offending Team Worker 3)

However, evidence-based practice, intervention guidance and toolkits tend to be quite prescriptive and are considered part of the risk paradigm. Again, this suggests that staff have a degree of reticence about 'how' and 'what' to do with children without a prescriptive guide, suggesting that even where staff are trying to move away from risk and embrace Child First approaches, they are still dependent on risk-based methods to mobilise this.

Finally, confusion emerged about how to strike the 'hard balance' between risk assessment and management, and Child First approaches:

> So, it's about relationship building really, isn't it? And it's about having the time and the space to do that and potentially the paperwork and the policies and procedures around managing risk can undermine that. Well, that's a contentious thing, isn't it? People don't bring in these things because they want to undermine risk management. But there's a balance, isn't there? You know, it's a tricky one. It's a hard balance to find. (YOT Worker 2)
>
> Yes, we've got to protect the public and we've got to protect the young person. But like I say, a change of terminology for a start off, that's got to change. Capture the same meaning, but just change it somehow. And if someone is scoring at high risk, then they've got to manage that. But we're telling him that he's risky, and if we're telling him that he's going to be risky, then he's going to act to be risky. So we need to change that somehow, but I don't know how. (YOT Resettlement Specialist)

Some sought to reconcile the 'hard balance' by focusing entirely on a child's identity shift and their future direction:

> I think they could come out and just focus straight on the future. I think while they're in custody, they get enough of, you're an offender, you've done this, and overcoming that offending behaviour. Coming out, I'd like to think that they come out into a community where they're treated exactly the same as everybody else and they should have the same opportunities. (YOT Education Worker).

Others had moved away from offending behaviour work completely towards trauma informed approaches, which they felt complimented the implementation of Child First Justice:

> And we just had a rethink and scrapped the lot. We don't do any offending behaviour programmes in ****** at all, we don't do any offence-specific interventions. We deal with the underlying causes, basically, so we

look at the [inaudible] and we look at attachment, we look at trauma, we look at relationships, we look at support networks.....

A final comment outlined how a YOT Senior Practitioner felt a child's 'risk' could be managed by completely embracing a Child First approach, and abandoning the risk paradigm:

> Probably one of our biggest challenges, is risk and how we define, how we manage risk. So, at the moment we've got a young person who carries a knife or something like that. We say we put him on the Knife Crime Programme, yes, calling it 'lives matter', and then we complete a safety plan with him. And that is how we say we're managing his risk. Now, on the flip side of that, being future orientated, we've got this kid, who may have been carrying a knife in the past. Well, what does he want to do?
> So, if we can get him involved in something within his community, whether it be education, some positive activity, if he gets involved in that and that's how he sees himself and if that where he sees his future going, I would say, he would stop carrying a knife, so you've managed his risk. . But I'm not sure how effective, I don't know any young person who walks around with their safety plan. But you know what, if I'm going to play football with my mates, I don't need to carry a knife. If I'm going to walk the street and I'm 15, 16, and I'm doing certain illegal activities, then actually, I'll carry a knife to protect myself. And you can write as many safety plans as you want, but that piece of paper isn't going to stop me from getting stabbed. (YOT Senior Practitioner)

In the above example, a child's risk is 'managed' anyway by using Child First approaches, but allows one to move away from bifurcated practice by removing the language, tools and processes of RFPP from front-line practice.

Conclusion

To effectively implement Child First Justice, a number of key challenges on the ground must firstly be addressed. One of the strongest themes from the interviews was that the 'balance' between risk assessment, management and offence focused work and Child First approaches was difficult to negotiate. Some staff could see the continuing role and importance of having some form of risk assessment and management as part of a youth justice practitioner's role; but the extent to which that directly impacted on the language used with children, and the work completed with them varied hugely. This difficulty appears to have been exacerbated by a growing awareness amongst front-line staff that the HMIP appears to prioritise risk assessment, risk management and the completion of offence focused work over Child First approaches in their inspections. This suggests a potential tension centrally between the Youth Justice Board and HMIP about where the focus on youth justice work should lie. Until this is resolved, the 'difficult balance' and lack of clarity for front-line staff and managers will persist. A central and clear policy narrative from the centre is crucial, as evidence emerged in this study that the contradictory messages are impacting on practitioners' abilities to spend time and build relationships with children, and much to the frustration of front-line practitioners and managers. It is crucial that, to resolve the divergent messages from the centre about whose approach takes precedence, both HMIP and the YJB involve front-line practitioners in this dialogue, given the difficulties it is causing. Recently, the YJB and HMIP published a joint statement (HMIP and YJB, 2022) in response to the challenge highlighted in this chapter and elsewhere (Day, 2022) which appears to highlight that HMIP and the YJB do not see their approaches as contradictory. Herein lies the challenge: this is irrelevant if their approaches are not clearly articulated and then clearly communicated to front-line practitioners. HMIP and the YJB, therefore, now need to focus on ensuring that their joint messaging is clear, and that this is understood by practitioners.

Equally, confusion about key terms such as desistance and Child First, and how they relate to other 'welfare based' approaches such as trauma informed practice, The Good Lives Model, Secure Stairs and person-centred counselling was evident. Further training and resources should be made available to front-line practitioners that clarify this confusion, for example by focusing on identity development.

Finally, the reasons for the reticence amongst some staff to move away from RFPP must be directly addressed. Evidence emerged in this study that RFPP has created a culture of fear amongst staff of 'getting it wrong', and that the risk assessment and management processes provided a degree of protection. Consideration, therefore, needs to be given to how staff can feel protected from wider scrutiny and criticism, whilst also being given the space to creatively work with children in ways that meet their individual needs and embraces Child First approaches.

This chapter has highlighted the importance of engaging in a meaningful dialogue with front-line youth justice practitioners about how and what impact changes in central policy narratives are having at the 'coal face' (Case & Hampson, 2019: 33). A number of obstacles and challenges are evident on the ground to implementing the YJB's vision to become a 'child first youth justice system' (YJB, 2021: 9). The confusion and concern caused by the competing narratives of the YJB and HMIP must be urgently addressed and resolved centrally by engaging in a dialogue with practitioners locally. The mobilisation of Child First is completely dependent on how youth justice practitioners and professionals interpret and understand this approach. However, until academics, policymakers and senior management structures meaningfully engage with practitioners about the challenges on the ground, there is a danger that the risk culture cloud will loom heavily over the emerging Child First world.

Bibliography

Bateman, T., & Pitts, J. (2010). New labour and youth justice: What Works or what's counted. In P. Ayre & M. Preston-Shoot (Eds.), *Children's services at the crossroads: A critical evaluation of contemporary policy for practice*. Russell House Publishing.

Bateman, T. (2020). *The state of youth justice*. Report, National Association for Youth Justice, London.

Bovarnick, S. (2010). How do you define a 'trafficked child'? A discursive analysis of practitioners' perceptions around child trafficking. *Youth and Policy, 104*, 80–96.

Burgess, R. G. (1984). *In the field: An introduction to field research*. Allen and Unwin.
Burnett, R., & Appleton, C. (2004). Joined-up services to tackle youth crime: A case study in England. *Youth Justice, 44*, 34–54.
Case, S., & Bateman, T. (2020). The punitive transition in youth justice: Reconstructing the child as offender. *Children & Society, 34*(6), 475–491.
Case, S., & Browning, A. (2021). *Child first justice: The research evidence-base (Full Report)*. Loughborough University. https://hdl.handle.net/2134/14152040.v1.
Case, S., & Haines, K. (2009). *Understanding youth offending: Risk factor research, policy and practice*. Routledge.
Case, S., & Haines, K. (2015). Children first, offenders second positive promotion: Reframing the prevention debate. *Youth Justice, 15*(3), 226–239.
Case, S., & Haines, K. (2016) Taking the risk out of youth justice. In C. Trotter, G. McIvor, & F. McNeill (Eds.), *Beyond the risk paradigm in criminal justice*. Palgrave.
Case, S., & Haines, K. (2021). Abolishing Youth Justice Systems: Children First, Offenders Nowhere. *Youth Justice, 21*(1), 3–17.
Case, S., & Hampson, K. (2019). Youth justice pathways to change: Drivers challenges and opportunities. *Youth Justice, 19*(1), 25–41.
Case, S. P., Drew, J., Hampson, K., Jones, G., & Kennedy, D. (2020). Professional perspectives of youth justice policy implementation: Contextual and coalface challenges. *Howard Journal of Criminal Justice, 59*(2), 214–232.
Charmaz, K., & Bryant, A. (2007). Grounded theory in historical perspective: An epistemological account. In K. Charmaz & A. Bryant (Eds.), *The Sage handbook of grounded theory* (pp. 1–25). Sage.
Cuneen, C., Goldson, B., & Russell, S. (2018). Human rights and youth justice reform in England and Wales: A systemic analysis. *Criminology and Criminal Justice, 18*(4), 405–430.
Day, A. (2022). 'It's a hard balance to find': The perspectives of youth justice practitioners in England on the place of 'risk' in an emerging 'child-first' world. *Youth Justice*. https://doi.org/10.1177/14732254221075205
Department for Education. (2004). *Every child matters*. Report for the Department for Education.
Evans, J., Kennedy, D., Skuse, T., & Matthew, J. (2020). Trauma-informed practice and desistance theories: Competing or complementary approaches to working with children in conflict with the law? *Salus Journal, 8*(2), 55–76.

Farrington, D. (2002). Developmental criminology and risk focused prevention. In M. Maguire, R. Morgan, & R. Reiner (Eds.), *The Oxford handbook of criminology* (3rd ed.). Oxford University Press.

Goldson, B. (2020). Excavating youth justice reform: Historical mapping and speculative prospects. *The Howard Journal of Crime and Justice, 59*(3), 317–334.

Goldson, B., & Randazzo, S. (2021). Global child and youth imprisonment: Histories, human rights standards, distributions, impacts, outcomes and replacements. *Incarceration and Generation, 1*, 75–102. Springer International.

Goodman, P., Page, J., & Phelps, M. (2017). *Breaking the pendulum: The long struggle over criminal justice.* Oxford University Press.

Haines, K., & Case, S. (2009). Putting children first in Wales: The evaluation of Extending Entitlement. *Revista de asistenta sociala, 4*(4), 65.

Haines, K., & Case, S. (2015). *Positive youth justice: Children first, offenders second.* Policy Press.

Haines, K., & Drakeford, M. (1998). *Young People and Youth Justice.* Red Globe Press: London.

Hampson, K. (2018). Desistance approaches in youth justice—The next passing fad or a sea-change for the positive? *Youth Justice, 18*(1), 18–33.

Hazel, N., & Bateman, T. (2021). Supporting children's resettlement ('reentry') after custody: Beyond the risk paradigm. *Youth Justice, 21*(1), 71–89.

Hazel, N. with Goodfellow, P., Liddle, M., Bateman, T., & Pitts, J. (2017). 'Now all I care about is my future'—Supporting the shift: Framework for the effective resettlement of young people leaving custody. Report, Beyond Youth Custody.

HMIP and YJB. (2022). *Joint statement from her majesty's inspectorate of probation and the youth justice board*, March 2022. Joint statement from HM Inspectorate of Probation and the Youth Justice Board (justiceinspectorates.gov.uk).

Loeber, R., Huizinga, D., & Thornberry, T. P. (1996). *Program of research on the causes and correlates of delinquency: Annual report 1995–1996.* Report prepared for the Office of Juvenile Justice and Delinquency Prevention, U.S. Department of Justice.

Maruna, S., & Mann, R. (2019). *Reconciling 'desistance' and 'what works'.* Report, Academic Insights Paper 2019/1, Her Majesty's Inspectorate of Probation: London.

Muncie, J. (2008). The 'punitive turn' in Juvenile justice: Cultures of control and rights compliance in Western Europe and the USA. *Youth Justice, 8*(2), 107–121. https://doi.org/10.1177/1473225408091372

Smith, R. (2006). Actuarialism and early intervention in contemporary youth justice. In B. Goldson & J. Muncie (Eds.), *Youth crime and justice*. Sage.

Smith, R., & Gray, P. (2019). The changing shape of youth justice: Models of practice. *Criminology and Criminal Justice, 19*(5), 554–571.

Smithson, H., & Jones, A. (2021). Co-creating youth justice practice with young people: Tackling power dynamics and enabling transformative action. *Children & Society., 35*(3), 348–362.

Taylor, C. (2016). *A review of the youth justice system in England and Wales*. Ministry of Justice.

West, D. J., & Farrington, D. P. (1973). *Who becomes delinquent?* Heinemann.

Weston, S., & Mythen, G. (2020). Working with and negotiating 'risk': Examining the effects of awareness raising interventions designed to prevent child sexual exploitation. *The British Journal of Criminology, 60*(2), 323–342.

Weston, S., & Mythen, G. (2021). Disentangling practitioners' understandings of child sexual exploitation: The risks of assuming otherwise? *Criminology and Criminal Justice*. https://doi.org/10.1177/1748895821993525

Wigzell, A. (2021). *Explaining desistance: Looking forward, not backwards*. Report, National Association of Youth Justice.

Youth Justice Board. (2019). *How to assess children in the youth justice system: Section 4 case management guidance*. Ministry of Justice.

Youth Justice Board. (2018). *How to make resettlement constructive*. Report, Ministry of Justice.

Youth Justice Board. (2021). *Strategic plan 2021–24*. Report, Youth Justice Board.

11

Cementing 'Child First' in Practice

Kathy Hampson

Introduction

'Child First' has now become the *'strategic approach and central guiding principle'* of youth justice in England and Wales (YJB, 2021a: 10), but how has this affected youth justice work with children? This chapter will consider how the development of, and move towards, 'Child First' justice has been experienced by professionals working at the coalface with justice-involved children in England and Wales, how much they understand the basic principles under which they are now supposed to be working, and what difficulties they see in changing the rhetoric into everyday practice. Through analysis of their responses and policies/practice of various youth justice agencies, the enablers, barriers and challenges of cementing Child First youth justice in practice will be identified and discussed.

K. Hampson (✉)
Department of Law and Criminology,
Aberystwyth University, Aberystwyth, Wales, UK
e-mail: kah47@aber.ac.uk

Context

To understand the perspectives of youth justice practitioners in England and Wales, some contextualisation is necessary, looking at structures and processes of youth justice system (YJS) agencies. These brief discussions—explored in more detail elsewhere in this book—aim to (1) give better understanding of the wider system and adaptations to the changing youth justice landscape in facilitating (or hindering) Child First justice and (2) demonstrate practitioners' understanding and experience, in terms of their professional/training backgrounds and how their perceptions have developed.

Youth Justice in England and Wales

Youth justice systems across the United Kingdom (UK) have developed differently since justice was devolved to Scotland and Northern Ireland, leaving England and Wales as one combined justice jurisdiction (despite calls for Welsh justice devolution; Thomas Commission, 2019). Since the Crime and Disorder Act of 1998 (CDA), youth justice in England and Wales has been predicated on 'risk' (conceptualisations of children as being 'risky' rather than 'at risk' and vulnerable), leaning heavily on positivistic aggregative research identifying a range of 'risk factors', which the 'risk factor prevention paradigm' (RFPP) theorised as key to reducing offending in children (YJB, 2005). The key 'aim' of this new YJS, as stipulated in the CDA was to prevent offending (CDA S37(1)), placing the ultimate emphasis on children's *offending* rather than their *best interests* (contrary to the United Nations Convention of the Rights of the Child (UNCRC, United Nations, 1989), Article 3). This established a system which, in seeking to prevent/minimise risk factors, was extremely negative its dealings with children (prioritising *prevention of risk* rather than positive encouragement of strengths and opportunities, responsibilising children rather than adults or wider systems) (Bateman, 2020).

The CDA also established agencies designed to fulfil the stated aim of preventing/reducing offending by children—the Youth Justice Board (YJB) was the overarching strategic body responsible for youth justice planning and achievement of CDA goals and Youth Offending Teams (YOTs, multiagency teams of professionals statutorily sourced from social services, education, health, police and probation) were designed to deliver face-to-face interventions to justice-involved children.

The YJB established practice guidance to ensure that YOTs and custodial establishments for which it was responsible[1] worked effectively in preventing and reducing offending. To this end, they produced 15 Key Elements of Effective Practice documents (KEEPs) on a range of practice areas, a pivotal one being 'Assessment, Planning, Interventions and Supervision' (APIS), within which risk emphasis was explicit: '*Managers should oversee decision-making and ensure that it is evidence-led and risk-based*' (YJB, 2008: 7). The YJB, with the Secretary of State for Justice, sets National Standards for YOTs, covering operational aspects like minimum contact requirements, timescales for reports and completing/reviewing assessments (cf. YJB, 2009). These prescriptive expectations (*administrative* justice) through the first decade of the new millennium left little to practitioners' discretion, potentially reducing their work to box-ticking and management oversight to applying National Standards, amounting to 'zombification' (Pitts, 2001).

YOTs, created statutorily as multi-agency (but also often encompassing non-statutory agencies where available, like substance misuse services and housing) operationalise YJB strategic plans, working to nationally prescribed effective practice measures, with research evidence largely limited to risk (and protection) factors in the form of the RFPP (YJB, 2005). This strongly influenced justice delivery to children, but whilst the evidence included the importance of protective factors on children's development and offending trajectories, this aspect seemed subsumed by

---

[1] Initially, the YJB monitored the operation of Secure Training Centres (generally privately-run custody for girls and boys from 12 to 17) and Young Offender Institutions (run by the prison service for older boys—and girls initially—aged 15 to 18) and for the placement of children in the most appropriate custodial institution (including commissioning beds in local authority-run Secure Children's Homes for younger and more vulnerable children). This changed following criticism that youth custody oversight was confused between the YJB, Ministry of Justice and National Offender Management Service ('*there is no definitive point of either leadership or accountability at system level*', Youth Custody Improvement Board, 2017: 3), in response to which the Youth Custody Service was established in September 2017.

risk (e.g. the APIS KEEP mentions 'risk' (towards others) 66 times but 'protective' factors only nine times). This loss was exacerbated by the YJB-mandated assessment tool—Asset.

Asset took 12 areas of children's lives (e.g., lifestyle, substance use, attitudes to offending) and required practitioners to score children based on how much each (dynamic risk) factor influenced their offending (note that this was entirely about *criminogenic* needs—exacerbates of offending, rather than more general needs of the child), between four ('very strongly associated') and zero ('not associated at all'). This score, added to a list of static risk factors, created a composite 'risk of reoffending' score, which directly impacted required contact between the child and YOT—the higher the score, the more intense (frequent) the contact. Protective factors were given just one section with an 'evidence' box and accompanying tick boxes—as a measure of how much protective factors were underplayed, guidance on completing Asset devoted over 17 pages to explaining assessment of 'risk' but less than one to protective factors (YJB, n.d.). Asset therefore severely limited professional judgement (through its actuarial scoring system) without effectively incorporating protective factors.

Training programmes were developed for the YJB, in theory to enable practitioners in becoming informed and knowledgeable in their dealings with children and provide in-house progression for practitioners on entry-level qualifications. In 2003, the Professional Certificate in Effective Practice (PCEP) was launched, but criticisms quickly identified aspects of one-sidedness which simplified 'what works' whilst denying controversies (Kubiak & Hester, 2009). In 2006, the youth justice foundation degree (encompassing PCEP material) began, written and delivered by the Open University, but remaining true to the (then) YJB preference for the RFPP, rather than allowing critical thinking development more normally typical of undergraduate study (Phoenix, 2011), potentially amounting to a hard-schooling in risk for YOT workers. The programme has since widened out to include full degree and postgraduate study, now provided by Unitas and validated through the University of Suffolk (unitas.uk.net/).

Inspections of YOTs are undertaken by HM Inspectorate of Probation (HMIP) working to a list of self-prescribed standards. Inspection processes developed from voluntary (in 2003) to a structured statutory process (by 2007). YOTs are rated from 'inadequate' to 'excellent' (Macleod et al., 2010; see also the archive of inspection reports, including relevant inspection criteria—National Archives, n.d.). HMIP also conduct thematic inspections (e.g. a thematic review of YOT work during the COVID-19 pandemic, HMIP, 2020), which has proved useful in developing new directions, discussed later. YOTs produce action plans after receipt of inspection reports indicating how they will address issues raised (HIMP, 2021a).

Developments Towards More Child-Friendly Approaches

Although post-CDA YJS development was very risk-focused (seeing children as risky offenders), there have been developments over the past decade towards more child-friendly working. Research showing system-contact to be inherently damaging for children (cf. McAra & McVie, 2007) contributed towards a resurgence[2] of understanding the importance of minimal contact (also chiming with efforts to reduce numbers of children entering the YJS by increasing prevention activity (interventions to *prevent* children from offending) and diverting from court wherever possible. This has led to impressive reductions of children entering for the first time and every subsequent stage of court disposal, including custody (MoJ, 2021). Changes in policy (e.g. Youth Restorative Disposal pilot 2008, cf. Haines et al., 2013) and legislation (e.g. Legal Aid, Sentencing and Punishment of Offenders Act 2012 provision for Youth Cautions and Youth Conditional Cautions) have provided more flexibility for diversion. In Wales, this sparked the development of the 'Bureau', maximising non-criminalising options for children committing low-level offences for the first time (Haines et al., 2013), whereas in England this catalysed 'Triage', where children arrested for low-level offences were diverted towards informal restorative outcomes through

---

[2] This is a resurgence because pre-CDA youth justice was much more focused on diversion as a response to low-level offending by children, in line with international guidance (cf. The 'Beijing Rules' Principle 11, UN, 1985).

negotiation between police and the YOT (Institute for Criminal Policy Research, 2012). Both options, although imperfect, offer alternatives to prosecution, contributing to the falling numbers of first-time YJS entrants (MoJ, 2021).

Another positive development has been desistance-focused research and practice in the adult sector (cf. Farrall & Maruna, 2004), now being applied to the youth estate (cf. Wigzell, 2021). In general, desistance-focused working concentrates on strengths-based approaches, societal reintegration and personal narrative transformation from pro-offending to non-offending. Application of this to children is a double-edged sword, however, since assuming children are hardened offenders who *need* personal narrative transformation is to consider them 'offenders' rather than 'children' with fixed offending identities, rather than drifting in and out of offending *behaviour* (Matza, 1964). This has adultised children—applying adult-centric concepts and considering children equally culpable for their actions. However, from this more child-friendly applications have been drawn (cf. Constructive Resettlement, YJB, 2018a)—a potential enabler for Child First justice. To facilitate a shift towards a more strengths-based working, the YJB commissioned a re-design of Asset which became AssetPlus, emphasising more children's strengths and interests (through specific sections on 'factors for desistance') and offering a foundation for later Child First changes. Over the past decade, the YJB has also softened National Standards, gradually moving away from prescriptive (tick-box) contact regimes, assessment, reviewing (etc.) towards judgement-based processes, giving practitioners more say over case management. This also allowed YOTs to find alternatives to breach (sending children back to Court for non-compliance) for children finding compliance challenging; now there are various initiatives to re-engage children without the need for breach action (see, e.g. Darlington YOT's 'breach re-engagement' process on the YJB Hub[3]).

---

[3] The YJB set up an effective practice 'Hub' as a forum for YOTs (and other agencies) to share good practice, which has been particularly well-used during the COVID-19 pandemic for the sharing of creative practice. For this example, see: https://yjresourcehub.uk/working-with-children-and-families/item/136-breach-re-engagement-materials-darlington-youth-offending-service.html.

Another keystone to developing a more Child First-ready YJS was growing awareness of the need for trauma-informed working. In England, this was often linked to consideration of Adverse Childhood Experiences (ACEs), acknowledging that most children within the YJS have experienced significant trauma and therefore have corresponding needs and issues (Wright & Liddle, 2014). In Wales Enhanced Case Management (ECM), based on the Trauma Recovery Model (cf. YJB Cymru, 2017) was piloted in three Welsh YOTs with encouraging evaluations resulting in a Wales-wide roll out (Cordis Bright, 2017; Glendinning et al., 2021). However, the danger of situating problems within a child is overlooking external factors, with identified ACEs becoming a new range of risk factors targeted for reduction/mitigation (reverting to a negative backwards-facing deficit model; Turner, 2019). This danger is true for both ACE and ECM approaches (cf. YJB, 2020a), so should be borne in mind in further development—very much currently a work in progress. The importance here lies in being able to see children as *vulnerable* (focusing on traumatic experiences) rather than risky (focusing on offences). These developments, therefore, took the YJS *towards* being able to see children as *children* rather than offenders, setting the scene for Child First justice.

The Evolution of 'Child First' (for a Fuller Discussion, See Earlier Chapters)

Child First youth justice is not new—seeing children as '*children first, offenders second*' was first proposed by Wales-based Haines and Drakeford (1998: 89) as a '*Children-First philosophy*'. This was adopted in the All-Wales Youth Offending Strategy—'*The strategy therefore promotes the principle that young people should be treated as children first and offenders second*' (YJB/WG, 2004: 3), allowing Wales to push forwards, even whilst the bigger picture was controlled by Westminster. Eventually, the YJB began a gradual adoption of this for the whole jurisdiction, with '*child first, offender second*' as a stated *aspiration* (YJB, 2018b: 7), whilst full incorporation without caveats soon followed: '*The YJB is committed to building a youth justice system that sees those in it as children first and offenders second*' (YJB, 2019: 7). The YJB Strategic Plan 2021–2024 developed this further, stating 'Child First' (note: offender nowhere; Case & Haines, 2021) to be '*Our strategic approach and central guiding principle*' (YJB, 2021a: 10), surely paving the way for 'Child First justice' to pervade all aspects of practice? However, the reality, whilst showing green shoots of change, also indicates significant barriers to a Child First-ready YJS.

The YJB followed up formal adoption of Child First with more nuanced model development (although this has been criticised by commentators as incomplete (cf. Bateman, 2020), it is the basis for 'Child First' hereon in), by identifying four strands (or 'tenets'; Case & Browning, 2021a), as detailed in previous chapters. For the YJS to be Child First-ready, all related agencies (e.g. YOTs, courts, HMIP) and professionals therein need to be aware of these tenets and appreciate the need to work actively towards their development and incorporation. Any aspect of the YJS not promoting them (all) risks derailing the realities of Child First truly becoming the '*strategic approach and central guiding principle*'.

Potential Barriers to Child First in Practice

The legislature must be on-board with Child First to truly cement it into practice since this is not in the gift of the YJB. Unfortunately, proposals in the current Government's 'Beating Crime Plan', whilst recognising vulnerabilities of children to criminal exploitation (e.g. through 'County Lines' drug gangs and investment in therapeutic responses), seek other changes potentially adversely affecting children, thereby moving *away* from Child First thinking. Examples include strengthening street policing (by increasing both numbers and powers) and harsher punishments—'*permanently relaxing conditions on the use of section 60 stop and search powers*' (UK Government, 2021: 6), despite this disproportionately affecting children within ethnic minorities, ignoring previous concerns over police misuse (ironically an issue simultaneously highlighted by justice inspectorates; HMICFRS, 2021). This Plan was eruditely criticised by the new Chief Executive of the YJB, Claudia Sturt:

'*The adult and youth justice systems serve different purposes. The youth justice system should work in the best interest of the child and to prevent offending and reoffending, but prevention requires a whole system approach, not just a justice response*' (YJB, 2021c). The fact that the legislature continues to seek to address youth crime, at least in part, through tougher justice responses, shows lack of understanding/acceptance of Child First tenets and the function of *youth* justice as focused on children's best interests (UNCRC 1989 Article 3). The difference identified by Sturt between adult and child systems also draws attention to inspection disparities, as YOTs are inspected by (adult-focused) *Probation* inspectorates.

The pitfalls of an adult (and justice) focused inspectorate are clear when looking at HMIP's inspection criteria, recently updated (July 2021). HMIP have acknowledged the importance of developing research in desistance and addressing re/offending through building desistance factors, incorporating this into inspection criteria (HMIP, 2021b). Their desistance thematic inspection (HMIP, 2016) helped raise awareness within the YJS of strengths-based approaches and embed YJB terminology ('desistance') within AssetPlus development. However, they do not acknowledge that most desistance literature is adult-centric, so applying what might fit probation to the YJS is problematic in terms of validity. Child First justice embraces strengths-based approaches within Tenets 1 and 2, but frames this within the context of 'pro-social development' (a positive goal), rather than 'desistance' (a negative goal, possibly not appropriate for children who are less likely to identify as 'offenders'). Research has expressed concern regarding understanding within the YJS of a more positive way of working; combined with confusing mixed messages from HMIP, workers also worried about the attitudes of courts, and whether judges/magistrates would understand pre-sentence report proposals for interventions not seeing the child as an offender (Hampson, 2018; see also Case & Browning, 2021b). Without training, courts would be unlikely to understand proposals for a Child First intervention plan, making them a potential barrier.

Whilst HMIP acknowledge Child First principles, there are confusions of model-base evident throughout its guidance documents (HMIP, 2021b). The YJB's risk-based approach developed into the Risk Needs Responsivity (RNR) model, which considers risks *and* needs (although largely *criminogenic* needs) (YJB, 2008); whilst this might be a softening of a hard-line RFPP approach, it still sees children as risky offenders, rather than as vulnerable (*at* risk). HMIP is clear that RNR is still at its heart (reflected in the inspection criteria) (HMIP, 2021b). This is illustrated by the following from case management guidance: '*There is some debate about the relative efficacy of the risk versus strengths-based models of delivery, with supporters siding with one or the other. In truth, both approaches have merit and a role to play*' (HMIP, 2021c). This is not unequivocal acceptance of/commitment to Child First—rather a version sullied by risk (specifically the RNR (adult) model; cf. Kemshall, 2021; HMIP, n.d.), justified in the term 'blended approach', but causing 'incongruence' (Case & Browning, 2021b: 8) through blending two *opposing* approaches, like an '*unhappy emulsion*' (Case & Hampson, 2019: 35). This undermines *youth* justice priorities highlighted by Sturt whilst refusing to see children as children (Tenet 1), arguably leading to poorer inspection reports where 'risk' has not been prioritised, even for out-of-court cases (cf. Case & Browning, 2021b). This indicates the inappropriateness of an *adult justice* inspectorate responsible for YJS standards, where aims are very different—it is surely more appropriate for YOTs to be inspected through education or social service inspectorates (proposed by Charlie Taylor in his 2016 YJS Review), without RNR muddying the Child First trajectory.

Changes (mentioned earlier) to Asset (AssetPlus) carried great potential, especially given Asset's risk emphasis, rendering it unsuitable for facilitating 'Child First'. The roll-out of AssetPlus was accompanied by YOT 'cascade' training (one staff member trained at a 'train the trainer' event then 'cascading' the learning to their team) to facilitate use of this new tool in a more positive, strengths-based way. Unfortunately, research has found that staff felt under-prepared for the changes, seemingly wrestling the new format back into more familiar risk-focused assessments, resulting in little change (Hampson, 2018). Rigorous training on underlying concepts was vital to achieve their aim of a positive 'desistance'-focus (despite issues with applying that concept to children). Concern was also expressed that AssetPlus was extremely time-consuming, with positive 'factors for desistance' tending to become lost within a negative narrative (Hampson, 2018). AssetPlus echoes the HMIP's 'blended' approach, being still largely risk-focused, adding 'desistance' as a bolt-on rather than pervading the whole assessment. Indeed, Baker (2012) was clear that AssetPlus specifically facilitates RNR. A tool reflecting the four tenets of Child First (and the '*different purposes*' of adult versus child justice) should surely incorporate them throughout; AssetPlus remains another potential barrier to cementing Child First justice in practice.

Current training arrangements within the sector may be a barrier to realising Child First. Unitas have formed the Youth Justice Institute (although rather obliquely), offering a selection of online courses, with some free introductory modules.[4] Encouragingly, they now offer a 'Trauma Informed Practice' module, which should further embed consideration of children's vulnerability (being 'at risk'). However, it was concerning to see the phrase 'young offender' used within the free 'Exploring Youth Justice' course, as well as very dated reading material, largely from the Unitas-published textbook (but also a YJB Strategic Plan from 2015 with old aims firmly around reducing offending—completely missing new Child First directions, but which have been indicated since 2018). The dated nature of these materials (available *currently* for youth justice practitioners and would-be YJS workers) means that Child First justice is not mentioned, despite the Unitas suite of training seeking to (according to the YJB Workforce Development Strategy) '*embed Child First principles into the workforce*' (YJB, 2021b: 3). This strategy actively encourages youth justice practitioners to undertake these courses, despite their lack of Child First material. Correspondence with YJB staff has confirmed that Unitas have been commissioned to provide a Child First module (presumably also to be delivered online and completed individually; both as stand-alone and as part of larger qualifications, like the Youth Justice degree). This might seem encouraging, but it is difficult to see how one module (amongst many others) on Child First can communicate this as whole system value-base, especially with other contradictory modules. Compartmentalising teaching/learning like this means that anything written before the adoption of Child First will not by definition be from that standpoint, whereas *every module* needs to be congruent

---

[4] See https://youthjusticeinstitute.co.uk/courses/.

with Child First justice as an overarching paradigm.[5] Anything else risks being tokenistic at best but at worst could undermine the whole direction of travel for practitioner-students receiving mixed messages, becoming a barrier to cementing Child First in practice.

To date there has been no Child First-related training provided by the YJB for practitioners, beyond a couple of short webinars staged during the pandemic (see, for example, YJB, 2020b) and a Welsh-centric session provided by Hwb Doeth[6] so it is difficult to see how practitioners could be operating with this as their *'central guiding principle'*. The realities of the YJS being Child First-ready therefore, in the terminology of HMIP's own inspection ratings *'requires improvement'*. Given these issues, it is important to see how practitioners at the coalface of youth justice working view and are experiencing the Child First revolution.

Views, Attitudes and Experiences of Youth Justice Practitioners

Methodology

To gain some understanding of how youth justice practitioners view these developments and to what extent they are experiencing the potential barriers outlined above, a small number of interviews were undertaken ($n = 5$; two practitioners from Wales, three from England). Following training on developing desistance approaches in youth justice (most recently incorporating the YJB's Child First context; cf. Hampson, 2018) given to a Welsh YOT in 2021, discussions on enablers and barriers to this kind of working (framing this both as 'strengths-based' and 'Child First') were discussed in that group context ($n = 12$), which have also

---

[5] A paradigm is defined by the Oxford English Dictionary as a 'world view' and is therefore wider/deeper than a model/set of guidelines; a Child First paradigm (world view) therefore affects every aspect of the way justice is done with children (representing a 'paradigm shift' from the RFPP; Case, 2021: 8).

[6] Hwb Doeth is collaborative organisation drawing together universities, YOTs and strategic policymakers (e.g. Welsh Government and YJB Cymru) in Wales regarding youth justice policy, practice and development, organised through the Welsh Centre for Crime and Social Justice (cf. https://wccsj.ac.uk/).

contributed. Clearly, such small numbers cannot gain a wide-ranging perspective on developments, particularly given local differences, but they can give an *indication* of understandings, perceptions and experiences; interviews and discussions taking place in both England and Wales also allowed some comparison between them, given their differential Child First development. Practitioners interviewed ranged from having sixteen years' experience to just three, with backgrounds including social work, youth work, substance use and child custody. The discussion group included practitioners from a wide range of backgrounds including police, probation, social work, youth work and health. Interviews were recorded and transcribed, and the discussion group notated (all used with permission of interviewees and attendees). Transcripts/notes were analysed for themes, particularly relating to the Child First tenets, and issues raised in the above discussions. To give practitioners a voice, significant space is devoted to their views through direct quotes, especially important in the light of one practitioner comment: '*The grunts at the coalface aren't going to do it* [create change] *because nobody listens to us*'.

Challenges in Awareness and Understanding

Practitioners need to be both *aware* of Child First justice (and the YJB four 'tenets') and *understand* its implications to be able to embed it into practice. It was somewhat surprising therefore to find very little cognisance of 'Child First' specifically, with none of those interviewed being aware of the four tenets. However, there was a noticeable difference in appreciation of the underlying values of Child First between the Welsh and English practitioners, possibly reflecting its Welsh origins. One English practitioner could not even recall being aware of 'Child First' as a term, where another conflated it (and the underlying values) with the values of the Council (not expressly Child First, although not specifically opposed), which emphasise being 'child-friendly'. Both Welsh practitioners were aware of the term, and whilst they could not name the four tenets *were* able to identify important aspects of them. That consideration of the UNCRC in policy relating to children is mandatorily embedded in Welsh policy/legislation (Welsh Government, 2015) may also have contributed to a better appreciation of this aspect of Child First justice (Tenet 1), illustrated by one Welsh practitioner:

> I think probably the first one is seeing children as children then and... that's all the information around UNCRC...the child's rights and...ensuring that the punishment doesn't...supersede those rights.

Despite not being specifically able to name the tenets, she was able to identify them all (e.g. 'seeing children as children—Tenet 1—as in the quote above) by thinking through YOT practice:

> Then I know that there is something in there around pro-social identity and supporting that identity shift...then...encouraging the young person to make those positive changes and...how we as practitioners can support that...That's a lot around pro-social modelling, showing them a different a different way...I think there must be something in there around...collaboration, working with young people...minimising the contact with the youth justice system so around diversion stuff.

As can be seen from these two quotes from the same practitioner, although she was not aware of exact terminology, her ability to identify all tenets through thinking about YOT practice illustrates that much of the Child First value-base *has* filtered through, certainly in this Welsh YOT. Interestingly, she also identified that this constitutes a *change* in working practice: '*we weren't working in this way before, and young people were labelled weren't they... hugely stigmatised*'. Differences clearly exist between Welsh YOTs, however, perhaps illustrating that cognisance of Child First justice depends on local practice, as the other Welsh practitioner could only contribute to this: '*we put the child's needs first rather than the offence first*'—a rather tautological understanding, not showing nuanced appreciation of all four tenets. She saw Child First just as being '*child-friendly or child-focused*'. Even the practitioner who said they had not heard of Child First was able to identify relevant aspects of practice:

> It's about the child's needs first over anybody else's so over systems...the Asset Plus training...talks about a strengths-based approach, which I

guess is Child First isn't it? So maybe it's not about the term it's about what we're actually doing.

The last point is an interesting one, which emphasises the importance of impact on practice—knowing about Child First without putting it into practice is clearly not helpful, but perhaps knowing *terminology* is not so important in assessing how much this change of direction affects the coalface. However, the fact that no training has yet been provided on Child First justice (and what this might look like) and that current case management guidance contradicts it[7] (despite being published after initial adoption of 'Child First'; YJB, 2019) is problematic, giving practitioners only partial understanding (e.g. less natural emphasis on children's rights in England than Wales). The provision of robust training (discussed later) on the four tenets their practical application is more likely to embed them systematically, with less room for (potentially problematic) local variation; relying on sound teaching and learning, rather than osmosis.

Importantly, several aspects of the Child First tenets were agreed upon by all practitioners, for example, the importance of seeing children as children (rather than offenders) and meeting individual needs (Tenet 1):

> It's about not seeing them as offenders then… it's about…looking at the reasons behind why… rather than punishing them. Within the five seconds…they just become the child. The offence just sits in the background to that because…you start…looking how the young person's mind works. Take into account their care history as well…their education, their learning needs. When I start to do an Asset [assessment] I never start with the offending stuff. I always start with the young person, their development, their history, family relationships, hobbies, lifestyle, identity, you know diversity.

This tenet includes *differences* between adults and children, meaning that children (considered children rather than as '*mini-adults*'; Case &

---

[7] Case management guidance is currently being rewritten, so hopefully it will reflect the YJB's own 'tenets' of Child First justice.

Haines, 2014: 7) do not have the same level of culpability, because their level of maturity is very different, as one practitioner expressed:

> I think 'why did you, what made you do those things? What were you thinking?'…it's just impulses that as an adult we learn to think 'oh that's not appropriate…or 'this would be the consequence' and it's just not there when you're a teenager.

There was also major agreement on the importance of building relationship with the child (Tenet 2) as a necessity for effective working:

> The child comes first, the offence comes second…So I can build a relationship with the young person rather than just focusing on the risk. If I focus on the positives and build a relationship with the young person-…that can help improve engagement. I spent a lot of time explaining the processes, reassuring, but I guess again that's relationship building isn't it. It's not time wasted.

An interesting point from the discussion group was the importance of being prepared to change an allocated worker if the relationship was stalling, because '*the relationship is key*'. However, both this group and another practitioner identified time constraints:

> A month isn't a long time to get to know anyone to be fair…you build a relationship over the next three months…but to build a relationship, it's difficult to get to know anyone in the first month isn't it?

Strengths-based working (and moving away from offence-focused work) featured strongly in most practitioners' understanding and experience of Child First, with one practitioner identifying the benefits as '*healing the brain by doing positive activities so they're not in fight flight all the time*'. Other comments regarding a positive focus show the ubiquitous acceptance of this aspect:

> We're looking at opportunities for young people rather than punitive measures…I think we are moving towards a more strength-based way of practising…you find something the kid likes… grab it and go…a lot

of the kids suffer from low self-esteem, anxiety and they don't want to be sitting there discussing all the things they've done wrong and all bad that's happened, because they get that from school, from parents...they want opportunity, they want positivity.

The importance of giving the child a voice, listening to their views and actively collaborating with them is a central aspect of Child First (Tenet 3) and acknowledged by practitioners:

...we're asking them to help us develop child friendly plans...there's a lot of participation stuff. Asking for their views and asking them to help develop new interventions. You do...your self- assessment questionnaire with a child...that's supposed to be the forefront of your work with the young person because it's their views...you base your work and your plan around what the strengths are building from that initial self-assessment.

But again, time constraints were mentioned by one practitioner as working against the feasibility of being able to base the work on children's views:

We're supposed to...have them inform the plan...but it's...directed by how much time you've got. So...you've got something like three weeks to get the assessment done for the panel...and then it says 'the young person should be involved in writing the plan' - you don't have time to involve them...The process is a barrier to the child being at the forefront of it, because of all the other things you've got to do.

This is also an example of where good training might significantly improve practice, given that the above quotes alone show a varying understanding of what meaningful collaboration/participation is: from designing logos and naming already-constructed programmes (minimal/tokenistic participation), to developing new interventions (more meaningful participation, depending on methodology). With research and practice developing apace in this area (cf. Creaney, 2020; Peer Power, 2020), training linked to Child First embedment would facilitate much-needed common understanding.

Tenet 4, recognising potential harms of the YJS itself by seeking minimal intervention and promoting diversion (away from the YJS), was also understood by practitioners as an important part of Child First:

> So you've got the out-of-court stuff, you've got the prevention stuff as well...I don't see the benefit in keeping a young person working with the youth justice team longer than they need to...there's other services that are better placed to work with them and we'd signpost them out to other services. Now you're getting stuff out-of-court that...years ago they would have been on a supervision order...it's so de-escalated, which is brilliant for the kids.

However, this reduction in criminalisation was recognised by one worker as part of the reason for a greater intensity of trauma-experienced children in the system: '*These days every single case I get is child in need, child protection, looked after, previous childcare involvement, child exploitation, criminal child exploitation*'. The analogy of a 'thickening soup' (Brewster, 2020) has been used to illustrate this change in cohort characteristics, but accompanied by growing awareness, as discussed earlier, of the need for trauma-informed working, which fits into the detail of Tenets 1 and 2:

> Once you start assessing the young person...no choice but to go to the background because you can't address...offending behaviour until other complex needs or risks are met. The child first stuff probably started to come out maybe around the time of us learning how to work in a trauma informed way...with the Enhanced Case Management. The value of looking at a young person as a child who has absorbed everything around them in terms of...their ACEs.

Several workers explained that when court personnel received training in trauma-informed working, their attitude towards the children changed, allowing more acceptance of Child First-focused court reports proposing more positive, strengths-based interventions:

> Local magistrates will have had training on enhanced case management and trauma recovery model...which has obviously helped their understanding...it has changed perhaps the way they deal with young people. I find that our courts, our magistrates here are fantastic with our reports...they've had training on the trauma recovery model now. That...has made a difference to a lot of practitioners in terms of understanding what young people can manage.

One challenge which these examples highlight is the importance of local actions in communicating these developments and offering training to such agencies as courts, which could increase inconsistency across the jurisdiction, tantamount to a postcode lottery for children regarding whether they receive a Child First response. For example, awareness of the need for trauma-informed practice was seen as problematic in some quarters (prevalent in the YOT discussion group, where concerns with police understanding were raised, as Inspectors expected offence-focused work in Community Resolution interventions[8]), indicating the need for continuing cross-agency awareness-raising and training (more helpfully led centrally to achieve consistency), as one practitioner expressed:

> You're mitigating the kids' needs with the police and say 'look, these kids when you pick them up...they're desperately traumatised and you want to be bearing that in mind when you're dealing with them'.

These discussions of different aspects of the four Child First tenets with coal-face practitioners working with children and the impact on everyday youth justice on the ground, illustrate general support (whether or not they were specifically aware of the tenets)—surely an enabler of Child First? As one worker put it: '*I think there's very much an appetite for it within our YOT...it has changed loads over the time that I've been there*' [13 years]; although another practitioner pointed out that this transition was perhaps more difficult for some than others, depending on professional background:

---

[8] A Community Resolution is described as '*an informal non-statutory disposal used for dealing with less serious crime and anti-social behaviour where the offender accepts responsibility*' (Sentencing Council, 2021), likely to be delivered by the police officer seconded to the YOT.

> There's colleagues within the team...who are...traditionally trained as probation officers, and that shift I think has been more difficult than perhaps for those of us who come more from a background around social work and...building on protective factors...I do find sometimes the police struggle with that...they are trained to deal with offenders and to...stop them from committing offences. So sometimes there's a clash of culture which I think is more around people who have been in their roles for a long time.

The issues reflected above should be acknowledged and addressed, as it shows the dangers of Child-First-by-osmosis, rather than intentional robust training in support of such a shift.

Barriers, Challenges and Enablers of Achieving Child First in Practice

Although much has changed over the last decade *towards* Child First thinking in terms of the way justice-involved children are seen and understood and best practice in supporting them, further barriers and challenges to truly cementing Child First in practice were both observed within practitioner responses, and explicitly identified by them as actively obstructive.

The emulsion of risk and Child First as a '*blended*' approach (Kemshall, 2021) has clearly caused confusion for practitioners who are on the one hand tasked with actualising the Child First as their '*strategic approach and central guiding principle*' (YJB, 2021a: 10; seeing children as children, at risk from others, particularly adults—*child* first), whilst also balancing the demands of risk management (which sees children as inherently risky—*offenders* first). Clearly, these two paradigms do not even meet in the middle, let alone blend without severe compromise. 'Risk' as a guiding principle was evident throughout the practitioners' responses, even when they were talking about Child First, still hinting at offence-focused work as an aspect, at least, of interventions (contrary to Tenet 2, which states that '*All work is constructive and future-focused*'):

11 Cementing 'Child First' in Practice 321

We put the child's needs first rather than the offence first. So, we'd look at what is going on in the child's life and the risk factors as to why the child would offend rather than focus directly on the offence itself. It's not that we forget about the offence, because you know of course there is work that has to be done there. So, you spend all your time in meetings and filling in risk panel reports and putting in contingency plans. I mean if there's high risks, like really high risks, then potentially *[there's a barrier]*, because we do have to focus on risk.

This contradiction was picked up by another practitioner, who said '*it should be a child first approach, whether it's high risks or not*', but perhaps how to actualise Child First in practice right up to very 'high risk' cases (children who have committed serious offences, or assessed as likely to in the future—a not unproblematic prophetic process) is a challenge which needs more development, in order to convince managers, police, courts and HMIP that Child First can apply throughout the gamut of justice-involved children. However, HMIP, as proponents this 'blended', but therefore ultimately compromised, approach was identified by one practitioner as a barrier for their YOT, after a rather damning inspection report of their out-of-court cases (so *not* 'high risk'):

The inspectors came along…said that…we were giving kids too much chance and not addressing the risk properly….we weren't robust enough in…risk assessments with…out-of-court disposals…social care were fuming because they turned around and said what we're doing…is…the new way of working with children to keep them out of the out of the justice system…they came along with the probation hats on and saw it as risk-taking with risky offenders, rather than being child-friendly and child first.

Practitioners' views on the *AssetPlus assessment tool* (see earlier discussion) were mixed, with some seeing the benefit when compared with its predecessor, Asset:

Yeah I think it does *[facilitate Child First]* more so now than the old Asset It's definitely miles better than the first Asset we had was, because the first one you started off with your offending and everything else was quite small after that and scoring...It didn't leave much room for professional judgment.

Another practitioner who had only been with the YOT since 2017 (so never experienced Asset) saying '*It's a very important tool. It gets the job done. It's a big part of the job so I've got no complaints about it*'. Another much more longstanding practitioner expressed frustration ('*It's huge, it's a massive monster...I can understand how it is meant to work but it's such a complex document that every time you tick a box, yes, you open another page with lots more questions*'); but also acknowledged that it was also about learning to approach the whole process differently, but that this can be challenging for practitioners used to the previous system: '*it's not supposed to be the monster it is, but when you've learned a certain way of writing it's hard to unlearn that*'. This view was echoed by another more long-standing practitioner: '*Practitioners have got to get used to writing in that child first way isn't it, and to show that, yes the child has contributed towards that, and that that can be hard sometimes*'. Exhaustion caused by the size of AssetPlus was also flagged by another practitioner as unhelpful:

> It's a long document, the AssetPlus...by the time you get to...the pathways and planning which is the most important part...sometimes people are quite exhausted...they're not maybe putting as much thought and effort into it as the earlier parts of it.

Another practitioner found AssetPlus unhelpful towards some aspects of Child First, especially the importance of involving the child with the embedded 'What do you think' self-assessment section:

> The self-assessment forms are just shocking. They're not child friendly are they? Yes...they're asking questions directly to the child, but they're not laid out in the most child-friendly way. They're lengthy...by the time they've reached the end they've lost the will to live...it's very different to everything else we do with the young people, like everything else we do is more creative or colourful.

One worker suggested that for collaboration to be effective, change is needed:

'Sometimes you forget about giving the child's point of view as well. So perhaps maybe some tweaks there could be useful'. *Another suggested change was needed in the planning aspect:* 'the AssetPlus intervention plan wasn't particularly child friendly so we...devised one that we could sit with the young person and they would put their bits on there, what they wanted, so it was very child-friendly'.

Practitioners, therefore, recognised some of the strengths (enabling characteristics) of AssetPlus, especially in comparison to its predecessor, Asset, but ultimately felt that the challenge still remained in making it more user- and Child First-friendly.

Unsurprisingly, since there has not yet been any national programme of *training* for Child First, all practitioners recognised that this would be an extremely important aspect of properly cementing it in practice, although they pointed out other training they had received, complementary to Child First justice (if not specifically focused on it), like trauma-informed working, using AssetPlus and embedding youth justice-focused 'desistance' principles. The YJB, when approached about this, stated that Unitas had been commissioned to produce training on this. However, as previously discussed, this needs to be approached holistically, as a Child First 'ethos' (Bateman, 2020) should pervade the *whole* Youth Justice System (and therefore all aspects of training). To answer this with the commissioning of a new distance learning (so, individual computer-based) module risks silo-ing Child First as *one aspect* of youth justice, rather than its '*strategic approach and central guiding principle*'.

The continued use of Unitas as the preferred training provider is worrying, given some of the issues discussed earlier, but even more so after talking to practitioners who have (recently) completed training, who identified several concerning aspects, like the requirement for the Unitas book as the basis of all submitted work (denying critical treatment; '*the assignments, basically they wanted you to re-word the Unitas book*'), preference throughout for the RNR model with its emphasis on risk and the complete lack of any reference to Child First:

> There's nothing about children first or nothing really on the positive side...risk is about everything. It is, it is about everything...and not really protective factors. It's quite negative. There's a lot about the risks and the strengths came second.

This seems to indicate that even if Unitas produced a good Child First module, unless the other course content also has Child First as core, it will essentially be contradictory and perpetuate barriers, exacerbating confusion already perpetuated by continued reference to blends of 'risk' and 'Child First'.

Practitioners when asked about what good training to enable Child First practice might look like were unanimous that a computer-based module would not be the best vehicle: '*I find they're the most ineffective...it doesn't grip me and I won't read it properly or give it the time*'. Effective training should be collaborative with colleagues (a point also made by Case & Browning, 2021b: 10), working through together what Child First looks like in practice, at all levels and stages:

> What I find is really good is...find out what people think is Child First Offender Second. Examples of practice where you might feel that it was child first offender second, or the other way around... how they've approached it, how they've engaged the young person, how they might have used a Child First approach. Having like case studies...how could staff work with that young person in a Child First way? So, what would you need to consider? How would you approach it? How would you engage that young person? How could they contribute to their plan? Maybe getting staff to think about in terms of possible outcomes for them around diversion or if there's a statutory court order, how could that be worked in a child first way?

Practitioners also identified several other potential challenges to cementing Child First in practice, for example, lack of funding (also a major talking point in the YOT discussion group):

> 'There aren't the resources because of the cuts to do the strengths-based stuff...it's down to the bare bones' *and the COVID-19 crisis:* 'None of the services that you would refer them to, to go mountain biking, walking,

Duke of Edinburgh – it's all been closed down. So, you're left with coming to the office and having a chat...Take them to the park and have a chat. It's ridiculous...it's all just come to a grinding halt'.

Hopefully issues related to the pandemic will be resolved, but others may not be so easy to address, with continued funding challenges (exacerbated by the pandemic) expected for years to come.

Conclusion

The practitioners interviewed and involved in the YOT discussion group were all very positive about Child First principles (perhaps the most significant enabler), agreeing that this was the only real way forward for youth justice practice. In many ways, much of what they described IS Child First in practice but there were still barriers and challenges which could at best slow down progress, but at worst bring the Child First revolution to a shuddering halt. One of the most concerning threats must be the dogged and continued adherence to RNR, somehow seeing this as compatible with Child First justice. This has clearly affected practitioners and their understanding of Child First (particularly in the void created by lack of specific and appropriate training). Related to this is the need for AssetPlus re-design to fully align with Child First (rather than trying to hold both RNR and Child First in balance—or tension). YOT ability to adhere to the tenets is severely hampered by an inspectorate which still values risk above Child First practice. So, to fully enable this shift, inspection guidelines need to be clear and properly Child First-focused. Whilst the YJB's whole-hearted adoption of Child First justice is a major enabler towards making it reality, there is still much work to be done in neutralising barriers and addressing the challenges which YOT practitioners are already experiencing.

References

Baker K. (2012). *AssetPlus rationale*. https://assets.publishing.service.gov.uk/government/uploads/system/uploads/attachment_data/file/367782/AssetPlus_Rationale_revised_October_2014_1_0.pdf. Accessed 22 August 2021.

Bateman T. (2020). *The state of youth justice 2020*. National Association for Youth Justice. https://thenayj.org.uk/cmsAdmin/uploads/state-of-youth-justice-2020-final-sep20.pdf. Accessed 3 August 2021.

Brewster, D. (2020). Not wired up? The neuroscientific turn in youth to adult (Y2A) transitions policy. *Youth Justice, 20*(3), 215–234.

Case, S., & Haines, K. (2014). Children first, offenders second: The centrality of engagement in positive youth justice. *The Howard Journal of Criminal Justice, 54*(2), 157–175.

Case, S., & Haines, K. (2021). Abolishing youth justice systems: Children first, offenders nowhere. *Youth Justice, 21*(1), 3–17.

Case, S. P., & Browning, A. (2021a). *Child first justice: The research evidence-base*. Loughborough University. https://repository.lboro.ac.uk/ndownloader/files/26748341/1. Accessed 5 August 2021.

Case, S. P., & Browning, A. (2021b). *The child first policy implementation project. Turning policy rhetoric into practice reality*. Loughborough University. https://repository.lboro.ac.uk/ndownloader/files/31020007/1. Accessed 25 October 2021.

Case, S. (2021). Challenging the reductionism of "evidence-based" youth justice. *Sustainability, 13*(4), 1735.

Case, S., & Hampson, K. (2019). Youth justice pathways to change: Drivers, challenges and opportunities. *Youth Justice, 19*(1), 25–41.

Cordis Bright. (2017). *Evaluation of the enhanced case management approach*. www.cordisbright.co.uk/admin/resources/170328-evaluation-enhanced-case-management-approach-en.pdf. Accessed 5 August 2021.

Creaney, S. (2020). "Game playing" and "docility": Youth justice in question. *Safer Communities, 19*(3), 103–118.

Crime and Disorder Act. (1989). www.legislation.gov.uk/ukpga/1998/37/contents. Accessed 5 August 2021.

Farrall, S., & Maruna, S. (2004). Desistance-focused criminal justice policy research: Introduction to a special issue on desistance from crime and public policy. *The Howard Journal, 43*(4), 358–367.

Glendinning, F., Rodriguez, G. R., Newbury, A., & Wilmot, R. (2021). *Adverse childhood experience (ACE) and trauma-informed approaches in youth justice services in Wales: An evaluation of the implementation of the enhanced case management (ECM) project*. Bangor University. https://yjresourcehub.uk/evaluation-library/item/download/1049_d5ec4ee08c1279aab5a132e2cc4c2042.html. Accessed 8 September 2021.

Haines, K., Case, S., & Charles, A. (2013). The Swansea Bureau: A model of diversion from the youth justice system. *International Journal of Law Crime and Justice, 41*(2), 167–187.

Hampson, K. (2018). Desistance approaches in youth justice—The next passing fad or a sea-change for the positive? *Youth Justice, 18*(1), 18–33.

Haines, K., & Drakeford, M. (1998). *Young people and youth justice*. Palgrave.

HMICFRS. (2021). *Disproportionate use of police powers. A spotlight on stop and search and the use of force*. Justice Inspectorates. www.justiceinspectorates.gov.uk/hmicfrs/wp-content/uploads/disproportionate-use-of-police-powers-spotlight-on-stop-search-and-use-of-force.pdf. Accessed 5 August 2021.

HMIP. (2016). *Desistance and young people*. www.justiceinspectorates.gov.uk/hmiprobation/wp-content/uploads/sites/5/2016/05/Desistance_and_young_people.pdf. Accessed 5 August 2021.

HMIP. (2020). *A thematic review of the work of youth offending services during the pandemic*. www.justiceinspectorates.gov.uk/hmiprobation/wp-content/uploads/sites/5/2020/11/201110-A-thematic-review-of-the-work-of-youth-offending-services-during-the-COVID-19-pandemic.pdf. Accessed 3 August 2021.

HMIP. (2021a). *Youth offending inspection—External guidance manual*. www.justiceinspectorates.gov.uk/hmiprobation/wp-content/uploads/sites/5/2021/05/Youth-Guidance-Manual-External-v5.2-May-2021.pdf. Accessed 3 August 2021.

HMIP. (2021b). *Inspection standards for youth offending services*. www.justiceinspectorates.gov.uk/hmiprobation/wp-content/uploads/sites/5/2021/05/Youth-Offending-Inspection-Standards-May-2021-v1.1.pdf. Accessed 5 August 2021.

HMIP. (2021c). *Case management in context*. www.justiceinspectorates.gov.uk/hmiprobation/effective-practice/youth-justice-case-management-effectiveness-in-inspected-cases/case-management-in-context/. Accessed 23 August 2021.

HMIP. (n.d.). *The evidence base—Probation services*. www.justiceinspectorates.gov.uk/hmiprobation/research/the-evidence-base-probation/. Accessed 5 August 2021.

Institute for Criminal Policy Research. (2012). *Assessing young people in police custody: An examination of the operation of Triage schemes* (Home Office occasional paper). https://assets.publishing.service.gov.uk/government/upl oads/system/uploads/attachment_data/file/116265/occ106.pdf. Accessed 5 August 2021.

Kemshall, H. (2021). *Risk and desistance: A blended approach to risk management*. HMIP Academic Insights. www.justiceinspectorates.gov.uk/hmipro bation/wp-content/uploads/sites/5/2021/06/Academic-Insights-Kemshall. pdf. Accessed 5 August 2021.

Kubiak, C., & Hester, R. (2009). Just deserts? Developing practice in youth justice. *Learning in Health and Social Care, 8*(1), 47–55.

MacLeod, S., Jeffes, J., White, R., & Bramley, G. (2010). *Analysis of youth offending team inspection reports* (LGA Research Report). Slough: NFER.

Matza, D. (1964). *Delinquency and drift*. Wiley.

McAra, L., & McVie, S. (2007). Youth justice? The impact of system contact on patterns of desistance from offending. *European Journal of Criminology, 4*(3), 315–345.

Ministry of Justice. (2021). *Youth justice statistics 2019–20*. https://assets.pub lishing.service.gov.uk/government/uploads/system/uploads/attachment_d ata/file/956621/youth-justice-statistics-2019-2020.pdf. Accessed 23 August 2021.

National Archives. (n.d.). *Youth offending team inspection reports*. https://web archive.nationalarchives.gov.uk/20100512162212/http://www.justice.gov. uk/inspectorates/hmi-probation/youth-offending-reports.htm. Accessed 3 August 2021.

Peer Power. (2020). *No decision without me*. www.peerpower.org.uk/wp-con tent/uploads/2020/12/PeerPowerAnnualReport2019-2020.pdf. Accessed 19 August 2021.

Phoenix, J. (2011). In search of a youth justice pedagogy? A commentary. *Journal of Children's Services, 6*(2), 125–133.

Pitts, J. (2001). Korrectional Karaoke: New labour and the zombification of youth justice. *Youth Justice, 1*(2), 3–16.

Sentencing Council. (2021). *Community resolution*. www.sentencingcouncil. org.uk/explanatory-material/magistrates-court/item/out-of-court-disposals/ 6-community-resolution/. Accessed 20 August 2021.

Taylor C. (2016). *Review of the youth justice system in England and Wales*. Ministry of Justice. https://assets.publishing.service.gov.uk/government/ uploads/system/uploads/attachment_data/file/577103/youth-justice-review-final-report.pdf. Accessed 8 September 2021.

Thomas Commission. (2019). *Justice in Wales for the people of Wales*. https://gov.wales/sites/default/files/publications/2019-10/Justice%20Commission%20ENG%20DIGITAL_2.pdf. Accessed 2 August 2021.

Turner, A. (2019, January 29). Good intentions but the right approach? The case of ACEs. *Public Healthy Blog*. https://publichealthy.co.uk/good-intentions-but-the-right-approach-the-case-of-aces/. Accessed 6 August 2021.

UK Government. (2021). *Home Secretary backs police to increase stop and search*. https://www.gov.uk/government/news/home-secretary-backs-policeto-increrease-stop-andsearch#:~:text=Permanently%20relaxing%20the%20conditions%20maintains,occur%20to%20%E2%80%9Cmay%E2%80%9D%20occur. Accessed 8 October 2022.

United Nations. (1985). *United Nations standard minimum rules for the administration of juvenile justice ("The Beijing rules")*. www.ohchr.org/documents/professionalinterest/beijingrules.pdf. Accessed 8 September 2021.

United Nations. (1989). *Convention on the rights of the child*. www.ohchr.org/en/professionalinterest/pages/crc.aspx. Accessed 6 August 2021.

Welsh Government. (2015). *Children's rights in Wales*. https://gov.wales/sites/default/files/inline-documents/2019-04/2_Rights_En.pdf. Accessed 19 August 2021.

Welsh Assembly Government and Youth Justice Board. (2004). *All-Wales youth offending strategy*. Cardiff: Welsh Assembly Government and Youth Justice Board.

Wigzell, A. (2021). *Explaining desistance: Looking forward, not backwards*. National Association for Youth Justice. https://thenayj.org.uk/cmsAdmin/uploads/explaining-desistance-briefing-feb-2021-final.pdf. Accessed 20 August 2021.

Wright, S., & Liddle, M. (2014). *Young offenders and trauma: Experience and impact*. Beyond Youth Custody. www.beyondyouthcustody.net/wp-content/uploads/BYC-Trauma-experience-and-impact-practitioners-guide.pdf. Accessed 20 August 2021.

YJB. (2005). *The role of risk and protective factors*. https://webarchive.nationalarchives.gov.uk/20110602000931/https://www.yjb.gov.uk/Publications/Resources/Downloads/Role_of_risk_and_protective_factors_fullreport.pdf. Accessed 2 August 2021.

YJB. (2008). *Assessment, planning, interventions and supervision*. https://webarchive.nationalarchives.gov.uk/20110601215227/https://www.yjb.gov.uk/Publications/Scripts/prodDownload.asp?idproduct=393&eP=. Accessed 2 August 2021.

YJB. (2009). *National standards for youth justice services.* https://webarchive. nationalarchives.gov.uk/20110601213908/https://www.yjb.gov.uk/Publicati ons/Scripts/fileDownload.asp?file=National+Standards+for+Youth+Justice+ Services%2Epdf. Accessed 2 August 2021.

YJB. (2018a). *Making resettlement constructive.* https://yjresourcehub.uk/cus tody-and-resettlement/item/download/723_b535da3b3f0716677b9964ec 93870ca6.html. Accessed 5 August 2021.

YJB. (2018b). *Youth Justice Board for England and Wales strategic plan 2018–2021.* https://assets.publishing.service.gov.uk/government/uploads/system/ uploads/attachment_data/file/706925/201804_YJB_Strategic_Plan_2018_ 21_Final.pdf. Accessed 8 September 2021.

YJB. (2019). *Case management Guidance.* www.gov.uk/government/collections/ case-management-guidance. Accessed 8 September 2021.

YJB. (2020a). *Why enhanced case management is 'child first'.* https://yjresourc ehub.uk/trauma-and-wellbeing/item/download/991_be523a13cc562c0819 7d30ff1f804a20.html. Accessed 8 September 2021.

YJB. (2020b). *Child first in theory and in practice YJB live session—Lancashire YJS and Lewisham YOS (November 2020).* Available on the YJB Resource Hub. https://yjresourcehub.uk/out-of-court-disposals-and-prevention/item/ 829-child-first-in-theory-and-in-practice-yjb-live-session-lancashire-yjs-and-lewisham-yos-november-2020.html. Accessed 6 August 2021.

YJB. (2021a). *Strategic plan 2021–2024.* https://assets.publishing.service.gov. uk/government/uploads/system/uploads/attachment_data/file/966200/YJB_ Strategic_Plan_2021_-_2024.pdf. Accessed 2 August 2021.

YJB. (2021b). *Workforce development strategy.* https://yjresourcehub.uk/workfo rce-development/item/download/1013_7aab6cf1b9ffd8d8486497a05bcb 5843.html. Accessed 23 August 2021.

YJB. (2021c, July 30). *YJBulletin,* Issue 186. https://youthjusticeboard.newswe aver.co.uk/yots2/zvp2eh43tletdt3xlq5agw?email=true&lang=en&a=11&p= 59920230&fbclid=IwAR2btz-WrkA7VWM5XP2epN2kcNHE3KGy76TtA U89k5FBP8HEZ5b30XIAqsA. Accessed 5 August 2021.

YJB. (n.d.). *Asset.* https://webarchive.nationalarchives.gov.uk/201106012 22228/http://www.yjb.gov.uk/Publications/Scripts/fileDownload.asp?file= Asset%2Epdf. Accessed 2 August 2021.

YJB Cymru. (2017). *Enhanced case management. Our approach to complex cases in youth offending teams.* https://yjresourcehub.uk/evaluation-library/item/ 441-evaluation-of-the-enhanced-case-management-approach.html. Accessed 5 August 2021.

Youth Custody Improvement Board. (2017). *Findings and recommendations of the Youth Custody Improvement Board*. https://assets.publishing.service.gov.uk/government/uploads/system/uploads/attachment_data/file/594448/findings-and-recommendations-of-the-ycib.pdf. Accessed 2 August 2021.

12

Embracing children's Voices: Transforming Youth Justice Practice Through Co-production and Child First Participation

Samantha Burns and Sean Creaney

Introduction

This chapter sets out to discuss the extent Youth Justice Services (YJS) affirm or deny children's participation in the commissioning, design, delivery and evaluation of the services they are in receipt of. This includes examining whether children are trusted with responsibility to adopt a key decision-maker role or whether professionals view children as too 'risky' or 'vulnerable' to meaningfully participate. This also includes the extent to which professionals are consciously receptive to children's

---

S. Burns
Department of Sociology, Durham University, Durham, UK
e-mail: Samantha.burns@durham.ac.uk

S. Creaney (✉)
Department of Law and Criminology, Edge Hill University, Ormskirk, UK
e-mail: sean.creaney@edgehill.ac.uk

preferences, and committed to challenging structural barriers and transforming assessment, intervention planning and supervision. In addition, we examine the ongoing risk discourses in YJS, which we argue can undermine children's priorities and concerns throughout supervisory and assessment processes, and wider organisation priorities.

By looking at these aspects of the YJS workforce, this chapter critiques professional interest in relinquishing power/control, authorising or facilitating children's choices/freedoms, and in co-creating legitimate participatory opportunities that can unlock children's expertise and capabilities as decision-makers. By addressing these aspects of YJS supervision, this chapter depicts how this 'plays out' in the field in what is often an adult-controlled and risk-dominated environment. Core themes include—but are not limited to—how youth justice professionals navigate or facilitate aspects of participatory work, such as shared decision-making, peer-led approaches, children's 'untapped' potential as 'knowers' or 'experts', and non-hierarchical empathic relationship building. We do this by theorising the efficacy of Child First participation principles and co-production in practice and by drawing on empirical evidence. We also present fascinating insights, knowledge and expertise of professionals working within youth justice, whereby we held conversations that enabled this chapter to dive deeper into key issues of participation in youth justice supervision. More specifically, through integrating these in-depth conversations into the discussions and arguments presented, this will help the reader to contextualise and digest some of the key issues around valuing children's voice and lived experience within participatory processes. The authors also examine how broader cultural, organisational and structural components contribute to particular barriers concerning risk and the accumulation of adult power.

We assert that children under youth justice supervision often experience types of capital deficit or hardship, especially in terms of cultural and economic power. Children's distinctive experiential or situated knowledge can be unfairly subject to disproportionate critique leading to spurious claims that their insights are not as credible as other forms of evidence collected and analysed through assessment processes or investigative practices (Creaney, 2020; Phoenix & Kelly, 2013). Crucially, the

Child First stance recognises children's capability to participate as collaborative partners. At the same time, Child First does not denounce the perspective of the adult professional. On the contrary, it provides a platform for front-line professionals to also exercise agency and specialist knowledge accrued through practice experience in the field. However, a significant barrier to overcome is that of managerialist bureaucracy and the dominant discourse of public protection preoccupied with judgement and 'symbolic violence' (Bourdieu and Wacquant, 1992). These two forces collectively restrict the professional's ability to help children accumulate their lived experience as capital and respond to children's needs in partnership through positive and progressive ways. As such, a form of 'hyper-bureaucracy' can present itself as a fundamental barrier to meaningful participatory practices within youth justice supervision (Armitage et al., 2016; Eadie & Canton, 2002).

Hence, this chapter is organised by firstly presenting a backdrop of Child First principles coming into the point of service delivery and identifies key characteristics of a shared decision-making approach, justifying why it is necessary for it to become included within core components of the Child First movement. By expanding on ideas of participatory work with children, it is argued that co-production principles and a focus on children as equal partners and co-creators (see Social Care Institute of Excellence, 2015) can be a progressive response to awarding equal value of both children and professionals' knowledge and experiences. The remainder of the chapter is guided by invigorating conversations with those youth justice professionals who have shared their lived realities of working in youth justice environments, drawing upon the critical issues and core themes of participatory opportunities, and clarifying the benefits of working with and recognising the immense value of children's voice and expertise.

Part 1: Responding to children's Voice

It is a fundamental right for children to be provided with opportunities to play a part in determining the response to the problems associated with their behaviour (Creaney & Smith, 2020). Likewise, children have the right to a voice which is heard and responded to by adults, and to be provided with opportunities to influence systems or processes that affect them. This was reiterated in a review of the Youth Justice System in 2016 (Taylor, 2016), which also asserted that children under supervision need to be viewed and responded to as 'children first' (Taylor, 2016: 48). In response to this review, the Youth Justice Board (YJB) crafted a revised definition of the 'Children First, Offenders Second' principle (i.e. 'Child First'—YJB, 2019; adapted from Haines & Case, 2015). At the heart of a Child First, philosophy is a steadfast commitment to the avoidance of tokenism and adult-centrism (Haines & Case, 2015). There has since been a concerted effort to promote children's participatory rights and invest in an agenda which would be capable of progressing positive forms of practice intervention and relationship-based supervision. This led to the YJB producing updated guidance reiterating the importance of treating children as active subjects (as opposed to passive objects who need 'fixing'), focusing on building children's strengths and capacities to facilitate their meaningful engagement in assessment, planning, intervention and supervision processes (YJB, 2019, 2021). This included an emphasis placed on tackling the underlying causes of crime by documenting the impact childhood adversity and trauma has on a person's life chances.

At this point, it is important to make readers aware that child-led practice has not been a fundamental feature of recent youth justice policy in England. The YJB's Participation Strategy published in 2016 set out to reverse this neglect by infusing a change in culture and giving credence to the voice of the child (Case et al., 2020). The strategy refers to children having a right to a voice, freedom to impart ideas and be listened to (Article 12 of the UNCRC, 1989). There was discussion within the document concerning the importance of children's substantive involvement in the design and delivery of services. There was acknowledgement of the barriers that may impede children's meaningful participation, including communication difficulties or children not feeling confident or comfortable to actively enact agency and decide a particular course of action. The YJB pledged to seek and value children's feedback on their experiences throughout all stages of the Youth Justice System. It set out several core principles which were intended to undergird decision-making and nurture a participatory culture within YJS. This included an emphasis on promoting children's ability to exercise agency/choice, and a concerted effort to assign dedicated participation champions to develop inclusive practices with children to enable them to exert influence, shape decision-making and consequently enhance provision (Creaney & Case, 2021).

The YJB's adoption of a 'child first' approach has been widely welcomed and endorsed by many in the youth justice sector, including the National Association for Youth Justice, the only UK charity that focuses exclusively on the welfare and rights of children in Youth Justice (see Bateman, 2021). The child's engagement is crucial to effective planning, intervention and supervision, and of equal importance is the co-creation principle, which is pivotal to sustain positive outcomes (Hazel et al., 2017). The YJB Child First model was informed by empirical evidence and co-constructed knowledge collated and presented in a series of published reports, collaborative and engaging resources as part of the Beyond Youth Custody project (Wright et al., 2014), notably the evidence-based key characteristics of support, including constructive, co-created, customised, consistent and co-ordinated practices. Moreover, the principled and progressive positive Youth Justice model of Child First, notably legitimate (fair, just, moral), meaningful participation and engagement (commitment, belief) in the planning and execution of effective services, underpinned the basis of the YJB's Child First approach and informed subsequent revisions to documents and strategies.

The YJB's current Child First definition consists of commitments towards the best interests of the child (cf. Article 3 of the UNCRC) and the application of the positive youth justice concept of child-friendly practice, which includes meaningful opportunities for children to impart ideas in both the policy realm and at the point of service delivery (Haines & Case, 2015; Brown, 2020). Also included in the YJB Child First definition is the promotion of positive behaviours/outcomes and strengths-based practices. Here, there is an acute focus on identifying and maximising positive aspects of children's lives through working with them, tapping into and building on their particular skill sets in a pro-social way. To help address structural inequalities and promote pathways to desistance, the development of a constructive child-practitioner relationship is viewed as a medium for change and a core component of effective practice. Facilitating participatory practices is of the utmost importance to the YJB, and this is reflected in their commitment to recognise children's ability to offer unique insights. For example, the YJB has created a Youth Advisory Network,[1] which seeks to provide opportunities for justice experienced children and young adults to improve outcomes for children and influence the youth justice delivery landscape (YJB, 2020). Pivotal to this is the acknowledgement that children are partners in the process, not disinterested 'objects'. Indeed, children have the right and the ability to co-construct knowledge throughout assessment processes and intervention planning. Finally, the YJB strategy seeks to promote a non-criminal identity by maximising routes to diversion, to avoid or discourage early (or escalating) criminalisation. Throughout this process, there is a spotlight on positive alternatives and the identification of underlying unmet needs thought to be driving behaviours and influencing outcomes, especially in relation to education, health and social care. The discussions, within this chapter, align to the third Child First principle: 'encourage children's active participation, engagement and wider social inclusion. All work promotes desistance through co-creation with children' (YJB, 2019, 2021). Crucially, it is argued that, children must be viewed capable, knowledgeable co-producers who can influence the process and work carried out.

Moreover, it has been proposed that there is a need to move away from a reliance on risk, strategic calculations or measures that purport to erase uncertainty by predicting the likelihood of the child engaging in future harmful behaviours (Case, 2018; Case & Haines, 2009). Following the Crime and Disorder Act 1998, within YJS there was an acute focus on identifying risk, and strategies to implement measures to curtail offending, almost 'akin to the prescription of doses or medicines' (Stephenson, 2018: 69). In particular, the risk-focused mechanisms that were created by the Crime and Disorder Act 1998 resulted in frontline practitioners being constrained by the mantra of managerialism and

---

[1] At the time of writing (May, 2022), the YJS the YJB will be working with as part of the YAN regional 'pilot' include: Southwark and Bromley, Camden, Devon, Ealing, Lancashire, North Lincs, Rochdale and Suffolk.

the dominance of neo-liberal bureaucratic processes, which consequently led to their discretion and expertise being 'neutered' (Smith, 2003: 3). Hence, by casting aside the outmoded idea of predicting 'risk', the nature and purpose of youth justice has been re-defined through the Child First philosophy (YJB, 2019, 2021), intuitively activating a Positive Youth Justice, which created a spotlight on children's participatory rights. Practitioners have been instructed to co-create practice with children and utilise their relative autonomy to initiative pro-social techniques and bespoke forms of intervention (Smithson et al., 2020). YJS have been encouraged to invoke a strengths-based approach and provide access to legitimate routes out of offending including potential pathways to positive outcomes. A participatory approach with children is viewed here as a foundation to improving children's outcomes and reducing offending.

When children experience difficulties in their lives, it is important that they receive support from adults to navigate those challenges. Yet, those under supervision have frequently been failed; often presenting with histories of victimisation, and a catalogue of unmet social, emotional and health needs (Taylor, 2016). As discussed, children deserve to a have a say in what happens to them when they enter the Youth Justice System, subject to police or court order requirements. Despite this commitment, there can be difficulty giving credence to the voice of the child in a context of enforcement and compliance enmeshed within bureaucratic processes which can restrict professional agency or limit autonomy to facilitate bespoke forms of practice. Therefore, it can be challenging to encourage children's participation and empower those in receipt of a service to express a view, given that they are to an extent mandated by the court to attend meetings or undertake certain schemes of work. While children are required to complete certain interventions or programmes, this should not be perceived as an entirely involuntary or wholly compulsory process. To enable children to meaningfully shape the decision-making process, they need to experience a sense of freedom and autonomy and not feel 'done to' (Haines & Case, 2015).

A key obstacle to promoting a pro-social self has been professionals who exert a powerful influence over young people, having reservations about 'handing over control' (Thomas, 2007: 202), which could undermine professional authority and their legitimate status as credible figures in the field. Professionals can aim to overcome this by being transparent about their roles and responsibilities and commit to creating a collaborative relationship, characterised by trust and empathy, ensuring that it is clearly and routinely communicated to the child that their viewpoint is of value. By being transparent and holding authentic dialogue with children, professionals can positively shine a light on power within relationships. Yet, it is likely that children will perceive their treatment by professionals as illegitimate if they are not provided with the opportunity to inform the process, and influence decisions that affect them. Conversely, when children perceive their treatment by the YJS as legitimate (fair, just, moral), they are more likely to both comply and engage with interventions (Haines & Case, 2015). Therefore, it is important to listen and respond appropriately to children's voice through a collaborative relationship with professionals where it is possible to co-create the way services are received by the child, which is why it is important to focus on professionals and the way they facilitate forms of participation with children.

In Focus: Voices of Professionals

Mifta Choudhury, founder of Youth Ink, discusses the tension of YJS worker's authority role: Mifta—*Within criminal justice, we have some young people who understand and know their rights; they are confident enough to challenge a YJS officer. Sometimes this can lead to issues for the young person as the YJS officer is unsure how to address the young person challenging the YJS officer. The role of the YJS officer is to enforce the court order, which means "YJS officer will tell the young person what to do". This makes it difficult as the YJS would like to befriend the young person, which would make the role of the YJS and YJS officer simpler as the young person would be compliant. It is disappointing that YJS teams do not teach a young person who comes to YJS on a court order the rights they have while they are on their order with the YJS. For example, if a young person waits more than 15 minutes for a YJS officer, the young person has the right to ask the YJS officer why they have waited over 15 minutes. However, some YJS's will not* *tell young people they have these rights and can ask questions and challenge officers.*

Forms of Participation

There are different forms of participation, with the suitability of each type influenced by a child's age and stages of their development. Definitions of what constitutes participation or how it is conceptualised can differ (Checkoway, 2011). For example, the concept can relate to shared decision-making and/or children's active involvement in the design, development and evaluation of activities. Participation can also be thought of as being listened to and/or consulted on the governance and delivery of services. Crucially, when practitioners engender a climate where children's meaningful participation in processes is encouraged, children are more likely to feel able to exert influence over decision-making and to have confidence that their expressions of agency are of value and have a degree of influence. As discussed, children's participation has been promoted, through the publication of the YJB's participation strategy (YJB, 2016), problematising the dominant view that 'professionals know best'. It was acknowledged that children can be active agents, capable of possessing credible expertise. It promoted or reinforced the need to elicit the child's viewpoint on matters that affect them and detailed the beneficial effects of their active participation and meaningful involvement in the planning, design, delivery and evaluation of youth justice services (YJB, 2016). Prior to this, children's right to influence service design tended not to be a core feature of policy or practice within YJS.

It is important to note that there can be concern regarding whether children's perspectives or input into the process makes a difference at the coalface. Professionals must be upfront and explicit about how involved children can be in the decision-making process, the steps taken to shine a light on and to combat unequal forms of power within relationships between stakeholders. This includes the impact children's voice will have on how the organisation operates, and a commitment to publicise how any suggested areas for development from children, as part of the consultative process, will filter through to practice. However, a barrier which often arises is that children may be suspicious of authority figures. To address any sense of distrust, it is important that professionals create an environment that is warm or welcoming that is free from judgement. This can help to instil belief that children's involvement is encouraged, and that their individual and collective experiences are of value to enhance service provision and to improve satisfaction. It is also vital that the professional skilfully engages the child and is alert to forms of resistance and intent on resolving any conflict by responding in a positive and constructive way. This involves adopting a child-friendly stance that recognises children's similar or divergent priorities and concerns, embracing approaches that build confidence and self-esteem.

It is possible to strive towards a fair and just partnership but inevitably the professional has the authority to exert particular influence including sanctions for non-compliance or trigger breech proceedings if dissatisfied with the nature of a child's input into processes, thus the child may continue to feel relatively powerless. Thus, to an extent, there may still be a level of uncertainty regarding whether children feel *entitled* to a voice and enabled to exert influence over the content and format of particular interventions. It is unclear whether children feel they are able to accrue and retain a level of control over the process or whether the type of support being offered results in children feeling empowered to shape a positive identity for themselves (Wright et al., 2014; see also Clinks, 2016). What appears indisputable, though, is that unless there is commitment to nurturing a relationship-based practice and an acknowledgement regarding its pivotal role in bolstering participation or engagement in supervision, it will be difficult for front-line practitioners to co-create a rich and contextualised understanding of the needs, wants, or circumstances of the child (Creaney, 2020; Wigzell, 2021).

In Focus: Relationship-Based Practice—Voices of Professionals

Andi Brierley, a former youth justice practitioner, talked about a group project he set up for and with *Children Looked After*. The project promoted a relationship-based practice, especially principles of trust and reciprocity, and provided opportunities for children to share their experiences of being justice-involved:

Andi—*it was a real success being from the children's point of view so we're getting the children to first of all, have two interviews to get them to think about their experiences of care and criminal justice, what they think could improve and so that was the first two weeks, and then for the next seven weeks, they put together a presentation so that they could deliver it to senior managers in both social care and criminal justice and say; "these are my experiences" and obviously with that particular group they've had numerous placement breakdowns and numerous relationships, often moved around the country, we have lots of kids from all the local authorities coming to [the area], and, to be honest, the stories that the children were telling were pretty bad, and It was delivered in a way that they wanted to deliver it, so sometimes, like because I worked in the justice system, I would be thinking like I don't know how it is going to be received!*

Building a non-hierarchical relationship involves an active conscious ongoing effort to breakdown power inequalities (Burns, 2019; Creaney & Case, 2021). Forging collaborative and constructive relationships is important when striving to assess cognitive ability and is vital as part of attempts to capture perspectives on preferred levels of participation or when the intention is to devise tailored and bespoke forms of support. The established evidence-base is highlighted in a recent report which documents and showcases the efficacy of Child First Justice (See Case & Browning, 2021a). Of note, elements that contribute to effective participatory practices include collaborative, trusting and reciprocal relationships, fair responses and meaningful incentives, and the equal sharing of power between all stakeholders. We can inject into the Child First paradigm the theory and practice of co-production.

Theory and Practice of Co-production and Co-creation

With Child First principles and a commitment to relationship-based practice, unequal power continues to still be a particular barrier to overcome. So, insights from co-production are useful to help fundamentally shift power within relationships to maximise the voice of the child and influence the transformation of service delivery to better meet children's needs. Co-production aligns with Child First as it allows for a specific focus on the changing role of adult professionals and challenges a deficit view towards children as incompetent and incapable (Tisdall, 2017). Furthermore, a co-production approach is underpinned by the belief that children are a valuable resource who possess a multiplicity of experiences, and whose insights, if captured and acted upon, can usefully enhance public service provision, viewing children as capable and knowledgeable experts (Brady, 2020; Tisdall, 2013). Co-production can also be a conceptual gateway to transformation, as these relationships between children and professionals become a democratic process of co-learning and co-creation (Percy-Smith, 2012). We can utilise co-production as a conceptual vehicle for emancipation, especially with children in the Youth Justice System who are seldom provided with meaningful opportunities to input into decision-making.

Child First approaches also intend to 'responsibilise adults' which complements co-production ideas. This is because through a co-production lens, the role of adult professional changes from professional expert to *co-constructor of knowledge* in an equal, reciprocal partnership (Percy-Smith, 2012). In co-production initiatives, the idea of 'shared responsibility' (Slay & Penny, 2014) is utilised to emphasise equality within relationships, although how this fits within a youth justice context is still contentious when there has been a historic over-responsibilisation of children (Goldson, 2000; Haines and Drakeford 1998). Nonetheless, these insights from co-production can allow a greater focus on the role of adult professionals in ensuring they recognise their reformed role while balancing and sharing responsibility with children in an equitable manner. However, AssetPlus (YJB, 2014), introduced in 2015, still privileges practitioner expertise, and is meant to directly enhance their ability to decide a course of action that is appropriate and warranted from their point of view. Front-line professionals may feel constrained by the real and perceived concerns surrounding the 'threat' children pose to society and unintentionally undermine children's knowledge and capabilities, while reducing their responsibility to transform their role for a participatory process to become equal and reciprocal.

Drawing on empirical data theorised through a Bourdieusian lens, one study found that models of co-production were problematic to implement in practice within a context of risk management (see Creaney and Burns, in press; see also Peer Power/Youth Justice Board, 2021). This was due in part to risk management processes being deficit-based, and the result of professionals as officers of the court being primarily concerned with the execution of approaches that are restrictive as opposed to enabling. Such approaches designed to reduce or 'manage' the risk of harm or vulnerability, do not appear to be entirely compatible with a strategy of co-production that is strengths-based and promotes characteristics of empathy and trusting relationships. Subsequently, more attention can be paid to the theory and practice of co-production within youth justice service provision. Not only can co-production transform children's agency, but it can also transform the way adults view children and how institutions affirm their cultural norms and values to involve young people in collective decision-making processes.

Furthermore, co-production can be fundamental to the transformative potential of Child First principles in practice by broadening its aim to challenge power inequalities and system harms. When the voice of the child is put at the core of assessment and intervention, it can still be a narrow, individualistic mode of participation, concerned with individual rights to access services and facilities, which means inclusion in existing adult-dominated institutions. While much work within youth justice services uses the one-to-one nature of working between the youth justice worker and child within assessment and intervention plans, this could be viewed as a building block towards further co-creation and co-production initiatives. This involves children being included within more strategic level decision-making processes, moving away from the hierarchal nature of youth justice service organisational structures. An example of co-production at a strategic level has been occurring across Greater

Manchester, whereby a participation framework has been co-designed in collaboration with and for children and young people (Smithson et al., 2020). Later in this chapter, we provide examples in practice where this is already happening within local youth justice services.

Alongside an emphasis on developing more strategic level participatory processes, which can include peer-led programmes, promoting pro-social attitudes and behaviours, it is vital that professionals assess and reflect on both themselves and the child's readiness to participate. In a recent research report by Peer Power, a recommended theme of 'rights and readiness' intended to highlight the importance of assessing the readiness of practitioners; *'to see themselves as agents for change with children rather than service providers for children. Ensure that accredited rights-based participation and empathy training is available for children involved in participation and co-creation'* (Peer Power/Youth Justice Board, 2021: 70). In line with the recommendation, it is imperative that those in authority sign up to forging both empathic and trusting relationships with children who are in receipt of supervision (Brierley, 2021); reiterating principles of trust and reciprocity. By utilising children's knowledge and expertise, those working within the collaborative project across Greater Manchester shared how they gained trust and empathy through the sharing of children's lived experiences (Smithson & Jones, 2021). This clearly exemplifies how principles of co-production can be utilised in the field of youth justice with those under supervision, which builds children's capital and values their contribution.

Essentially, by reflecting on the concept of co-production, the role of the professional becomes less about being a 'fixer' of problems and more about being a 'facilitator' and 'collaborator' of solutions (New Economics Foundation, 2009). However, as alluded to, it cannot be assumed that all professionals are supportive of co-production; willing and capable to co-produce and co-create with children under supervision. Advocating co-production as a conceptual basis for children's participation requires a reconceptualisation of both adults and young people's capabilities alongside institutional structures and cultures which support it (Tisdall, 2017).

In Focus: Voices of Professionals

Anne-Marie Douglas, Founder and CEO of Peer Power, an empathy led charity that engages young partners with two goals in mind; individual change and system change. It facilitates recovery from trauma, provides safe platforms for voices to be heard and responded to, and supports young partners in getting skills, experience and training to become future leaders. Together, they support those delivering, designing or commissioning services in responding to the experiences of young people; driving empathetic and participatory approaches across the youth sector. Anne-Marie reflected upon the opportunities and challenges for co-production in the youth justice context:

> *I'm seeing often 'co-production' being used interchangeably with participation to explain any type of involvement with children at a service. "We are co-producing xyz…" when the reality of the involvement is somewhere between informing, educating and consultation. It can be helpful, particularly in a youth justice context, to be intentional and explicit in communicating to children about the types and breadth of involvement activities, and importantly the tensions that exist therein. For example, around power, access, and structural limitations in justice settings. This is about more than speaking truth to power, it is bringing power to light together, speaking about it, examining it, owning it. Using different types of involvement in a youth justice context is to be expected, being realistic and transparent as to the level of influence and change making for each involvement activity is imperative in developing trust in the process.*
>
> *At Peer Power, young partners are involved in change making at various levels. Peer Power Experts describe themselves as having experienced injustice and inequality through childhood adversity and social and economic factors. They are passionate about peer support and using their experiences in positive and powerful ways to improve social care, justice and health services by voicing issues for and with other young people. They identified practitioners not understanding co-production properly as a problem, and decided that they wanted to design, develop and deliver experiential co-production and empathy training for practitioners to help them improve their understanding and practice. This training is followed up by coaching sessions delivered by Peer Power Experts that provide support, challenge and problem solving to support services on their individual journeys in embedding co-production.*

Before embarking on the co-production journey, services must reflect upon and assess their 'readiness' to achieve tangible system change in organisational culture and if meaningful relationships and outcomes are to be achieved with children. This means looking at all aspects of the service, how far can they really go in sharing power? Are the linked support agencies on that same journey? Are they doing the work internally to dismantle racism and oppression, and are there safe spaces for children to challenge power, discrimination and have the difficult conversations? Empathy offers opportunity to understand each other deeply and enable difficult conversations to happen. How might the service offer remuneration and reward for the expertise and emotional toil involved to embed the key co-production principle of reciprocity? The lived experiences of children must not be exploited in the name of service development. In this work, we must do no harm. How are we asking children that may have been harmed by services and systems to play a role in the fixing of them, and who benefits? Services that are already working from a trauma responsive and relational approach will have the foundations in place for embedding meaningful involvement. They must engage with children and practitioners involved regularly, reflect on their practice, the ethics and safety of the work. Storytelling must be prepared for and facilitated ethically, safely and with clear boundaries. Personal stories or questions risk reducing children to being defined by what happened to them, rather than what they can contribute, and risks further trauma through the telling, both to themselves and to others. Thus, preparation, readiness, support and a trauma responsive approach is key throughout the co-production journey.

Part 2: Participation in Practice: Navigating the Challenges

A commitment to Child First is pivotal to sustain a meaningful focus on children's participatory rights, and more specifically, to legitimise and assert children's ability to express agency and enact choice throughout decision-making processes (Case et al., 2020). At this point, it is important to acknowledge that there can be a degree of disparity in the way youth justice services promote and deliver participation work. A commitment to participation work in practice can range from it being an additional duty for a YJS worker towards a commitment to employing a dedicated participation worker, or by resourcing an independent organisation partnership to manage and deliver participatory projects alongside the priority work of youth justice services. For example, the organisation 'Youth Ink' have a mission to ensure that co-production and lived experience is at the heart of working with children that come into the criminal justice system (Youth Ink, 2021) and model 'peer navigators' to work alongside children as a type of mentoring.

These differences account for a major challenge of the value placed upon participation by professionals and barriers of the wider organisational structures and culture, which requires some navigation to ensure that participatory processes are co-created in partnership and the role of the professional is transformed. Without dedicated time and resources for participatory approaches, professionals are constrained in their ability to be a facilitator of solutions with children. This section now describes the roles of professionals who contributed to this chapter and explains the importance of having a dedicated participation worker to facilitate children's voice and knowledge into decision-making processes, while the remainder of the chapter draws upon power inequalities, the dominance of risk and peer support as one remedy for strengthening Child First and co-production practices within YJS.

In Focus: Voices of Professionals

Sherry Davis, a youth engagement manager in a London-based youth justice service, runs a 'Voices in Partnership' group with children who have come into the service. Sherry explains this group and how she understands the specific challenges in YJS of time and resources.

Sherry—*the group that I run is called the VIP which means 'voices in partnership' and they [children] made that name up years ago. I think it's such an amazing name because it means that they are treated as special but also we're partnering together and their voices are being heard. I'm really, really passionate about making sure that young people are involved in service delivery, but in a way that is meaningful to them. And a way that really does benefit them down the line so marrying up the idea of 'okay let's contribute* *to the service but also let's make sure that they're either remunerated financially or they do it to develop a skill or gain a new opportunity as a result. Young people need to know that their views aren't just added to reports that disappear into the ether, but that suggestions are actioned wherever possible. We are beginning to move away from conversation-based engagement and taking a more creative approach to involving young people, using music, art and film. This approach has had a huge impact not just on the quality of feedback from young people who produce powerful and relevant work that is celebrated by professionals, but it has broadened horizons for the young people involved in the process, because they gain paid work experience that looks amazing on a CV.*

I don't think my role exists in every single YOS, but I know that every youth offending service has a mandate to engage with young people, so if you don't have a person that's dedicated to that role it just becomes harder to do [participation work] because my colleagues already in London are inundated with loads of work and admin, and so I think if the structure of youth offending services had to include a youth engagement worker, I think that would definitely increase the level and the quality of engagement with young people in the service, but also budgets as well. The budget to bring in service providers and pay young people for all of the work they do has been significantly reduced over the past 5 years. It means I have to approach potential providers and ask if they have a budget either to provide workshops, or if they want to consult with young people, to pay them living wage or vouchers. In some cases, they can, which is great.

Andi Brierly, a former youth justice practitioner, raised important concerns about how participation and relationship-building can be undervalued:

Andi—*Relationship building, it's just something that's not valued enough, and the other participation worker, he did it for a period of time and then decided he didn't want to do it anymore, because he realized that to climb the professional career ladder, he knew that in the youth justice system, seen as doing the participation work, I don't know how to put this, but you know it is seen as 'not real work'*

Child First Participation: Concerns and Remedies

To enable a culture of participation and co-production to flourish there must be equal weight given to the perspectives and insights of both children and professionals. Throughout decision-making processes, it is also vital that children are able to experience a sense of ownership of progressive and principled co-creative practices. The implications of the Child First agenda and how this creative discourse 'plays out' in a context of 'high risk' management processes is not only little understood but a growing cause for concern (see Creaney & Burns, in press; Day, 2022; Peer Power/Youth Justice Board, 2021). Subsequently, it is important to discuss and reflect on balancing a focus on navigating Child First as a guiding principle alongside a child-friendly 'risk-led' strategy to prevent offending. Some professionals feel that it is still necessary to include risk management as a tool for responding to children's complex and adverse lives.

In Focus: Voices of Professionals

Lesley Tregear is a former Head of Youth Justice and Chair of the Association of YOT Managers (AYM), for whom she now works. During a conversation with Lesley, she expressed her concerns of moving away from risk management.

Lesley—*'it is difficult to move away entirely from risk… Because at the end of the day some of the behaviours that children present with are risky. If you take a child centred approach and you look at protective behaviours and all the support mechanisms that will help to ameliorate some of those issues then that is fine, but you still have to balance the fact that trauma is something that happens, not necessarily, but quite often over a long term, and certainly takes a long time to overcome. If you don't manage the risk then I think we are in danger of going back to those early days of children's services and juvenile justice where unmanaged risk resulted in ongoing offending; you do need to balance the scales. We have to recognise that those risks are there and need to be managed. The way that you manage them I think is* the important thing. If you take a punishment approach, it is a very restrictive approach and won't provide the necessary support. So, it is more about building up the protective factors around the child, identifying what they need, what will work for them. We know that child development says that adolescents in particular don't understand risk and the consequences of it, so using only a restrictive regime really won't work, that's when you get rebellion and resistance, because it just doesn't work for them. By addressing their needs and building up the protective factors around them I think you can achieve managing risk but from a child centred perspective'.

Viewing children's behaviour as risky is understandable when this has been the dominant normative throughout practice over the last 20 years and fits into the narrative of understanding children's needs and protective factors, which provides a certain focus on children's welfare and trauma (Stephenson & Allen, 2018). However, maintaining the binary of risk and protective factors raises a concern that a public protection agenda can dominate discussions, especially amongst management or officialdom, and create a situation which may force aspects of the Child First agenda to be held in abeyance (Creaney & Case, 2021). This can then mean that professionals, as the dominant agents who wield significant amounts of power and influence, conserve power and reproduce their privilege status as 'expert' who understands children's needs more than the child, despite the child being an expert in their own life circumstances. More specifically, professionals may feel they can protect and uphold the legitimacy of risk-led practices by promoting and defending the public protection and managerialist agendas (Peer Power/Youth Justice Board, 2021). Yet, this may be at the expense of negating from children's voice and influence on service delivery. We use 'High risk' management processes to evidence this.

'High risk' management processes are primarily adult-led, concerned with harm reduction; either detecting and monitoring safeguarding concerns, or reacting to intelligence received, that children are judged to be displaying undesirable behaviours. Despite efforts to ensure the child is enabled and has a degree of control over proceedings, professionals may rebuke proposals of this sort, being of the view that there is a need to retain a focus on risk, which intentionally or otherwise serves to reinforce a distinction between the official categories of 'low', 'medium' and 'high' risk (Creaney & Case, 2021). A risk-averse environment can constrain and bear upon professionals, resulting in defensible decision-making to minimise risk of harmful behaviours occurring to or from the child (Wood & Kemshall, 2008), leading to children more likely to be in receipt of repressive interventions. While the voice of the child in risk management processes has not escaped conscious recognition, this challenge continues to merit particular attention.

Thus, there is a need for research into this vexing problem to uncover to what extent professionals feel it incumbent upon them to involve children as partners in this process. It is of note that a study by Peer Power/Youth Justice Board (2021), problematised the application of the 'high risk' term when capturing the thoughts and feelings of practitioners, concerning the nature and extent of participation and co-production in practice. The authors of the report recommended a re-think concerning language, in the light of changes to the participation strategy and guiding principles. Others have raised similar concerns about the Child First guiding principle being underdeveloped in practice (Case & Browning, 2021b). The commitment to Child First is tempered by a culture of risk management, deficit-based environments and due to decision-making being disproportionately shaped 'by approaches derived from earlier, risk based, and much more punitive, understandings of youth justice intervention' (see Bateman, 2021). This is disconcerting given that measures that are non-consultative and controlling can be damaging and aggravate matters and lead to resistance, increasing risk of reoffending, compromising public safety (Haines & Case, 2015).

It appears that risk-based practices have not been consigned to the past (albeit certainly weakened) in that 'public protection' continues to vex professionals on the ground.[2] What persists is a strategy of surveillance and control to prevent a perceived impending threat of a child's violence

---

[2] The inspection framework continues to privilege risk-led strategies and approaches (see HMIP, 2020). There is a sense that participation and co-production are viewed by the inspectorate as of lesser importance. A mindset persists that 'effective' offender focused strategies need to be conceptualised and implemented to reduce the 'threat' children pose to society and consequently to prevent various forms of harm being caused. Case and Browning (2021a) shined a light on how risk-based assessments and interventions are anathema to principled, progressive, children first practice in the YJS. That said, during fieldwork the inspectorate does conduct a deep dive of governance, leadership and multi-agency partnership arrangements, and following a

or self-harm. Indeed, this aspect of the risk model is not on the periphery or on the margins of consciousness. It retains a powerful role, shaping how practitioners think and act in the field. While some may criticise the risk-focused model for its pathologising and 'offender focus' and essentially limited scope for the exploration of children's strengths and positive attributes (see Case, 2018), it is difficult to move away entirely from risk. Moreover, a focus on risk at the practice level has at least been partially retained by multi-agency YJS.

Child First and desistance-focused practices appear to an extent to still be trapped within a risk-focused mindset (Bateman, 2020; Wigzell, 2021).

The 'high risk' management process is a case in point. Arguably, for 'high risk' panels to be inclusive and participative, there is a need to align the purpose and strategy of these processes with a Child First ethos. More specifically, this involves injecting a participatory rights-based discourse into decision-making and prioritising treating children as equal, reciprocal partners in a co-production process. Valuing children's input during 'high risk' meetings to deeply listen and understand what works for them and their circumstances can result in positive outcomes, including: meaningful participation, increases in self-esteem and confidence, and motivation to change (Creaney & Case, 2021). The benefits of trusting, constructive child-practitioner relationships can be supplemented by Child First peer mentoring. This progressive and principled practice involves those with lived experiences of system contact providing advice and support to their peers experiencing issues that they can relate to. Peer mentors can be an 'authentic' and 'credible' voice, an inspiration to others that change is possible and support their peers to influence the decision-making process. This type of approach places value on expertise borne of experience (Lister, 2000) by treating children not as passive objects who are 'done to' (e.g. through non-consultative arrangements) but as co-producers whose insights are of critical importance to how organisations operate and how professionals care for and respond to children.

---

series of conversations with a range of stakeholders aims to offer judgements on the quality of relationship-type practices.

Progressing Child First Peer Mentoring

Peer mentoring can be described as a participatory and strengths-based practice. It can be used to reconcile any lack of engagement or experiences of disempowerment. Children who have experienced challenges, overcome adversity and forged a positive path for themselves despite obstacles and unfortunate circumstances, can accrue experiential knowledge (Creaney, 2018; CYCJ, 2021; Deakin et al., 2020; Duke et al., 2022). Subsequently, children as peer mentors are 'experts by experience', capable of providing unique insights, sharing knowledge and experiences of using justice services. This can be defined as 'know how' of how to navigate life's challenges and system demands. Peer mentoring can also be a valuable tool of enhancing co-production with YJS, because it values children's resources and can bring them into more equal relationships both with YJS staff and other children.

Peer mentors can be vital influencers, able to relate to mentees in similar circumstances or situations and forge a meaningful connection with those experiencing a comparable phenomenon (Lopez-Humphreys & Teater, 2018: 193; see also Buck & Creaney, 2020). Thus, they can inspire their peers and assist them in the change process, demonstrating to them that it is possible to overcome problems and live a meaningful and productive life. They can be an empowering role model who influences attitudes and behaviours in a positive way. When speaking to both Mifta and Andi, they shared their lived experience within the criminal justice system, and through their stories, they were able to view the importance of 'having someone who has been in your shoes and understands what you are going through', who can facilitate healing, growth and identity transformation (Hazel et al., 2017).

For some children, becoming a peer mentor or peer navigator can be an opportunity to improve their communicative/inter-personal skills, provide future employment opportunities and build up their role and reputation within the community. It is essential that they are provided, though, with appropriate guidance and are able to access training and support. Alongside this, professionals should set up a thorough, screening and selection process and reflect carefully and critically on the process of mentor/mentee matching. Essentially, as Austria and Peterson (2017) note, mentors require effective relationship-based support and guidance. Alongside effective relationship-based support, it is equally necessary for professionals to see the value of peer mentors, incentivise appropriately for their time and commitment, while also bringing them into the service; developing their sense of belonging and contributing to the desistance process.

In Focus: Voices of Professionals

Mifta (Youth Ink) explains his view on the role of peer mentoring as an example of co-production and concerns about how to ensure children are valued for their role.

Mifta—... *it's not just about designing a program with a young person and delivering it to other young people...if you imagine for a moment, you have an ex service user and a YJS officer standing together coming to see a young person. And one goes and I am the YJS officer this is what we're going to be doing and I'm going to talk you through this, but I want to introduce you to another person, he's an ex service user who came through the program. He's going to talk to you about what he's doing now and how we're going to be working together as a YJS and ex-service user. If you can just imagine for a minute what that would be like for that young person sitting on the opposite side, just to hear that right at the beginning. And that's what co creation and co-production is...*

I think service users (young people) are used to not being valued by the criminal justice system. Why would you not train up young people, up-skill young people. If the young person is 16 plus why would you not train them as a volunteer and value them for what they bring to you? Young people are struggling to get jobs, to feel part of their community. At Youth Ink we value young people who come to us. We are prepared to train young people, to upskill them. When the young person is ready we will step in to support the young person either by offering them some sessional work to support them, or to support them in other areas. It is not about the job for the young person it is about the support, the pro-social skills they will learn they can develop their CV, giving young people a better chance of getting a job or getting back into education or training.

However, alongside a concern that professionals may not value the contribution of peer mentors, there are still several points regarding the effectiveness of implementing the model of peer mentoring into practice. First, professionals may be selective in terms of who they recruit to positions of authority. This practice may result in vulnerable and disadvantaged children being excluded from adopting key decision-making positions. Thus, a 'diversity of voices' may not be captured and a challenge remains to some professionals around how to engage children to become peer mentors. Except, this challenge would be alleviated immensely with Child First principles and relationship-based approaches where children trust that professionals value their knowledge and expertise. Second, there may be concern that mentors romanticise about their involvement in 'crime' and thus may be considered unsuitable to guide their peers on a positive trajectory.[3] Although this second point is reconciled by organisations who use this co-production model, as they invite new peer mentors to become experts through training programmes which discuss how to talk to other children about their lived experience and encouraging other children to not engage in criminality, while also ensuring there is a sufficient knowledge base around children's participation rights.

Overall, a key feature of peer mentoring practices is seeing children not as 'part of the problem' or who have 'cognitive deficits' that need treating (Graham & McNeill, 2018: 441) but crucially as 'part of the solution' (LeBel et al, 2015: 118) with copious amounts of potential. Thus, the focus of peer mentoring is the aiding of recovery through forging empathic inter-personal relationships. Crucially, children are not viewed as 'sources of fear', 'posers of risk to others' or a threat to society or objects of concern (Drakeford & Gregory, 2010; Haines & Case, 2015; Whyte, 2009). The ethos is one of aspiration, emotion-based hope and

---

[3] In the desistance literature, there is emphasis on helping perpetrators of crime to 'knife off' from one's past, disconnecting from association with so-called pro-criminal or delinquent peers (Robinson, 2016). This is deemed to be influential in stopping them being the perpetrator of further harms inflicted on victims/society (Göbbels et al., 2015: 67). Stopping offending (desisting) is a negotiated process, not a 'one off event'. Desistance is concerned with how professionals assist children to move away from crime and live a fulfilling life. Attention is not so much directed at achieving short-term change but rather long-term transformation and promotion of positive outcomes in the form of individual and structural change.

inner peace (Lopez-Humphreys & Teater, 2018). Peer mentors aim to enhance the child's ability to reflect on their emotional state, with a view to them feeling empowered and resilient in the face of adversity, able to take control of decisions that affect them and their life. Peer mentors can also support in ensuring that children's participation rights are adhered to and that children are influencing services in a meaningful way.

Conclusion

This chapter has presented a critical perspective on forms of participation, co-production and Child First practices in youth justice. It has offered insight into the challenges involving children in the design and delivery of services by reflecting on key barriers and facilitators, which can enhance or hinder children's involvement in decision-making. Furthermore, it was discussed how a break from 'risk' and deficit-based practice is being realised through a new ethos of enhanced participatory practice undergird by co-production and a strengths-based pedagogy. The chapter has explored how children can be enabled to exert a degree of influence, empowered to co-create practice, critique the status quo and disrupt systems with a view to ignite individual and structural change. While it can be challenging for children to accrue a degree of power not least given that attendance at appointments is often mandatory and there is an unequal power relationship, if they are enabled to participate without feeling judgement or experiencing symbolic violence, this can be a crucial formative step in the quest to help them thrive and overcome forms of adversity. Structural inequalities limit potential. Thus, is incumbent upon professionals to acknowledge and respond to forms of injustice.

Conversations have been integrated within the chapter to illustrate the enablers, barriers, challenges and opportunities for Child First participation and co-production in Youth Justice. This is important for two substantial reasons. On the one hand, it helps to bring to life the types of practices being formulated and implemented in the real world. Secondly, it reaffirms or strengthens the argument that policies are created and practice strategies negotiated between those working in the field at the local level—by stakeholders who seek to preserve their interests and participate in a struggle to disrupt systems or conserve power (Goldson & Briggs, 2021).

It is a recent development that the YJB has directed YJS to halt what has been a dominant focus on risk. The non-departmental public body have drawn attention to children's participation and cemented the belief that it is paramount those under supervision are involved in the design, delivery, and evaluation of services. This has led to the 'adult knows best' mentality being replaced by a new Child First standpoint that consistently puts children's priorities and concerns front and centre and is ultimately receptive to children being in positions of power and influence.

We have argued in this chapter that Child First is a concept which has potential to alter field conditions and transform practice and supervision *from* adult-led and non-participatory *to* co-creative and non-hierarchical. Child First is anti-risk, anti-stigma and pro-participation, which engenders child-friendly and child appropriate responses to offending by children. Front-line professionals and managers must be committed to relationship-based practice which invokes trust, reciprocity and empathy, while being viscerally opposed to 'box ticking' which is detrimental to a participation culture, outright tokenistic and can be harmful to children's lives. Professionals must also consciously avoid using techniques that inadvertently or otherwise devalue children's agency in the decision-making process. We have noted here that high risk management meetings exemplify how risk can still immerse into the way professionals respond to children which can detract from their voice being heard and decision-making being shared equally in partnerships. How to navigate risk management strategies with participation and co-production principles will be a continued challenge in practice, with more to be learnt about whether these can co-exist within youth justice services.

It is important that organisational strategies and interventions are principally focused on encouraging children's meaningful participation throughout assessment processes, intervention planning and supervision and professionals transform their role into co-constructors of knowledge with children, which has the potential for the co-creation of institutional and cultural change in youth justice services. In addition to these important considerations and other discussions on elements of effective participatory practice, practitioners must not lose site of the potential force of cultural and structural constraints impacting children's ability to participate. Thus, the youth justice workforce should give equal consideration to both internal and external forces, aspects that can either facilitate or impede children's ability to input into processes, provide insight and negotiate the way they receive services.

Finally, we provided an overview of experiential forms of Child First peer support and discussed opportunities for justice-involved children to share experiences and reflect on their feelings and emotions. It is crucial that peer mentoring is aligned with Child First precepts and associated positive Youth Justice mechanisms. In particular, that experiential forms of peer support are a meaningful collaboration between those involved, and a type of practice that is observable and measurable against the Child First tenets. More specifically, this must involve a strategic and practice focus on the creation of legitimate and fruitful opportunities for children to actively participate and engage as partners in the process. This type of approach places value on expertise by experience while treating children not as passive objects who are 'done to' (e.g. through non-consultative arrangements) but as co-producers whose insights are of critical importance to how the organisation operates and how professionals care for and respond to them. Here, children are at the heart of the approach and awarded a degree of power. They are viewed as 'knowers' who are able to express choice, not least regarding how services or interventions are designed, delivered and evaluated. Children are encouraged to enter into a reciprocal partnership, with a practitioner who is committed to the principle of equality of opportunity and a positive youth justice, is sincere and emotionally available, approachable and prepared to provide consistent support to repair any fractured relationships.

Acknowledgements Thank you to Mifta Choudhury, Sherry Davis, Lesley Tregear, Andi Brierley and Anne-Marie Douglas for their valuable insight into the lived realities of working with children across services and their vision of participation and co-production in the Youth Justice System.

References

Armitage, V., Kelly, L., & Phoenix, J. (2016). Janus-faced youth justice work and the transformation of accountability the Howard. *Journal of Crime and Justice, 55*(4), 478–495.

Austria, R., & Peterson, J. (2017). *Credible messenger mentoring for justice-involved youth*. www.thepinkertonfoundation.org/wp-content/uploads/2017/02/Pinkerton-Papers-credible-messenger-monitoring.pdf. Accessed 24 November 2017.

Bateman, T. (2020). *The state of youth justice 2020*. Report, National Association for Youth Justice.

Bateman, T. (2021). *Bridging the care-crime gap: Reforming the youth court?* Report, National Association for Youth Justice.

Bourdieu, P., & Wacquant, L. (1992). *An invitation to reflexive sociology*. Polity Press.

Brady, L. (2020). *Embedding young people's participation in healthcare*. Policy Press.

Brierley, A. (2021). *Connecting with young people in trouble: Risk, relationships and lived experience*. Waterside Press.

Brown, A. (2020). *A rights-based analysis of youth justice in the United Kingdom*. Unicef.

Buck, G., & Creaney, S. (2020). Mental health, young people and punishments. In P. Taylor, S. Morley, & J. Powell (Eds.), *Mental health and punishments: Critical perspectives in theory and practice*. Routledge.

Burns, S. (2019). Young people as co-producers in policing across England. An evaluation of the 'youth commission' on police and crime. *Children & Society, 33*(4), 347–362. https://doi.org/10.1111/chso.12312

Case, S. (2018). *Youth justice: A critical introduction*. Routledge.

Case, S., & Browning, A. (2021a). *Child first justice: The research evidence-base* [Full report]. Loughborough University.

Case, S., & Browning, A. (2021b). *The child first strategy implementation project: Realising the guiding principle for youth justice* [Full report]. Loughborough University.

Case, S., & Haines, K. (2009). *Understanding youth offending: Risk factor research, policy and practice*. Willan Publishing.

Case, S., Creaney, S., Coleman, N., Haines, K., Little, R., & Worrall, V. (2020). Trusting children to enhance youth justice policy: The importance and value of children's voices. *Youth Voice Journal*, ISBN: 978-1-911634-23-2.

Checkoway, B. (2011). What is youth participation? *Children and Youth Services Review, 33*(2), 340–345.

Clinks. (2016). *Clinks' submission to the review of the youth justice system.* www.clinks.org/sites/default/files/2018-10/clinks_taylorreview_final.pdf. Accessed 16 July 2017.

Creaney, S. (2018). Children's voices—Are we listening? Progressing peer mentoring in the youth justice system. *Child Care in Practice, 26*(1), 22–37. https://doi.org/10.1080/13575279.2018.1521381

Creaney, S. (2020). "Game playing" and "docility": Youth justice in question. *Safer Communities, 19*(3), 103–118. https://doi.org/10.1108/SC-01-2020-0002

Creaney, S., & Case, S. (2021). Promoting social inclusion: Participatory rights alternatives to risk discourses in youth justice. In P. Liamputtong (Ed.), *Handbook of social inclusion research and practices in health and social sciences*. Springer.

Creaney, S., & Smith, R. (2020). Social work and youth justice. In J. Parker (Ed.), *Introducing social work*. Sage.

CYCJ. (2021). *A guide to youth justice in Scotland: Policy, practice and legislation.* https://www.cycj.org.uk/wp-content/uploads/2021/06/Section-15.pdf

Day, A.-M. (2022). It's a hard balance to find: The perspectives of youth justice practitioners in England on the place of 'risk' in an emerging 'child-first' world. *Youth Justice*.

Deakin, J., Fox, C., & Matos, R. (2020). Labelled as 'risky' in an era of control: How young people experience and respond to the stigma of criminalized identities. *European Journal of Criminology*. https://doi.org/10.1177/1477370820916728

Drakeford, M., & Gregory, L. (2010). Transforming time: A new tool for youth justice youth justice. *Youth Justice, 10*(2), 143–156.

Duke, K., Gleeson, H., Dabrowska, K., Dich Herold, M., Rolando, S., & Thom, B. (2022). Building cultures of participation: Involving young people in contact with the criminal justice system in the development of drug interventions in the United Kingdom, Denmark, Italy and Poland. *Youth Justice*. https://doi.org/10.1177/14732254221075206

Eadie, T., & Canton, R. (2002). Practicing in a context of ambivalence: The challenge for youth justice workers. *Youth Justice, 2*(14), 14–26.

Göbbels, S., Thakker, J., & Ward, T. (2015). Desistance in offenders with mental illness. In J. Winston (Ed.), *Mental health, crime and criminal justice: Responses and reforms*. Palgrave Macmillan.

Goldson, B. (Ed.). (2000). *The new youth justice*. Russell House Publishing.

Goldson, B., & Briggs, D. (2021). *Making youth justice: Local penal cultures and differential outcomes—Lessons and prospects for policy and practice*. Howard League for Penal Reform.

Graham, H., & McNeill, F. (2018). Desistance: Envisioning futures. In P. Carlen & L. A. França (Eds.), *Alternative criminologies*. Routledge.

Hazel, N., Goodfellow, P., Liddle, M., Bateman, T., & Pitts, J. (2017). *Now all I care about is my future—Supporting the shift: framework for the effective resettlement of young people leaving custody*. Report, Beyond Youth Custody.

Haines, K., & Drakeford, M. (1998). *Young people and Youth Justice*. Macmillan.

Haines, K. R., & Case, S. P. (2015). *Positive youth justice: Children first, offenders second*. Policy Press.

HM Inspectorate of Probation. (2020). *A thematic review of the work of youth offending services during the COVID-19 pandemic*. https://www.justicein spectorates.gov.uk/hmiprobation/wp-content/uploads/sites/5/2020/11/201 110-A-thematic-review-of-the-work-of-youth-offending-services-during-the-COVID-19-pandemic.pdf. 7 December 2020.

LeBel, T. P., Richie, M., & Maruna, S. (2015). Helping others as a response to reconcile a criminal past: The role of the wounded healer in prisoner reentry programs. *Criminal Justice and Behavior, 42*(1), 108–120.

Lister, R. (2000). *Participation should be a reality, not just a buzz word*. https://www.theguardian.com/society/2000/dec/07/comment

Lopez-Humphreys, M., & Teater, B. (2018). Peer mentoring justice-involved youth: A training model to promote secondary desistance and restorative justice among mentors. *The International Journal of Restorative Justice*. https://doi.org/10.5553/IJRJ/258908912018001002002

National Association for Youth Justice. (2019). *Manifesto 2019/2020* [online]. https://thenayj.org.uk/manifesto-2019-final.pdf

New Economics Foundation. (2009). *A guide to co-producing children's services*. New Economics Foundation.

Peer Power/Youth Justice Board. (2021). *Co-creation and participation in practice project*. Peer Power/YJB.

Percy-Smith, B. (2012). Participation as mediation and social learning. In C. Baraldi & V. Iervese (Eds.), *Participation, facilitation, and mediation children and young people in their social contexts* (pp. 12–29). Routledge.

Phoenix, J., & Kelly, L. (2013). 'You have to do it for yourself': Responsibilization in youth justice and young people's situated knowledge of youth justice practice. *British Journal of Criminology, 53*(3), 419–437.

Robinson, A. (2016). Growing out of crime? Problems, pitfalls and possibilities. In A. Robinson & P. Hamilton (Eds.), *Moving on from crime and substance use: Transforming identities*. Policy Press.

Slay, J., & Penny, J. (2014). *Commissioning for outcomes and co-production: A practical guide for local authorities*. London.

Smith, R. (2003). *Youth justice: Ideas, policy, practice*. Willan Publishing.

Smithson, H., Gray, P., & Jones, A. (2020). 'They really should start listening to you': The benefits and challenges of co-producing a participatory framework of youth justice practice. *Youth Justice*. https://doi.org/10.1177/1473225420941598

Smithson, H., & Jones, A. (2021). Co-creating youth justice practice with young people: Tackling power dynamics and enabling transformative action. *Children & Society*, 1–15.

Social Care Institute for Excellence. (2015). *Co-production in social care: What it is and How to do it*. https://www.scie.org.uk/publications/guides/guide51/at-a-glance/

Stephenson, M. (2018). 'Evidence-based Practice and Effective Practice'. In M. Stephenson, & R. Allen (Eds.), *Effective Practice in Youth Justice*. 3rd edn. Unitas.

Stephenson, M., & Allen, R. (Eds.). (2018). *Youth justice: Challenges to practice*. UNITAS.

Taylor, C. (2016). *Review of the youth justice system in England and Wales*. MoJ.

Thomas, N. (2007). Towards a theory of children's participation. *International Journal of Children's Rights, 15*(2), 199–218.

Tisdall, E. K. M. (2013). The transformation of participation? Exploring the potential of 'transformative participation' for theory and practice around children and young people's participation. *Global Studies of Childhood, 3*(2), 183–193.

Tisdall, E. K. M. (2017). Conceptualising children and young people's participation: Examining vulnerability, social accountability and co-production. *The International Journal of Human Rights, 21*(1), 59–75.

Wigzell, A. (2021). *NAYJ briefing: Explaining desistance: Looking forward, not backwards*. National Association of Youth Justice.

Whyte, B. (2009). *Youth justice in practice: Making a difference*. Policy Press.

Wood, J., & Kemshall, H. (2008). Risk management, accountability and partnerships in criminal justice. In B. Stout, J. Yates, & B. Williams (Eds.), *Applied criminology*. Sage.
Wright, S., Hazel, N., & Bateman, T. (2014). *Engaging young people in resettlement: A practitioner's guide*. Other, Beyond Youth Custody/Nacro.
Youth Ink. (2021). *Youth Ink: At the heart of the community* [online]. https://www.youth-ink.org.uk/. Accessed 1 August 2021.
Youth Justice Board. (2014). *AssetPlus*. YJB.
Youth Justice Board. (2016). *Participation strategy: Giving young people a voice in youth justice*. Youth Justice Board.
Youth Justice Board. (2019). *Youth justice board for England and Wales: Business plan 2019–2020*. Youth Justice Board.
Youth Justice Board. (2020). *How to join a youth justice stakeholder group*. [online]. https://www.gov.uk/government/publications/how-to-join-a-youth-justice-forum/how-to-join-a-youth-justice-stakeholder-group . Accessed 12 December 2021.
Youth Justice Board (YJB). (2021). *Strategic plan 2021–24*. Report, YJB.

13

Postscript—Progress and Challenges for Progressing Progressive Child First Youth Justice

Neal Hazel and Stephen Case

The Progress of Child First

Child First is now the guiding principle for all policy and practice across the Youth Justice System of England and Wales (YJB, 2021a). At the time of writing (2022), it is also being formalised as the key reform principle for youth justice in Northern Ireland and is increasingly influential as a shaper of policy and practice in a host of Western justice systems (e.g. Scotland, Ireland, Australia, New Zealand, Canada, certain states of the USA). This edited text has brought together a collection of eminent

---

N. Hazel (✉)
School of Health & Society, University of Salford, Salford, UK
e-mail: n.hazel@salford.ac.uk

S. Case
Criminology, Sociology and Social Policy,
Loughborough University, Loughborough, UK
e-mail: s.case@lboro.ac.uk

© The Author(s), under exclusive license to Springer Nature
Switzerland AG 2023
S. Case and N. Hazel (eds.), *Child First*,
https://doi.org/10.1007/978-3-031-19272-2_13

authors from across academic, research, policy, strategy and practice to provide insights on Child First as an evidence-based innovative approach to modern youth justice. Each author has been at the forefront of the evolution of Child First, and each offers their own perspective of the development, current position and challenges to this approach.

As has already been noted by authors in this book, it seems inappropriate to write a conclusion for reform in youth justice that is still on a journey of development through academia, policy and practice. However, it does seem appropriate to collate and reflect in a postscript on progress and some of the key challenges for Child First moving forward that have been highlighted in the preceding chapters.

Reforming policy and practice is a slow process, and various chapters in this book have described the development of Child First as a not being a straightforward or immediate process (e.g. Chapters 4 and 6). At the time of writing, it has been a generation since Haines and Drakeford (1998) first proposed a 'children first, offenders second' (CFOS) approach that can be seen as the genesis of Child First. Indeed, some authors in this book were still children themselves at that time. While the concepts within CFOS were incorporated relatively quickly into Welsh policy discourse (e.g. in Welsh Assembly Government, 2004), and developed into practice at a local level in Wales (Haines & Case, 2015), they have been slower to be embedded in national Welsh policy and practice (Chapter 4) and even slower to gain political traction in England and the UK government context (Chapter 6). As different authors here argue, this was because until 2018 (Chapter 7), although much of the groundwork had been set (Chapters 6 and 11), the academic concepts and evidence involved had not been translated clearly into the policy context, and also lacked a clear 'theory of change' for how working in a CFOS way would lead to 'preventing offending' (the statutory aim of the Youth Justice System; Crime and Disorder Act 1998).

In short, the essence of CFOS was that responses to children who offend should be constructed with the recipient's status as 'child' at the forefront (see Chapter 3 for a more detailed explanation). The concepts in the literature associated with CFOS represented a critical challenge to the dominant 'risk paradigm' in research and youth justice discourse that treated children primarily as offenders or potential offenders. The risk paradigm responsibilised and adulterised children as 'risky' individuals in a way that failed to take account of the developmental status of children and the responsibilities of adults for their behaviour. Consequently, when the Youth Justice System developed the primary aim of 'preventing offending', it was assumed by policymakers that this could be done directly by making them accountable and managing them as offenders, rather than through achieving their positive outcomes as children. CFOS reversed this assumption—if adults enable positive child outcomes (i.e. helped to thrive in a childcare sense) and behaviour, then the prevention of offending would be a by-product. CFOS literature critiqued the dominant paradigm and proposed approaches to achieve positive outcomes for children including those in trouble.

The mid-2010s saw a slow increase in references in English and UK central policy to the need to treat those under the age of 18 as 'children first', or espousing other concepts engaged by researchers advocating CFOS. Case (Chapter 3) notes that the 2015 National Police Chiefs' Council's Child Centred Policing national strategy stated that all children's encounters with the police should see them treated as children first, and that 2017 Sentencing Council guidelines stated that sentencing should be focused on the child rather than the offence. Most significantly for the development of Child First as the guiding principle for youth justice in England and Wales, the Youth Justice Review commissioned by the Ministry of Justice recommended a 'new system in which young people are treated as children first and offenders second' (Taylor, 2016: 48).

In the two decades since Haines and Drakeford suggested CFOS, the evidence base around what was important and effective in youth justice had grown to broadly reflect the key concepts they had heralded (see Case & Browning, 2021a). Consequently, in 2018, the YJB was able to use CFOS concepts as they had been developed (Byrne & Case, 2016) to structure a guiding principle for youth justice that was based on contemporary research evidence and understanding (see, Chapter 7). Indeed, the principle was called CFOS, since shortened to Child First. The four tenets of the Child First principle are listed in full and explored elsewhere in this book (including Chapter 1 and Chapter 7), but are currently being summarised by the YJB in the following ABCD mnemonic:

Tenet 1—**A**s children.
Tenet 2—**B**uilding pro-social identity for positive outcomes.
Tenet 3—**C**ollaborating with children.
Tenet 4—**D**iverting from stigma.

In terms of the development of a progressive Youth Justice System, the formal adoption of Child first by the YJB is described by Bateman (Chapter 2) as a 'seismic shift that deserves to be applauded'. The progress achieved from the point of formalising Child First as the guiding principle has been noted across several chapters in this book. Particularly, notable indicators of the progress made include:

- Child First underpins the National Standards for youth justice (MOJ/YJB, 2019) for custody and community youth justice, and ongoing revisions of the Case Management Guidance (YJB, 2022a) for local Youth Offending Teams (YOT) staff responsible for supervising children.
- Child First is now built into training for all new youth justice professionals with a new module in the Effective Practice Certificate.
- Local authorities' statutorily required annual youth justice plans must now self-assess against the four tenets of Child First and demonstrate how the 'ethos' is woven throughout service delivery (YJB, 2022b).
- The Youth Custody Service has Child First underpinning its new policies (e.g. early and late release) and has adopted the development of children's pro-social identity as its theory of change (tenet 2).
- In Wales, Child First is additionally the first principle in the Youth Justice Blueprint for Wales (Welsh Government & Ministry of Justice, 2019).

Of course, it should be recognised that while Child First has and continues to be on a developmental journey, we are also all adapting to evolving insights and progressive discourse involved with a nascent approach. Perhaps such a paradigm shift is like learning any new language, when we all at first try to translate these new insights into our existing frameworks of reference, before eventually becoming more comfortable and fluent thinking in a new discourse. Of academics,

Haines and Case have admitted that they used the concept of risk factors, now recognised as deficit-focused, for their evaluations of 'prevention' interventions in the early days of CFOS (Chapter 4). Similarly, the first author to this chapter has published on what prevents offending after children are released from prison in a decontextualised way (cf. Hazel et al., 2002), before recognising the need for an explanatory theory of change (Hazel & Bateman, 2020). At the policy level, it is noted that the YJB, where the Child First principle was formulated, still occasionally slipped into 'language previously used' (Chapter 7).

In the end, Child First is intended to produce a 'common language' with which all constituents in and around the Youth Justice System can make decisions in an evidence-informed way that will lead to positive outcomes and behaviour for children, and so prevent offending. Indeed, a literal shift in discourse prompted by the Child First is a basic but useful measure of progress in culture change at the levels of policy and practice. While Bateman is correct in noting (in Chapter 2) that the Ministerial Foreword to the National Standards for youth justice (MoJ/YJB, 2019) still refers to 'offenders' once at the beginning, it then goes on to refer to 'child' or 'children' nine times. Not perfect, but progress from the norm of 'young offenders' in previous ministerial discourse (e.g. MoJ, 2016). Moreover, in the most recent ministerial speech to date on youth justice (Atkins, 2022) Child First is much more cemented in the political discourse. When discussing under 18s, the minister referred to 'children' and 'childhood' eleven times, 'boys' and 'girls' three times, 'young people' twice and 'offenders' not at all.

Challenges to Embedding Child First in Policy and Practice

For all its progress to date, authors in this book have warned of a number of challenges to be faced and navigated if Child First is to be embedded sustainably in policy and practice to ensure that the Youth Justice System is informed by contemporary understanding. These challenges are not just for practitioners to face alone.

For Academics

For academics, not only is there a need to continue to build an evidence base of outcomes from applying Child First concepts with different children in different ways, but we also need to recognise that there are still debates about concepts within Child First that need to be played out—that is, of course, how any field of knowledge progresses. At the time of writing, for instance, there is a debate about how much Child First youth justice can be aligned with the concept of 'desistance theory' which first emerged from the adult literature (Chapter 10; Wigzell et al. (Eds.), forthcoming). Similarly, within this volume, Kilkelly makes some challenges and suggestions for children's rights to be more embedded in the principle (Chapter 5). It is noted (Chapter 4) that as policy and practice further operationalise Child First, there are and will be differences between conceptions (e.g. over the extent that any incarceration of children is acceptable) that will need to be navigated by academics and other stakeholders. Additionally, as the evidence base and contemporary understanding in youth justice research grow, the academic community will need to continue to be fully engaged with how new insights should be interpreted for policy and practice and incorporated into the Child First principle. The YJB's newly established Academic Liaison Network of more than sixty leading international youth justice-related academics is already proving a valuable resource to this end in the academic-policy nexus.

For Policymakers

At the policy level, while there is a growing acceptance of both Child First as an approach and the overall messages contained in the four tenets, there have still been concerns and challenges raised that have related specifically to how these might impact on others' imperatives and agendas (e.g. victims). For academics, this brings the challenge that these diverse agendas do not fit neatly with existing analytical models built on the traditional welfare vs justice dichotomy that framed much of the academic discourse about seeing children as children or offenders

(Chapters 2 and 7). At the policy and practice levels, as Child First is increasingly embedded and draws in wider stakeholders there is a continued need to navigate these diverse concerns that are not focused directly on children's positive outcomes (Chapter 4).

Bateman notes (Chapter 2) that research and statistics showed how the existing system punished disadvantage, with the large majority of children subjected to the most punitive disposals having backgrounds characterised by poverty (Jacobson et al., 2010) and being from minority ethnic backgrounds (Youth Custody Service, 2021). This is, at least in part, because the system sees children as offenders or potential offenders, where vulnerability and structural barriers are assessed as risk factors for crime that responsibilise children and trigger more intense criminal justice interventions. In a world more enlightened by the Black Lives Matter movement, there is an even clearer need across jurisdictions for a Child First approach that sees vulnerability, including disadvantage through diversity, as a barrier to positive child outcomes and the responsibility of adults to remove.

A significant barrier at both policy and practice levels is that there continues to be discourses of 'good practice' provided centrally that are based on a view of excellence that is deficit-focused directly on offending, and based on a particular methodology—the quasi-experimental Random Control Trial (or systematic reviews favouring that methodology). For example, the Home Office funded Youth Endowment Fund's (YEF) critical appraisal tool for assessing the quality of impact evaluations of interventions for reducing 'youth violence' is based on adherence to this model (White et al., 2021). Case (Chapter 3) details the dangers of this methodology, including how it downplays the broader range of criminogenic factors, including structural and interactional influences. Relatedly, it tends to focus on whether the practice in question makes a difference on average to offending outcomes, and fails to investigate what it is about the intervention that makes the difference (the theory of change). One key failing of this decontextualisation is that the methodology downplays or ignores understanding of how outcomes differ with diversity, which is unacceptable in a society that recognises its importance, including how Black Lives Matter. We would contend that a Child First evidence base would need to measure evidence not based on purity with a quasi-experimental positivist method, but on (a) whether it makes a difference to positive child outcomes and (b) whether it can usefully explain why and how it makes a difference, and to which children, including the recognition of contextual influences. However, even with this substantial barrier, there is hope of recognition and movement with the influence of Child First. Referring back to the example above, the YEF has been engaged with the YJB and others to try to ensure that publications adhere to the contemporary understandings in Child First, and now has academics writing in this book on its advisory panels. A recent systematic review funded and co-written by the YEF noted the limitations and negative implication of the risk-factor paradigm, while acknowledging that the importance of understandings brought together in Child First 'cannot be overstated' (Ullman et al., 2022: 6). Furthermore, a recent YEF and Department for Education 'systems [as opposed to programmes] evidence and gap map' takes a broader approach to evaluating evidence, thus allowing a wider range than the risk paradigm, and notes that the most prolific contributor to its evidence base is this this book's co-editor, Case (Jain et al., 2022). Admittedly, the systems' gap map is not Child First in the way that it treats children as potential offenders 'at risk of or involved in violence', but there is clear progress from engaging with the Child First initiative.

Related to a shift in methodology, Child First's move from a deficit-based model to one that is focused on positive child outcomes requires an accompanying change in performance indicators by which the system can measure success (Case & Browning, 2021b). At the moment, the key performance indicator for child outcome is reducing the offending rate (YJB, 2022b), which is deficit-focused and measures a long-term symptomatic aim rather than positive objectives that staff can achieve more directly. No indicator corresponds to the positive child outcomes and development of pro-social identity that will eventually lead to reduced offending. It would be, of course, naïve to expect a system with the overall aim of 'preventing offending' and the responsibility of the Ministry of Justice not to measure offending rate. We do not suggest that this is not measured; Child First tenet 2 notes that following its theory of change leads to desistance (and so, safer communities and fewer victims). However, there is a need to develop appropriate measures and indicators that will capture positive child outcomes, including the development of their pro-social identity, that youth justice professionals can support directly. We know that this is acknowledged but not yet solved by the YJB because in the specifications for the statutorily required Youth Justice Plans from each local authority, the YJB asks them to add to the standard performance indicators, 'locally agreed performance indicators that evidence positive outcomes for children' (YJB, 2022b). However, it is for policymakers (with help from academics) to establish and adopt indicators appropriate to our contemporary understanding of what it is important to improve, as defined in Child First.

We have already noted the importance of discourse and lexicon in reformation of policy and practice and associated culture change in the youth justice sector. Haines and Thomas (Chapter 4) remind us that a maturing Child First system will need to review terms in youth justice that stem from the risk-paradigm but are not widely problematised, possibly because they largely refer to practices that are in themselves appropriate to Child First. Their chapter provides us with a list of terms including 'prevention', 'diversion' and 'alternatives' to prosecution and to custody, which are all justice-related terms that see negative outcomes as the norm. There is similarly regular confusion in our discussions with policymakers and practitioners over 'protective factors' which are positive in themselves, but in discourse are protecting against a deficit, still seeing children as potential offenders. Again, it's part of the learning curve that we are all on towards a Child First common language.

At the Practice Level

In relation to engaging practitioners as stakeholders, the point is well made (Chapter 4) that some practitioners will have been trying to work in a Child First way, even within an offender-first system, and may be alienated by the YJB and other advocates coming to the party late. The YJB and other policy-level advocates need to be clear that the intention is for the Child First principle and associated national standards and case management guidance to enable practitioners to do what they may well know through their experience is important for effectiveness and to remove elements that undermine that work by increasing criminogenic stigma.

For new youth justice staff, although it was noted above that the Effective Practice Certificate for all new youth justice staff now contains a Child First module, more work needs to be done to ensure that wider training and workforce development is compatible with Child First. At the time of writing, the Youth Justice Skills Matrix (YJB, 2021b), which is designed to be used for job descriptions, appraisals, training needs analysis and restructures is largely in contradiction with the guiding principle for youth justice and the National Standards for youth justice (MoJ/YJB, 2019) in its deficit focus. The associated National Occupational Standards (e.g. SFJ ED5) similarly focus on risk factors for offending rather than positive child outcomes and behaviour. While this issue will shortly be reviewed (now that it has been recognised), it does suggest that there is still some way to ensure that national guidance for workforce development is in line with Child First, let alone it being embedded at the practice level (Chapter 11). Meanwhile, there is no widespread mandatory training for police in working with children, nor specific mandatory training or experiences needed for Crown Court judges to sit in cases involving children (Chapter 8), let alone training on Child First.

Influenced by CFOS concerns around the risk paradigm, the YJB updated the youth justice case assessment tool, Asset, to AssetPlus in 2014, which incorporated more content on strengths as 'protective factors' against offending. However, as 'protective' implies, the tool was and is still fundamentally deficit-focused, assessing children as potential offenders to be managed rather than developing positive outcomes and behaviours as children. It was not the 'game changer' away from a bulky risk-paradigm tool that the YJB was hoping for (Chapter 6). Authors in this book repeatedly stress the importance of revision of the assessment tool for a Child First approach to be embedded in practice fully and meaningfully (Chapters 6, 9, and 11). At the very least, in the short term, there is a need to revise current AssetPlus content within Child First discourse and focus, reframing assessment in relation to positive outcomes (with 'risk factors' as barriers to those). However, Byrne calls for a single recording and assessment system integrated with children's services (Chapter 9).

Concerns are repeatedly raised by authors in this book for how Child First is to become embedded into practice in bodies not under the auspices the YJB through grant funding, such as the courts or youth custody (Chapters 5, 6, and 11). The implication is that compliance with the principle for the Youth Justice System may not be system-wide where the principle's primary sponsor to date does not have monetary or other levers. The point is rightly made that not having all state bodies in the field of youth justice expressly adopt Child First could result in policy confusion and mixed messages. The example is given repeatedly of how YOT professionals interpret messages contradicting or limiting Child First from HM Inspectorate of Probation criteria (Chapters 6, 10, and 11). Of course, the YJB does have a statutory duty to inform the sector more widely than YOTs, but inevitably, embedding Child First into policy and practice more widely relies on a process of engaging stakeholders, disseminating the principle within the discourse of contemporary evidence and understanding, and the navigating of stakeholder concerns that was started in the framing of the four tenets (Chapter 7). There are clear examples of this having already happened successfully to some extent, in the Youth Custody Service's adoption of Child First for guiding its policy on early release (HMPPS, 2022), and in the HM Inspectorate of Probation/YJB (2022) joint statement on 'risk of harm'. In 2021–2022, the YJB held a series of events with stakeholders to develop maps in England and Wales of support across the current Youth Justice System (and beyond) to help understand where improvements can be made and Child First better embedded in order to inform subsequent business (YJB, 2022b). It is almost certain that this engagement will need go beyond the criminal justice system, to ensure that wider systems (including children's services, youth services and third sector) can support the emphasis on developing a pro-social identity that requires children to experience new constructive activities, interactions and roles (fresh AIR; see Hazel et al., 2020).

A related, but perhaps bigger challenge, is to help those practitioners wider than YOTs to recognised *how* they can operationalise Child First in their respective roles. While the YJB's review of the Case Management Guidance provides guidance on implementation to YOT staff (YJB 2022a), there is currently a lack of understanding about what Child First means for other practitioners and how they can operationalise it. Again, there has been little public pushback on Child First from stakeholders associated with the police, courts, or other partners within and associated with the criminal justice system, but our engagement with these practitioners (c.f. Case & Browning, 2021b, and in non-academic roles) has made it clear that they need focused ideas on what they have to do differently for their work to be compatible with Child First. There is an urgent need for work to be done (perhaps convened by the YJB) to help these wider practice stakeholders to understand what to do, then ensure that it is embedded through guidance, tools or adapting processes as appropriate. There are some tools available to help practitioners to work in a constructive way (e.g. Hazel et al., 2020), but not clear guidance how the 'common language' of Child First is voiced in their specific contexts.

Perhaps the most basic challenge to practitioners, fundamental to the success of any work, is how to better achieve children's engagement and meaningful collaboration at all stages (tenet 3). At the policy level, there has been some considerable progress in involving children to deliver their unique insights, mainly through the YJB's Youth Ambassadors and Youth Advisory Network. There is now a pilot involving the latter working to advise a number of YOTs on the planning and delivery of their services (Chapter 12). It will be a significant challenge to enable children's individual engagement throughout the Youth Justice System. Even in terms of just ensuring that children understand what is happening to them, let alone being engaged in it, Hollingsworth notes how there is an 'overwhelming evidence of unmet communication needs' and very little child-focused support available to child defendants in court (Chapter 8). Burns and Creaney (Chapter 12) note the 'power' implications of more meaningful collaboration, with professionals having some reservations about 'handing over control'. Along with the greater involvement of peer support, perhaps this suggests the answer lies in the wider culture shift from the 'risk paradigm' that will enable a workforce to see success in terms of working *with* rather than *to* children, which is necessary in order to help them develop their pro-social identity.

At the System-Wide Level

Child First is a principle intended to guide decision-making at both the policy and practice levels. It is noted (Chapter 7) that while this is intended to address how to achieve positive outcomes within the current Youth Justice System, Child First could be used in the future to guide answers to questions more fundamental to the nature of the system as a whole. Indeed, perhaps having such contemporary understandings from research will inevitably lead to policymakers asking themselves those bigger questions for reform, just as they have been raised by the chapter authors at various points in this book.

This includes the recognition that system context may limit the extent to which a truly Child First system can operate. In particular, Bateman questions whether the Youth Justice System is 'bound by its close relationship with the adult justice system and the punitive overtones which such a relationship imparts' (Chapter 2). This may ultimately ask the question of whether a Child First justice system should operate within a 'justice' environment at all, or rather be integrated with children's services. While Bateman argues that the separation has meant attention and resources have been ensured for children with the most complex needs, Byrne argues that separation is untenable once we understand that positive outcomes as children are required, and would not mean dissolving specialist functions or ignoring public protection responsibilities (Chapter 9). Relatedly, Byrne raises the question of whether youth justice should mirror children's social care and education by falling within the purview of the Department of Education in England and be devolved to the Welsh Government rather than the responsibility of the Ministry of Justice. Similarly, reflecting the proposal in the Taylor report (2016), the question is raised of whether inspections of children's youth justice services should be carried out by an inspectorate of children's services rather than an inspectorate of probation services (Chapter 9).

Hollingsworth starts her analysis of compatibility of current court processes with Child First (Chapter 8) with her conclusion that the very fact children are sent to the criminal courts is counter to the principle by being adulterising, responsibilising, and criminogenically stigmatising. Consequently, it is necessary for her to instead consider the barriers and possibilities for change within a system that fundamentally treats children as offenders first. However, her damning spoiler does raise the question of what a Child First decision-making body would look like, and policy-makers could look at systems elsewhere within England (e.g. problem-solving courts), elsewhere (e.g. the Children's Hearing System in Scotland or Family Group Conferences; see Hazel, 2008), or require a new bespoke model to take account of contemporary understandings in youth justice.

A longstanding question in the literature that may be further highlighted as Child First is embedded is whether fundamental change is required to ensure that children are only imprisoned as a last resort for a minimal amount of time where they pose a serious risk to others and there are no alternative options to mitigate that risk in the community. In relation to custody being a last resort, although the government contends that this is assured by the current sentencing framework, dozens of children are imprisoned for minor offences such as handing stolen goods and possession of cannabis (Chapter 2). In relation to being for the minimal amount of time, children are tried in the crown court and subjected to the maximum adult sentence including life sentences (albeit with variance—see, Chapter 8), which the United Nations Committee on the Rights of the Child has argued are 'cruel, inhuman or degrading' (UNCRC, 2019: 13).

Where children do need to be held in custody, the Child First understanding of being appropriate to the needs of the child and minimising criminogenic stigma would point to a secure provision that is child-focused and as similar to a 'normal childhood' as possible (tenet 4). There is widespread agreement that Young Offender Institutions (YOIs) and Secure Training Centres (STCs) are not fit for purpose. At the time of writing, the government is committed to closing these types of institutions, but there is no sign of this policy being implemented. Although Bateman points out that the government and pressure groups have pointed to Secure Children's Homes (SCHs) coming closest to a best practice therapeutic environment, we know from inspection reports that having this type of institution per se does not necessarily correspond to a Child First culture that promotes welfare and pro-social identity development (cf. Ofsted, 2022). In additional, under current commissioning rules, SCHs can refuse to take individual 'justice' children; a situation which saw a number of girls being transferred to an all-male YOI following the recent closure of the STC that had previously accommodated them. Nevertheless, Bateman makes the argument that using SCHs, where vulnerable children outside of the criminal justice system can also be held, rather than an institution exclusive to the criminal justice institution, like the proposed Secure Schools, will minimise criminogenic stigma and transition to a pro-offender identity.

The most fundamental question that is raised for any Youth Justice System is the age of criminal responsibility at which individuals can enter the criminal justice system. As Hollingsworth argues (Chapter 8), with limited conceptual differences between the accountability given to children and adults, the criminal system is effectively premised on seeing children above the age of criminal responsibility not as children but as offenders. In England and Wales, set at ten years old, we have one of the youngest ages of criminal responsibility in the world (Hazel, 2008). Moreover, with the removal (in 1998) of the *doli incapax* we no longer have the child development-related protection of a presumption of incapacity until the age of fourteen. Informed by the Child First principle and associated evidence-base (including recent research on brain development), the YJB's position on the age of criminal responsibility is that the current level is too low, that there is sufficient evidence to merit a review, and that from the evidence it would support a rise to at least 12 years old.

Final thoughts—A 'Bulwark' Against Swinging Back and Provoking Action to Embed

Child First continues to gain traction as the guiding principle for the Youth Justice System in England and Wales, allowing for progressive policy and practice reform in line with the contemporary evidence base. Perhaps the biggest question for all those working to embed the principle further is whether this momentum can continue moving forward.

In his Foreword to this book, Charlie Taylor notes that attitudes have 'undoubtedly changed', but warns that 'the pendulum can quickly swing back'. It is recognised that this can be a highly politicised policy area, internationally, subject to various pressures from outside of the justice system (Hazel, 2008). Authors here discuss the importance of framing the Child First tenets in a way that could accommodate and navigate the concerns of stakeholders and gain traction in the political context (Chapter 7). However, we are also warned that the sustainability of Child First still has to be tested in the face of changed political discourse, such as a reactionary turn by the media, the election cycle where there could be an 'arms-race' on which party could be tougher on crime, or significant events like a horrific crime committed by a child. Bateman (Chapter 2) reminded us of the 'punitive turn' in the wake of a moral panic triggered by the 1992 murder of toddler James Bulger by two ten-year-old boys that saw a rapidly expanding use of child imprisonment. Indeed, that tragic event, thirty years before the writing of this book, still has an influence over youth justice policymaking, with ministers telling us privately in recent years that this would, for instance, make it politically unacceptable to consider raising the age of criminal responsibility to above that of those boys. Even when a prominent children's charity recommended in 2010 raising the age of criminal responsibility, they felt it necessary to include the caveat that this need not be applied to the most grave crimes (Barnardo's, 2010). We hope that Taylor is right to conclude his Foreword with the assessment that this book's 'consolidated body of learning will serve as a bulwark' against any such future punitive turn.

To this point, however, the journey of Child First has been one of maturation in content, status and application over the past generation. As 'children first, offenders second', it started as an academic concept that built into a powerful and detailed critical commentary exposing the dangerous state of youth justice policy and practice in England and Wales and the 'risk paradigm' that underpinned it. There then developed an evidence base of research that supported CFOS to the extent that it largely found itself articulating contemporary academic understanding of what was important in youth justice. Since being translated into the policy and practice context, and with a theory of change of developing pro-social identity to achieve the overall system aim of 'preventing offending', Child First is now the guiding principle for the Youth Justice System, informing policy decisions and underpinning the standards to which youth justice professionals are to adhere. It will now, of course, need to be embedded into policy, practice, discourse and system culture and faces the challenges outlined throughout this book and specifically in this chapter. Keith Fraser, in his Foreword, expresses the hope that readers of this book will be 'provoked' into both considering these challenges and 'taking action to embed Child First in practice'. As Child First is further embedded as the guiding principle for decision-making *within* the Youth Justice System, it is likely if not inevitable that more fundamental questions will be raised for and by policymakers *about* the system. As always, these will be debated politically, but can likewise be guided by this established and accepted principle and discourse based on contemporary research evidence and understanding.

Child First has proven to be an effective vehicle for evidence-based progressive reform in youth justice in England and Wales. Moreover, its progress so far has been made within existing legislation (which is still offender-focused), and with the context of uncertainty from political and economic upheaval (Brexit) and a global pandemic (COVID-19). While undeniably still on a journey of development, it has already been demonstrated that there is clear potential for the Child First model to serve as a valid and sustainable blueprint internationally for a cutting-edge, principled and 'positive' approach to working with children who come into contact with youth justice systems.

References

Atkins, V. (2022, June 15). *Speech to the modernising criminal justice conference.*
Barnardo's. (2010). *From playground to prison: The case for reviewing the age of criminal responsibility.* Barnardo's.
Byrne, B., & Case, S. (2016). Towards a positive youth justice. *Safer Communities, 15*(2), 69–81.
Case, S. P., & Browning, A. (2021a). *Child first: The research evidence-base.* Loughborough University.

Case, S. P., & Browning, A. (2021b). *The child first strategy implementation project: Realising the guiding principle for youth justice.* Loughborough University.

Case, S. P., Creaney, S., Coleman, N., Haines, K. R., Little, R., & Worrell, V. (2020, November). Trusting children to enhance youth justice policy: The importance and value of children's voices. *Youth Voice Journal.*

Haines, K. R., & Case, S. P. (2015). *Positive youth justice: Children first, offenders second.* Policy Press.

Haines, K. R., & Drakeford, M. (1998). *Young people and youth justice.* Macmillian.

Hazel, N. (2008). *Cross-national comparison of youth justice.* Youth Justice Board.

Hazel, N., & Bateman, T. (2020). Supporting children's resettlement ('reentry') after custody: Beyond the risk paradigm. *Youth Justice, 21*(1), 71–89.

Hazel, N., Hagell, A., Liddle, M., Archer, D., Grimshaw, R., & King, J. (2002). *Assessment of the detention and training order and its impact on the secure estate across England and Wales.* Youth Justice Board.

Hazel, N., Drummond, C., Welsh, M., & Joseph, K. (2020). *Using an identity lens: Constructive working with children in the criminal justice system.* Nacro.

HM Inspectorate of Probation/YJB. (2022). *Joint statement from HM inspectorate of probation and the youth justice board.*

HMPPS. (2022). *Early and late release for detention and training orders policy.* MOJ/HM Prison and Probation Service.

Jacobson, J., Bhardwa, B., Gyateng, T., Hunter, G., & Hough, M. (2010). *Punishing disadvantage: A profile of children in custody.* Prison Reform Trust.

Jain, S., Skinner, G., Laksminarayanan, M., Alva, D., Bond, A., Oprea, E., & White, H. (2022). *Technical report: An evidence and gap map of research and literature related to systems of support for children and young people who are at risk of or involved in violence.* Youth Endowment Fund.

MoJ. (2016). *The government response to Charlie Taylor's review of the youth justice system.* Ministry of Justice.

MoJ/YJB. (2019). *Standards for children in the youth justice system 2019.* Ministry of Justice.

Ofsted. (2022). *Full inspection of Vinney Green secure children's home.* Ofsted.

Taylor, C. (2016). *Review of the youth justice system in England and Wales.* Ministry of Justice.

Ullman, R., Lereya, T., Glendinning, F., Deighton, J., Labno, A., Liverpool, S., & Edbrooke-Childs, J. (2022). *Youth crime and violence.*

United Nations Committee on the Rights of the Child. (2019). *General Comment No. 24 replacing General Comment No. 10. Children's rights in juvenile justice.* UN.
Welsh Assembly Government. (2004). *All Wales youth offending strategy.* Welsh Assembly Government/Youth Justice Board.
Welsh Government and Ministry of Justice. (2019). *Youth justice blueprint for Wales.* Welsh Government.
White, H., Saran, A., Verma, A., Oprea, E., & Babudu, P. (2021). *Evidence and gap map of interventions to prevent children getting involved in violence: Technical report on the* (1st ed.). Youth Endowment Fund.
Wigzell, A., Paterson-Young, C., & Bateman, T. (Eds.). (forthcoming). *Understanding children's pathways away from offending: critical reflections on desistance and children from theory, research and practice.* Bristol University Press.
YJB. (2021a). *Strategic plan 2022–2024.* Youth Justice Board.
YJB. (2021b). *Youth justice skills matrix.* Youth Justice Board.
YJB. (2022a) *Case Management Guidance.* Youth Justice Board
YJB. (2022b). *Business plan 2022–2023.* Youth Justice Board.
Youth Custody Service. (2021). *Monthly youth custody report—June 2021: England and Wales.* MOJ.

Index

A

assessment 5, 9, 12, 32, 54, 56–58, 67, 70, 74, 76, 86, 87, 122, 153–155, 159, 160, 162, 163, 191, 192, 225–227, 244, 248–250, 256–262, 272–276, 279, 280, 282–289, 291, 293, 295, 296, 303, 304, 306, 310, 311, 334, 336, 338, 345, 353, 359, 376, 382

Asset 57, 58, 99, 154, 155, 159, 160, 275, 304, 306, 310, 321–323, 376

AssetPlus 99, 159, 160, 163, 248, 249, 256–258, 276, 280, 285, 288, 289, 306, 309–311, 322, 323, 325, 344, 376

B

barriers 12, 17, 19, 68, 124, 140, 183, 186, 188, 222, 242, 246–248, 250, 251, 255, 259, 272, 275, 291, 301, 308, 309, 311, 312, 320, 321, 324, 325, 334–336, 342, 344, 349, 358, 373, 374, 376, 379

C

case management 38, 190, 192, 256, 257, 306, 310, 315, 375

challenges 2, 5, 7, 13, 16, 18, 19, 25, 27, 28, 33, 35, 45, 61, 68, 70, 72, 74, 94, 95, 103, 104, 111, 169, 171, 172, 177, 192, 193, 222, 227, 237, 240, 242, 243, 245–249, 255, 257, 259, 264, 272, 273, 287, 294–296,

301, 319–321, 323–325, 339,
 344, 345, 347–349, 353, 355,
 357–359, 368, 371, 372, 377,
 378, 383
Child First 1, 2, 7, 9, 11–20, 25,
 27–31, 33, 35, 37–40, 42, 44,
 61, 63, 65, 67, 72, 73, 93,
 97–104, 110, 111, 118–130,
 139–143, 146, 149, 151, 158,
 160–164, 169–175, 177–194,
 204, 205, 214–217, 220,
 222–225, 227, 228, 237–243,
 245–264, 271–274, 276–279,
 281, 282, 284–289, 292–296,
 301, 306–325, 335–339,
 343–345, 348, 349, 351–354,
 357–360, 367–383
Child First justice 15, 18, 274–276,
 278–280, 284, 289, 290,
 292–294, 302, 306–309,
 311–315, 323, 325, 343, 379
child-first offender second 10, 174,
 175, 188, 190, 263, 277, 290
Child First participation 19, 334,
 351, 358
child-focused 12, 17, 67, 73, 103,
 124, 139, 142, 143, 147,
 149–151, 154, 156, 157, 160,
 163, 207, 213, 242, 274, 275,
 378, 380
Children first 11, 12, 14, 25, 63–67,
 70–75, 96, 101, 120, 129,
 186, 245, 271, 274, 336, 369
children's rights 14, 16, 17, 63, 68,
 98, 99, 109–111, 113–117,
 123–127, 129, 130, 178, 191,
 204, 205, 211, 213, 214, 217,
 228, 277, 315, 372

co-creation 183, 337, 338, 344,
 345, 359
co-production 19, 160, 287, 292,
 334, 335, 343–347, 349, 351,
 353–359
Crown Court 18, 39, 41, 205,
 208–210, 214, 217–221, 376,
 380
culpable 16, 29, 35, 306
custody 2, 4, 5, 9, 12, 31, 32,
 39–41, 43, 44, 85, 86, 92, 95,
 101, 103, 105, 121, 122, 141,
 143, 144, 147–149, 152–155,
 157–159, 161, 162, 181, 183,
 186, 189, 215, 223–225, 227,
 254, 255, 276, 283, 293, 303,
 305, 313, 370, 375, 377, 380

D

desistance 12, 44, 122, 138–140,
 149, 155, 159, 180, 272, 273,
 275, 276, 279, 280, 285, 289,
 292, 295, 306, 309–312, 323,
 338, 354, 356, 357, 372, 374
diversion 1, 4, 10, 13, 16, 31–33,
 37–39, 44, 65, 67, 73, 85, 86,
 89, 90, 92, 100, 104, 109,
 110, 117, 119, 120, 122, 123,
 125, 129, 138–141, 147, 149,
 161, 184, 224, 242, 252, 261,
 274, 275, 279, 305, 318, 338,
 375

E

embracing children's voices 19, 333
evidence-based 2, 5, 8, 10, 11, 16,
 18, 51–56, 58, 59, 62, 63,

69–71, 73, 75, 93, 102, 126, 292, 368, 383
experiential peer support 360

H
hegemony 162

I
incarceration 31, 33, 40, 104, 147–149, 151, 152, 223, 244, 254, 372
influence 6, 10, 15, 19, 53–55, 57, 59, 64, 66, 68, 91, 93–98, 102, 113, 149, 153, 158, 161, 174, 193, 194, 212, 215, 221, 228, 240, 256, 263, 264, 276, 278–281, 303, 304, 336–342, 344, 352, 354, 355, 358, 359, 373, 374, 376, 382

J
judges 69, 207–209, 211, 215, 217–219, 221, 222, 226, 309, 376
juvenile justice 85, 116, 141

M
magistrates 41, 69, 205, 208–210, 217, 222, 226, 309
mentorship 261, 349, 354–358, 360
minimal intervention 13, 120, 140, 184, 190, 275, 318
minimum age of criminal responsibility (MACR) 28, 33–36, 114, 118, 212, 228

N
neo-correctionalism 5, 6
new orthodoxy 4, 94

P
partnership 9, 11, 63, 69–71, 73, 75, 88–91, 96, 119, 153, 157, 158, 247, 260, 261, 273, 335, 342, 344, 349, 353, 359, 360
policy 2, 8, 11, 14, 16–19, 30, 33, 36, 52, 53, 55, 59, 62, 64, 69, 71, 72, 74, 75, 85–87, 90–96, 98–105, 117, 118, 120, 121, 123, 126, 128–130, 138, 139, 141–149, 151, 153, 155–157, 163, 169–176, 181, 184, 185, 189, 192–194, 228, 238, 244, 247, 251, 253, 255, 263, 264, 272, 273, 277–279, 281, 305, 312, 313, 337, 341, 367–369, 371–373, 375, 377–381
policymaking 171, 183, 193, 194, 382
policy narratives 272, 276, 278, 281, 295, 296
popular punitivism 141, 162
Positive Youth Justice 8, 11, 16, 19, 62, 63, 67, 68, 72, 102, 110, 119, 120, 337, 339, 360
practice 2, 4, 8, 10, 13, 14, 16–19, 25, 27, 28, 30, 44, 52, 53, 55–62, 64, 66, 68–70, 73, 75, 85, 87–91, 93, 95–105, 110, 111, 116, 117, 119, 121, 123, 126, 127, 138, 140–143, 147, 149, 153, 155, 160, 161, 163, 170, 171, 174–176, 178, 179, 182, 183, 185, 187, 192, 194,

206, 207, 219, 221, 222, 224, 227, 228, 239, 241, 243–247, 249–251, 253, 256, 258–260, 272–275, 277, 278, 280–283, 286, 288–290, 292, 294, 295, 301, 303, 306, 308, 311–315, 317, 319–321, 323, 324, 334–337, 339, 341–345, 348, 352–355, 357–360, 367, 368, 371–373, 375–382
Progressive Universalism 142
public policy 123, 169, 171
punitive 3–7, 14, 15, 18, 27–29, 31, 32, 35, 36, 38, 39, 41, 43, 52, 64–66, 69, 85, 95, 98, 120–122, 125, 151, 157, 161, 211, 214, 239, 240, 246, 353, 373, 379, 382

Q

quango 142

R

reductionism 14, 55, 57–59
research 2, 8, 53–57, 60–62, 68–70, 87–91, 99, 104, 105, 116, 117, 122, 129, 130, 138, 170–175, 177, 181, 182, 184, 186, 188, 190, 192–194, 207, 272, 274, 278, 281, 288, 302, 303, 305, 306, 309, 310, 317, 346, 353, 368, 369, 372, 373, 379, 381–383
responsibilisation 5, 6, 53, 63, 71, 86, 119, 141, 274, 344
risk 4–6, 16, 18, 19, 30, 32, 41, 44, 53–61, 63, 66, 67, 70, 72, 74,
86–88, 91, 95, 99, 103, 110, 119, 122, 138, 154, 155, 171, 173, 177, 181, 182, 186–188, 206, 208, 223–225, 227, 239, 240, 256, 263, 272–284, 286–289, 292–296, 302–305, 307, 309–311, 320, 323–325, 334, 338, 339, 345, 349, 351–354, 358, 359, 369, 371, 373–376, 380
risk factor prevention paradigm (RFPP) 16, 18, 32, 55–61, 66, 70, 239, 272, 273, 277–279, 283–286, 289, 294, 296, 302–304, 310
risk management 1, 5, 6, 10, 12, 13, 16, 38, 51, 54–56, 58, 60, 61, 63, 66, 69, 70, 74, 119, 187, 283, 284, 293, 295, 320, 345, 351, 353, 359

S

safeguarding 162, 186, 240, 241, 243–246, 250, 257, 262, 263, 284, 352
sentencing 6, 11, 17, 18, 26, 30, 31, 38–40, 65, 67, 73, 118, 122, 157, 211, 212, 214, 215, 217, 218, 224, 272, 369, 380
strength-based 154, 160

T

textual reflexivity 170, 174, 192, 193
third sector 8, 62, 91, 93–97, 99–101, 377

Index

U

UK Government 18, 52, 53, 92, 96, 98, 103, 238, 252, 253, 271, 277, 278, 308, 368
United Nations Convention on the Rights of the Child (UNCRC) 5, 8, 16, 34, 41, 62, 68, 71, 75, 99, 101, 102, 109, 113–117, 123–129, 149, 209, 239, 277, 302, 309, 313, 336, 337, 380

W

Wales 7–9, 13, 15–18, 25, 33, 41, 52–54, 56, 57, 61, 62, 72, 74, 85, 90–92, 96–98, 100–104, 110, 116, 118, 122, 126, 149, 169, 175, 183, 190, 192, 205, 214, 240, 244, 248, 252, 253, 264, 272, 275, 277, 279, 283, 289, 301, 302, 305, 307, 312, 313, 315, 368–370, 377, 381–383
Welsh Government 8, 62, 88, 92, 96–98, 100–102, 184, 253, 264, 312, 313, 379

Y

YJB Cymru 8, 62, 91, 92, 97, 98, 100, 307, 312
youth court 32, 39, 41, 152, 177, 205–211, 214, 219, 222, 226
youth justice 1–20, 25–27, 29–33, 35, 37, 51–58, 60–75, 83, 85–87, 92–99, 102–104, 109–111, 114–124, 128–130, 137–139, 141–144, 146, 149–154, 156, 157, 160–163, 170, 171, 173–175, 177–186, 188–190, 192–194, 237–241, 244, 246–251, 253–257, 260, 262–264, 272–274, 276–283, 285–289, 295, 296, 301, 302, 304, 305, 307, 310–312, 319, 323, 334, 335, 337–339, 343–349, 353, 358–360, 367–372, 375–377, 379, 380, 382, 383
Youth Justice Board (YJB) 17, 18, 26, 27, 35, 37–39, 52, 53, 56–58, 61, 62, 67, 70, 73, 74, 89–92, 94, 96, 97, 100, 103, 111, 121, 122, 124, 130, 138, 139, 142, 143, 145–148, 154, 155, 157, 163, 174, 179, 180, 185, 188, 192, 237–239, 249–251, 256–259, 271–273, 275, 276, 279–281, 287, 288, 290, 295, 296, 302–304, 306–309, 315, 320, 323, 325, 337–339, 341, 344, 345, 351–353, 359
youth justice inspections 247, 256, 280
youth justice policy 13, 17–19, 25, 27, 28, 44, 56, 58, 61, 67, 72, 75, 91, 96, 99, 142–145, 147, 149–153, 156–158, 160, 161, 170, 171, 239, 272, 275, 336, 382
youth justice practice 11, 19, 55, 62, 63, 67, 69, 74, 125, 140, 146, 151, 154, 169, 238, 241, 243, 244, 248, 279, 280, 283, 287, 289, 325

youth offending 7, 13, 18, 28, 52, 59, 63, 64, 70, 247, 248
Youth Offending Teams (YOT) 2, 8, 10, 26, 37, 38, 62, 68, 69, 74, 88–91, 94–100, 102, 138, 139, 147, 148, 152, 153, 155, 156, 159, 163, 181, 189–192, 194, 226, 242–250, 255, 262, 272, 279, 280, 287, 288, 303–310, 312, 314, 319, 321, 322, 324, 325, 370, 377

Ingram Content Group UK Ltd.
Milton Keynes UK
UKHW041421220323
418987UK00001B/135